Radical essays
on
Nigerian literatures

Malthouse critical titles

H. Otokunefor & O. Nwodo (eds), *Nigerian Female Writers: A critical perspective*
Tanure Ojaide, *The Poetry of Wole Soyinka*
Tayo Olafioye, *The Poetry of Tanure Ojaide: A critical appraisal*
Kanchana Ugbabe, *Chukwuemeka Ike: A critical reader*

Radical essays on Nigerian literatures

Edited by

G. G. Darah
*Professor of oral literature and folklore
Department of English and Literary Studies
Delta State University
Abraka, Delta State
Nigeria*

malthouse

Malthouse Press Limited
Lagos, Benin, Ibadan, Jos, Port-Harcourt, Zaria

Malthouse Press Limited
43 Onitana Street, Off Stadium Hotel Road,
Surulere, Lagos, Lagos State
E-mail: malthouse_press@yahoo.com
malthouse_lagos@yahoo.co.uk
Tel: +234 (01) -773 53 44; 0802 600 3203

All rights reserved. No part of this publication may be reproduced, transmitted, transcribed, stored in a retrieval system or translated into any language or computer language, in any form or by any means, electronic, mechanical, magnetic, chemical, thermal, manual or otherwise, without the prior consent in writing of Malthouse Press Limited, Lagos, Nigeria.

This book is sold subject to the condition that it shall not by way of trade, or otherwise, be lent, re-sold, hired out, or otherwise circulated without the publisher's prior consent in writing, in any form of binding or cover other than in which it is published and without a similar condition, including this condition, being imposed on the subsequent purchaser.

© G.G. Darah 2008
First Published 2008
ISBN 978 023 254 0

Distributors:
African Books Collective
Oxford, United Kingdom
Email: abc@africanbookscollective.com
Website: http://www.africanbookscollective.com

Acknowledgements

The idea of this book was conceived in the late 1980s at the Obafemi Awolowo University, Ile-Ife, Nigeria. I was on the staff of the Department of Literature in English which inaugurated a seminar series under the headship of Professor Biodun Jeyifo. Some of the seminar papers were published under the title, *Ife Monographs on Literature and Criticism*. In 1984 I presented the paper, "Ideological Orphanage, the Intelligentsia and Literary Development in Colonial Nigeria" which is reprinted as chapter 13 in this volume. A shorter version of it was published in the Yemi Ogunbiyi (ed.) *Perspectives on Nigerian Literatures: 1700-the Present: Volume One*, (Lagos, 1988) Guardian Press Limited. Work on the paper challenged me to search for materials on Nigeria's national literatures and the outcome was truly rewarding.

Under Jeyifo's leadership, the Department attracted radical lecturers, especially of the Leftist/Marxist persuasion. Among these were Professor Ropo Sekoni, a specialist in semiotics whose essay appears in this volume as chapter 2, and Professor Adebayo Williams. Professor Oyin Ogunba, one of the foremost scholars of oral literature and drama, was the academic *iroko* tree under whose liberal plumage we all gathered to argue and disagree productively. Other departmental colleagues were Professor Mary Kolawole, Professor Desmond Macbeth, Professor Ben Ibitokun, Professor Segun Adekoya, and Dr. Chima Anyadike.

Our radical fellow travellers in the Department of Dramatic Arts were Professor Kole Omotoyi and Dr. Yemi Ogunbiyi. Professor Sope Oyelaran, Professor Akinwumi Isola and Professor Karin Barber were in the Department of African Languages and Literatures. Professor Geoff Hunt in Philosophy had a keen interest in African literature. Professor Segun Osoba (History) was the acknowledged elder of the community of radical lecturers and anti-imperialist activists in the Faculty of Arts in particular and the University in general.

Some of us belonged to the Ibadan-Ife group of socialist thinkers which included Professor Femi Osofisan and Odia Ofeimun. The most prodigious Marxist scholar at Ibadan in the 1970s was Professor Omafume Onoge who pioneered the teaching of courses on Marxist Sociology of Literature. For the work on this book, I am indebted in many ways to all my mentors, colleagues and students who shared exciting moments with us in those heady days of ideological disputation and engagement.

The decision to edit this anthology of essays was helped by my October 1989 newspaper article in the Nigerian *Sunday Times* on the eve of that year's convention of the Association of Nigerian Authors (ANA) which took place in Calabar. The title of the article was "200 Years of Nigerian Letters", being a synoptic account of the various phases of Nigerian writing from 1789 when Olaudah Equiano, Nigeria's freed slave in England, published his autobiography, later issued by Heinemann as *Equiano's Travels*.

Chinua Achebe's "What has literature got to do with it?" is the text of his 1986 Nigerian National Merit Award Lecture. The version reproduced as chapter 1 in this volume was first published in *Tapping Nigeria's Limitless Cultural Treasures* edited by Frank Aig-Imoukheude (National Council for Arts and Culture, Lagos, 1988). Professor Ropo Sekoni's "The semiotics of class and gender struggle in pre-colonial narrative systems" (chapter 2) was seminar paper delivered in the Department of Literature in English, Ile-Ife, in the 1980s, with minor reworking for the purpose of this book.

The following papers were first presented at conferences of the Nigerian Folklore Society where I was the national president from 1988-1995: "Myth and the formation of social consciousness: the *Bayajida* of the Hausa" (chapter 3) by Maikudi Karaye; "Towards understanding *Ndi Igbo* and their cosmology" (chapter 4) by Ichie Ezikeojiaku; "Egalitarian ethos in Tiv folktales" (chapter 8) by Tar Ahura; "Social and ethical values of story-telling among the Berom of Plateau State" (chapter 9) by Abu Abarry; and "Feminism and oral literature: the example of Igbo birthsongs" (chapter 10) by Afam Ebeogu. I am grateful to the authors and the Nigerian Folklore Society for permission to use these materials.

Akinwunmi Isola's "Children's oral literature and socialisation in Yoruba" (chapter 11) and Karin Barber's "Style and ideology in Fagunwa and Okediji" (chapter 15) were seminar papers presented at the Department of African Languages and Literatures, Ile-Ife. I thank Glendale Press, Dublin, for permission to reprint Isidore Okpewho's "Once Upon a Kingdom": Benin in the heroic traditions of Bendel State, Nigeria" which was first published in *The Heroic Process: Form, Function, and Fantasy in Folk Life*, edited by B. Almqvist, S. O'Cathein, and P. O'Healai (1987).

"Principles of the Igbo oral epic: a study in traditional aesthetic and oral literary criticism" (chapter 6) by Chukwuma Azuonye was first presented at the 1986 Second International Seminar on Igbo Literature organised by the Society for Promoting Igbo Language and Culture at the University of Nigeria, Nsukka. The essay is used here with the permission of the author. Sam Asein's "Literature and society in Lagos: (late nineteenth-early twentieth century" (chapter 12) is reprinted from *Nigeria Magazine*, No. 117-118, 1975.

I am eternally grateful to my fellow folklorists at Ahmadu Bello University, Zaria, Professor Aderemi Bamikunle and Professor Abba Aliyu Sani for their enthusiastic support for the book project. Sani's two essays (chapters 16 and 20) and Bamikunle's (chapter 18) were commissioned for this volume. Mohammed Sokoto, now at the National Institute for Strategic Studies, Kuru, Jos, was in the Department of Sociology, Zaria, when he wrote the essay in chapter 14. It was developed from research materials he gathered for his MSc thesis.

Professor Dandatti Abdulkadir was our senior professional colleague, former president of the Nigerian Folklore Society, Vice-Chancellor of Bayero University, Kano, and Nigeria's Ambassador to Libya. His scholarly depth, commitment and humility inspired us immensely. His "The life and works of Sa'adu Zungur" (chapter 17) is reproduced from his bio-critical study of Zungur, *The Life, Works and Opinions of Sa'ad Zungur* published by the Northern Nigerian Publishing Company, (Zaria, 1974). Emmanuel Obiechina's "The impact of the newspaper and cinema on Onitsha Market Literature" (chapter 19) is taken from his book, *Literature for the Masses: An Analytical Study of Popular Pamphleteering in Nigeria* (Enugu: Nwankwo Ifejika & Co Publishers, 1971).

"The indigenous publisher and the future of culture in Nigeria" (chapter 21) by Kole Omotoso is reproduced from chapter VII of the book, *Indigenous Publishing for National Development*, edited by G.O. Onibonoje, Kole Omotoso, and O.A. Lawal (Ibadan: Onibonoje Press and Book Industries (Nig) Ltd, 1976). "Domestication of an opiate: Western paraesthetics and the growth of the Ekwensi tradition" (chapter 22) by Femi Osofisan was initially published as an essay in the journal of the Ibadan-Ife group, *Positive Review (A Review of Society and Culture in Black Africa)* Vol. 4, 1981.

The final chapter (23), "The retrospective stage: some reflections on the mythopoeic tradition at Ibadan" by Omafume Onoge and G. G. Darah was presented at a conference on African literature at the University of Ife, (now Obafemi Awolowo University, Ile-Ife) in 1977. It was published in *Ch'Indaba*, Vol. 3, No. 1, October/December. 1977, a journal edited by the Nobel Laureate, Wole Soyinka.

Preface

This anthology of essays brings together original critical comments on Nigerian literatures written in the 1970s and 1980s. I started sourcing for the materials in the early 1990s. Most of the essays had not been published at that time. Some were commissioned by me for the purpose of the anthology. Eight of the essays had been published in one form or the other and their sources are duly acknowledged.

My initial plan was to have the book in two volumes. This first volume contains materials dealing with Nigerian literatures from their earliest beginnings to the first decade after Nigeria's independence in 1960. The second volume will feature essays covering the period from 1970s to the present. This division is done for the purpose of editorial convenience. Some of the essays such as those by Chinua Achebe, J.P. Cark, Chukwuma Azuonye, and Karin Barber deal with contemporary literary traditions.

The 23 essays in this volume examine two distinct traditions of Nigerian literary heritage – the oral and the written. Achebe's essay in Chapter 1 serves as a prolegomena for the entire project. However, Chapters 2 to 11 represent the oral tradition while Chapters 12 to 23 focus on the tradition of letters. The chapters provide a historical perspective on the diversity and growth of Nigeria's literary culture over the ages.

The essays are organised around the thematic locus *radical*, an ideological label which helps to foreground the political imperative that informs the interpretation emphasised by the contributors. My critical bias in this respect has benefited from the robust debates and exchanges amongst Nigeria's literary scholars in the last quarter of the twentieth century. During the period there was a sharp divide between radical, neo-Marxist interpreters of African culture and literatures on the one hand and their conservative counterparts on the other. The epithet *radical* is also used in the classical Marxian sense to mean original, deep, and comprehensive.

The ideological debates were healthy for the growth of Nigeria's literatures and their evaluation in academic publications and the mass media. These public exchanges influenced the thematic and stylistic orientation of many writers and artists. Wole Soyinka's winning of the Nobel Prize for Literature in 1986 intensified the discourse, especially with the rising tide of mass revolts against military juntas of the time. Soyinka himself was often a target of harsh comments by some of the younger, more ultra-left critics. He was later to pay tribute to that tempestuous era with the publication of his book, Art, Dialogue & Outrage: Essays on Literature and Culture, (Ibadan, New Horn Press, 1988) In choosing the essays for this volume, I have placed premium on interpretations that draw attention to the political and ideological foundations of the materials examined.

The value of the critical discourse represented by the essays can be gauged by the fact that all the contributors were at one time or the other engaged in Nigeria's academic institutions. All the authors, except Abu Abarry and Karin Barber are Nigerian nationals. After editing the essays, I left the university system and became a practising journalist in Lagos (1991–2001). My attention was diverted from the book project during that decade and thus it suffered awful delay. I would like to urge the contributors to pardon me for this lapse. In the interval of a decade and a half, some of the authors would have published their works elsewhere.

I regret to point out that three of the distinguished contributors passed away during the period. These are Professor Samuel Omon Asein of the University of Ibadan, Professor Aderemi Bamikunle of Ahmadu Bello University, Zaria, and Dr. Tar Ahura, formerly the Provost of the College of Education, Katsina Ala, Benue State. The publication of their essays will serve as tribute to their contribution to the development of Nigerian literatures.

Notwithstanding the delay in the publication of the book, the essays will be useful to students and researchers on Nigerian literatures. It is noteworthy to observe the amount of work that has been done on Nigerian literary development in the past two decades. There is now ample material for a second volume and more. To invoke the words of Chinua Achebe on Nigerian literatures, it is morning yet on creation day.

G.G. Darah
Delta State University,
Abraka, 2007.

Contents

Acknowledgements
Preface
Introduction

Chapters

1. What has literature got to do with it? - *Chinua Achebe* 1
2. The semiotics of class and gender struggle in pre-colonial narrative systems -*Ropo Sekoni* 13
3. Myth and the formation of social consciousness: the Bayajida of the Hausa - *Maikudi Karaye* 25
4. Towards understanding Ndi Igbo and their cosmology - *Ichie P.A. Ezikeojiaku* 35
5. 'Once Upon a Kingdom…': Benin in the Heroic traditions of Bendel State, Nigeria - *Isidore Okpewho* 49
6. Principles of the Igbo oral epic: a study in traditional aesthetic and oral literary criticism - *Chukwuma Azuonye* 75
7. Poetry of the Urhobo Dance Udje – *J.P. Clark* 105
8. Egalitarian ethos in Tiv folktales - *Tar Ahura* 11
9. Social and ethical values of story-telling among the Berom of Plateau State - *Abu Abarry*
10. Feminism and oral literature: the example of Igbo birth-songs - *Afam Ebeogu*
11. Children's oral literature and socialization in Yoruba - *Akinwumi Isola*
12. Literature and society in Lagos (late 19th - early 20th Century) - *Samuel Omo Asein*
13. Ideological orphanage: the intelligentsia and literary development in Colonial Nigeria - *G. G. Darah*
14. The songs and poems of the Satiru Revolt c. 1894-1906 - *Abubakar Sokoto Mohammed*

15. Style and ideology in Fagunwa and Okediji - *Karin Barber*
16. Abubakar Imam and the conservative conscience - *Abba Aliyu Sani*
17. The life and works of Sa'adu Zungur - *Dandatti Abdulkadir*
18. Twilight in the homestead: the drama of Ene Henshaw - *Aderemi Bamikunle*
19. The impact of the newspaper and the cinema on Onitsha Market literature - *Emmanuel Obiechina*
20. Cultural imperialism and publishing in Northern Nigeria: 1903-1960 - *Abba Aliyu Sani*
21. The indigenous publisher and the future of culture in Nigeria - *Kole Omotoso*
22. Domestication of an opiate: western paraesthetics and growth of the Ekwensi tradition - *Femi Osofisan*
23. The retrospective stage: some reflections on the mythopoeic tradition at Ibadan – *Omafume Onoge and G.G. Darah*

Bibliography
Index

Contributors

Abarry, Abu is at the Department of African-American Studies, Temple University, Philadelphia, United States of America. He was formerly at the University of Jos, Nigeria.

Abdulkadir, Dantatti was the Vice-Chancellor of Bayero University, Kano, Nigeria. He is a Professor of Hausa literature and folklore and was the President of the Nigerian Folklore Society.

Achebe, Chinua is Africa's foremost novelist and man of letters. His *Things Fall Apart* novel (1958) inaugurated the vigorous tradition of African fiction. An erudite essayist and poet, Achebe is acknowledged world-wide as the most distinguished African voice of colonial and post-colonial discourse.

Ahura, Tar was a radical scholar of theatre and drama. He was a leading researcher on indigenous theatrical forms and idiom, particularly of the Tiv nationality of Nigeria. He was the Provost of the Benue State College of Education, Katsina-Ala.

Asein, Sam was Professor of literature at the Department of English, University of Ibadan. The literature of apartheid South Africa was one of his major areas; he did his doctorate degree on the works of Alex La Guma.

Azuonye, Chukwuma is Professor and Chair of the Department of Black Studies/Africana Studies, University of Massachusetts, Boston, United States of America. He is a leading scholar of Igbo folklore and oral literature.

Bamikunle, Aderemi was a Professor of English at the Ahmadu Bello University, Zaria. African drama was one of his fields of inquiry.

Barber, Karin is a Professor in Birmingham University, United Kingdom. She was a lecturer in the Department of African Languages and Literatures at the Obafemi Awolowo University, Ile-Ife, Nigeria.

Clark, J.P. is Nigeria's poet laureate and one of Africa's most outstanding dramatists and literary theorists. His deep understanding and creative use of Ijaw and Urhobo folk traditions have earned him international recognition as a gifted playwright, translator and essayist.

Darah, G.G. is Professor of oral literature and folklore at the Department of English and Literary Studies, Delta State University, Abraka, Nigeria. He is former President of the Nigerian Folklore Society and chair of the editorial boards of the *Daily Times* and *The Guardian* newspapers in Nigeria.

Ebeogu, Afam is Professor in Abia State University, Uturu, Nigeria and a former editor of the *Journal of Nigerian Folklore*.

Ezikeojiaku, Ichie, a leading scholar Igbo culture and language, is a lecturer in the Abia State University, Uturu, Nigeria.

Karaye, Maikudi of the Centre for the Study of Nigerian Languages, Bayero University, Kano, is an expert in Hausa oral traditions and literature.

Isola, Akinwumi, a Nigerian national laureate of literature and major playwright in Yoruba, was of the Department of African Languages and Literatures, Obafemi Awolowo University, Ile-Ife, Nigeria.

Mohammed, Sokoto, formerly of the Department of Sociology, Ahmadu Bello University, Zaria, was Senior Research Fellow at the Nigerian Institute for Policy and Strategic Studies, Kuru, Jos, Nigeria.

Obiechina, Emmanuel was former Deputy Vice-Chancellor, University of Nigeria, Nuskka. He was a Distinguished Visiting Scholar at the University of Pittsburgh, the University of Kansas at Lawrence, and Harvard University, Cambridge, in the United States of America. He was also a Research Fellow at the W. E. B. Du Bois Institute for Afro-American Research.

Okpewho, Isidore is the Distinguished Professor in the Humanities and Professor of Africana Studies, English, and Comparative Literature, Binghamton University, State of New York, New York. He is former President of the International Society for the Oral Literatures of Africa.

Omotoso, Kole is a novelist, playwright and essayist. He is former President of the Association of Nigerian Authors. He was of the Department of Dramatic Arts, Obafemi Awolowo University, Ile-Ife, Nigeria. Since the 1990s, he has been in South Africa and was lately in the University of Cape Town.

Onoge Omafume, Professor of Socio-Anthropology, former Executive Director of the Centre for Advanced Social Science, Port Harcourt, Nigeria, pioneered the teaching of Marxist courses on Sociology of Literature at the University of Ibadan.

Osofisan, Femi is a Professor of drama and theatre at the University of Ibadan. He is a radical and prolific playwright, producer, and translator. He is former President of the Association of Nigerian Authors and General Manager of the National Theatre, Lagos.

Sani, Abba Aliyu, is Professor and former Head, Department of English at the Ahmadu Bello University, Zaria, Nigeria. He was Secretary of the Nigerian Folklore Society.

Sekoni, Ropo is of the Department of English and Mass Communication, Lincoln University, Pennsylvania. An authority on trickster tales and narrative systems, Sekoni was at one time in the Department of Literature in English, Obafemi Awolowo University, Ile-Ife, Nigeria.

Introduction

- *G. G. Darah*

This book is a celebration of Nigeria's contribution to the world's heritage of letters.

The twenty-three essays in it explore the fundamental role of the intelligentsia in defining and describing the nation state in space and time. The contributions represent some of the best and most articulate assessments of Nigeria's literary discourses in their pre-colonial and colonial phases. The various ideological reflections in the essays reveal significant details about the intellectual and imaginative processes that have gone into the shaping of Nigeria over the centuries. The diversity of themes examined, the historical epochs covered and the geo-political spread of the contributors add to the uniqueness of the volume.

It is appropriate, therefore, that the volume opens with Chinua Achebe's seminal essay, "What had literature got to do with it?" which discusses the place of culture and the arts in the transformation and development of society. Achebe is, without doubt, one of the foremost thinkers of Africa in the sphere of culture and civilization. His acclaim is more easily acknowledged in the field of fiction, particularly in the genre of the novel in which his *Things Fall Apart* (1958) set aesthetic standards for the rest of the continent. In his fictive images, Achebe underscores the central thesis of the critical choices that faced colonized Africa in its unequal exchange with imperialist Europe. In all his novels we discern his abiding concern with the challenges of development and change. His critical essays on literature show a similar passion. In the imaginative and critical works, Achebe grapples with the enigmatic question of an African response to the consequences of the rupturing of African societies in their encounter with capitalist Europe.

In this provocatively titled essay, Achebe restates the thesis of the most appropriate route to Africa's emancipation from the disastrous effects of its conquest by foreign powers. In a style so graceful, simple and profound, he urges the African elite to construct the ideological vehicle that can ferry their nations across the divide that separates neo-colonial Africa from regions of the world that have achieved capitalist modernization. This historic burden is placed on the shoulders of the artist who has used his/her creative genius to affirm and renew humanity through the ages. According to Achebe,

> The universal creative rondo resolves on people and stories. People create stories create people; or rather stories create people create stories.

This point is buttressed with Achebean anecdotes and analogical references. We learn from the essay that before the Japanese had a breakthrough into technology, they first uncovered the wisdoms locked up in their folklore. They collected the oral traditions and translated them for critical attention. This act of cultural rehabilitation was achieved by restoring a primacy of place to the Japanese language as the medium of national discourse. Achebe observes that when the United States of America felt challenged by the pioneering efforts of the former Soviet Union in space exploration in the early 1960s, President John F. Kennedy boosted government subvention for the sciences, yet he did not order a halt to the support for the humanities. In both countries, the arts and sciences marched together to produce the thoughts and ideas that advanced technological innovation. The allusion in these references is to Nigeria of the 1980s when the military government took deliberate steps to undermine the study of the arts and history in favour of the sciences. This misguided policy was a failure, for, as Achebe quips, "What kind of science can a child learn in the absence, for example, of basic language competence and an attendant inability to handle concepts?"

In his prognosis Achebe allies himself with the views of Frantz Fanon and other radical thinkers on the question of mental decolonisation. Literature is an essential ideological weapon in this discourse of development. Properly executed and directed, literary works can free the mind and aid it in the journey of self-discovery and quest for change. Achebe provides samples of folk narratives to illustrate this hermeneutic function. Thus literature is both an inspirer and companion of development or modernization. For literature to serve this function effectively, it should not only educate; it should reveal and amplify abiding values. This is how Achebe describes the art: development nexus:

> ...*I am saying that development or modernization is not merely, or even primarily, a question of having lots of money to spend on blueprints drawn up by the best experts available; it is in a*
>
> critical sense a question of the mind and the will. I am saying that the mind and the will belong first and foremost to the domain of stories. In the beginning was the Word, or the Mind, as an alternative rendering has it. It was the Word or the Mind that began the story of creation.

The imaginative world of literature can serve as an alternative reality for humanity, thus pointing the way to the future that the mind dreams of. Achebe's concluding paragraph puts the issue more graphically:

> Literature, whether handed down by word of mouth or in print, gives a second handle on reality; enabling us to encounter in the safe manageable dimensions of make-belief the very same threats of integrity that may assail the psyche in real life; and at the same time providing through the self-discovery which it imparts, a veritable weapon for coping with these threats whether they are found within our problematic and incoherent selves or in the world around us. What better preparation can a people desire as they begin their journey into the strange, revolutionary world of modernization?

The theoretical issues raised by Achebe recur as analytical props in the essay by Professor Ropo Sekoni in Chapter 2. His quarry is the corpus of Yoruba oral narratives of the pre-colonial discourse. Leaning on scholars such as Terry Eagleton, Edward Said, and Vladimir Propp, Sekoni foregrounds his presentation with the affirmation that literature "is essentially a means of social indoctrination of the consumer by the producer." He immediately adds that "the literature of every community reflects in its totality the values and counter-values that characterize that community in a given period." This view echoes through all the contributions in the volume. As the themes of the folktales referred to by Achebe illustrate, the world of each narrative is divided into competing interests and desires craved or resisted. Sekoni calls this the politics of hierarchy that defines the infrastructure of literary production because "literature as a site of struggle between different groups in a politically divided society is in fact overly announced through the names of different genres of literature."

Sekoni adopts the socio-semiotic strategy that identifies sign-types and their manipulation in individual tales selected from the repertoire of *Ifa* divination narratives of the Yoruba. The *Ifa* corpus is a compendium of data comprising myths, historical legends, pedagogy, fiction, and poetry. On the basis of studies done by scholars such as William Bascom and 'Wande Abimbola, the *Ifa* discourse is comparable to that of the Bible or the Koran in terms of thematic range and stylistic complexity.

Sekoni first tackles the limited perspective of pioneers in the study of this very rich tradition of oral literature who concentrate their critical gaze on elementary literary features. Sekoni observes that Professor Abimbola's studies, for example, fail to recognize "that the ritualization of experience often made possible by the narration of anthropomorphic experiential categories in *Ifa* discourse leads more logically to the examination of the ethico-aesthetic objectives of *Ifa* tales." Sekoni states the matter thus:

> ...the divination discourse shows evidence of a specific that aspires to teach the values of hegemonic politics: monarchy, patriarchy and a socio-economic system of the domination of the community by the privileged class. The discourse also occasionally provides tales that challenge and resist the politics of domination.

The representation of gender relations is one site where ideological contests are articulated. Sekoni reviews tales in which the issue of patriarchy features, adding that "the appropriation of social power by men to the exclusion of women and the inferiorization of women by men" is one way of justifying the subordination of women. Besides cosmogonic narratives, there are others which explore the reality of class-structured existence such as the issues of finance, politics, knowledge or hermeneutics. Some of the tales, says Sekoni, "valorize capital over labour, celebrate primitive accumulation of capital, preach the superiority of man of political power over his subjects and the power of the slave owner over the destiny of the slave." A number of tales dealing with the theme of capitalist accumulation are analysed.

Sekoni's analysis enables us to gauge the age of the history of class and ideological discourse in pre-colonial Yoruba ontology. The chapter demonstrates the utility of Marxist aesthetics in the study of oral texts. The *Ifa*, he says, "constitutes an indigenous system of African philosophy and thought" and therefore deserves a more serious scrutiny than scholars have given to it thus far. Sekoni's concluding remarks underline this point:

> ...whatever else the *Ifa* discourse may be, it is a site for the contestation of values in a politically heterogeneous polity like Yoruba space in which the tension of gender and class relations abounds. In this capacity, the *Ifa* discourse constitutes archaeology-goal field in which social contradictions are mimed to reflect and refract the antagonism that is inherent in a continual struggle between hegemonic and counter-hegemonic interests.

Maikudi Karaye's discussion of the *Bayajida* epic of the Hausa (Chapter 3) takes us to another cultural site which yields interesting information on the link between mythopoeic thinking and the formation of political institutions. Like the Yoruba, the Hausa in Northern Nigeria are a large and coherent linguistic group, with an extensive lore of narratives, institutions and other accomplishments of civilization. The Yoruba live in the rainforest region of the south-west of the country while the Hausa occupy the open savannah and semi-desert territory of the central and north-west regions. The Hausa established an advanced state system before the advent of the Fulani and Islam to the area in the eighteenth century. A number of important books on Hausa tales and legends have appeared, yet there has been no attempt to subject the material to the kind of analysis Karaye offers in this essay.

The *Bayajida* myth was treated in the doctoral thesis by the late Professor Ibrahim Yahaya of Bayero University, Kano. The myth has also featured in the works of scholars such as Mohammad Hambali Jinju, W. K. R. Hallam, and Abdullahi Smith. In Karaye's view, these attempts are limited by their undue reliance on the formalist method of analysis. Karaye observes that the "scientific study of myth recognizes, first that myth belongs to the superstructural level of society, that is, the ideological level which those who listen to or recount the story are generally conscious of." Karaye warns that the plot or narrative logic of the myth should not be isolated outside it but should be examined in the context of the totality of the world in which the mythological tale exists and has meaning.

Several variants of the *Bayajida* myth recorded over a period spanning several decades are examined. From these, Karaye distils the anthropomorphic and ideological meanings hidden in the plot and the text. In one variant, Bayajida appears as an archetypal culture hero who saves a community from an imminent threat and goes on to establish a new order and civilization. In another, the hero, Auta, takes on the image of an Oedipian saviour who subdues a villain and is rewarded by being made a heir-apparent (*Galadima*). The resolution of the conflict in the narrative discloses information about the early stages of state formation. Elements such as walls and gates indicate the institutions of culture which Karaye contrasts with nature. This binary opposition structures the plot of each narrative. There is a predictable teleology in the tales – a character in distress flees home, encounters and overcomes a danger to a community and ends up reinstating the order that was subverted by the external threat. The agent representing the threat stands for anti-culture while its opposite validates culture and human progress.

Karaye's radical epistemology lays stress on the issue of contradiction that is inherent in all social formations. The interface and clash between the opposed forces of destruction and reconstruction produce a dialectical outcome which could lead to progressive change. In the variants of the myth, culture is symbolized by walled towns, home, marriage, traditional titles, etc., while the symbols of anti-culture are snakes, goblins, witches, ogre, etc. From this welter of images we can detect the hidden ruling class ideology prevalent at the time the tales originated or gained literary currency. Karaye interprets the matter thus:

> ...by referring to the social organization and economic activities of the Hausa during the nineteenth century when Hausaland was controlled by the Fulani aristocracy, it is possible to demonstrate that these symbols appear because they represent the interest of the aristocracy. Hausa society then was divided into two distinct classes – the Fulani aristocracy and the Hausa peasantry which also roughly correspond to the distinction between town and countryside respectively.

The Bayajida myth serves other political functions in contemporary Nigeria. Conservative Hausa political leaders deploy the myth to segregate non-Hausa groups. The idea of the myth is used to justify discrimination against people living in the southern fringes of Hausa territory who "are generally described as unbelievers, witches and cannibals who may thus be enslaved or eliminated." This interpretation leads Karaye to conclude that, as a myth,

> ...Bayajida shapes and influences the way and manner Hausa people think and react to social change and is therefore the counterpart of Nigeria's modern myth of development, democracy, national unity, and so on, which are propagated as the true yearnings of the people.

Although his textual evidence is rather sparse, Ichie Ezikeojiaku (Chapter 4) applies a method similar to Karaye's in his commentary on the link between mythological thinking and history in Igbo society. He establishes the cosmological system that structures Igbo beliefs and folklore. Igbo cosmology, he says, "seeks to explain the existence of things in the world and their specific infrastructural and religious order." The principle of dualism is an important element of this cosmology. The Igbo world is divided into two segments, namely, the visible and the supersensible or metaphysical. Both of them interact in a dynamic manner.

The belief in ancestors and other spiritual entities derives from this structure. Ritual is the communicative channel that connects the two worlds. Citing the views of the anthropologist, Victor Uchendu, Ezikeojiaku observes that the relationship between the two hemispheres is usually a realistic one. The dead members of the community are addressed and petitioned as if "they are there". An excerpt of incantatory verse is provided to illustrate this type of communicative event. Other texts of benediction and prayer examined attest to the folk knowledge of the worlds indicated. The first set of texts deals with the acknowledgement of the existence of *Chukwu*, the supreme God of the Igbo.

Several deities, major and minor, are identified in the world of spirits. The geography of their distribution indicates how widespread their influence was during the pre-colonial era of Igbo society. The Igbo society described by Ezikeojiaku was an agrarian one where nature and its worship occupy a pre-eminent place in the cosmology. The world of man or humans is one of the tiers in the mythological order. The angle of emphasis chosen by Ezikeojiaku is somewhat biased in favour of the male gender. In Igbo mythopoesis, man is "half iron and half wood" and is therefore expected to possess the attributes of strength, ingenuity and the spirit of endurance. The symbol of *ikenga* embodies these elements. The fearless nature of the Igbo person, in Ezikeojiaku's view, is so strong that he/she does not cower before God, rather he/she speaks boldly to, and sometimes, cajoles the gods.

What Ezikeojiaku has said of the Igbo in this essay is generally well known. However, he has brought fresh insight by focusing attention on how the texts of folklore and oral literature can provide good material for demonstrating the interface between world-view and the intellectual constructs that derive from them.

Professor Isidore Okpewho has established himself as the most outstanding scholar of oral literature studies in Africa. At a time when many European researchers expressed doubt about the legitimacy of the African heritage of oral literature, Okpewho made a path-breaking intervention with his authoritative work, *The Epic in Africa: Toward a Poetics of the Oral Performance* (1979). His *Myth in Africa: A Study of Its Aesthetic and Cultural Relevance* (1983) further expanded the field of inquiry, so did his *The Oral Performance in Africa* (1990), and *African Oral Literature: Backgrounds, Character, and Continuity* (1992).

The essay on Benin heroic traditions (Chapter 5) exhibits the quality of intellectual depth and originality for which Okpewho's critical work is well known. The essay offers a comprehensive survey of the heroic narratives of the cultural geography of the old Benin Empire. This essay has been expanded into a book form with the title, *Once Upon a Kingdom: Myth, Hegemony, and Identity* (1998). Okpewho defines the historical and cultural networks of the languages and nations in this rain forest region of West Africa. The old Benin Empire was one of the strongest and most dreaded in Africa. Its power and wealth drew the first set of European explorers to the West African coast in the late 15th Century. For four hundred years, Europe's dealings with the region made Benin a pivotal point of contact. Yet accounts of these relations hardly acknowledge the presence of a rich repertoire of literary traditions here uncovered by Okpewho.

The monumental image of Benin as a cultural reference point has been recreated, stored, transmitted and enacted over the centuries throughout the entire region. Okpewho raises the enigmatic question: "How did Benin come to loom so large in the narrative imagination" of the people of the western Niger Delta? He unravels the question by suggesting that the memory of Benin remains dramatic and pervasive because the experiences the various peoples had was "so harsh that the Oba, as Benin in general, frequently emerges as the menace which must be confronted and overcome."

Okpewho tracks the heroic motif in the narratives throughout the region. The material is sourced from stories of various genres – historical accounts, war memoirs, legends, folktales and sundry memorabilia – all of them using Benin as a core image. The published sources include works by the distinguished Benin historian, Jacob Egharevba, J.E. Sidahome's *Stories of the Benin Empire* (1968), and Dan Ben-Amos's *Sweetwords: Story-telling Events in Benin* (1975). Illustrative material is also obtained from J.P. Clark's *The Ozidi Saga* (1977), one of the finest samples of the oral epic genre in Africa.

These published sources are supplemented with field recordings of heroic narratives gathered from researches conducted by students supervised by Okpewho at the University of Ibadan in the 1970s. By scanning these diverse sources, Okpewho is able to assemble a rich store of information on the pervasiveness of the image of Benin in the imagination of the various peoples who have had contacts and relations with the old empire over the millennia.

The inventory of wars and conflicts engendered by events in the empire is wide-ranging and fascinating. Some of the wars resulted from internal feuds amongst chieftains and interest groups within the ruling class of the empire. Others deal with the tension that ruled the relations between the Oba and the palace on one hand and powers and principalities at the periphery of the monarchical authority. Most of the stories relate the city-countryside dichotomy and the fate of the heroic figures associated with rebellions against the autocratic and authoritarian regimes of the monarchs of the various epochs.

One of the mythical figures celebrated in the stories is Agboghidi. Okpewho scrutinizes variants of tales in which the Agboghidi personage appears and assumes local colours, depending on the locale of the narration. In one Etsako story in the Auchi district of the empire, the account of Agboghidi's revolt against discrimination and oppression in the Oba's palace bears striking resemblance with the revenge mission of Ozidi in the Ijo epic of the same name. In fact, the name Agboghidi appears in the Ozidi story. Aruanran is another folk hero that features in many of the stories. As a prince who was cheated of his birthright by being denied the opportunity to ascend the throne, Aruanran inspires sympathy as a tragic hero.

Okpewho points out the contrasting views about the heroic personage to illustrate how the representation in the tales varied from narrator to narrator and from region to region within the empire. Palace courtiers and historians such as Egharevba give the figure scant mention in their accounts. On the other hand, autonomy-seeking sections of the old empire valorize him as a symbol of freedom and justice. In Urhobo narratives, Aruanran features as Arhuaran or Oduaran; the latter name connotes a stout heart and courage. Urhobo, Benin, Esan (Ishan), and Isoko epics describe him as a giant with twenty toes and twenty fingers. In the Udu district of Urhobo, Arhuaran is known as Ovo, a warrior of extra-ordinary strength who combined with Onirhe to found the Udu section. Benin, Urhobo, and Isoko accounts agree that the hero committed suicide by drowning in a lake in Udo area which was his military headquarters and place of refuge when he was sacked from the palace. In Clark's *Ozidi*, he is represented as Ogueren or Oguaran while Igwara is the name used in Ukwuani tales.

Okpewho's perceptive study has offered us new insights and knowledge on the epic genre in West Africa. Here we have an excellent proof of the epic as a quintessential literary form, an embodiment of the best that the human imagination can create, store, and reproduce. Fresh light is thrown on the history of the Benin empire and its relations with neighbouring peoples and kingdoms. Warfare and various forms of weaponry are highlighted. Institutions of politics, culture, administration, and coercion are described. International and diplomatic relations featured in the narratives give us a picture of societies that had all the essential attributes of statehood.

No less enthralling is the manner Okpewho establishes the dynamic interfaces that link history, myth, legend, folktale, drama and other forms that constitute the oral literary heritage. In his conclusion, Okpewho invites us to reconsider the theoretical issue of the boundary between history and fantasy and how scholars should handle such a puzzle within the context of the material under consideration. As he remarks, in the world of the epic and heroic narratives, one man's history is another's fantasy.

Professor Chukwuma Azuonye's essay on the principles of the Igbo oral epic (Chapter 6) is a fitting companion piece to Okpewho's. While Okpewho's study covers the western stretch of the rain forest region of southern Nigeria, Azuonye extends the discourse to an examination of the manifestation of the form in the eastern section of the region. His specific area of investigation is the Ohafia district in the upper reaches of the Cross River basin.

The Ohafia heroic songs are a variety of the genre of war songs *(abu-aha)*, which together with heroic music *(iri-aha)* constitute what the Ohafia people regard "as the highest form of literary art in their culture..." Azuonye first defines the aesthetic principles that govern the composition and delivery of the epic songs. He does not merely apply some formal and *universal* features to local variants; rather he interrogates both the songs, the bards who perform them, the listeners who hear the performance and the culture that produces and appreciates the songs. As Albert Lord once observed, Azuonye takes us into the artistic universe of a living tradition. The result is truly original and refreshing.

From extensive field interviews, Azuonye identifies four epic principles. These are the principles of familiarity, authenticity, clarity, and creative variation. The principle of familiarity concerns the impact the songs have on the community when the heroic deeds of achievers are celebrated. As one of the bards interviewed says, "Whenever this particular type of *iri* is performed, our hearts brim with joy because it is the umbilical cord with which we were born." This sense of nationalism and pride, remarks Azuonye, helps "to ensure the continuance of their heroic spirit from one generation to another."

The principle of authenticity emphasizes the closeness of artistic image to the heroes valorized in the presentation. The singer is expected to present the "literal truth of the history which is common knowledge, the facts of an event or situation which other witnesses can corroborate." Here, indeed, is an aesthetic demand that could constrain creative freedom. Yet there is always room for innovation and graceful abstraction. As Azuonye explains, "like the cartoonist, what the singer needs to do in order to win the approval of his audience is to emphasize a dominant feature of a character, object, place or situation by means of a mythopoeic, descriptive or associative epithet or other formula, especially formulas of the particularized category..."

The other important aesthetic principle is that of clarity which deals with the ability of the bard to put things in a way that they would be clearly perceptible to the listener. This means that the singer has to elaborate, "to add as many details as possible so that the listener will never, at any stage, be at a loss in following the plot of the story as a whole or any stage of its development." The ability of the bard to vary his songs and themes is referred to as the principle of creative variation. The utility of this method is lucidly explained in the analogical reference applied by the poets Azuonye interviewed. Kaalu Ikpo compares the method to a church choral singing; Egwu Kaalu conveys the idea in the imagery of shifting cultivation or the art of going through school. Hear Egwu Kaalu: "After going through one page you turn to another and after going through that page you turn to another, and so on. The same is true of our poetic practice."

We can stretch the analogy a little. What Azuonye has done in unravelling the poetics of Ohafia epic songs is comparable to going through a school of the aesthetics of oral literature. The field evidence he has brought out is fresh and unique. His understanding of Ohafia culture is deep just as his evaluation of the material is profound.

The essay is a fitting tribute to the celebrated bards of the Ohafia Igbo – Kaalu Igirigiri, Ogbaa Kaalu, Egwu Kaalu, and other socio-aestheticians whose creative genius and intellect produced this excellent epic tradition for the world.

Professor J. P. Clark's "Poetry of the Urhobo Dance Udje" (Chapter 7) was one of the first radical articulations of the discourse of African oral literature that was emerging in the early 1960s. This was the time when debates were raging over the identity and academic integrity of the corpus of written African literature in foreign languages. The status of oral literature was problematic in those years. Clark's poetry and drama made incisive impact on the temper and direction of the discourse. He was the first to draw the attention of the literary world to the riches of Udje song-poetry and performance. He had recorded the classical works of celebrated Udje exponents in the Ughievwen (Jeremi) district. The material examined in this essay is a fitting tribute to the poetic genius of the oral artists.

The introductory section of the essay describes the conventional and technical differences that distinguish oral poetry from the tradition of English poetry that dominated the curriculum of degree courses at the time. Clark defines the oral tradition thus: "From the engendering of the word to its rendering as a poem, this is poetry that is delivered by mouth and aimed at the ear to move the whole body. In place of paper, it relies for its propagation and preservation on performance and memory." On strategies of composition and delivery, Clark says that Udje song-poetry is "...topical poetry saved from obscurity and turned into common currency for its immediate public as well as for the stranger from the outside by reason of its having been masterfully minted from particular ores to an alloy of fluid meaning and function."

These aesthetic principles exemplify the originality of Clark's theoretical and exegetical grounding in oral literary poetics. The next section of the essay contains English transcriptions of three sample pieces, followed with a brief analysis of each song, revealing how the "language of each works by images, metaphors, similes, proverbs and a whole gamut of figures of speech." Clark's gifts as a leading African poet are evident in the graceful and ornate rendering of the poems in English language.

It is pertinent to add that Clark's pioneering essay provided a thematic thrust for my doctoral thesis on the Udje genre which was completed for the University of Ibadan in 1982. The insights of his scholarly writings on Udje have inspired more field work and academic interpretations of the tradition. Professor Tanure Ojaide, another notable Nigerian poet, published his book, *Poetry, Performance and Art: Udje Dance Songs of the Urhobo People* in 2003 and my *Battles of Songs: Udje Tradition of the Urhobo* appeared in 2005.

Chapters 8 and 9 explore the exciting world of the genre of the folktale. Both focus on the theme of moral values as exemplified in the tales of the Tiv of Benue State and the Berom of Plateau State in Nigeria. The two language groups are in the Middle Belt region, the veritable linguistic Tower of Babel in the country. The folktale and other fabulary narratives have excited humanity over the ages. Works on African traditions have been coming out since the 1960s. The major ones are H. A. S. Johnston's *A Selection of Hausa Stories* (1966), Ruth Finnegan's *Limba Stories and Story-telling* (1967), Joseph Sidahome's *Stories of the Benin Empire* (1968), Harold Schueb's *The Xhosa Ntsomi* (1975), and Dan Ben-Amos's *Sweetwords: Story-telling Events in Benin* (1975).

Johnston's anthology provided good evidence for assessing the range and quality of material available in the Hausa-speaking areas of Northern Nigeria. But for a long time, little was known of the narrative traditions in the other 300 languages in that geographical region of the country. Thanks to Dr. Tar Ahura and Professor Abu Abarry, we now have information on two of the language groups. The two essays are important because they help to direct critical attention to the oral literature of the so-called minority peoples of Northern Nigeria who are usually neglected in mainstream academic discourse on the area.

Ahura's study of the themes in Tiv folktales is set against the background of the socio-cosmological outlook of the people. Tiv tales are told to celebrate and uphold the spirit of moral purity and egalitarianism. A narrator employs the medium of the fictive experience to create "an alternative world in which those who use their power and influence recklessly are exposed and brought under control." To appreciate how this didactic purpose is achieved, Ahura provides a brief sociological portrait of the Tiv people. The stories explore a cultural site where the tension between the individual and the group is mediated and managed to ensure group solidarity and unity. In this agrarian environment, there is no room for the expression of fierce individualism and egoism. An individual attains a leadership position only if he or she has the qualities that are cherished by his or her kin.

The powers the individual possesses are useful to the extent that they "contribute to the general good of the community." The spirit of co-operation is so strong that "no member of the society usually towers above the others, because to the Tiv, to be unique is tantamount to being evil." Marriage contracts, for example, were arranged in a manner that placed stress on balance and fairness amongst the parties. This system of delicate equilibrium is reflected in the themes and plots of stories.

Ahura observes that Tiv arts of song, dance and story-telling constitute the most positive, life- and value-affirming forces. This is why every household tries to train one or two drummers and performers. Story-telling events and their accompanying songs are occasions "in which powerful members of the community are usually ridiculed and disgraced by the less powerful, thus offering a moral lesson that in human life reckless display of power and influence to the disadvantage of the less fortunate is wrong..." The institutional status accorded these events explains why story-telling sessions are sometimes held in the public square so that their impact can be widely felt. The satirical targets of the stories are people who deviate from communal norms. "That is why" says Ahura, "many Tiv tales are structured on a binary scale of struggle between vice and virtue, with virtue triumphing over vice." The Hare is the trickster personage of the Tiv. Ahura gives the synopsis of two fables to illustrate the core element of social justice in the folktales.

It is important that Ahura has introduced a caveat in the concluding part of the essay. The egalitarian traits codified in the folktale images come from the remote past. The world "fictionalized in the tales predates the present era in which individualism has supplanted communal well-being, at least at the level of national politics." Considering the conflicts and tensions explored in the tales, it would appear that signs of social differentiation were already visible in the society. However, the teleology of the tales shows that "at all times, the display of privilege was considered an anti-social behaviour which attracted penalties." British colonialism and the economic system of capitalism have ruptured what used to be Tiv society. With the advent of British colonial rule, social classes developed in Tiv land. Ahura observes that capitalism has brought no real transformation to the land and, so, "the ethos of a peasant society has survived into the modern era and thus given a contemporaneous relevance to the themes of the folktales."

Abarry begins his analysis (Chapter 8) with remarks on how the concentration on the history and culture of the larger nations of Hausa/Fulani, Kanuri and Nupe made the literatures of the minorities relatively unknown. The Berom, for example, who live in the Jos area of the Plateau have a distinct culture, world-view, national pride, and a sense of cultural continuity. Their folktales offer us a delightful entry into their fascinating world of fear, hopes and aspirations. The themes the stories explore help us to better appreciate how the Berom have been able to fashion intellectual and ideological responses to the challenge of living in their environment.

Berom folktales are grouped into two broad typological categories – the fictitious (Ya) and the true (Ha). Narratives in the first group are dominated by animal characters, with the Hare as the stereotyped folk hero. The Berom employ the Hare personage as a trope to depict human attributes of cunning, agility, resourcefulness and naughtiness. Hare, says Abarry, "exploits his craftiness and wit to subdue stronger, bigger and more ferocious creatures." A narrator employs this image to "promote certain models of behavioural conduct, emphasize the observance of social custom, and instil healthy moral principles in the audience."

/The "Ha" tales, on the other hand, are legendary accounts which "seek to explain past historical events or enable the people to comprehend serious philosophical problems of life pertinent to the Berom world-view." The distinction Abarry seeks to establish here is useful for the purpose of analysis. But he tends to overstretch the point when he says that the fictitious tales are merely for entertainment, "devoid of strong and deliberate moral sentiments" while the so-called true stories "are serious tales which seek to probe the origin and nature of things, both tangible and intangible." The point ought to be made that in the context of performance, both satirical and serious tales can engender a critical response that challenges the average listener to re-examine philosophical problems of life. The antics of the trickster hero usually instigate this kind of intellectual response.

From the background of his Ga people of Ghana, Abarry draws parallels of form and narrative technique. This analogy helps to underscore the core aesthetic principles by which the performance of folktales is judged, at least in the West African cultural region.

As Abarry observes, the demand on the story-teller is "to communicate to the audience in a manner as to persuade and influence them." This is the kind of ideological indoctrination Sekoni says is the central purpose of a literary enterprise. Realism in Berom tales is achieved through the deft "use of an aesthetically patterned language, splendid characterization, narrator-audience rapport and creative spontaneity." The ultimate success of a performance event is determined by how the raconteur transforms the tale "into a unique experience" for the listener. As in the case of the *ntsomi* narrator studied by Scheub, the Berom artist "manipulates core-clichés, episodic patterns, oratory, narrator-audience dynamics, drama, song, and his own mood to ensure a successful performance with a lasting impact on his audiences."

Afam Ebeogu's essay in Chapter 10 is a novel and radical attempt to extend the discourse of feminism to the analysis of oral literature. As he observes in a note, the feminist debate has enjoyed a copious space in Marxist critical theory. Whereas the popular trend is to posit women issues and views as the polar side of a class-divided society, Ebeogu employs the term *feminism* to represent "women's point of view" rather than a class doctrine. For him, Igbo birth-songs afford women an opportunity to represent "their own honest, realistic and constructive perception of order and stability in the society." Like Professor Azuonye, Ebeogu bases his analysis on field material obtained from practitioners and patrons of this brand of oral poetry.

The essay first deals with the occasion for the performance of birth-songs and the medium through which they are realized. The medium includes music and dance. Our appreciation of the poetic quality of the songs is enriched by Ebeogu's analysis of the form, structure and idiom of representative fragments. The examination of the themes of the songs throws more light on how they reflect women's perception of their gender status and role in society. *Mma nwayi ba nnwa* is the Igbo expression for children being the reward of a marriage contract. Another phrasing of the same idea emphasizes that the best way for a woman to satisfy a man is to bear children for him. The values of marriage are celebrated in the songs.

The women also use the songs to articulate their heroic role in the regeneration of humanity. The sexual act that leads to pregnancy is described in one of the songs as the "market of the night/bed". In some songs, this task is referred to metaphorically as the hill of child birth which only the strong and brave can surmount. Thus through the songs the women celebrate life and joys of womanhood. The responsibility of parents is also highlighted in some of the songs. As Ebeogu says, "a good number of the songs emphasize that it is not enough to have a child; it is equally important to give the child much adequate training as would enable it to be useful in life."

The child is both a gift to the family and the community at large, a point conveyed in the remark, "*O nuru akwa nnwa gbata/Na o bughi otu onye nwe nnwa*" Ebeogu concludes his assessment of the genre by returning to the initial distinction he makes between the feminist impulse in Igbo all-women songs on one hand, and the doctrinaire proclamation of an emancipation agenda in women literature in class-divided societies. For Ebeogu, "what these songs project is a kind of mature, positive and benign feminism that could fearlessly ask relevant questions about, and make significant comments on, the nature of the society without seeking to undermine or otherwise subvert cherished traditional values."

Not everyone will agree with Ebeogu that Igbo women want change, "but not the kind of change that would topple in one fell swoop the essential values that sustain the culture to which they are part." No less contentious is Ebeogu's observation that Igbo women prefer the method of urbanity, wit and group confidence to the brazen confrontational attitude in the modern feminist movement. The impression created in these remarks is that women in Igbo belong to one homogeneous, undifferentiated community of interest and that they all have the same stake in preserving "cherished, essential values".

Children are also the subject of Professor Akinwumi Isola's essay in Chapter 11. His focus on the socializing role of literature reiterates Achebe's thesis on the humanizing function of the arts in general. Isola, a Nigerian national laureate of letters, is a leading playwright, critic, poet, and translator. His creative and scholarly works on Yoruba are widely used in educational institutions. In this essay he laments the poor quality of literary material offered for children at the formal and informal levels of education. He situates his analysis in the context of the neo-colonial system in Nigeria, a factor which he says prevents the members of the educated elite from giving to children "a body of written literature that can equip them adequately for the future..."

To establish the contrast between the modern times and the past, Isola takes us to the rich repertoire of genres and traditions of Yoruba oral literature for children. Illustrative material is provided on the various ways poetic language was employed in the socialization of children. In the oral tradition, rhythm and movement were essential elements of the communication process. Teaching of children included drills in pronunciation, tongue-twisters, and mnemonic devices. Poems involving repetition and use of sound effects helped a child to acquire the rudiments of speech. Isola recalls how the allegorical fantasy in folktales, especially of the aetiological variety, was exploited to "awaken the child's creative interest and ability" as the child grew up to fit into society.

The introduction of British colonial education changed all that. Isola observes that as a result, the "old social institutions that ensured the continuity of certain cultural practices have become irrelevant..." Ceremonies connected with the traditional cultural institutions have either been discontinued or altered in ways that do not give room for the expression of artistic material. Much of Yoruba oral poetry for children has disappeared in the process. In Isola's view, what is offered to children in the formal school system is a "parody of Euro-American nursery rhymes taught by half-baked local teachers..."

Isola does not spare Christianity and Islam for alienating the Yoruba from their cultural roots. Belief in these religions, he says, has become an opium that makes the poor and oppressed to move from one religious sect to another looking for salvation from problems caused by the oppressive economic system. Fanaticism is growing, inducing most people to "rely on religious teachings to supply... songs and poetry" used during worship and social occasions. In a sarcastic tone, Isola shows that instead of learning folk rhymes, lyrics, folktales and other suitable oral forms, the Yoruba child now chants " *O se Jesu*" (Thank you, Jesus)

Now that Christian and Islamic songs have virtually replaced Yoruba traditional songs at marriage, funeral, and other ceremonies, what is to be done? Isola is realistic enough to admit that the era of pristine Yoruba culture is gone for good. Yet there are pragmatic steps that can be taken to record extant forms of oral literature. These include lullabies, nursery rhymes, tongue-twisters, counting mnemonics, games, riddles, jokes, proverbs, and folktales. Writers for children are to be encouraged to utilize the material to produce books and teaching aids, provided that the writers take advantage of advances in science and technology in the presentation of the material. Many Yoruba writers, including Isola, have attempted to do this over the years. But support for their endeavour has so far been too meagre and uncoordinated to yield the kind of result that can equip the Yoruba to effectively combat the menace of cultural alienation engendered by neo-colonialism in all spheres of Nigerian life.

Professor Sam Asein's survey of literature and society in Lagos (Chapter 12) brings us into the early phases of the scribal or written traditions of literatures in Nigeria. Asein's essay is one of the first attempts to assess how Lagos, the capital of Nigeria from colonial times to 1990, became the beach-head for the propagation of British cultural values in the country. The importance of the essay is enhanced by the copious references the author makes to the views which defined British colonial policy for about half a century.

One key finding of Asein's survey is the role played by institutions of colonial administration, the church and the popular press of the time. These were the primary ideological institutions the British employed to construct a Nigerian state in their own image. Together, they helped to produce an elite which, in the words of Wole Soyinka, tried to "out-Europe Europe" in manners and taste. The products of the colonial education were weaned to accept the superiority of European culture and world-view. Professor Emmanuel Ayandele, the noted historian of missionary education in Nigeria, once described the elite of the period as deluded hybrids who believed that only Shakespearean English was worth speaking. As Asein observes, the policy of the church mission and the government schools was to groom native Englishmen rather than Nigerians. Thus in their literary output, the elite produced poor imitations of European classics.

The essay devotes considerable space to how the various colonial institutions promoted literature. The newspapers were the main avenues. Some of them regularly carried advertisements for essay competitions and literary contests "to teach the refinements of style to the new literates and the emphasis was on correctness of diction and, especially in the theatre, on 'pronunciation and articulation'" The attempt to make Nigerian youths of the time learn Roman and Greek models of literature was condemned by sections of the national press as a mad gamble in which the youths bartered away their Africanity. The Nigerian educated elite who strived to imitate Europeans are referred to as "Black Victorians"; the reigning British monarch at the time was Queen Victoria.

The press also promoted the emerging age of enlightenment and helped to shift attention from the oral tradition to the written one. It was truly an era of a people in transition. The names and ownership of the newspapers reflected the spirit of the age, for example, *The African Times* and *The Anglo-African*.

Literary clubs offered incentives for creative writing. Their names, too, are a commentary on the ideological outlook of the period. There were, for example, the Brazilian Dramatic Company, the Melodramatic Society, and the Aurora Club. The clubs featured concerts "to develop in the community an interest in dramatic literature and to acquaint the audience with that genre." Asein points out that the production of concerts "showed a conscious effort to imitate such styles and mannerisms as were current in Europe..." and the "criteria for critical judgment were those which were considered acceptable to public taste in the mother country." The stress on didactic literature continued into the first decades of the twentieth century.

Darah's essay (Chapter 13) extends the insights in Asein's. But whereas Asein's quarry is the Lagos colonial community, Darah's probe covers all the major cultural zones of the country from the early twentieth century to the eve of independence in 1960. The analysis brings to critical limelight fresh information on various epochs of Nigerian letters and the political and ideological issues that the writers responded to. Professor Omafume Onoge's "The Crisis of Consciousness in Modern African Literature: A Survey" offers a continent-wide treatment of the subject. (See Chapter Two in Georg Gugelberger (ed) *Marxism and African Literature,* Africa World Press, 1985)

Darah's theoretical standpoint is anchored on the concept of "ideological orphanage", a phrase that sums up the process through which the Nigerian intelligentsia became subordinated to and made hostage to the world-view fostered by colonialism and foreign religions and their mediating institutions. Asein concentrates on the Christianised elite; Darah begins from an earlier period of the Islamic Jihad in Northern Nigeria and the intellectual ferment that grew from it. The conquest of the Hausa states by the Uthman Dan Fodio-led Jihad around 1804 introduced a form of cultural imperialism. Following this political transition, the mythology of the Middle East became the basis for validating intellectual activity. The role of the "Black Victorians" already treated by Asein is also examined.

What kind of literature could such alienated elite produce? Material from both the northern and southern halves of the country is examined to show how the themes and styles of the works betrayed the ideological outlook of a conquered intelligentsia. Writing in indigenous languages was one way the elite tried to create a distinct national tradition of literature. Yet the output of notable writers in Hausa and Yoruba reveals that the Bible and the Koran had a strong grip on their imagination.

It was the Hubert Ogunde itinerant theatre that first struck out on a trajectory for a truly national tradition of literature. Ogunde's career points to a trend in which the arts were a handmaiden of politics in the era of anti-colonial mobilization. The vigorous support the theatre received from the indigenous press indicated the possibilities that awaited the country had the mission of the nationalist struggle not been betrayed by the compromised elite as Frantz Fanon would have it.

An initiative similar to Ogunde's was started in the east of the country in what is now known as "Onitsha Market Literature". This ferment occurred in the market town of Onitsha which, like Harlem in New York of the 1920s, hosted a literary renaissance. The Onitsha tradition produced over 200 titles in two decades. Yet the themes and aesthetics of the works exhibit the ideological dependency of the authors. Unlike Chinua Achebe who was educated in the same area and who was to inaugurate a solid tradition for the African novel, the authors of the Onitsha chapbooks were influenced by the works of English popular writers such as Rider Haggard, Edgar Wallace, and Evelyn Waugh. Of course, the cinema, as Professor Emmanuel Obiechina points out in Chapter 19, was a major foreign influence.

The alienating power of education is further illustrated by the contrast Darah seeks to make between Amos Tutuola, for example, and the generation of university-trained writers. Tutuola took over the narrative form of European literature and domesticated it to communicate Yoruba folklore and imagination. Darah says that in spite of their prolific output, many of the writers educated at Ibadan were obviously indebted to the aesthetic canons of the Anglo-Saxon heritage in which they were schooled. The difficulty some of the early writers faced can be gleaned from the power wielded by foreign publishers and critics at the time. In all likelihood, the dependency on imperialist institutions of cultural and intellectual production did considerable harm to the emergent national literature. The issue is examined in detail in Abba Sani's essay on "Cultural Imperialism and Publishing in Northern Nigeria" in Chapter 20 below.

Historians have given copious accounts of the Islamic revolution that swept through northern Nigeria in the early nineteenth century. There are also extensive comments on how the British colonial forces under the command of Frederick Lugard subdued the fierce resistance mounted by the Sokoto Caliphate from the end of the 1890s to the dawn of the twentieth century. Yet chroniclers of the era have hardly acknowledged the significance of the peasant uprising during those wars. Perhaps, for the first time, Dr. Mohammed Sokoto (Chapter 14) gives us a sensitive interpretation of the decade-long rebellion. It is instructive that it was the most oppressed classes – the slaves and peasants – that achieved this historic feat. The Satiru revolt, as it is called, was "initially directed against the aristocrats of the Sokoto Caliphate and later, with the imposition of British imperialism on the society, was aimed at overthrowing British colonial rule." It is even more revealing that Mohammed Sokoto has sourced his evidence from the repertoire of songs and poems created by that revolutionary ferment.

The essay situates the rebellion in the context of the Mahdist ideology of liberation which is central to Islamic movements in Africa. The unique character of the Satiru uprising is defined as an attempt to rupture both the decaying feudal system and the new colonial order being established by the British. The Satiru movement had the attributes of the Paris Commune which sought to throw off the yoke of the feudalists and the bourgeoisie in France from the late 1780s. There is another unique feature of the Satiru uprising. Most peasant revolts, Dr. Sokoto Mohammed points out, "merely made economic demands but that of Satiru was aimed at seizing the political power of the Sokoto Caliphate" The *talakawa* or oppressed classes also targeted the institutions of British colonialism – taxes, military conscription, compulsory labour, etc.

Exhausted and overwhelmed, the *Satirawa* were finally defeated in the battle of March 10, 1906. Thousands of peasants were massacred; about 3,000 women and children were handed over to the Sultan of Sokoto for disposal. Lugard said the massacre was necessary because "the military situation demanded a signal and overwhelming victory for the restoration of British prestige and prevention of any such rising in the future." The crushing of the Satiru rebellion is one of the bloodiest episodes in what historians call the conquest of Nigeria.

The detailed background given by Dr. Sokoto Mohammed helps the reader to appreciate the themes and idioms of about eight representative fragments of songs discussed in the rest of the essay. For example, the English rendering of one of the songs captures the brutality of the massacre:

> Look at how people are being hunted like antelopes
> As if it were antelopes being hunted in Satiru
> Look at how people are being slit like gourds
> As if it were gourds being slit at Satiru
> Look at how a whole town is so red and glistening
> As if it were alharimi spread out in Satiru...
> Look at how the settlement of bastards developed into a town
> Today only foxes are waiting in Satiru.

The symmetry, imagery and sense of urgency conveyed in the song attest to the magnitude and horror of the massacre. The eighth song fragment gives a contrary view to the version of the Satirawa. The poem, apparently composed by a loyalist of the feudal regime, attempts to discredit the leaders of the uprising. The poet says that "Unorthodox knowledge is insane/Which was typical of the leaders of the Satiru". Later, the poet rejoices that "Thanks be unto Allah for wiping the clique of the devilish dwellers of Satiru". But the final comment on the war is taken from the perspective of the heroic but vanquished peasants. They lost the war, but achieved a feat by killing Hillary, a British commander:

> Satirawa!
> > Heathens of the hard plains
> > Despite your annihilation, you have killed Hilliri.

Professor Karin Barber's "Style and ideology in Fagunwa and Okediji" (Chapter 15) opens with an affirmation of the basic Marxist thesis that all art is ideological. Barber says this is so because "every work of literature reveals a configuration of beliefs and assumptions about the nature of the world..." As she puts it, whether the author is conscious of it or not, his/her position "serves particular social interests by legitimizing, tacitly or explicitly, certain social structures." Barber adds the important caveat that this does not mean that the works of literature produced by members of the same class express an identical configuration of beliefs." All literary critics of Marxist persuasion duly recognize this warning.

It is against this methodological background that Barber examines the works of two Yoruba leading novelists of the twentieth century – Daniel Olorunfemi Fagunwa and Oladejo Okediji. Barber's conclusion is anticipated in the following remarks:

> Fagunwa is solidly conservative, upholding with eulogistic
> fervour the established authority structure and values that maintain it. Okediji
> is relatively radical, expressing disgust with the state of the society and
> calling for action from the under-privileged to put things right. Okediji,
> unlike Fagunwa, is able to transcend the values of his own interest group (the
> elite) to ally in sympathy with the rest of society.

Again, following Marx, Barber says that besides individual talent, there are socio-historical circumstances that account for the different ideological standpoints manifested by the two writers. Fagunwa wrote in the 1940s and 1950s when British colonial ideology held sway. Okediji's two novels were published in 1969 and 1971, the period when the Nigerian civil war (1967-70) had shattered myths about the country's capacity to manage inter-group conflicts. Fortuitous wealth from oil had intensified class differences, making conspicuous consumption a trademark of the emergent national bourgeoisie. Fagunwa and Okediji belonged to the fraction of the elite – educators and academics – which had suffered a sharp decline in fortunes as a result of the economic crisis of the war years.

The thematic and stylistic reflections of the changes indicated above are reviewed in the rest of the essay. On characterization, for example, Barber explains that while Fagunwa's heroes "inhabit a stable social world which they temporarily leave, and always return to..." the hero in Okediji's novels lives in "an unstable and hostile social environment" where he trusts no one but himself, where he "suspects traps and betrayals at every step." This is the world of neo-colonial capitalism in Nigeria, a world where society, in Barber's view, is "a competitive jungle through which the individual has to pick a dangerous path." The assessment of Fagunwa's aesthetics is made more vivid by Barber's close reference to the text of the novels. There have been numerous comments on Fagunwa's writings, yet none has the acuteness and clarity in this essay.

The stylistic nuances in Okediji's works are evaluated in the context of the socio-historical ferment already indicated. The tensions and pressures of urban life are reflected in the manner the protagonists respond to them in thought and action. The plots of the narrative, says Barber, "move at break-neck speed..." with "brief pauses for rest and reflection merely accentuating the narrative's headlong pace." The elements of the thriller are manifest in the use of interior monologue and flashbacks. Fagunwa's leisurely form suits his sermonizing purpose just as Okediji "chooses a form which best allows him to express his conception of society's moral crisis." Barber describes Okediji's strategy as the "efficacy of action" while that of Fagunwa supports the ethic of "social immobilism".

The use of language by both authors also reveals their moral social sympathies. In Barber's judgment, "Fagunwa erects an imposing artificial façade of style which keeps the reader at a distance, Okediji is a master of the colloquial." Students of Fagunwa and Okediji will benefit immensely from the detailed textual analysis attempted in this section. Barber concludes by expressing a bias for Okediji whose "apparently natural, speech-like style does more than reveal understanding of, and sympathy with, the common man: it makes a specific moral point."

The late Abubakar Imam is to written Hausa literature what Fagunwa is to Yoruba letters. Both pioneered an aesthetics that has continued to influence the production and appreciation of indigenous tradition of writing. Just as Fagunwa wrote to promote an ethic that reinforced the world-view of the conservative substratum of the Yoruba Christian elite so did Imam devote his career as creative writer and editor to the defence of the British colonialists and their feudal allies in Northern Nigeria. The two writers were beneficiaries of the teacher training education which suited the colonial mandate of subordinating the emergent national elite to the overall design of British imperialism. They were rewarded for their labours by winning the Margaret Wrong Memorial prize for creative writing. In 1979, Imam received the Nigerian National Merit Award.

Professor Abba Aliyu Sani examines in Chapter 16 what he describes as the conservative conscience that made Imam a prodigious figure in the intellectual firmament of Northern Nigeria. The essay offers fresh and illuminating information on Imam's fictional writings and the comments in the Hausa language newspaper, *Gaskiya Ta Fi Kwabo* (Truth is worth more than a penny). Imam did not just write to influence public opinion in favour of the colonial system; he was an active political figure for several decades. Sani provides important details of Imam's political career.

Imam was a member of the Northern Region House of Assembly and served as General Secretary of the Northern Peoples Congress (NPC) which was the ruling party in Nigeria from 1957-1966. Imam was also the first Superintendent of the Northern Regional Literature Agency (NORLA) which promoted literacy and publishing. This strategic position enabled Imam to influence a tradition of writing that orientated readers to share the world-view of the British colonial regime. This was during the decisive decade of 1950-60 when the anti-colonial struggle in Nigeria was at its peak. Imam authored about seventeen books, including those of fiction, travelogue, religion, history, biography and journalism.

Sani goes into rare archival sources to support his thesis that Imam promoted the colonial project in Northern Nigeria. The first sources are the pages of *Gaskiya* which, during Imam's editorship, served the propaganda needs of the British. Also highlighted are Imam's views against the pro-independence demands championed by nationalists such as Dr. Nnamdi Azikiwe.

In the second segment of the essay, Sani reviews Imam's most important fictional work, the three-volume story, *Magana Jari Ce* (The craft of story-telling is a valuable asset). The story was published in the 1930s before Imam became an editor. The book celebrates the superiority of the pen (writing) over the gun (force). This didactic message is conveyed through the persona of the parrot in the tales. In Sani's view, the "dominance of emirs and palaces as the centre of all activities, be they legal, economic, political or cultural...allows Imam to restate and reinforce the significance of monarchical and traditional leadership." He adds that Imam's glorifying portrait of the feudal institutions "presents emirs as the bastions of justice, fair play and the defenders of the people against oppression." In contrast to this image, peasants and other lower classes are stereotyped as lazy, poor and undesirable. Yet it is these "wretched of the earth" of northern Nigeria whose frequent revolts have continued to undermine the legitimacy of the feudal aristocracy. Sani's perceptive analysis helps us to understand the intellectual roots of the ideology that has kept this section of the population in bondage several decades after Nigeria attained independence from British colonial rule.

Sa'adu Zungur whose life and works are reviewed by Professor Dandatti Abdulkadir in Chapter 17 was a contemporary of Abubakar Imam in politics. Although Sa'adu also used the medium of poetry to mobilize public opinion, he was always on the radical side of the political spectrum. He belonged to the intelligentsia of the Northern Elements Progressive Union (NEPU), the party he founded with the late African revolutionary, Mallam Aminu Kano. Dandatti Abdulkadir was a member of that radical circle based in Bauchi. He did his doctorate degree on the political and literary career of Sa'adu Zungur. This chapter is taken from Abdulkadir's bio-critical book, *The Poetry, Life and Opinions of Sa'adu Zungur*, published by The Northern Nigerian Publishing Company, Zaria, in 1974.

Sa'adu Zungur was a member of the Nigerian Youth Movement which pioneered the anti-colonial struggle in Lagos in the 1930s. Sa'adu also served as the secretary of the National Council of Nigeria and the Cameroons (NCNC), the party that spearheaded the independence movement in the 1940s and 1950s. He was the first student from Northern Nigeria to be admitted to the Yaba

Higher College, now Yaba College of Technology, the only institution of higher learning in the Nigeria at the time.

Professor Abdulkadir brings a rich background into the analysis of Sa'adu's poetry.

Information is provided on the sociology of the written word during this era. There is a summary of the fierce political debates that raged in Northern Nigeria in the 1950s and the role poetry and public commentary played in shaping political opinion. Sa'adu was reared in a homestead of poetry and learning, his father was a scholar and teacher of the Koran. Iconoclast and rebel with a cause, Sa'adu, in the words of Abdulkadir, "found it difficult to fit into the society in which he lived." An advocate of radical reforms, he worked hard to see that the poor and oppressed people felt the impact of the social "revolution that was taking place..." He argued that without access to education "Northerners would lag behind their counterparts in the South."

Sa'adu founded the Zaria Literary Society, the first of such in the north of the country. The NEPU which he founded with Aminu Kano, Maitama Sule, and Abubakar Zukogi in 1950, was dedicated to the reform of the Native Authority system, the emancipation of the down-trodden masses (*talakawa*), and the provision of welfare schemes in the Northern region. Sa'adu started the translation of the Koran into Hausa in order to enable the masses to understand it. Although he died in 1958 at 43, Sa'adu remains a revolutionary icon, a man who, in the words of Professor Abdulkadir, "awakened his people so that they might take their rightful position in Nigeria."

The highlights of Sa'adu's eventful political career serve Abdulkadir well in the assessment of the themes and idioms that make his poetry a unique tradition in Hausa literature of the twentieth century. Textual evidence is sourced from the long poem, "Wakar Maraba da Soja", a tribute to the heroism of Nigerian soldiers who fought in the 1939-45 Second World War. The narrative format of the poem enables Sa'adu to combine the eulogy of the soldiers with commentary on burning issues of the time. Imam, as we have seen, also used his writings to drum up support for Britain in that global conflict. Whereas Imam represents Nigerians as subject people who were expected to be grateful to their colonial overlords, Sa'adu extols the Nigerian soldiers for fighting to "preserve freedom and save humanity from destruction." As Abdulkadir observes, Sa'adu supported the fight for freedom because he wanted its benefits to reach Nigeria:

> Useless is freedom where there is poverty...
> Never while men are scorned, never while they are hungry,
> never till these are ended, can freedom endure.

Cosmopolitan flavour is another feature of Sa'adu's poetry. His poems on the Second World War have references to countries and personalities involved. We learn of Adolf Hitler's Germany that started the war and its allies such as Italy and Japan. There are allusions to the invasion of Ethiopia by Italy, the occupation of France by Germany, battle scenes in India and Burma, and the American use of the atomic bomb on Japanese cities. The mention of these historical episodes enriches the poems as the work of an intellectual. For example, besides the alliterative resonance in the Japanese names, there is a thrill in this paragraph describing the devastation caused by the bomb:

> What devastation the atom bomb has wrought in the city of Hiroshima!
> Fire as far as Wa'kayama, yes and even to Yokohama;
> northwards of Fujiyama, all the way to Tanega and Kogoshima like the flame of Jahima...

It is only someone of Sa'adu's intellectual stature who was current in international politics and the details of the military campaigns that could reveal this much information in four lines.

With the staging of his play, *This is Our Chance*, in 1945, James Ene Henshaw (a medical doctor) inaugurated Nigeria's written tradition of drama in English. Hubert Ogunde emerged on the scene at about the same time. More than a decade was to pass before Wole Soyinka and J.P. Clark became established as leading playwrights. Henshaw published no less than seven plays in 25 years. Yet the discourse of Nigerian drama in English hardly recognised his contribution until about the mid 1980s. This gap is what Professor Aderemi Bamikunle attempts to fill in Chapter 18.

Like most writers who came after him, Henshaw was motivated to write to promote the project of cultural rehabilitation. He had a clear view of the responsibility that faced African artists in the colonial period. As Henshaw explains, "it was far more important today for Africans (*sic*) to explain Africa to each other." But Henshaw is realistic enough to admit that only the positive and progressive elements of African culture should be preserved and that aspects of Western/foreign culture can be grafted to the African one to create what Bamikunle calls "a vibrant and dynamic contemporary culture which will meet the needs of the present as well as the future."

A synopsis of Henshaw's seven dramatic works follows the general introduction. The summary serves a useful purpose as the gamut of the playwright's themes is laid out for appreciation. The dramaturgy of African plays in European languages has been vigorously debated since the 1960s. The debts the playwrights owe to other traditions have been well acknowledged. Soyinka, Clark and Ola Rotimi have written essays and books to explain the African idioms and techniques of their works. Bamikunle examines the attempts made by Henshaw to incorporate elements of African theatre into his plays. One such element is ritual, a dramatic short-hand in which we encounter the merging of the spiritual and the human worlds.

Henshaw enhanced the African flavour of his plays by re-interpreting materials from folklore – myths, legends, fables, songs, drumming and dances. He experimented with the use of a "suitable language" to convey the thought processes of his characters. Bamikunle concludes the essay with a pertinent comment on Henshaw's original contribution to the dramaturgy of Nigerian English language drama. Whatever the more celebrated playwrights such as Soyinka, Clark, Rotimi, Wale Ogunyemi, and Femi Osofisan have done is "like building on the foundation laid by Ene Henshaw." In this way, Henshaw "made bold and original attempts to arrest the twilight in the cultural homestead in the hope of fortifying the structures of creative adaptation to a new and changing environment."

Chapter 19 dealing with the influence of the newspaper and the cinema is taken from Professor Emmanuel Obiechina's fascinating study of the tradition of popular writing now known as Onitsha Market Literature. The focus is on the ways the mass media of newspapers and the cinema influenced the themes, styles and outlook of the authors of the miscellany that constituted that unique tradition. The Onitsha renaissance in letters covered the period of the mid 1940s to 1966 when the military coup of that year set in motion a chain of events that ultimately destroyed the social and economic foundations of the literature and its patrons. Obiechina observes that the authors of the pamphlets drew the portraits of their popular heroes from the newspapers, the radio and other mass media, "but these were reinforced by the soap-box, the pulpit, and above all, the biblical tradition."

A section of Darah's essay has already evaluated the output from Onitsha. A thematic survey of the over 200 titles fostered at Onitsha shows that contemporary politics was a favoured subject for the writers. No less than eight titles were based on the dramatic events of the 1960 Congo crisis in which the first Prime Minister, Patrice Lumumba, was killed. Political events that culminated in the military coup d'etat in Nigeria in 1966 were documented in about six titles. Obiechina observes that a "detailed study of these pamphlets shows that as well as fostering a political consciousness, the newspapers have contributed considerably to the conditioning of the attitudes of their readers to political events in Africa and elsewhere."

Cinema houses offered entertainment to urban dwellers in the years under review. The cinema facilities were owned and run mostly by Lebanese businessmen. The films they showed were from America and Europe. Yet they enjoyed tremendous patronage from the youths and other sections of the urban populace that needed modern forms of art and leisure. In this way, the cinema became the primary source of education for city dwellers. The cinema shaped attitudes to dressing and fashion. Images of romantic love came from the films. The variety from India was very popular. The definition of material success was based on what people saw in the films. The orientation fostered by the cinema valorized values and styles from Western capitalist societies. The spectacular images of American and European life style served as models for the elite.

Obiechina points out that the films portrayed the glamour and opulence of Hollywood. The American super star was an icon. The devil-may-care toughness of the heroes, and the slick efficiency of the gang-leaders were admired. According to Obiechina,

> The man who is successful with women, the successful gangster, the man of action, the man...who drinks hard, chain-smokes, overdresses and talks tough is the hero after whom film-going adolescents and those adults who are committed to acquiring the new style of life model their lives.

The cinema also popularised new ideas about feminine beauty, with film stars serving as models for young men and women. Obiechina says that the popular writers' "ideal of feminine beauty is the film actress, and when they describe beautiful women, the wasp-waisted, mascara-groomed, scarlet-lipped woman is their model." Obiechina makes an important remark that many of the pamphlets carried photographs of European and Indian film stars on their cover pages, a marketing technique borrowed from the "Indian popular pamphlets on which the African equivalents were originally modelled." The music tracks in the films became the favoured songs referred to by the authors. It was fashionable at the time for many school boys and girls to own record song books which they displayed conspicuously on their parlour tables and spent considerable part of their holidays singing the songs.

Although Obiechina underlines the manner these commercially-inspired media debased popular tastes and promoted cultural alienation, he points out how the pamphlets transformed "tradition-bound attitudes and outlooks into those which 'liberate' individuals and invest them with a certain ubiquitous vitality and assertive autonomy." In the long run, the literature influenced by the mass media in Onitsha reflected some measure of progress to modernity by broadening the vistas of human experience.

Professor Abba Sani's incisive analysis of the conservative impulse in the writings of Abubakar Imam has already pointed to how literature was used to control the outlook of the educated elite in Northern Nigeria during the colonial period. In Chapter 20, Sani assesses the influence of British cultural imperialism on the region. In the words of Sani, "the subordination of the Northern Nigerian elite to the likeness of their conquerors was achieved not just through military superiority but also through the subtle structures of education, religion, and the technology of the printing and publishing of literature."

The British encouraged local writing by translating story-books from Arabic and English into Nigerian languages, particularly Hausa. For the non-Hausa language groups, this amounted to double linguistic colonization. The Zaria

Literature Bureau was set up for this purpose. It organized writing competitions which produced manuscripts for publication. The generation of writers fostered by the Bureau includes Abubakar Tafawa Balewa, Nigeria's first prime minister, Abubakar Imam, Tafida Wusasa, Bello Kagara, and Muhammadu Gwarzo. Nearly all of them turned out to be apologists of the British colonial regime.

The North Regional Literature Agency (NORLA) was set in 1953 to publish and distribute seventeen news-sheets in major languages in the region. As Sani points out, with the exception of Sa'adu Zungur, "all the authors promoted by NORLA deemed themselves as having enormous stakes in the survival of the colonial system." NORLA also promoted Hausa language to the position of a lingua franca in the Northern region. The Agency also insisted on publishing religion-based literature in Arabic or *ajami* because of its perceived relevance to the masses. The undisclosed reason, in Sani's view, was that "the works helped to consolidate colonial exploitation and domination."

Sani's detailed study discloses the subtle political and structural instruments the British manipulated to undermine the emergence of a vigorous national publishing industry in northern Nigeria. That process took place during the sixty years of colonialism (1900–1960). The resultant damage was so severe that four decades after Nigeria's independence, both the popular press and book publishing in the north of the country are still comparatively underdeveloped.

In Chapter 21, Professor Kole Omotoso strikes a more optimistic note in his assessment of the opportunities and responsibilities of the indigenous publisher in the post-colonial milieu. His analytical thrust leans on the enigmatic riddle posed by Achebe in the first chapter, to wit: what kind of development project can a people conceive and execute in the absence of confidence in indigenous language and culture? Omotoso extends that thesis by observing that if language is a fundamental vehicle of culture, how can a people or country develop its culture and civilization when its thoughts are conveyed in an alien tongue or medium?

To tackle the problem requires a programme of cultural decolonization, a project which Omotoso says "implies seeking redefinition in our own languages." The works in these languages should be made available by a national publishing concern. Sani has shown how such an initiative in Northern Nigeria produced results that tightened the neo-colonial noose on the area. In the absence of a national publishing company, Omotoso advocates the intervention of "a conscious and conscientious publisher, a nationalist educator…"

Omotoso ties the search for the "conscientious publisher" to the larger agenda of trying to construct an alternative system to the one employed by imperialist powers to dominate former colonies. Citing the views of Frantz Fanon, Amilcar Cabral and other authorities on culture and the colonial question, Omotoso says that this kind of publisher has to denounce his or her class roots to stay with the oppressed majority and "make his enterprise available to them for the furtherance of their revolutionary struggle."

Yet there are difficulties and impediments. The publishing industry is technology-dependent. Even the most patriotic of publishers relies on imported machinery and skills to remain in business. Marketing outlets for books are controlled by foreign publishing houses. As Omotoso admits, a successful indigenous entrepreneur needs the backing of a radical political movement. By the second decade of independence, nearly all such projects in Africa had collapsed as soon the original thinkers and leaders were out of power. Notwithstanding these obstacles, Omotoso thinks that the indigenous publisher can make some headway. Investment in literacy programmes in local languages is one such avenue. Omotoso says that the work of translators is crucial in this respect because "the process of converting the present oral cultural manifestations of the masses of the people into writing must witness radicalizing programmes..."

How would the conscientious publisher sustain his enterprise in a profit-oriented, capitalist milieu? Omotoso's advice is that he or she should not "enrich himself beyond the recognition of his society" because if the publisher were involved in "the struggle of the people, he would know that the people's profit is his gain in the long run." Although Omotoso recognizes that an atmosphere for this kind of altruism did not exist in Nigeria at the time he wrote, he urges that "the indigenous publisher...must help towards the creation of such a society, a society in which books, like garri and plantain" will be both available and affordable.

The context of Omotoso's optimistic prognosis should be understood. This was in the middle of the 1970s when much of Africa was in a renascent spirit with regard to the anti-colonial struggle. Guerrilla armies of liberation had won significant victories in Mozambique, Angola, and Guinea-Bissau and Cape Verde. The anti-apartheid movement was at an irreversible trend in Zimbabwe, Namibia and South Africa. The Organisation of African Unity had a coherent voice on the total liberation of the continent. Even neo-colonial Nigeria was astir with radical thinking and popular activism. The teaching of Marxist courses in universities was fostering a new generation of elite that clamoured for radical change in class and social relations. The universities in Ibadan, Ife and Zaria were the main centres of the discourse. The influence of this intellectual ferment is obvious in Omotoso's idiom and projections.

Barely ten years after this essay was first published, the economy of most African countries collapsed under pressure from the World Bank and the International Monetary Fund. The fortunes of the elite and middle class also declined. Many indigenous publishing establishments suffered as a result. One of the casualties was the Onibonoje group in Ibadan which sponsored the book containing Omotoso's controversial essay.

A quarter of a century after the book appeared, the socio-economic crisis in most of Africa is so grave that it will be difficult to find an indigenous publisher who would ignore the cold logic of the balance sheet and make books available and affordable.

Chapter 22 is a tribute to Cyprian Ekwensi and a critique of the aesthetic popularized by his writings. This is an engaging essay by Professor Femi Osofisan, one of Africa's most radical playwrights and theatre theoreticians of the twentieth century. The essential features of the phenomenon Osofisan calls "paraliterature" are manifested in the Onitsha market literature examined by Obiechina. This genre of popular writing is a product of a cosmopolitan culture that developed in the 1940s in Nigeria and reached maturity in the 1970s. The goal of this writing, he says, is to "lure the reader temporarily into a world of sensual fantasy, in which the familiar social and moral order is threatened, but ultimately restores itself, thanks to the reader's *alter ego*, the Superhero."

Osofisan first establishes the theoretical moorings of the genre as a product of the universal quest for leisure, a substitute for edifying experience. The appeal of popular literature derives from humanity's primordial instinct for the "gratification of our inherent lust." Osofisan's insightful description is worth recalling in part:

> We relax very rarely to enrich our mind, but frequently to stupefy it, to shield it away from the nuisance of consciousness. Always we relax in order to forget, to cushion ourselves from quotidian realities...
> It is no wonder then that the undefinable anguish of modern industrial state, particularly in the capitalist and capitalist-supportive countries, is daily drowned, before the para dawn's rude awakening ,in the wash of sex, alcohol, and tawdry art. Para literature, like drugs, like television, like a night's whore, creates its own illusion of freedom, a cocoon of assurance for the battered psyche, and it thus partakes of the deceptive ritual of escapism in the modern city. It is because this drama is only a trance, because the catharsis is manqué, and the illusion never lasts, and because the refuge provides no lasting solution to the problems of living, that the literature sold to the masses is appropriately regarded as socio-political opiate.

The origin of the form is traced to western Europe of the eighteenth and nineteenth centuries. The socio-demographic forces that helped its growth are mentioned. As the population of the poor increased in the cities, those living in the squalid slums needed new forms of art as spiritual analgesia. In Osofisan's view, this is the milieu where popular "theatres and music halls flourish, newspapers, pamphlets and penny dreadfuls flood the market; it is the age of Zola, Dickens and Turgenev,..." He observes that the commercial interests that made the literature to proliferate also cheapened its stylistic quality and aesthetic value. Similar developments occurred in Nigeria in the post-civil war years of the 1970s.That was the era when, in Osofisan's words, "our nations were sinking fast in the clutches of the capitalist economies of the West." As a result,

Preliminary matter xliii

"our societies are splitting up rapidly into more defined, more antagonistic classes; the cities are dividing into ghettoes on one side and well laid out elite plots on other; 'development' to our ruling class takes shape in the openly promoted westernization of our countries."

The publishing firms in Nigeria were aware of the changes and capitalized on the situation to win more readers. In the 1960s, the literate audience was made up mainly of the educated, petty bourgeoisie, "by the 1970s the bulk of the reading public was to be found lower down the social ladder, comprising the class of secretaries, nurses and the equivalent spectrum of the lower middle class." This is how Osofisan concludes his description of the era:

> The climate of taste has changed, both the aspiring writer and the profit-hungry publisher were bound to take notice. The new public outside the universities devours Hadley Chase, not Shakespeare; it cares little for Okigbo or even Aluko, not to talk of Soyinka and Echeruo: away from the schools' curricula, it is not the Heinemann Educational Series, but the opportunistic collections of Macmillan's 'Pacesetters' and the Fontana African Novels which top the best-sellers' list.

The second part of the chapter examines Ekwensi's pioneering role in domesticating this tradition of popular literature. Ekwensi is certainly Nigeria's most sensitive chronicler of urban life; he is acknowledged by Osofisan as "paradoxically the most *relevant*...and the most contemporary of the authors of the first generation." Ekwensi, he adds,

> ...was the first to understand the demands of the evolving society, and to make attempts to come to terms with the character of the metropolis. This is why his art...appears to transcend the fragile morality of his contemporaries, why today's interesting ferment is, in a vivid sense, the legacy of his pragmatic vision.

As he does with the background to the emergence of the popular fiction in Europe, Osofisan delineates the social landscape of Nigeria, pointing out the link between leisure and the various forms of junk, commercialized cultural products:

> Hollywood, Indian (and now Chinese) films, pop music, pulp fiction are, with religion, the drugs which the masses consume in moments when they are not toiling or starving. And because of the massive spread of Western culture into the cities all over the globe, our own masses in the third world have come too to be corrupted by these same inferior, mind-drugging means of entertainment.

From Ekwensi's biography and professional career, Osofisan gleans information to reconstruct the materials that influenced his style and aesthetics.

The sources include the reading menu at the Government College, Ibadan, which featured Western thriller writers such as Rider Haggard, Edgar Wallace, Charles Dickens, Sapper and Bates. Ekwensi's cosmopolitan outlook was shaped too during his days at the Yaba Higher College and at Achimota College, Ghana (formerly the Gold Coast). The adventure stories and travelogues have traces of Ekwensi's experience as a forester, an engagement which took him to various parts of the country. Osofisan remarks that with his extensive travels in the "prairies of the north, as well as the cult-infested rain forests of the south, and particularly, the city of Lagos" Ekwensi wrote the manuscript of his first work, *When Love Whispers*, in three days.

The success of the book spurred the author on to celebrate the vibrant and pulsating rhythm of life of passion and aggression of Lagos. This urban milieu leaves its imprint on Ekwensi's linear and episodic style, "combining swift, simple prose with highly dramatic action, exploiting suspense, violence and sex..." Although Osifisan attributes these elements in Ekwensi to writers such as Haggard, Alexandre Dumas, and Earnest Hemingway, the matter of borrowing should not be overstressed. In any case, the truly talented writer or creative artist is a gifted editor and interpreter of ideas and techniques from previous endeavours.

Whatever may be the sources of Ekwensi's aesthetics, Osofisan is right to acknowledge him as "indisputably our most modern writer...a writer of the modern metropolis." He was the first creative writer to place "the city as his centre of action". The Lagos in his works is vivid and alive, with almost "an independent personality that becomes a narrative 'hero' in its own right". Osofisan adds that "city and Eros mesh in Ekwensi, to such a point that each assumes the aspect of the other, both feline, seductive, corrupting."

The portrait of the city as grand theatre of action and change distinguishes Ekwensi from other African writers of his generation. Perhaps, it is only in South African fiction that we have such parallels.

In the concluding section of the essay, Osofisan casts a prospective glance at new writing fashioned after the Ekwensi tradition. He detects the same thematic preoccupation with crime, sex, and adventure. Among the new authors are Kalu Okpi, Adaura Ulasi, Agbo Areo, and Kole Omotoso. Although a few of the writers seem more technically informed than Ekwensi, Osofisan thinks that not much progress has been made in the genre. He fears that in some cases, "progress is backwards from the achievement of Ekwensi." He notes, for example, that where Ekwensi "is careful to be authentic, to capture the exact nuances and levels of speech appropriate to a Nigerian setting, it is customary to find the new writers parroting the speech patterns and mannerisms of cheap American gangster novels."

A more frightening element is the spell eroticism and pornography have over some of the writers. Whereas Ekwensi shows ethical concerns in his use of such material, Osofisan remarks that his "heirs assault our sensibility continuously with their vulgarity, mistaking such for boldness and originality." This trend shows how much the decadence of foreign popular culture has overwhelmed the country's landscape. The writers of the Onitsha chapbooks portrayed these manners as the ultimate in modernity. In Nigeria of the 1990s, the models of culture, dressing, speaking, music, and gladiatorial sports came from the western world, especially the United States. Osofisan's alarm is well timed:

> To judge by the direction being taken by Western art, however, this popular Western art that is serving as model to our authors – it is not unlikely that this unleashing of Eros in all its crudity will soon be common-place among us, and that around it will gather most of our future writers. If that happens, it will be the final ironic tribute to Ekwensi's success as a pioneering artist in the domain of Nigerian paraliterature.

The final chapter, "The retrospective stage: some reflections on the mythopoeic tradition at Ibadan" by Omafume F. Onoge and G. G. Darah was written in the heat of the ideological polemics that hallmarked the discourse of African literature in the 1970s. The paper was delivered at a conference on African literature held at the University of Ife, now Obafemi Awolowo University. This was when Nigeria was just recovering from the political convulsion occasioned by the 1967–70 Civil War. The intelligentsia in the country was caught in a whirlwind of ideological adjustment. The nation's elite was polarized between conservative and radical/progressive camps.

The neo-liberal section favoured the option of growing a country along the familiar path of capitalist development. The radical, Left-oriented segment supported liberation from the neo-colonial strictures that made Nigeria "look big for nothing" in global affairs as the coup plotters of January, 1966, described the situation. The Nigerian Left called for a revolutionary reconstruction, with a socialist economic agenda. The clashes between the two ideological divides echoed in academic debates in the university campuses and the mass media. This paper was an opportunity for the two polar points of the discourse to interact and challenge each other. The response to the presentation of the paper bore all the drama that the event generated.

As the introduction indicates, the paper was done in the year of the Second Black and African Arts Festival, otherwise known as FESTAC 77 which was held in Lagos. Africa was then in the turmoil of anti-imperialist uprising with the main theatres in apartheid South Africa and the Portuguese colonies in Angola, Mozambique, and Guinea Bissau and Cape Verde. Drama and theatre were active platforms for this political and intellectual engagement. The plays and other artistic works of the time reflected all the tensions indicated above.

The paper benefited from insights of Marxist epistemology and literary criticism fostered at Ibadan by Professor Onoge's courses on the sociology of literature. Onoge was in the social sciences and I was doing my doctoral research on Urhobo oral literature at the Department of English at Ibadan. Our collaboration on the conference paper turned out to be very fruitful. Our immediate focus was to examine the plays staged at the University theatre during the period, showing how their themes and aesthetics reflected the contending ideas of the time. Understandably, we were unsparing on what we considered to be an *undialectical* refraction of the historical and political events and epochs that informed the playwrights' choice and treatment of the issues. We took a class-partisan position as shown in this passage:

> ...in class societies more than one image exists for reflection in the mirror. The various classes project different and contradictory images of the society and its dynamics. The image projected by the privileged exploiter classes *conserves* the status quo, while that projected by the exploited classes *subverts* the status quo. And the burden of our argument has been that, even within the restricted limits of the mirror theory of art, the mirrors contained in the contemporary retrospective stage at Ibadan provide only a one-sided reflection of our past and present realities. They reflect only the consciousness of the privileged exploiter.

It is my hope that readers of this volume will find good enough material to justify the title, *Radical Essays on Nigerian Literatures*.

Chapter 1

What has literature got to do with it?*

- Chinua Achebe

Man is a goal-setting animal. Alone or in concert with his fellows he does frequently tend to select and tackle his problems in graded priorities. He identifies personal goals, family goals, community goals, national and international goals; and he focuses his attention on solving them. At the national level, for example, he has invented short-term annual budgets and long-term five- or ten-year development plans; and for good measure, we do have in this country chiliastic expectations, such as health for all in the magic year 2000.

Setting goals is a matter of intelligence and judgement. Faced with a confusing welter of problems all clamouring for solution at once, man's most rational strategy is to stay as cool as possible in the face of the confusion and attack the problems singly or in small manageable groups, one at a time. Of course the choice of what he must assault first or what he can reserve for last is of the utmost importance and can determine his success or failure.

The comprehensive goal of a developing nation like Nigeria is, of course, development, or its somewhat better variant, modernization. I don't see much room for argument about that. What can be, and is, vigorously debated is the quickest and safest route for the journey into modernization and what items should make up the traveller's rather limited baggage allowance.

But the problem with goals lies not only in the area of priorities and practicalities. There are appropriate and inappropriate goals, even wrong and unworthy goals. There are goals which place an intolerable strain on the pursuer. History tells us, for example, of leaders who in their obsessive pursuit of modernization placed on their people such pressures as they were unable to bear — Peter the Great of Russia, Muhammad Ali of Egypt and others. Out of contemporary China rumours have come that the national goal of the one-child family which was set to combat a disastrous population problem has come into

---

* Being text of the 1986 Nigerian National Merit Award Lecture. Reprinted from *Tapping Nigeria's Limitless Cultural Treasures*, edited by Frank Aig-Imoukhuede, National Council for Arts & Culture, 1988, pp. 25-29

conflict with the desire of ordinary rural parents for male children and has apparently led to the large-scale secret murder of female children. It is clear from these and similar examples that a nation might set itself a goal that puts its very soul at risk.

At the Tokyo Colloquium in October 1981, under the theme of 'Diversified evolution of world civilization,' Professor Marion J. Levy of Princeton University, known for his study of the history of modernization in Japan and China, made the following remark about Japan:

> Well over half a century ago when everyone else was occupied with describing Japan in terms of the warrior and merchant classes, Yanagida Kunio took the position that the real heart of Japan was in the customs of the Japanese farmer.[1]

If Kunio was right, the point made by Professor Levy is very instructive. The mercantile and militaristic (but particularly the militaristic) goals of Japan in the first half of this century would then seem to have been at variance with the real heart of Japan, or perhaps one should say that the heart of Japan was not fully in them. This is of course an area of discourse where firm proof and certainty would be unattainable. But I think that Kunio's view does gain credence from the fact that Japan, whose celebrated militarism suffered one of the most horrendous defeats ever visited on an army in modern, or indeed any, times, was yet able to survive and muster the morale to become in twenty-odd years a miracle of technological and economic success, outstripping all comers. A very colourful metaphor comes readily to mind-snatching victory out of the jaws of defeat.

The history of Nigeria from, say, 1970 to 1983 can be characterized by contrast as a snatching of defeat from the jaws of victory, if one considers how nearly 100,000 million naira went through our hands like so much sand through the fingers of a child at play on the beach. How do we begin to explain that? Did we not have goals? Did we not have development plans? Did we not have experts to guide our steps on the slippery slopes of modernization?

But we did have all those things — annual budgets, development plans, the lot. We were not short on experts, either. If we didn't have the particular kind we required, surely we had the money to hire him. What went wrong then? Our heart? Our mind? It seems our heart was not in it. Perhaps we suffered a failure of imagination. Perhaps psychologically we did not really wish to become a modern state; we saw the price of modernization and subconsciously decided we were not prepared to pay it.

Let us examine one or two of these suppositions, beginning with the question of the expert. No nation which contemplates modernization can neglect the role of the expert. He is needed; he must be paid for and he must be given adequate

---

[1] Proceedings of the Tokyo Colloquium, October 1981

protection of tenure as well as respect so that others inferior to him may be motivated to strive and attain his expertise rather than hope through cheap politicking to manoeuvre themselves into his seat. But having an expert among us does not absolve the rest of us from thinking. To begin with the expert is generally an expert only in a narrow specialism. He can build a bridge for us perhaps, and tell us what weight of traffic it can support. But he can't stop us from hiring an attendant who will take a bribe and look the other way while the prescribed weight is exceeded. He can set up the finest machinery for us but he can't create the technician who will stay at his post and watch the controls instead of going for a chat and some groundnuts under a mango tree outside. So there is a limit to what an expert can do for us. In 1983, just before the overthrow of President Shagari's administration, I gave an interview for a television programme which subsequently caused some offence in certain quarters. One of the questions put to me was what did I think about the President's Green Revolution programme. And I said then, as I would say today, that it was a disaster which gave us plenty of food for thought and nothing at all in our stomach. Whereupon a certain fellow, with a lot of grouse in him, wrote in the newspapers that I should not have been asked to comment on agriculture because I was not an expert in that field. Well, we do not really need a PhD in agriculture to tell us when our stomach is empty, do we? If we are in reasonable health we should all carry around with us reliable in-built alarm systems popularly called hunger to appraise us of our condition to appraise us of that fact!

I must say in this regard that the best experts do not themselves encourage us to have foolish and superstitious faith in their ability to solve our diverse development problems. In an essay published by the *American Economic Review* in 1984, Sir Arthur Lewis, one of the foremost development economists in the world and no stranger by any means to problems of African underdevelopment, did highlight in his inimitably elegant fashion the sheer plethora of prescriptions among development experts of differing persuasions:

> Every school has offered its own candidates for driver of the engine of growth. The Physiocrats, agriculture; the Mercantilists, an export surplus; the classicists, the free market; the Marxists, capital; the neo-classicists, entrepreneurship; the Fabians, government; the Stalinists, industrialization; and the Chicago School, schooling.[2]

To sum up this marvellous passage I have composed a couplet which I beg pardon to inflict on you:

> There! We have it on the best authority.

---

[2] W. Arthur Lewis, 'The State of Development Theory,' *American Economic Review*, 1984; reprinted in *Economic Impact*, 49, 198, p. 82

Theorists of development cannot agree.

I will turn now to another world-famous economist, John Kenneth Galbraith, for a different kind of testimony. Interestingly, John Kenneth Galbraith is the current President of the American Academy of Arts and Letters. I must crave your indulgence to quote a fairly long extract from his address to the Academy in 1984 about the role of the arts in industry:

> Finally, let no one minimize the service that the arts render to established industry. In the years since World War II there has been no economic miracle quite like that of Italy. That lovely country has gone from one political disaster to another with one of the highest rates of economic growth of any of the industrial lands. The reason is not that the Italian government is notably precise in its administration, that Italian engineers and scientists are better than others, that Italian management is inspired or that Italian trade unions are more docile than the AFL-CIO. The Italian success derives from the Italian artistic tradition. Italian products over the widest range are superior not in durability, not in engineering excellence, not in lower cost. They are better in design. Italian design and the consequent industrial success are the result of centuries of recognition of — including *massive subsidy* to - the arts.[3]

In concluding his address Galbraith made the following affirmation:

> The arts are not the poor relation of the economic world. On the contrary they are at the very source of its vitality.

Before I leave these foreign references I must return very briefly to that other miracle, Japan, to which I have already made reference. If "there has been no economic miracle quite like that of Italy", there has been none to match Japan's in dramatic suddenness and awesomeness of scale. It has been uniquely salutary also for thoroughly debunking all the bogus mystique summoned to explain western industrialism - the Protestant ethic, the Graeco-Judaic tradition, etc. We, the late-comers (as Marion J. Levy calls us), have every reason to pay special attention to Japan's success story as we take our faltering steps to modernization.

In the 1981 Tokyo Colloquium which I spoke about earlier we were attempting, among other things, to define the cultural ingredient, or as one of the Japanese scholars put it, the "software" of modernization. One of the observations that made a particularly strong impact on me in this connection was a little family anecdote by Professor Kinichiro Toba of Waseda University:

---

[3] J.K. Galbraith, in *Proceedings: American Academy and Institute of Arts and Letters*, second series, No. 35, New York, 1984

My grandfather graduated from the University of Tokyo at the beginning of the 1880s. His notebooks were full of English. My father graduated from the same university in 1920 and half of his notes were filled with English. When I graduated a generation later notes were all in Japanese. So...it took three generations for us to consume western civilization totally via the means of our own language.[4]

If Professor Toba's story is at all typical of the last 100 years of Japanese history (and we have no reason to believe otherwise) we can conclude that as Japan began the countdown to its spectacular technological lift-off it was also systematically recovering lost ground in its traditional mode of cultural expression. In one sense then it was travelling away from its old self towards a cosmopolitan, modern identity, while in another sense it was journeying back to regain a threatened past and selfhood. To comprehend the dimensions of this gigantic paradox and coax from it such unparalleled inventiveness requires not mere technical flair but the archaic energy, the perspective, the temperament of creation myths and symbolism.

It is in the very nature of creativity, in its prodigious complexity and richness, that it will accommodate paradoxes and ambiguities. But this, it seems, will always elude and pose a problem for the uncreative, *literal* mind (which I hasten to add is not the same as the *literary* mind, nor even the merely *literate* mind). The literal mind is the one-track mind, the simplistic mind, the mind that cannot comprehend that where one thing stands, another will stand beside it, the mind which (finally and alas!) appears to dominate our current thinking on Nigeria's need for technology.

The cry all around is for more science and less humanities (for in the narrow disposition of the literal mind more of one must mean less of the other). Our older universities have been pressured into a futile policy of attempting to allocate places on a 60:40 ratio in favour of science admissions. In addition we have rushed to create universities of technology (and just as promptly proceeded to shut down half of them again) to demonstrate our priorities as well as confusions.

Nobody doubts that the modern developed world owes much of its success to scientific education and development. There is no doubt either that a nation can decide to emphasize science in its educational programme in order to achieve a specific national objective. When the Russians put the first man in orbit in 1961, John Kennedy responded by doubling United States space appropriations in 1962 and intensified a programme of space research which was to land Americans on the moon within the decade. But Kennedy did not ask the universities to starve out America's liberal arts education. As a matter of fact, he had previously demonstrated sufficient awareness of the national need for the arts when at his inauguration he broke with tradition and gave pride of place to a

---

[4] Proceedings of the Tokyo Colloquium, published in *The Daily Yomuiri*, 18 November 1981.

reading by Robert Frost, the great New England poet.

Furthermore, it is important to realize that because a country like America with a well-developed and viable educational system may safely switch emphasis around in its educational programme it does not therefore follow that Nigeria, whose incipient programme is already in a shambles can do the same. What kind of science can a child learn in the absence, for example, of basic language competence and an attendant inability to handle concepts?

Have we reflected on the fact that in pre-independence Nigeria, the only schools equipped adequately to teach science, namely the four or five Government Colleges not only produced doctors and engineers like other schools but held an almost complete monopoly in producing novelists, poets and playwrights?

Surely if this fact proves anything it is that education is a complex creative process and the more rounded it is, the more productive it will become.[5] It is not a machine into which you fed raw material at one end and pick up packaged products at the other. It is, indeed, like creativity itself, "a many-splendoured thing."

The great nineteenth-century American poet, Walt Whitman has left us a magnificent celebration of the many-sided nature of the creative spirit:

> Do I contradict myself?
> Very well then I contradict myself
> (I am large, I contain multitudes) ...[6]

The universal creative rondo revolves on people and stories. *People create stories create people;* or rather, *stories create people create stories.* Was it stories first and then people, or the other way round? Most creation myths would seem to suggest the antecedence of stories - a scenario in which the story was already unfolding in the cosmos before, and even as a result of which, man came into being. Take this remarkable Fulani creation story:

> In the beginning there was a huge drop of milk. Then the milk created stone; the stone created fire; the fire created water; the water created air. Then Doondari came and took the five elements and moulded them into man. But man was proud. Then Doondari created blindness and blindness defeated man...

A fabulously rich story, it proceeds in stark successions of creation and defeat to man's death through hubris, and then to a final happy twist of redemption when death itself, having inherited man's arrogance, causes

---

[5] The Vice Chancellor of University of Ibadan, Professor Ayo Banjo, was reported as making the point that Ibadan does not teach mass communications and yet 'has produced most of the best writers in Nigerian journalism today.': *Sunday Concord*, 16 February 1986.

[6] Ulli Beier (ed.) *The Origin of Life and Death*, London, Heinemann Educational Books, 1966.

Doondari to descend a third time as Gueno the eternal one, to defeat death.

So important have such stories been to mankind that they are not restricted to accounts of initial creation but will be found following human societies as they recreate themselves through vicissitudes of their history, validating their social organizations, their political systems, their formal attitudes and religious beliefs, even their prejudices. Such stories serve the purpose of consolidating whatever gains a people or their leaders have made or imagine they have made in their existential journey through the world; but they also serve to sanction change when it can no longer be denied. At such critical moments new versions of old stories or entirely fresh ones tend to be brought into being to mediate the changes and sometimes to consecrate opportunistic defections into more honourable rites of passage.

One of the paradoxes of Igbo political systems is the absence of kings on the one hand, and, on the other, the presence in the language and folklore of a whole range of words for "king" and all the paraphernalia of royalty. In the town of Ogidi where I grew up I have found two explanatory myths offered for the absence of kings. One account has it that once upon a time the title of king did exist in the community but that it gradually fell out of use because of the rigorous condition it placed on the aspirant, requiring him to settle the debt owed by every man and every woman in the kingdom.

The second account has it that there was indeed a king who held the people in such utter contempt that one day when he had a ritual kolanut to break for them he cracked it between his teeth. So the people, who did not fancy eating kolanut coated with the king's saliva, dethroned him and have remained republican ever since.

These are perhaps no more than fragmentary makeshift accounts though not entirely lacking in allegorical interest. There is, for instance, a certain philosophical appropriateness to the point that a man who would be king over his fellow should in return be prepared to personally guarantee their solvency.

Be that as it may, those two interesting fragments of republican propaganda played their part in keeping kings' noses out of the affairs of Ogidi for as long as memory could go until the community, along with the rest of Nigeria, lost political initiative to the British at the inception of colonial rule. Thereafter a new dynasty of kings rose to power in Ogidi with the connivance of the British administration, thus rendering those mythical explanations of republicanism obsolete. Except perhaps that they may have left a salutary, moderating residue in the psyche of the new rulers and those they ruled.

I shall now, with your indulgence, present two brief parables from pre-- colonial Nigeria which are short enough for the present purpose but also complex enough to warrant my classifying them as literature. I chose these two particularly because they stand at the opposite ends of the political spectrum:

> Once upon a time, all the animals were summoned to a meeting. As they
> converged on the public square early in the morning one of them, the fowl,

was spotted by his neighbours going in the opposite direction. They said to him, "How is it that you are going away from the public square? Did you not hear the town-crier's summons last night"?

"I did hear it," said the fowl, "and I should certainly have gone to the meeting if a certain personal matter had not cropped up which I must attend to, I am truly sorry, but I hope you will make my sincere apologies to the meeting. Tell them that though absent in body I will be there with you in spirit in all your deliberations. Needless to say that whatever you decide will receive my whole-hearted support."

The question before the assembled animals was what to do in the face of a new threat posed by man's frequent slaughtering of animals to placate his gods. After a stormy but surprisingly brief debate, it was decided to present to man one of their number as his regular sacrificial animal if he would leave the rest in peace. And it was agreed without a division that the fowl should be offered to man to mediate between him and his gods. And it has been so ever since.

The second story goes like his:

One day a snake was riding his horse coiled up, as was his fashion, in the saddle. As he came down the road he met the toad walking by the roadside.

"Excuse me, sir," said the toad, "but that's not the way to ride a horse."

"Really? Can you show me the right way then?" asked the snake.

"With pleasure, if you will be good enough to step down a moment."

The snake slid down the side of his horse and the toad jumped with alacrity into the saddle, sat bolt upright and galloped most elegantly up and down the road. "That's how to ride a horse," he said at the end of his excellent demonstration.

"Very good," said the snake. "Very good indeed; you may now come down."

The toad jumped down and he snake slid up the side of his horse back into the saddle and coiled himself up as before. Then he said to the toad, "Knowing is good, but having is better. What good does fine horsemanship do to a fellow without a horse?" And then he rode away in his accustomed manner.

On the face of it those are just two charming animal stories to put a smile on the face or, if we are fortunate and have a generous audience, even a laugh in the throat. But beneath that admittedly important purpose of giving delight there lies a deep and very serious intent. Indeed, what we have before us are political and ideological statements of the utmost consequence revealing more about the societies that made and sustained them, and by which, in the reciprocal rondo of creativity, they were made and sustained, revealing far more than any number of political science monographs could possibly ever tell us. We could literally spend hours analysing each story and discovering new significance all the time. Right now, however, we can only take a cursory look.

Consider the story of the delinquent fowl. Quite clearly it is a warning, a cautionary tale, about the danger to which citizens of small-scale democratic systems may be exposed when they neglect the cardinal duty of active participation in the political process. In such systems a man who neglects to lick his lips, as a certain proverb cautions us, will be asking the harmattan to lick them for him. It did for the fowl with a vengeance!

The second story is, if you will permit a rather predictable cliché, a horse of a different colour altogether. The snake is an aristocrat in a class society in which status and its symbols are not earned but ascribed. The toad is a commoner whose knowledge and expertise garnered through personal effort, count for nothing beside the merit which belongs to the snake by some unspecified right such as birth or wealth. No amount of brightness or ability on the part of the toad is going to alter the position ordained for him. The few but potent words left with him by the snake embody a stern, utilitarian view of education which would limit the acquisition of skills to the (arbitrary) availability of scope for their practice.

I have chosen those two little examples from Nigeria's vast and varied treasury of oral literature to show how such stories can combine in a most admirable manner the aesthetic qualities of successful work of imagination with those homiletic virtues demanded of active definers and custodians of society's values.

But we must not see the role of literature only in terms of providing latent support for things as they are, for its does also offer the kinetic energy necessary for social transition and change. If we tend to dwell more on stability it is only because society itself does aspire to, and indeed requires, longer periods of rest than turmoil. But literature is also deeply concerned with change. That little fragment about the king who insulted his subjects by breaking their kolanut in his mouth is a clear incitement to rebellion. But even more illuminating in this connection, because of its subtlety, is the story of the snake and the toad which at first sight may appear to uphold privilege but at another level of signification does in fact contain the seeds of revolution, the portents of dissolution of an incompetent oligarchy. The brilliant makers of that story, by denying sympathetic attractiveness to the snake, are exposing him in the fullness of time to the harsh tenets of a revolutionary justice.

I think I have now set a wide-ranging enough background to attempt an answer to the rhetorical question: What has literature got to do with it?

In the first place, what does **it** stand for? Is it something concrete like increasing the GNP or something metaphysical like the **It** which is the object of the question in Gabriel Okara's novel, *The Voice*?

I should say that my **it** begins with concrete aspirations like economic growth, health for all, education which actually educates, etc. etc., but soon reveals an umbilical link with a metaphysical search for abiding values. In other words, I am saying that development or modernization is not merely, or even primarily, a question of having lots of money to spend or blueprints drawn up by the best experts available; it is in a critical sense a question of the mind and the will. And I am saying that the mind and the will belong first and foremost to the domain of stories. In the beginning was the Word, or the Mind, as an alternative rendering has it. It was the Word or the Mind that began the story of creation.

So it is with the creation of human societies. And what Nigeria is aiming to do is nothing less than the creation of a new place and a new people. And what she needs must have the creative energy of stories to initiate and sustain that work.

Our ancestors created their different politics with myths embodying their varying perceptions of reality, people everywhere did the same. The Jews had their Old Testament on account of which early Islam honoured them as the people of the Book. The following passage appears in a brilliant essay in *Publications of the Modern Language Association of America*:

> The ideals that Homer portrayed in Achilles, Hector and Ulysses played a large role in the formation of the Greek character. Likewise when the Anglo-Saxons studied around their hearth fires, stories of heroes like Beowulf helped define them as a people, through articulating their values and defining their goals in relation to the cold, alien world around them.[7]

In the essay from which I took that passage the authors set out to demonstrate in detail the potentiality of literature to reform the self in a manner analogous to the processes of psychoanalysis: eliciting deep or unconsciously held primary values and then bringing conscious reflection or competing values to bear on them. The authors underscore the interesting point made by Roy Schafer that psychoanalysis itself is an essay into story-telling. People who go through psychoanalysis tell the analyst about themselves and others in the past and present. In making interpretations the competent analyst re-organizes and retells these stories in such a way that the problematic and incoherent self consciously told at the beginning of the analysis is sorted out to the benefit and sanity of the client.

It would be impossible and indeed inappropriate to pursue this perceptive and tremendously important analogy between literature and psychoanalysis any further here but I must quote its concluding sentence:

> ...If as Kohut, Meissner and others suggest, the self has an inherent teleology for growth and cohesion, then literature can have an important and profound positive effect as well, functioning as a kind of bountiful, nourishing matrix for a healthy, developing psyche.[8]

This is putting into scientific language what our ancestors had known all

---

[7] M.W. Alcorn and M. Bracher, 'Literature, Psychoanalysis and the Reformation of Self: a new direction for Reader-Response Theory,' *Publications of Modern Language Association of America*, New York, May 1985, p. 350
[8] Ibid., p. 352

along and reminds one of the common man who on being told the meaning of 'prose' exclaimed: "Look at that! So I have been speaking prose all my life without knowing it."

The matter is really quite simple. Literature, whether handed down by word of mouth or in print, gives us a second handle on reality; enabling us to encounter in the safe manageable dimensions of make-believe the very same threats of integrity that may assail the psyche in real life; and at the same time providing through the self-discovery which it imparts, a veritable weapon for coping with these threats whether they are found within our problematic and incoherent selves or in the world around us. What better preparation can a people desire as they begin their journey into the strange, revolutionary world of modernization?

Chapter 2

The semiotics of class and gender struggle in pre-colonial narrative systems

– *Ropo Sekoni*

Several researches in cultural communication have emphasized an umbilical relationship between what is often referred to as fiction or literature and the values (dominant and resistant) of the society about which poems, stories or plays are composed, written, or performed. Scholars such as Terry Eagleton, Edward Said, and Vladimir Propp have demonstrated in varying degrees the fact that literature - oral or written, folk or elitist - is essentially a means of social indoctrination of the consumer by the producer. To these writers and others who share their perception of culture and cultural production, the literature of every community reflects in its totality the values and counter-values that characterize that community in a given period.

With specific reference to oral literature, which in the context of Yoruba culture, is essentially a pre-colonial aesthetic construct, the status of literature as a means of reproducing the preferences of a dominant group and the resistance of those of the dominated group in an ethos characterized by the politics of hierarchy is perhaps more evident in pre-colonial era than in a post-colonial system where the control of the infrastructure of literary production is more assured for the dominant class than in what obtained in oral societies. In oral societies, the infrastructure for producing poetry, story, and drama is available to every able-bodied member of the community, unlike in post-colonial ethos where the means of producing literature are largely alienated from most members of the community.

Different genres of oral social discourse — from the almost sacred divination discourse to the flippantly secular trickster-tale narratives — have pointed at the character of fiction as a discourse of persuasion of the dominated by the dominator on the one hand, and on the other, as the resistance to the values of the dominator by the dominated. The phenomenon of literature as a site of struggle between different groups in a politically divided society is in fact captured in the names of different gen'es of literature. For example, the contrast between the Yoruba *Oriki* and the *Efe* portrays the possibility of competing or opposing "emotivities" within given cultural groups.[1]

This study will examine the semiotics of class struggle in Yoruba version of *Ifa* discourse. More specifically, the essay will attempt to demonstrate the notion of struggle over cultural signification by pro-hegemonic and counter-hegemonic forces in the divination tale of the Yoruba in both its "pristine" and contemporary manifestations.

The methodology that will guide the examination of the rhetoric of class struggle in the tales selected for analysis will be the socio-semiotic strategy which identifies sign-types and their manipulation in individual tales. As the focus of the study is on the narrative dimension of *Ifa* corpus, the "conflictualization" of the field of desire in *Ifa* tales or the choice of protagonists and the resolution of such conflicts will be seen as signs produced to represent and evoke specific emotional perception of social reality.

In the discussion of *Ifa* chants by other scholars, adequate attention has been paid to the divination discourse as an aesthetic object. Wande Abimbola's discussion of the poetic features of individual *Odu* chants constitutes the most elaborate discussion of the relationship between the *Ifa* discourse and the aesthetic manipulation of the divinee by the diviner-poet.[2] However, Abimbola's notion of aesthetics is unduly narrow in focus and objective. It examines only such basic poetic devices as pun, parallelism, repetition, simile, hyperbole, and other related elements. Abimbola's notion of aesthetics is, in other words, limited to specific artistic methods of de-familiarization and does not extend to the possibility of aesthetics as a general system of prefiguring and circumscribing the response to art objects in a manner that also delimits response to social system. Moreover, Abimbola's consideration of aesthetics in *Ifa* discourse hardly examines the fictive dimensions of the divination process. It is the view of this writer that each *Ifa* chant *(Odu Ifa)* is as much of a narrative system as it is a poetic one.

Another assumption underlying this study, and which Abimbola ignores, is that the ritualization of experience often made possible by the narration of anthropomorphic experiential categories in the *Ifa* discourse leads more logically to the examination of the ethico-aesthetic objectives of *Ifa* tales. In addition to the general significance of the Yoruba *Ifa* discourse as a literary and philosophical system,[3] the divination tale shows evidence of a specific objective

---

[1] See, for example, Olatunji, O.O., *Features of Yoruba Oral Poetry*, Ibadan, University Press Limited, 1984, p. 5-8.

[2] Abimbola, 'Wande, *Ifa: An Exposition of Oral Literary Corpus*, Ibadan, Oxford University Press, 1976

[3] Abimbola 'Wande, *Sixteen Great Poems of Ifa*. UNESCO, 1975, p. 32

that aspires to teach the values of hegemonic politics: monarchy, patriarchy and a socio-economic system of the domination of the community by the privileged class. The discourse also occasionally provides tales that challenge and resist the politics of domination. Another aspect of this chapter is to demonstrate that it is the simultaneous presence of the affirmation of dominant values and of the negation of such values that reveals the sociogonic character of *Ifa* discourse and, more importantly, its status as a site of changing and competing "emotivities" or emotional perceptions of human action and behaviour. For example, some of the *Ifa* tales used for ritualizing the experience of primordial or pre-temporal personages that divinees are asked to identify with evoke such values as class or gender domination, primitive accumulation as means of capital formation,, he deception of consumers as a marketing strategy, while other tales (usually fewer) countermand such values.

Patriarchy, as the appropriation of social power by men to the exclusion of women and the inferiorization of women by men as a way of justifying the subordination of women, is a recurrent theme in the Yoruba divination tale. In "Okanransode" ("*Okanran-ogbe*"), patriarchy and patrilocality are ontologized through a tale that illustrates how Orunmila (male) beats or cheats Osun (female) in the race for the acquisition of wisdom or cosmic knowledge. In this tale, Osun was the first person to discover the icon of intelligence. In one variant, Orunmila and Osun were asked to sacrifice their shirts. Orunmila did but Osun refused. At night a rodent bore holes in the pocket of Osun's shirt. The following day, Osun was the first to sight the icon of intelligence believed to have been dropped by Olodumare. She dropped it in her pocket and alerted Orunmila to the fact of her acquisition of the icon. Just as she moved in space ahead of Orunmila, the icon dropped through the hole caused by the rodent. Orunmila saw the icon drop, quietly picked it and produced it after Osun's discovery of its disappearance. Orunmila then claimed proprietary rights over the icon and only agreed to share part of it with Osun after the latter had been blackmailed into marrying Orunmila and agreeing to turn a friendship between equals to one of subordination and colonization.[4]

What this tale does is to draw attention to the cultural practice of subjugation of women or their marginalization with respect to social power through a story in which supernatural reward of eternal value (knowledge) is given to a male character that accepts to offer sacrifice to the gods and to deny a female character who refuses the same, of the benefits of her earlier advantage of speed of response, alertness and aggressiveness. This tale exposes the divinee to the benefit of offering sacrifice and indirectly teaches the syntax of social experience favoured by phallocracy and phallocentrism. The male divinee feels congratulated and assured of his power over women while the female divinee is

---

[4] See Babayemi, S.O. and Adekola, O.O. (eds.), *Isedale Awon Odu Ifa*, Ibadan, Institute of African Studies, 1988, p. 125

encouraged that her alienation can be reduced or eliminated through marriage, which is capable of giving her a share in the domination of the world by men.

Another thematization of phallocracy is attempted in "*Obara-meji*".[5] In this aetiological tale that explains the origin of the use of kolanut for the settlement of quarrels, the kolanut is primordialized as a woman and wife of Abemo, the celestial diviner who was a friend of Ajo the terrestrial diviner. Both of them were asked to make a sacrifice each for the possession of wealth and children. At first, Abemo sacrificed only for wealth, had money but failed to make Obi, his wife, pregnant. Obi later deserted him for Ajo on earth. Ajo offered sacrifice for children and not for wealth. He succeeded in making Obi pregnant within one year. At the end of the year, Ajo went to Abemo for an annual conference. He took Obi with him. Abemo was angered to find out that Obi had been living with Ajo for one year without any explanation from his friend. They both fought until they were sapped of energy. Abemo then appealed to Ajo and persuaded him to recall an earlier divination for them which warned them against Obi's danger to their friendship. At this point, both Abemo and Ajo agreed to a truce and decided to settle their rift on a once-and-for-all basis by killing Obi.[6]

The choice of images constitutive of this story shows a phallocentric sensibility. Obi in its primordial and contemporary state represents an icon of either erotic or gastronomic desires. In its pristine form, it is a woman shared by two friends and later slaughtered as a way of forestalling the defeat of a male character in front of a female character that has shared the secrets of both males. In its second phase the woman is depicted as kolanut, which still serves as an icon for the lessening of tension and a means of facilitating social intercourse. The demonization of the woman is thus subtly projected in an odu that encourages trust among men and distrust between men and women. The qualmlessness of Ajo (male) in sleeping with the wife of his friend (Abemo, also male) is blamed on Obi (female) whose desire for children (further humanization of the world) is ignored or, at best, interpreted as a cosmically disruptive promiscuous act. With this tale of Obara-Meji, the divinee is overtly warned of the need to solidify a materially useful relationship and covertly reminded of the psychic inferiority of women.

The theme of gender inequality takes more overt turn for the scopophilic depiction of women in other divination narratives. For example, in one of the tales of "Ogbe-Ate," Yemowo, another primordial female-figure, made along with other women in a pre-temporal females-only town, some sacrifice towards the cultivation of friendship with men in a neighbouring males-only town. As soon as the women approached the men's town, the men were surprised to see such beautiful figures and immediately set out to chase the women into the bush. They finally overpowered the women. They took all the women to Obatala in

---

[5] See Lijadu, M.O., *Orunmila,* Ado-Ekiti, Ajisafe Press, 1908, p.4
[6] Ibid., p.36

Ife. He chose their leader Yemowo and distributed the others among the men. The sacrifice offered by the women before leaving their town fructified by making it possible for them to experience heterosexual relationship without having to articulate their desires as well as by making men very enthusiastic in expressing their desire for heterosexual association.

However, this tale, which often prescribes sacrifice for women that desire husbands, also teaches heterosexuality from a phallocentric perspective. First, the woman is incapable of living without men. Women are also projected in the tale as exotic, beautiful and desirable by men. The women in the odu were also too timid to express their own desires and had to be content with their status as objects of male desire. Men rather than women did the choosing of heterosexual partners.

In another tale from Ika-turupon,[7] a woman of enormous wealth who did not believe in heterosexual relationship with men was violated through psychic manipulation. After refusing offers of friendship with gods such as Ogun, Obatala, and Orunmila, Orunmila decided to hypnotize her into having an erotic relationship. He used magical powers to destabilize the tight security in the woman's sixteen-room house at night and then to violate her. The woman, surprised at the magnitude of the powers that must have gone into this act, felt worried and insecure and developed a dependency complex to the extent that she later accepted Orunmila's marriage proposal.

In this tale, a woman that is self-sufficient and is opposed to heterosexuality is forced into it. This tale discourages not only sexual deviance but also any attempt by successful single women to refuse men as sources of support against dangers that may not be material or social in nature. To a male divinee, this tale is capable of emboldening him to approach a socially superior woman for friendship as this will facilitate his own access to social and economic power. To a female divinee on the other hand, the tale spells out the threat to life and limb that is inherent in a life that is, in spite of all manifestations of fulfilment, not subjected to male direction or supervision.

As a site of affirmation and contestation of dominant values, the Ifa discourse also evokes some tales that illustrate the sociogonic status of the tales of phallocentrism. In "Osa Meji," which is one of the principal cosmogonic tales, the invincibility of female energy is mimed. In this tale about the emergence of anthropomorphic experience on earth, the first set of male supernatural personages to be anthropomorphized came to the earth as inferiors or subjects of their female counterparts. Orunmila and the other divinities were harassed by the Iyami (witches, for lack of a better translation). The domination of the male forces by female forms of energy became so humiliating that Orunmila had to run back to Olodumare (God) for additional power. No such power was available. Orunmila was only briefed about the history of the

---

[7] Lijadu, M.O., *op. cit.*, p. 58

extreme power of women and urged not to fight them but to placate them. Finally Orunmila, as the intellectual giant of his world, could only enter into an agreement for a truce *(Ipihun)* with the primordial female energy. The female force up till this day in Yoruba religious practice cannot be resisted *(ba tile);* they can only be appeased (be).

.As a cosmogonic tale in contradistinction to the sociogonic ones discussed in the preceding section of this paper, "Osa Meji"[8] is capable of reminding female divinees of the intellectual and psychic superiority of the female. Even though this power is presented as a-causal and a-moral, it is also depicted as *a sine qua non* of cosmic and social stability and progress. When related to the story of the rivalry of Osun and Orunmila over the icon of knowledge, it simultaneously explains Osun's first and natural access to wisdom as well as Orunmila's second and dishonest acquisition of psycho-cognitive power. Such juxtaposition of the two tales also suggests the need for the inferiorization of the woman as a programme of justifying male dominancy for purpose of sublimating male fear of fair competition with their female counterpart.

In a tale from one of the minor *(amulu)* Odu, "Iwori-bara," the resistance of the female-world to the domination of the male-universe is enacted through an anthropological tale that illustrates how the cat becomes a predator of the mouse. In this tale,[9] a female cat was captured during a war by a male mouse who later brutalized and abused her for no other cause than that the cat was a wife to the mouse. After many years of harassment, one of the children of the cat in her previous marriage made some sacrifice after a divination and was given eight blades to mount on her fingers. She was also encouraged to attack the mouse any time he brutalized her mother. She did this and succeeded in killing the mouse which he was later encouraged by Esu to eat.

Although this tale is not about human characters, the depiction of the animal characters in the image of libidinal economy: wife, mother, daughter and husband, reveals its objective as an anthropogonic tale that is designed to challenge some sociogomic tales as those of the emergence of gender oppression in Yoruba society. The revelation at the beginning of this tale that the cat became a victim of the mouse because she failed to make necessary sacrifices and the final resolution of the conflict in favour of the cat after a long period of oppression by the mouse attempt to capture the ever complex character of historical male-female power struggle among the Yoruba. Traditionally, most Yoruba kingdoms have divided their space of power into two; the political one dominated by men and the economic space dominated by women. To the male divinee, this *Odu* preaches reorganization and re-fortification against being swamped by a strong wife. On the other hand, the female divinee is warned that she has to be of good behaviour so as not to incite the wrath of her husband. In

---

[8] In Ibie, C.O., *Ifism: The complete work of Orunmila*, Lagos, Efehi Limited, 1986, p. 191
[9] In Lijadu, M.O., *op. cit.*, p. 49

both cases, the tale explains the tensional character of gender relations, especially the rise of phallocentrism as a recognition and fear of the woman's power.

Ifa also mimes tales of class or group domination where the source of advantage over others derives from financial, political or cognitive power. Some of such tales privilege capital over labour, celebrate primitive accumulation of capital, preach the superiority of a man of political power over his subjects, and the power of the slave owner over the destiny of the slave.

One tale in which the politics of hierarchy and the oppression of the powerless by the man of power is enacted is in the tale of Irosun-sa.[10] In this story, Oba Ado was treated by his junior chiefs and the people of Ado only as a first among equals. His chiefs and subjects did not pay obeisance to him. He felt humiliated by this and offered prescribed sacrifices that would bring him the power to terrorize his subjects into accepting his authority. After the sacrifice, he, during a meeting with his chiefs, killed his Lisa (Prime Minister) and threw the head at the chest of Jomu (his defence minister). The people of the town became very fearful of the Oba because of his sudden lust for blood. The subjects scattered into the bush and later agreed to go back to heaven to implore Olodumare to kill them. On their way to heaven, they met a man who asked for their mission and told them that their total population of 120,000 was considerably less than the 200,000 normally required for the morning sacrifice to Olodumare. The people then agreed to go back to Ado with loads of gift of food and animals for their Oba. They also assured their Oba that they would'2 bring such gifts annually and that they would acknowledge his superiority to them by standing up during, the duration of their stay in his palace.

In the manner of sociogony, this Odu enacts the transformation of what could have been an egalitarian political system in which the polity was managed by a cabinet of equals into a system of extreme hierarchization. The absoluteness of the power of the Oba is being made tolerable through the depiction of a more ruthless leadership at the gate of heaven. Narratees of this tale are being urged to accept the authority of their political culture on the basis of the fact that it is better than that of what is normally expected to be a better place in heaven.

In another story under the series of tales in the *Odu* of Ofu-Gutan,[11] the moral turpitude of an Oba is covered up solely because of his social position. In this tale, Onibara was asked to sacrifice some goats in order to forestall an embarrassment that *a femme fatale* he was planning to marry could cause him. The Oba refused to make the sacrifice. He later got enticed by a very attractive woman whom most of his subjects disapproved of. Onibara married this woman whose diet only consisted of animal protein. So enamoured of her beauty was

---

[10] Ibid., p. 57
[11] Ibid., p. 60

the Oba that he acceded to the woman's expensive taste. Before long, Onibara depleted his own stock of goats, sheep and chicken. To keep this woman, he decided to buy a talisman that made it possible for him to change into a tiger. During one of his nocturnal activities in the form of a tiger, some of the town's security men shot at the tiger as he was about killing a goat. On the following day, the citizens discovered the corpse of their Oba covered by a tiger's skin in front of his palace. The corpse was secretly buried and his new wife was killed at the Oba's grave.

Although this tale summarized above adopts the device of aesthetic deviation by giving more attention to the woman at the end of the story, the demonization of the woman is an attempt to justify covering up the extreme indiscipline and irresponsibility of the Oba. As a man of power, the Oba is shielded even in death from the disgrace he had attracted and the woman is projected as *femme fatale* that is ready to bewitch an otherwise respectable man.

Tales that valorize socio-political power are occasionally challenged by tales of resistance that address the emotivity of the deprived. In one of the tales of Ogbe-Wonrin,[12] ancient Ife used to celebrate the advent of the New Year with a lot of eating and drinking. Slaves were forbidden from taking part in this seven-day ritual. After a long period of frustration, the slaves organized themselves into a union of common interests and decided to poison the atmosphere around the grove. For years, Ife indigenes died in the hundreds after coming into contact with poisonous bacteria deposited in the grove by the slaves. So depopulating was this epidemic that Ife elders had to consult Orunmila. After finding out that tradition of this festival had always denied slaves of participation, Orunmila prescribed some sacrifice and ordered that the festival should be celebrated by both indigenes and slaves, unlike in the tale of Ofu-Gutan in which the excesses of the ruler are explained away through the mechanism of projection. In the Ogbe-Wonrin tale summarized in the preceding paragraph, the excesses of the ruling class, especially those relating to mass cheating and repression, are problematized. The tale enacts a successful rebellion by members of the abused and oppressed class. It also illustrates that a class-divided polity breeds dehumanization, misdirection of resources and chaos, all of which can be eliminated only through political reorganization that accepts mutual respect and enrichment between capital and labour.[13]

The notion of capitalist accumulation as a source of social advantage and power is examined in several *Ifa* tales. For instance, one of the tales of Irosun-egutan, the hunter of heaven who was a friend of the hunter of the earth used to meet and interact at the junction between heaven and earth. On one occasion, the earthly hunter scouted the forest all day without any luck. On the same day,

---

[12] Ibid., p.56
[13] Lijadu, M.O., p. 3

his heavenly counterpart spotted during his hunting activity five large eggs. He called to the earthly hunter to come for two of the eggs which he had left for him, at their usual meeting place. The earthly hunter who was hungry most of the day, cooked the two eggs for food while his friend saved his own three eggs in a well protected place. On the following day, the heavenly hunter went back to where he kept the eggs and met hundreds of cowries-money surrounding each egg. He cleared all the money and left the eggs intact. After several visits to the eggs, he became extremely rich. He then called to find out the experience of his earthly counterpart with his eggs. He was disappointed to hear that the latter had eaten them. When the heavenly hunter told his friend about the wealth he got from the eggs, the latter responded that "it is only heaven that knows who will be turned into a rich person."

In this tale which ends in a matter-of-fact acceptance of material reward regardless of the labour input of the individual, the value of capital formation through primitive accumulation is also suggested. As this story preaches the value of investment through the juxtaposition of the saving of some eggs with the eating of some by a starving hunter, the tale also implicitly discountenances the importance of labour to the process of accumulation.

In another tale from the cluster of tales belonging to Ogbese,[14] the superiority of capital to labour is also underscored. In this tale Obatala who was experiencing poverty consulted an *Ifa* priest who asked him to accept without any complaint or argument whatever he was offered by a seller. A cripple-slave was later offered for sale to Obatala who because of the injunction given to Orunmila's earlier accepted the offer. After staying for some time with Obatala, the cripple decided to plant some maize in Obatala's backyard. In that year, most of the corn land in the area was affected by drought. It was only the maize planted by Obatala's slave that thrived. All the parrots in the country looking for maize sighted Obatala's maize farm. The cripple saw the parrots as they attacked this farm. He succeeded in scaring them away by shouting. He then planned against their return by uprooting most of the corn stalks and standing them against each other. As soon as the parrots returned in their thousands and perched, the corn stalks gave way and the parrots found themselves on the ground. As parrots were believed to be incapable of flying once their feet touched the ground, Obatala's slave crawled to the spot to collect and keep the parrots for his master. Obatala removed the red tail-feather of the parrots and sold them at exorbitant prices to other divinities and kings who were much richer than he was. After several of such sales, Obatala became the richest divinity whose wealth in its ever-blooming character supplied an image in the prayers offered by businessmen and women: "May my wealth be the wealth of the cripple," the wealth that comes to stay.

This tale praises capitalist accumulation while relegating the importance of

---

[14] See Babayemi and Adekola, *op. cit.*, p. 126

labour. By making Orunmila the tale's protagonist rather than the slave, the tale prioritizes acquisition of the slave as a high risk investment. The depiction of the slave as a cripple — and thus a worthless person being rescued by Obatala with his money — suggests the low rating of labour in a pre-capitalist ethos that characterizes the world mimed in this tale. The system of reward which marginalizes the worker (the cripple) as a slave whose labour power has been bought for perpetual exploitation further points to the priority that capital has over labour and the owner of capital over the worker. The deformity of the slave constitutes an icon suggestive of the inferiority of labour to capital.

However, in the character of cultural discourse as a site of confrontation between competing classes or groups, the *Ifa* discourse also addresses the centrality of labour to all forms of production. The same technique of hyperbole used for centring capital or capital owner and marginalizing other dimensions of production is also employed in several chants to valorize labour at the expense of other productive forces. For example, labour is praised as the most important force in production in the opening section to one of the poems of Ikanran-sa:

> Awon oko ko left ara won r 'oko, afi awa enia tii se elegbe lehin won, afi awa enia. Aake ko le gbiyanju tefetefe, afi awa enia tii se elegbe lehin re, afi awa enia. Awon ada kole ft ara won san inu igbo lo, awa enia nii se elegbe lehin won, awa enia. A mu isu wa ile, odo ko le tikarare gun un niyan, afi awa enia tii se elegbe lehin won, aft awa enia. Nje kinii se elegbe lehin enia, aft Ajalorun afi enia, a daa fun erin, a bu fun enia: nwon ni ki erin ru ki enia ma le muu. Erin ko, ko ru: enia gbo enia ru.

> Hoes cannot weed on their own; it is human beings that make them work. Axes cannot cut trees on their own; it is human beings that make them work; cutlasses cannot eliminate bushes on their own; it is human beings that make them work. A mortar cannot turn a piece of yam into paste on its own; it is human beings that make the mortar work. What makes human beings tick? It is God and man himself. A divination was done for the elephant and for man. The elephant was asked to offer some sacrifice so that he would not be subject to man's powers. The elephant failed to offer any sacrifice but man did.

In the above chant, an extreme form of humanism in which it is only God with whom human beings share power is promoted. More significantly, this *odu* accepts the instrumental status of all forms of capital to production while it celebrates the centrality of human labour in the productive process. Labour is seen as a form of power without any parallel in the human life-world.

The prioritization of labour over capital is also evident in *Ifa* tales that can be characterized as metatales, that is, tales in which the central tenets of *Ifa*: sacrifice, religious worship and practice of divination as an occupation or profession are subjected to critical review. Some of such tales are those selected from *Odi-meji* group of chants below:

A ko ile koto fun oritsa, ki orisa ki o gba bee. Bi orisa ba ni ko to, ko tikarare ki ada mole li oorun gangan, ki o wo igbo lo, ki o pa iko, kio pa okun. Ki oft on ja igbo bo wale, ki o ri bi agara ti idq ni; o difa fasamo a bu foodimo. Ifa ni ki afire f'orisa nla.

If a small house is built for a god, the god must accept it as such. If he feels that such house is not adequate, he should take a cutlass himself on a sunny day and head for the bush to cut roofing sticks 9nd ropes. He should experience the inconvenience of moving through a thick forest to the town so that he can experience first-hand the discomfort of self-exertion that characterizes production. *Ifa* says that some offerings should be made to Obatala.

A be igi ti inu igbo, o di olowo eni, kerekere aworan di onile aworan d'eni akunlebo. A difaf'Ooni Alakanesuru ti nwon ni ki o ru igbin, eiyele ati ewe owo ki o ma baa sin laiye. Nwon ni eetiri? O ni, enyin ko mope: "ninu igi ti a be wa ile li afr nse onje fun igi.

A tree that is cut and brought home from the bush becomes one's boss. Gradually, an art object becomes the owner of the house. an image becomes an object of worship. A divination was made for King Alakanesuru who was asked to sacrifice snails, pigeons and *owo* leaf (leaf of respect) so that he would not go to the world to slave for others. The king asked for justification for this. He was told that it is out of the wood that he brought home from the forest that some is used for cooking for some other wood designated as religious icon.

In the first chant, the issue of religious sacrifice is used in commenting on the centrality of labour to cultural production, that is, the production of human goods and services. This chant states almost too overtly that all values outside of labour are sheer reifications. The second chant attempts to mime and emphasize the process of reification by showing how it can only be sequel and secondary to labour or production.

There are several conclusions to make from a study of *Ifa*, as an aesthetic or symbolic communication. One of such conclusions is Abimbola's often quoted statement that the *Ifa* constitutes an indigenous system of African philosophy and thought.[15] A more specific conclusion derivable from this particular study is that, whatever else the *Ifa* discourse may be, it is a site for the contestation of values in a politically heterogeneous polity like the Yoruba space in which the tension of gender and class relations abounds. In this capacity, the *Ifa* discourse constitutes an archaeological field in which social contradictions are mimed to reflect and refract the antagonism that is inherent in a continual struggle between hegemonic and counter-hegemonic interests.

---

[15] Abimbola, Sixteen Great Poems of *Ifa*, UNESCO Publications, 1975, p. 32

Chapter 3

Myth and the formation of social consciousness: the *Bayajida* of the Hausa

- *Maikudi Karaye*

The problem of determining the extent of foreign involvement in the formation of Hausa states or of determining the actual historical connection between a Bayajida and the origin of the Hausa people and language has not been fully resolved by Hausa scholars. Muhammed Jinju drew attention to this problem in 1985 at a conference organized by the Centre for the Study of Nigerian Languages, Kano.[1] He argued that the Bayajida story is a mere folktale, full of contradictions, which assigns false Arabic origin to Hausa people and their language. Earlier scholars, especially Palmer, Hallam and Johnston, prefer to regard Bayajida as a real person who they 'identify' as Abu Yazid Ibn Khaidad Al-Zanati (884-947), believed to have arrived at Daura in the tenth century. They then proceeded to determine the degree of correspondence between the content of the Bayajida story and modern or ancient Hausa social formations. Hallam, for example, speculates that "...it is reasonable to assume that Bayajida alias Abu Yazid...came to Daura in the tenth century."[2]

Nor is Hallam alone in assuming that mythical figures such as Bayajida are real people. Abdullahi Smith, for example, believes that these "great men" were responsible for the formation of several states and that scholars should discover not only who they were but what secret powers they had:

> But who these the Sefs, Bayajidas, Oduduwas and Kisras and Tseodos and Oranmiyans actually were, what was the secret of their powers and in short just how they managed to produce the states that we know in Hausaland, Bornu, Yorubaland, Nupe, Benin and elsewhere has hardly been enquired.[3]

---

[1] See Hambali Muhammad Jinju, "Asalin Hausawa," unpublished paper presented at a conference on Hausa Language and Culture held from 17th to 21st August 1985 at Kano, p. 3.
[2] W.K.R. Hallam, "The Bayajida Legend in Hausa Folklore," *Journal of African History*, Vol. VII, No. 1, 1966, p.49.
[3] Abdullahi Smith, "Some Considerations Relating to the Formation of States in Hausaland," *Journal of the Historical Society of Nigeria*, Vol. V, No. 3, 1970., p. 329.

The basic contradiction noted by these scholars, which the method they use cannot resolve, is clearly stated in the following opinion of Ibrahim Yahaya, himself a believer that Bayajida did exist:

> We can hardly take Bayajida who is proved to have prevailed in the tenth century as the progenitor of the Hausa, since, in the first place, the legend itself is contradictory in that at the time of Bayajida's arrival in Daura, he found native inhabitants with a strong institution of Sarauta (rule, authority) headed by a *sarauniya* (queen) and these natives had their own language of communication which was almost certainly Hausa.[4]

It is precisely because these scholars have taken for real what is probably mythical that the contradiction in the Bayajida story persists. The situation confronting Hausa scholars with reference to Bayajida is similar to the one Radin faced in his attempt to interpret "Four Winnebago myths,"[5] namely, whether there is any correlation between the social structure alluded to in the myth and an actual Winnebago society that exists or might have existed. Levi-Strauss traces Radin's theoretical problem to Boas' *Tsimshian Mythology* which led anthropologists to assume that "a full correlation exists between a given society and its culture."[6] Rather than Boas, it is Malinowski who, in his *Myth in Primitive Psychology,* clearly formulated the functionalist framework in which the explanations offered by these Hausa scholars are couched. This functionalist framework as formulated by Malinowski is based on the belief that Myths have meaning in themselves and reflect society in a direct sense, that is, each myth corresponds to an actual rite or social activity. In Malinowski's word's,

> ...an intimate connection exists between the Lord, the mythos, the sacred tales of the tribes on the one hand, and their ritual acts, their moral deeds, their social organization, and even their practical activity on the other.[7]

It is by applying this functionalist framework whether consciously or not that many Hausa scholars inevitably find themselves assigning the Bayajida story the status of actual history as well as mistaking the social structure alluded to in the story of the real Hausa state system. In spite of the fecundity of the speculative method employed by earlier scholars such as Palmer, Hallam, Johnston, Smith, Yahaya and Jinju who either attempted to interpret or explain away the Bayajida story, recent developments in the scientific analysis of myth makes it possible and necessary to offer a different explanation using a new method.

---

[4] I.Y. Yahaya, "Oral Art and the Socialization Process: A Socio-Folkloric Perspectives of Initiation from Childhood to Adult Hausa Community Life," unpublished Ph.D. thesis, Ahmadu Bello University, Zaria, 1979, p. 68.
[5] See, Claude Levi-Strauss, "Four Winnebago Myths," in Richard and Ferdinand De George (ed.) *The Structuralists from Marx to Levi-Strauss,* Doubleday, New York, 1972 p. 200-201.
[6] Ibid. p. 201.
[7] B. Malinowski, *Myth in Primitive Psychology,* Wesport, Connecticut, 1971, p. 11.

The scientific analysis of myth recognizes, first, that myth belongs to the superstructural level of society, that is, the ideological level which those who listen to or recount the story are generally unconscious of. Consequently, myth is defined neither in terms of native classification nor of any textual or contextual properties but in terms of its logic. Secondly, the plot of a story or its component part(s) has no meaning in itself nor should it be interpreted relative to an isolated object outside it but in terms of the totality of life necessary for its production and maintenance. This totality comprises the whole world of mythology, that is, the series of myths which logically belong to the same type of real world which provides the experiential basis for the production and reproduction of the mythological world itself. Third, the implication of accepting the first and second principles is to reject all previous explanations in favour of the application of the following operations:

a) discover the unconscious level of the story, that is, the message in the story which both the narrator and his audience (which includes our learned scholars) may not be aware of. The message of the myth (i.e., the problem it is trying to solve) is uncovered by referring to the Hausa mythical world where series of stories exist which by virtue of their logical structure belong to the "Bayajida type"; b) account for the contradictions existing in the Bayajida myth as well as the one in the attempts to explain it by referring to the economic base necessary for sustaining different forms of social formations and their "myths" among the Hausa.

Method of analysis

Several variants of the Bayajida story are recorded and summarized in their shortest possible form such that no essential aspect of their meaning is lost. Each variant is then given an index number such as Bl, B2, B3 and so on. The approximate date and place of its collection are then given while an end-note[8] provides full reference in cases where the variant has been published or recorded in manuscript form. All the variants discussed except on (Bl) are the types normally classified by scholars as folktales rather than legend. This does not pose a problem since, according to the method applied here, a myth is defined in all its variants. Indeed, if this definition were to be taken too far not only these variants but Palmer, Johnston, Smith, Hallam and so on should all be included — as Levi-Strauss argued, should have been done to Freud in respect of the

---

[8] See, for BI, *Hausawa da Makwabtansu, Book I*, Zaria, Northern Nigerian Publishing Company, Zaria, 1971, p. 1-2; for B2, H.A.S. Johnston, *A Selection of Hausa Stories* Clarendon Press, Oxford, 1966 p. 75-77; for B3, Malam Barau, unpublished manuscript Book III; for B4, "Tatsuniyar Auta," Author's collection; for B5, "Yaro da Dodanniya," Barau, Manuscript; for B6, 'Auta Founded Town' R.S. Rattray, *Folklore, Customs and Proverbs* 2 Vols., Oxford Clarendon Press, 1913, p. 162-184.

Oedipus myth.

There are several variants of "the Bayajida legend" recorded in a number of works and one of them, recorded in 1971 in central Hausaland, reads,

> B1 A Prince of Baghdad, Bayajida, together with his troops, were dispersed by warring unbelievers. They arrived at Bornu where Bayajida married a princess. The king of Bornu feared his growing influence and planned to kill him. Bayajida escaped and finally arrived at Daura in Northern Nigeria.
>
> At Daura there was a snake living in the only well in the town. This snake prevented people from drawing water except on Fridays. Bayajida killed the snake and married the Queen as his reward. His offspring founded the seven Hausa states.

The next variant, B2, is an example of the type commonly classified as 'folktale,' and was recorded C.1910 in north-western Hausaland,

> B2 Auta and his sister left home for another town because their parents died. In this town there was an ogre preventing people from drawing water from the only well. Every year a daughter of the chief was sacrificed to the ogre. At night the ogre came, took the girl and dropped her inside the well. He then went round the town daring anyone to challenge him.
>
> Auta challenged the ogre and a fight was about to commence. But Auta threw red-hot stones at the ogre. The ogre swallowed several of these stones and fell dead. Auta was rewarded by being allowed to marry the chief's daughter and was appointed heir-apparent (*Galadima*). The chief in turn married Auta's sister.

A glance at the surface level of B1 and B2, that is, their plot, reveals that the principal character in each story leaves home for a foreign land where he kills a villainous character and finally becomes accepted into the aristocracy through his marriage with one of its members. In the case of Bayajida, it is interesting to note that it is his offspring that established the Hausa states. I will argue that all the other variants shown on the table below belong to the same plot. The minor changes in the forms of reward or in the type of principal character are simply differences in emphasis which are accounted for by an analysis of the "deep structure." The plot of B6 is typical of the "Bayajida type" except that there are nine brothers at the beginning but, later, it turns out that the youngest brother (*Auta*) is indeed the principal character since he kills a villainous character before finally becoming an aristocrat who, significantly, builds the first walled town.[9]

It is interesting to note that actual walls and the gates leading into major

---

[9] See, H. R. Palmer, *Sudanese Memoirs,* London, 1967, p. 132-134; Also S.H. Hurriez, "The Legend of the Wise Stranger: An Index of Cultural Unity in Central Bilad-al-Sudan," Khartoum, December, 1977, p. 5-6. Also, H.A.S. Johnston, *A Selection of Hausa Stories,* Oxford, 1966, p. 111-113. Also *Hausa da Makwabtansu Book I,* Northern Nigerian Publishing Company, Zaria, 1971, p.2-4.

Hausa cities, especially Kano, are today preserved as symbols of "culture". Incidentally, the term "culture", which features prominently in this chapter, is used in a sense similar to that developed by Levi-Strauss in his *Elementary Structures of Kinship*. In this work, he regards Nature and Culture as opposites. He argues that everything which is universal and spontaneous belongs to Nature while everything which is subject to rules belongs to Culture.[10] This Nature/Culture dichotomy emerges with the appearance of marriage exchange which is, for him, the first Cultural act. The term Anti-Culture however, has been suggested by me to refer to the distinction within Culture itself. In other words, unlike the opposition between Nature and Culture - which is of a fundamental nature - that between Culture and Anti-Culture is a division within Culture itself:[11] an opposition between those who represent Culture and those forces which seek to undermine them.

With reference to the stories under consideration, the table below summarizes B1 and B2 and the variants discussed:

No.	1	2	3	4
B1	Bayajida left home pursued by unbelievers	A snake prevents people from drawing water	Bayajida slays snake with a sword	Bayajida marries queen and offsprings establish Hausa States
B2	Auta left home because his parents are dead	An ogre prevents people from drawing water	Auta kills ogre with heated stones,	Auta marries king's daughter.
B3	Boy driven away by an ogre	The ogre eats human flesh	Boy meets Zarkallah who kills ogre by emerging through his navel	Boy returns home.
B4	Auta left his home for the town because of an ogre.	The ogre threatens to eat people	Auta kills ogre with heated stones.	Auta rewarded with slaves.
B5	Boy escapes from goblin mother.	The goblin eats human flesh.	Boy meets hedgehog who kills goblin.	Boy goes back home.
B6	Nine brothers leave home to	Witch threatens to eat the	The youngest brother (Auta)	Auta made heir-apparent and he

---

[10] See, C. Levi-Strauss, "Language and the Analysis of Social Laws," in, *Structural Anthropology*, London, Penguin 1962, p. 62.
[11] See, Maikudi Karaye, "The Structural Characteristics of the Gizo in Hausa Folktales," unpublished M.A. Dissertation, Khartoum, 1979, p. 44-45.

| visit girl-friend. | brothers. | kills witch, | builds the first walled town. |

Reading columns one to four vertically reveals the following relations. First, all the characters in column one lose their homes. Second, in column two, all the characters can be seen as representing Anti-Culture since they threaten to destroy Culture. Third, in column three, Anti-Culture is overcome. Finally, in the fourth column, Culture is re-established.

The fundamental contradiction in the myth of Bayajida is that Culture must exist amidst Anti-Culture and for it to survive (column 4) Anti-Culture (column 2) has to be eliminated (column 3) through the mediation of some Anti-Cultural elements (column 1). Those mediators necessary for the survival of Culture possess or acquire certain qualities or tools and at the same time lack essential cultural attributes like home, wife or title which they can only acquire after eliminating some Anti-Cultural element. In other words, the philosophy behind the Bayajida myth is that representatives of culture must exist amidst Anti-Culture since they need some of them to eliminate others while the Anti-Cultural elements have to eliminate others to acquire Culture or face elimination themselves. Thus, Culture is symbolized by walled towns, states, home, marriage, traditional title, etc., while the symbols of Anti-Culture are snakes, goblins, witches, ogres, etc. This contradiction between Culture and Anti-Culture and the various symbols identifying (=) each can be summarized as follows:

Culture = walled town, slave, home, marriage, title, states, etc.
Anti-Culture = Snake, goblin, witch, ogre, etc.

At this stage one might ask why Culture and Anti-Culture are represented by these symbols. At first sight, one might be tempted to say that these symbols are elaborate articulations of the fertile imagination, characteristic of the human mind. Here, one might conjecture that it is because the Hausa have walled towns, had slaves and cherish traditional titles on the one hand, and abhor any form of cannibalism and witchcraft on the other, that these symbols appear in their mythology. However, by referring to the social organization and economic activities of the Hausa during the nineteenth century when Hausaland was controlled by the Fulani aristocracy, it is possible to demonstrate that these symbols appear because they represent the interest of the aristocracy. Hausa society then was divided into two distinct classes - the Fulani aristocracy and the Hausa peasantry[12] which also roughly corresponded to the distinction between town and countryside respectively. The dominant ideology[13] was Islam and

---

[12] See, M.G. Smith, "The Hausa System of Social Status," *Africa*, Vol. XXIX, p. 247.
[13] M.G. Smith, "Historical and Cultural Condition of Political Corruption Among the Hausa," *Comparative Studies on Society and History* 1964, Vol. VI, p. 164-194.

economic production among the aristocracy was based on the exploitation of captive labour.[14] Among the peasantry it was based on the communal working of a piece of family land *(gandu)*.[15]

Traditional titles, slaves and walled towns appear as symbols of culture in Hausa mythology because slavery provides labour and warriors for the aristocracy while free peasants with surplus agricultural products surrender them to the aristocracy to acquire titles. Walled towns provide shelter during raids and both townsfolk and rural dwellers give a portion of their produce annually to ensure this protection. Furthermore, during the dry season each family provides labour for the maintenance and extension of these walls. The myth thus shapes the Hausa thinking, directing it to believe that humanity is synonymous with living in walled towns, acquiring slaves, titles, etc. while the political structure ensures conformity. In this manner the social arrangement where the interest of the aristocracy reigns supreme is reproduced and maintained.

Home and marriage appear as symbols of culture to reflect the organization of production among the peasantry. Here labour is provided by the number of kinsmen available at home. To ensure the continuity and prosperity of the peasant family its members must remain at home and marry as early as possible to produce the muscle power necessary for tilling the *gandu*. Even slaves kept by the rich peasantry are allowed to marry and are given quasi-kinship term. Since the aristocracy must exist amidst peasants, the ideology maintaining it has to ensure the continuity of the peasantry, albeit in a dominated position. In this way both the peasantry as a social class and its opposite - the aristocracy - are reproduced and maintained.

With reference to Anti-Culture, the goblins, witches and ogres raise an interesting fundamental issue since they eat human flesh and can, on this account, be related to the universal problem of anthropophagy. Professor Arens made the observation that no proof of actual cannibalism exists but that people of different races living all over the world under varying social formations discredit their political rivals by referring to them as cannibals. As Arens put it,

> ...rather than being an actual deed, cannibalism existed as an aspect of political ideology and was employed in the process of attempting to discredit political rivalry.[16]

Arens also made the important observation that in societies where there is division of labour, exploitation and domination, opposing classes describe each

---

[14] M.G. Smith "A Story of Hausa Domestic economy in Northern Zaria," *Africa,* 1952, Vol. XXII p. 333-347, also, A.D. Goddard, "Changing Family Structures Among Rural Hausa," *Africa,* 1973, Vol. XLIII, p. 207-218. Also, P.E. Lovejoy, "The Characteristics of Plantations in the Sokoto Caliphate," 1977, unpublished.
[15] See, Goddard, 'Changing Family Structures'; also Lovejoy, 'Plantations in Sokoto Caliphate.'
[16] See, W. Arens, "The Man-Eating Myth," *Anthropology and Anthropophagy,* 1980, Oxford University Press, p. 94.

other negatively with the poor and powerless usually described in terms closely related to those I call Anti-Cultural qualities.[17] Arens' view on this matter deserves to be quoted:

> With the most complex social systems characterized by some form of internal division based upon the unequal distribution of wealth and/or power, the oppressed or oppressing classes see each other through a vision clouded by moral judgements. The poor and the powerless are thought to be ignorant, lazy, dirty and possess a host of other related characteristics.[18]

When a social arrangement requires a constant supply of slaves to maintain its productive capacity, the need to justify slavery and the continuous in-flow of slaves can hardly be disputed. By postulating the existence of Anti-Culture Hausa mythology, provides justification for raids to confiscate property *(camel)* as well as to acquire slaves. In other words, within Hausaland, calling a political rival a witch justifies his elimination or being sold into slavery. Incidentally the Fulani aristocracy itself came to power in Hausaland by eliminating Hausa chiefs whom they called unbelievers practising traditional religion, that is, witchcraft. The snake at Daura is the counterpart of Satan in religious symbolism who is synonymous with disbelief.

In considering the relationship between the Hausa and their neighbours the Bayajida myth provides a form of national consciousness which unites all Hausas whom the myth describes as different from the others. These others, the myth submits, are witches or cannibals. People occupying the southern fringes of Hausaland are generally described as unbelievers, witches and cannibals who may thus be enslaved or eliminated. This partly accounts for the fact that during dry seasons, Hausa rulers of old led expeditions down south to acquire slaves. One may even be tempted to conclude that this is the reason why even the states to the South-West of Hausaland are called *Banza Bakwai* (illegitimate seven) and can thus be enslaved at will.

The remaining influence of this myth on the thinking of the Hausa is still manipulated by the elites to gain political control. This is done by calling all non-Hausa uncultured, with some even described as cannibals and, of course, unbelievers (of Islamic faith). When the differences in language and region are added the transformation of the myth into its modern variant is complete. In this way votes are secured, strikes averted or encouraged, and representation at various companies and committee obtained. As a myth Bayajida shapes and influences the way and manner Hausa people think and react to social change and is therefore the counterpart of Nigeria's modern myths of development, democracy, National Unity, and so on, which are propagated as the true yearnings of the people. It is only when the economic foundations responsible

---

[17] See, M. Karaye, MA. Thesis, p. 55, 64.
[18] W. Arens *The Man-Eating Myth* p. 158

for the creation of a myth are changed that the mythical thinking disappears. Meanwhile, Bayajida lingers and baffles our scholars just as the aristocracy that gave birth to it is baffled by the momentum of the new social arrangement characteristic of capitalism which is bent on eliminating it.

Bibliography of works mentioned

Abdullahi, S. "Some Considerations Relating to the Formation of States in Hausaland," *Journal of the Historical Society of Nigeria,* Vol. V, No. 3, 1970, p. 329-346.
Arens, W. *The Man-Eating Myth; Anthropology and Anthropophagy,* Oxford University Press, 1980.
Goddard, A.D. "Changing Family Structures Among Rural Hausa," *Africa,* 1973 Vol. XLVIII p. 207-218.
Hallam, W.K.R., "The Bayajida Legend in Hausa Folklore," *Journal of African History,* 1968, Vol. VII No. 1., p.47-60.
Hurriez., S.H. "The Legend of the Wise Stranger; An Index of Cultural Unity in the Central Bilad-as-Sudan," paper presented at the 3rd International Conference on Central Bilad-as-Sudan, Khartoum, 1977.
Jinju, H.M. "Asalin Hausawa," unpublished paper presented at Conference on Hausa and Culture, Kano, August, 1985.
Karaye, M. "The Structural Characteristics of the Gizo in Hausa Folktales," unpublished thesis, 1979.
Levi-Strauss, C. *Structural Anthropology,* London, Penguin, 1966.
- "Four Winnebago Myths", in R. and P. De George (ed.), *The Structuralists From Marx to Levi-Strauss,* Doubleday Anchor, New York 1972.
Lovejoy, P.E. "The Characteristics of Plantation in the Sokoto Caliphate," unpublished paper presented at "Symposium on Slavery in Africa," Princeton University, 1977.
Malinowski, B. *Myth in Primitive Psychology,* Connecticut, Negro University Press, 1971.
Northern Nigerian Publishing Company, *Hausawa da Makwabtansu Book I,* Zaria, NNPC. 1971.
Palmer, H.R. *Sudanese Memoirs,* London, Frank Cass, 1967.
Smith M.G. "A Study of Hausa Domestic Economy in Southern Zaria" *Africa,* 1952, Vol. XXII, 333-347.
- "The Hausa System of Social States," *Africa,* 1959, Vol. XXIX, pp. 231-252.
- "Historical and Cultural Condition of Political Corruption Among the Hausa" *Comparative Studies in Society and History,* 1964 Vol. 6, p. 164-194.
Yahaya, I.Y. "Oral Art and the Socialization Process: A Socio-Folkloric Perspective of Initiation from Childhood to Adult Hausa Community Life." Unpublished Ph.D. Thesis, ABU, 1979.

Chapter 4

Towards understanding *Ndi Igbo* and their cosmology

- Ichie P.A. Ezikeojiaku

Introduction

Lack of literary records makes it difficult to ascertain the date of the origin of a stock of the Kwa group of the Niger Congo called *Ndi Igbo*. Not only does this dearth of written records affect their origin, it also affects the means of interpreting and understanding their cosmology and religion. And a better understanding of this world view will help their neighbours in appraising how *ndi Igbo* react to national and non-national issues. The only records available are oral history, myths, legends, etc., though in more recent times the works of Isichei,[1] Afigbo,[2] Uchendu,[3] Onwuejeogwu[4] have become available. An examination of the above mentioned recorded oral accounts reveals a persistent and systematic similarity which points to a common origin of this stock. But while there are still other speculations proposed by some investigators, the following hypotheses seem to stand out clearly.

First, there is the Jewish origin theory proposed by Njaka,[5] and the Egyptian origin hypothesis proposed by Meek who claims that 'many traits of European culture have begun to filter through the Igbo communities in the 16th century.'[6] Second, Basden has proposed the Semitic theory which states that the Igbo have closer association with the Semitic race than any other and that the successive waves of invasion from the north-east of Asia down through Egypt must have driven them into their present geographical location. The effect of these waves of migration was such that 'they, *ndi Igbo* were borne onwards until, finally,

---

[1] Isichei, E., (1977), *Igbo Worlds,* London: Macmillan Educational Publishers Ltd.
[2] Afigbo, A.E. (1981), *Ropes of Sand*, Ibadan: University Press Ltd.
[3] Uchendu, V.C. (1966), *The Igbo of South-east Nigeria*, New York: Holt Rinehart and Winston. p. 3.
[4] Onwuejeogwu, M.A., (1981), An Igbo Civilization: Nri Kingdom and Hegemony, Benin, Ethiope Publishing Corporation, p. 3.
[5] Njaka, E.N., (1974), *Igbo Political Culture*, Evanston, p. 4
[6] Meek, C.K., (1937), *Land and Authority in a Nigerian Tribe*, London, p. 5.

they came to rest where we find them today and throughout the ages, generations to generations.'[7] There is also the Israelite theory of origin which argues that from the ritualistic point of view as well as judging from their industry and ingenuity, *ndi Igbo* are a stock from Israel. A typical Igbo village person, however, would say the Igbo were created where they find themselves today — and that would be the end of the matter.[8] There may be other speculations but all of them have been rejected by many historians, anthropologists and linguists because they tend to lack concrete historical or scientific proof.

Apart from the glimpse of proof from the Igbo-Ukwu finds by Shaw,[9] and the linguistic evidence adduced by Armstrong in 1976, the origin of the Igbo still remains uncertain, though the dominant view is that *ndi Igbo* are of Nigerian origin. This theory is supported by the linguistic evidence that the Igbo are of the Niger Congo group of languages which separated from this group about 6000 BC.

Other stocks in Nigeria and outside tend to misconstrue and misinterpret *ndi Igbo* in their behavioural relations simply because of an improper understanding of them and their world view. Since only a sound understanding and interpretation of their cosmology can provide appreciation of their behaviour in their relationship with other nationalities, we shall attempt here to present an outline of this world view. And to achieve this objective, we shall try to explore the world of God, the world of spirits, the world of nature and the world of man, each as conceived by *ndi Igbo*.

Igbo and not Ibo

In spite of the lack of historically recorded evidence about their origin, the word "Igbo" (and not "Ibo") is often used in three senses: to refer to the territorial location, the people themselves, and finally to the language. In terms of geographical space and population, the Igbo is considered as one of the great ethnic nationalities in Nigeria, and, indeed, in Africa. Onwuejeogwu has described *ndi Igbo* as those whose ancestry has roots in the Igbo culture area and whose *Igboness* conforms with the criteria by which this culture area is defined.[10] *Ndi Igbo* are, therefore, those who are found in the Igbo culture area, who speak the same language and subscribe to the same traditional, social,

---

[7] Basden, G.T., (1966, ed.); *Niger Igbos*, London, p.414
[8] Late Nze Ezeonyirimba Ezembaji of Umuaniji in Umuogwugwu of Uhuala kindred in Ihitenansa Autonomous community in Orlu Local Government Area of Imo State was interviewed on this issue in 1975 and he held the same view.
[9] Shaw, T., (1968) *Igbo - Ukwu: Account of Archaeological Discoveries in Eastern Nigeria*, Vols. I & II, London: Faber and Faber.
[10] Onwuejeogwu, M A., *op. cit.*

religious, political, economic, cosmological and cultural themes.

Cosmology

Ndi Igbo have a ritual system and, therefore, a structure of religion consonant with and adequate for their needs.[11] This means that ritual is religion-based and religion is built into their cosmology which is as old as their ancestry. Cosmology has been defined by Onions as a theory of the universe.[12] Igbo cosmology is, therefore, concerned with the discussion of their origin, structure and space relations in the universe.

Theorizing about the origin of the universe (the physical world), for example, does not seem to pose as serious a problem as theorizing about the non-physical world to the Igbo. They have, for example, an expression which says that *he nwere mbido ga-enwe niedebe* ("whatever has a beginning will have an end") To *ndi Igbo,* this expression implies that the universe must have a beginning and an end space-wise. The Igbo watch things come and go; a child is born, matures and after living, at most, a hundred years or a little more passes away. The animal and plant kingdoms are ruled by the same cycle. From the observance of the process of the coming-to-be and ceasing-to-be of visible reality, the Igbo draw the obvious inference that whatever has a beginning has an end. Thus, the Igbo thinker conceives the possibility of a beginning for all visible entities.

Perception

It has been observed that the behavioural patterns of *ndi Igbo* derive from their conception or perception of their world-view. To understand the world-view is, therefore, to understand how they behave in any society they find themselves. And to make the Igbo aware of the resources at their disposal; and to motivate and energize them to collectively utilize such resources for the improvement of their spiritual and material conditions of living (which is the import of mobilization), a clear understanding of their cosmology is crucial.

To understand a people's cosmology, is to understand both their temporal and non-temporal evaluation of life and the whole complex of their beliefs and practices concerning the nature and inter-relational structure of life in the universe with particular reference to the people. A thorough perception of this cosmology does not only provide *ndi Igbo* with a charter of action, but

---

[11] Nwoga, D.I., (1985), *The Supreme God As Stranger in Igbo Religious Thought*, Hawk Press, Ekwereazu, Ahiazu Mbaise, Imo State, p. 67.
[12] Onions, C.T., (ed.) (1979), *The Oxford Dictionary of English Etymology*, London, p. 218.

ultimately, also, with guidelines for their behaviour in the community. In its complexity, the Igbo cosmology seeks to explain the existence of things in the world and their specific infrastructural and religious order. The cosmology also seeks to evaluate the behaviour of man with reference to God, the divinities and the ancestors.

Uchendu views the Igbo cosmology under three aspects: as an "explanatory device," since cosmology theorizes about the origin and character of the universe; as a 'system of prescriptive ethics,' it prescribes what the Igbo ought to do and what they ought not to do, and finally as an 'action system' - which reveals what the Igbo actually do as manifested in their overt and covert behaviour.[13] This accounts for the importance which *ndi Igbo* attach to their ethical beliefs and practices, community rules and regulations, norms and taboos and respect to constituted authorities such as the *Ozo* and *Eze* institutions.

According to the Igbo, the universe is comprised of two worlds which interact with each other, namely, the visible world and the super-sensible world. All the beings known in Igbo ontology belong to one or the other of these two worlds. The visible world, represented by all the natural phenomena, is peopled by men while the super-sensible world is the spirit world.[14] But in this same world-view there is no distinctive and exclusive demarcation between the two worlds. Man dies to regenerate. Therefore, to *ndi Igbo,* if there is no death, there would be no birth and vice versa. Birth is interwoven with death just as death is interwoven with birth; hence both are related to each in a dialectic.

The living lives with the dead, in same way that the dead lives with the living. This accounts for why, before he eats, an Igbo traditionalist throws out bits of food outside to the waiting and hungry ancestors and spirits who should eat first before him. While he throws out bits of food as ritual, according to *Ezeonyirimba Ezembaji* the Igbo says,

Nna a ha	My dead father and others.
Ndi mbu	The ancient
Na ndi egede	And the antic
Rienu nke unu	Have your share of the food.
Ndi O ka agu	Those who are more hungry
Na ndi o nag/ti agu	And those who are not hungry
Riena nke unu	Have your share of the food.
Ka o ga-abu	So that
Anyi riwe nke anyi	When we start eating ours,
Mmire agaghi afa	There should be
Anyi n'eze	No mishap on us
Ihaa!	So let it be.

---

[13] Uchendu, V.C., *op. cit.*
[14] Iloanusi, O.A., (1984), *Myths of the Creation of Man and The Origin of Death in Africa*, European Universities Study Series XXIII, Theology Vol/Bd 222, p. 71.

The import of the above excerpt is that, according to Uchendu, "the Igbo world is a 'real' one in every aspect." There is the world of man peopled by all created beings and things, both animate and inanimate. The spirit world is the abode of the Creator, the deities, the disembodied and malignant spirits, and the ancestral spirits. As observed earlier, between these two worlds there is constant interaction. In the world of the spirits activities continue. The inhabitants of the world of the spirits manifest in their behaviour and thought processes that they are 'living.' The dead continue their lineage system just like those on earth. In his morning kolanut ritual an Igbo traditionalist addresses the dead as if they are there with him, as evident in the excerpt below:

Chukwu Abiama bia taa oji	God, the Son of Abiama come and take kola.
Nna a ha, unu mukwa anya?	My grandfathers, I hope you are all vigilant.
Nbu na Egede taanu oji	The ancient and the antic take kolanuts
Ohu mmuo na nnu mmuo	Twenty and four hundred spirits
Ngwanu were oke unu	Proceed and take your share of the kolanuts.
Nna a ha werenu nke unu	My grandfathers, take your share.
Werenu nke Chukwu Abiama	Take, the share of God, the son of Abiama,
Nyeruo ya	And send to Him.
Werenu oji kee ohu mmuo	Take kolanuts and share among spirits of all types.
Anyi kezuru ekezu	In our sharing we applied equity.
Ikpe omuma abughi nke anyi	Blame is not ours.
O buru na unu ekezughi	If you fail to apply equity in your sharing,
Ikpe omuma buzi nke unu	Then blame is yours.
Ebe anyi nyezuru unu oke unu	Since we gave out all your shares
Jirinu ndu kwuo anyi ugwo	Pay us with life.
Jirinu ahuike kwuo anyi ugwo	Pay us with good health
Ka O ga-abu chi fo anyi efo	So that when the day dawns we exist with it.
Ihaa!	So let it be.

There are also what *ndi Igbo* perceive in their cosmology as *ndi akariogeri,* spirits. These are believed to be the dead whose funeral ceremonies have not been completed. To this group belongs another sub-group of people who, while on earth, did not marry; or if married, did not beget children and took no important titles such as *Ozo* and other similar titles. The dead remain in this sphere until their burial ceremonies have been completed. This could be called a temporary condition in the spirit world. To the Igbo, this sphere of temporary stay is like the Christian concept of purgatory. The Igbo does not only believe in the above mentioned worlds but also in unborn lives. The frequent interaction between the two worlds influences the action of each individual in both the urban and the rural communities.

We have noted that *ndi Igbo* perceive the universe as having two worlds - the visible and the super-sensible worlds - which can further be divided into four, namely, the world of God, the world of spirits, the world of nature and the world of man. The last section of this chapter will attempt to further examine these worlds of *ndi Igbo* for a better appreciation of the behaviour of the Igbo toward those who come in contact with them.

The world of God

In the past, many authors have attempted to deal with such questions as: From where does the idea of God originate? Is this idea indigenous to the Igbo? Does he believe in one God or are there many gods besides the absolute God? Can this idea be traced back to Christianity or Islam?

Talbot,[15] Equiano,[16] Anozie[17] and Basden[18] provide some answers to the above questions and their views are supported by the fact that the traditional religious belief of *ndi Igbo* is indigenous. For, in spite of the existence of Christianity and Islam, neither of these religions has adversely influenced the religion of *ndi Igbo* which Onuoha describes as not only natural but ancestral, indigenous and oriented towards personal and community development.[19]

Therefore, the idea of God is indigenous to the Igbo, having originated from them and for them. The Igbo believe in the existence of a 'big' God with other gods, deities and ancestors helping him in his onerous task of ruling and guiding the universe. In this respect, one can argue that, among *ndi Igbo,* the idea of God is not traceable to either Christian or Islamic influence.

A look at the following sketch, adapted from Iloanusi,[20] can help us summarize our points and also guide the reader to understand and appreciate the cosmology under discussion:

---

[15] Talbot, P.A., (1969), *The Peoples of Southern Nigeria*, London, Vol. 11 (1926), p. 14.
[16] Equiano, O., (1967), *Equiano's Travels or The Interesting Narrative of the Life of Oluadah Equiano or Gustavus Vasa, The African*, London, 1789, 2nd ed., ed. by Paul Edwards, London, p. 10.
[17] Anozie, I.P., (1968) "The Religions Import of Igbo Names." (Unpublished Dissertation) Rome, p. 45.
[18] Basden, G.I., (1966, ed.), *op. cit.*
[19] Onuoha Enyeribe (1984), "The Philosophy of Igbo Religion," a paper presented at the Congress on Igbo Religion, University of Nigeria, Nsukka, on August, p. 3.
[20] Iloanusi, O.A., *op. cit.*

God	Chukwu	Sky	Eluigwe
Earth	Ala	Underworld	Alammuo
Human World	Uwa	Sprit World	Alammuo
Ancestors	Ndiichie	3rd Burial	Okwukwa ato
2nd Burial	Ikwukwa abuo	1st Burial	Okwukwa mbu
Death	Onwu	Old Age	Okenye
Puberty	Ntorobia	Boyhood	Umuaka
Birh/Reincarnation	Omumu/Alulouwa		

A Sketch of Igbo Idea of his Cosmology Eserese Nghota Uwa Onye Igbo

The Igbo concept of the four worlds in their cosmology can also be perceived from the themes contained in the morning prayers of an Igbo traditionalist and philosopher named Ezeonyirimba Ezembaji of Orlu, Imo State, from whom the following text was recorded in 1975:

Chukwu Abiama	God, the son of Abiama
Onye nwe uwa	The owner of the world
Chi na Eke	God and Creator
Eke kere Igwe na Ala	Creator of heaven and earth
Eke kere ihe di adi	Creator of things that exist
Eke kere ihe adighi adi	Creator of things that do not exist.
Ana m akpoku unu	I am invoking all of you
Igwe na Ala	Heaven and Earth
Anyanwu na Eze elu	The Sun and the king of the sky
Mmuo bi n'elu	Spirits that live in the sky
Ndi mbu na ndi egede	The ancestors and the antic
Arusi bi n'elu	The forces that live in the sky
Arusi bi n'ala	The forces that live on earth
Bianu za m oku	Come all and answer my call.
Ihe ekere eke	Created things
Na ihe di adi	And existing things
Ihe oma na ihe ojoo	Good and bad things
Ezi omume na ajo omume	Good and bad manners
Eziokwu na okwuasi	Truth and falsehood
Bianu tara oji ututu	Come all and take morning kolanuts.
Onu nwoke, onu nwanyi	The voice of males and the voice of females
Onu nze, onu okoro	The voice of *eze* and that of the untitled.
Onu agadi, onu umuazi	The voice of elders and that of children.

Bianu mbiko tara oji	Please, come and take kolanuts.
Anyi lee anya n'ihu	We look into the future
O buru anyi ihe oma	And it is blessing for us.
Anyi lee anya n'azu	We look into the past
O buru anyi ihe oma	And it is blessing for us.
Onye siri anyi adila	He who says we should die
Ya buru okuko uzo lakpuo ura	Should die before us
Ihaa!	So, let it be.[21]

Put in a simpler sketch, the Igbo idea of their cosmos can be represented thus:

Igbo Cosmology	World of God	World of Spirits	World of Nature
Human	World of Man	Spirits	Human

To the Igbo, both the visible and the invisible worlds were created by a Supreme Being known and addressed variously by these names:

Chi + Ukwu	=	Chukwu, God, Great Determiner
Chi + na + Eke	=	Chineke, God, the Creator
Ezechi + to + Eke	=	Ezechitoke = King Creator
Onye + Okike	=	Onyeokike, the one-who-creates;

Iphe + Meru + nemadru = Ifemeremmadu, The Being that made man;

Obasi-di-n'elu = Obasidin'elu,

The Great-One-who-lives-in-the-universe;
Onye + nwe + uwa = Onyenweuwa, Owner of the Universe;
Onye + oghorogbo + Anya = Onyeoghoroghoanya,

The Big-eyed one (omniscient)

Onye + Okike =   Onyeokike, the one-who-creates;
Iphe + Meru + nemadru = Ifemeremmadu,

The Being that made man;

Obasi-di-n'elu = Obasidin'elu,

The Great-One-who-lives-in-the-universe;
Onye + nwe + uwa = Onyenweuwa, Owner of the Universe;

---

[21] Ezeonyirimba Ezembaji, *op. cit.*

Onye + oghorogbo + Anya = Onyeoghoroghoanya,

The Big-eye one (omniscient)

Onye + O + na-abu + e + kpesiara + O + gwu = Onyeanaabu-ekpesiaraogwu,

The - Ultimate - Resort - Beyond - whom - there - is - no - other

Oji = mma + jide + ji = Ojummajideji,

Alpha and Omega, All-in-All, All Determiner.

The world of spirits

Next in the rank is the world of spirits which *ndi Igbo* also conceptualize in their world view. The Igbo recognize and worship lesser gods — divinities, deities, spirits, and oracles. The Igbo believe that these spirits are appointed by *Chukwu* to help him in the onerous task of administering and supervising both the visible and the invisible worlds which he created. The *ndi Igbo* derive their traditional religion, rituals and sacrifices from this conceptualization of many gods. So, in this world-view, the world of spirits is not only recognized but revered and respected. For, it is believed that if such reverence is not accorded the actors in the world of spirits, such actors would bring about bad omen into the worlds of nature and man. And when such bad omen occurs, the evil can only be averted by first of all ascertaining the grievances of the spirits through divination, and second, appeasing them by means of sacrifices consequent on divination. This partly explains the origin of divination in Igbo land.

An important aspect of the ancient Greek religion was the prevalence of ritual divination and the existence of numerous oracles and deities supposed to give voice to the will of providence. Among the famous oracles were those of Apollo at Delphi and of Zeus at Doldona (all in Greece) and that of Zeus Ammon in Upper Egypt. The oldest oracle in Greek mythology appears to be that at Doldona where the responses of the god were interpreted by priests from the rustling of Oak trees in the wind.

Like the ancient Greek, the Igbo recognize two categories of deities in their traditional religion, namely, the major and the minor ones. The following major deities are recognized and revered: *Ibinukpabi* of Arochukwu in Abia State of which Patridge reports that, according to a man from Obinkita, 'the great god was a huge snake called Ebeni-kpavi.'[22] But the shrine of this great god, whose influence was felt throughout the former Eastern and Western regions of

---

[22] Patridge Charle, (1905), *Cross River Native*, London, p.54.

Nigeria, was maliciously destroyed in 1906 by the white imperialists. The next major deity is the *Agbala* of Awka with its old shrine at Ezi Awka in Anambra State. Others are the *Igwekala* of Umuneoha in Mbaitolu Ikeduru local government area and *Amadioha Ozuzu* in Owerri in Imo State; the *Ojukwu Diobu* in Port Harcourt; the *Oshimiri* of Asaba in Delta State, and the *Onojo* of Oboni in Anambra State. Despite the vandalism of the white imperialists on these oracles, people continue to worship them till today though not as enthusiastically as before. The Igbo recognize these strong deities as agents of the Supreme God.

Also, in this world view, minor gods are recognized according to locality and they are seen as performing the same function as the major deities. Ancestral rites are usually performed to the following: *Chi,* personal god, represented by a person's shadow; *Ogwugwu,* god of peace; *Otammiri,* a river god; *Okide,* a river god; *Urasi* and *Imo,* river gods; *Agwunsi,* god of medicine and health; and *Ajoala,* evil god, etc. These gods serve local needs; they guide, protect and provide other services to actors in the worlds of man and nature.

The world of Nature

The Igbo perception of the world of nature is characterized by hills, rivers mountains, caves, anthills, trees, forests, shrubs, animals and insects and in some of these natural phenomena reside the major and minor deities. Among the Igbo, it is believed that spirits and gods transform into animals such as the lion, leopard or tiger. This act is called *ihi agu,* as in Uturu, Okigwe in Imo State; transforming into the boa and some other snakes, *ihi agwo/eke;* into the evil bird, *ajonnunu;* the owl, *iwi;* the vulture, *udele,* etc. This is why some Igbo communities do not eat the boa, the owl, the evil bird, the vulture, etc. These are regarded as sacred animals. There are also sacred trees such as *he ngwu* which people are forbidden to cut; hence the Igbo proverb: *Oma uma egbu ngwu mma anaghi adiri ya nko* ('One who attempts to kill an innocent person never succeeds'). This literally means that one never cuts the sacred tree, *ngwu,* without performing some sacrifices. The sacredness of these natural phenomena - fauna and flora - is responsible for the Igbo idea of norms and taboos. For example, in Uli, Ihiala local government area of Anambra State, it is taboo to kill a boa. When such an abomination is committed, the dead boa is given burial rites appropriate to a man. This is so because the people believe that to kill a boa is to kill the spirit of Otammiri Uli to whom they owe their existence. It,is also forbidden to kill a lion or a tiger in Uturu, because of the belief that *ndi Uturu na-ehi agu,* "the people of Uturu transform into lions and tigers." In some other Igbo communities, it is a taboo to kill a kind of python called *abuala.* In such places, it is believed that the animal is the spirit of a particular deity. In the whole of Igbo land, the evil bird *ajonnunu* and the vulture *udele* are not eaten.

The cry of the evil bird is usually interpreted to be a presage of some disaster likely to befall the people. Whenever its cry is heard, people predict that some one is likely to die.

In this cosmology, there is what is called the evil forest *ajoohia* (cf. Achebe)[23] into which people who commit abominations or suffer from infectious diseases are thrown. And, the physical features of the ecology determine which items in the world of nature are conceptualized as abodes of spirits and gods or, on the other hand, as gods and spirits to be recognized and revered as such.

The world of man

The *ndi Igbo* recognize the world of human beings which can be called the world of man - *uwa mmadu,* as opposed to the world of spirits - *uwammuo.* Man, as perceived in this world view, ought to be intelligent, strong in body and spirit; hence the proverbial expression, *isi ike na mmadu sie na mmuo.* To the Igbo, man is supposed to be of 'half iron and half wood,' i.e. *Okara igwe, Okara osisi.* In other words, man is conceived as one who is even ready to face all odds of life; he is ready for good as he is for ill. It is claimed by some analysts that this attribute made many *ndi Igbo* people survive the vagaries of the civil war (1967-1970). The binary nature of things, acts and behaviours in this world, seems to be manifest in an ideal Igbo man. This kind of man, who has his *ikenga,* the cult of the right arm and symbol of ingenuity, adventure and success in life, is a personality to be reckoned with. *Ikenga* has been described by Afigbo as "the hand with which (an Igbo) man hacks his way through the jungle of sweet and bitter experiences known as life."[24] According to this cosmological concept, a weakling has no *Ikenga* to ward off man-made evils and spirits, whereas a man with strong will is believed to have an *Ikenga* because he understands that it is he (man) who becomes the spirit/ancestor at death. Such a man does not, therefore, fear these spirits and his fellow human beings. This explains the much-talked-about fearless nature of the Igbo - a trait that makes them live and thrive in distant parts of Nigeria and Africa. Armed with this feat of daring and adventure, an Igbo often questions his ancestor or *Chi* (personal god). This is manifest for example, in the folktale figure "Ojaadili" (an epitome of the Igbo spirit) who wrestled with the most renowned human wrestler and defeated him, went to the animal world and defeated the chimpanzee in another wrestling match; went into the spirit world and defeated all the famous spirit wrestlers including a spirit with seven heads. Still feeling unfulfilled, fearless Ojaadili

---

[23] Chinua Achebe, (1958), *Things Fall Apart*, London, Heinemann Educational Books.
[24] Afigbo, A.E., (1986), 'Ikenga: The State of our knowledge,' Rada Publishing Company, Owerri, p. 2 or *Ikenga-Obo* and we are told that *Obo* is hand. On this plane of concept, *Ikenga* appears, from present evidence, to be very widely distributed in the forest lands of Nigeria. At least it appears to exist amongst all the peoples east of Yorubaland and south of the Northern border of Igala land. It has been reported among the Bakuba.

opted to engage in the most dangerous and fearful wrestling match of all - one with his personal god, *chi* - who finally defeated him.[25]

This fearless trait is also manifest in an Igbo man's peculiar way of praying in which he warns and even scolds his God, especially when he has done his own bit of an assignment and the other bit is expected to be done by God. In the ritual excerpt that follows, the artist invokes the spirit of equity and natural justice thus:

Agwu akwaraala m	*Agwu*,[26] I have provided you with all
gi ibu gi	the items of sacrifice.
Buruzie kesaa ndi	Take them and share with all
mmuo ibe gi	other spirits.
Emeela m nke diri m	I have done my own bit
Mezie nke diri gi	Do your own bit.
Ofo o fo n'aka	*Ofo*[27] if what remains is with you
Fo gi n'ukwu	Or it is under your feet
Amaghi m	I do not know
Abu m mwata	I am a baby
Ana m aghu	I do my washing first
Ahu n'afo n'afo	From my belly. (I plead innocent)
Ka unu giri ja-eme	For you to ignore
Ihe anyi kwuru	What we have pleaded for
Ofo ekwekwala unu	Let *ofo* prohibit you
Ala ekwekwala unu	Let *Ala* prohibit you
Ihaa!	So, let it be.[28]

The Igbo sense of recognizing the fact of a "beginning of beginnings" is portrayed in a folktale narrative which is usually introduced or set thus:

N'oge gboo gboo   *N'oge uwa adighi*

O buso mdi mmuo di ("In a long long time ago when the visible world was not; only the unseen were"). Here, the Igbo narrator begins his story by setting it at an undatable moment, *N'oge gboo gboo. . .* a familiar expression used to refer to the very distant past when there was nothing in existence, indicated by the 'before,' the time prior to the beginning of beginnings.

---

[25] Odunke Artists, (1975), *Ojaadili*, Ibadan: Oxford University Press Ltd.
[26] Agwunsi is the malevolent-benevolent spirit in charge of medicine and health. It is also in charge of divination.
[27] *Ofo* is a symbol of authority in the Igbo cosmology and it is usually held by the eldest in the family, especially the first son who is called *diokpara*.
[28] This text was collected from Mmeke Okpara of Uhuala Ihitenansa in Orlu Local Government of Imo State on September, 15, 1988.

The Igbo world view acknowledges that even before visible beginnings, the unseen realities were in existence...*O bu so ndi mmuo di* ("Only the unseen beings were"). What, then, is the relationship between the unseen beings and the fact of the origin of visible realities? As we pointed out earlier, there exist two broad types of world in this cosmology and the relationship between them gives rise to the Igbo ancestral religion. This duality in the Igbo perception of their universe is also evident in the following common expressions:

Uwa a na uwa ozo ("This world and another world"), *eluigwe na ala* ("the top of the sky and the earth"), *mma na njo* ("good and evil"), *Oke na nwunye* ("male and female"), *Ofo na Ogu* ("the symbol of authority and the symbol of natural justice"), *Onwu na ndu* ("life and death"), *Onwu oma na onwu ojoo* ("good death and bad death"); *nwata na Okenye,* ("the child and the elder") etc. These negative and positive oppositions characterize the Igbo world view and are observed in their traditional religious practices, beliefs and ethical values.

We have earlier examined some of the objects of the Igbo traditional religion, which include gods and deities which the Igbo regard as messengers of the Supreme God. Whenever an Igbo is disappointed in his link with the Supreme God by these middle spirits, he does not hesitate to say, *Arusi m jiri aka m wube hapu oru diiri ya, efopu m ya wube nke ozo* ("When I have done my part and the spirit fails to do his, I must remove its shrine and install another in his place"). This trait in an Igbo person ensures effectiveness in carrying out assigned duties among fellow human beings, among spirits and ancestors, even in his relationship with the Supreme Being Himself. This accounts for the Igbo's zest for industry, ingenuity, and hard work because everyone wants to play his or her part well. The result is that an Igbo is like the *Uboogu* which survives in any ecology; he prunes here and draws there in every part of Nigeria to ensure good living habits.

The *Ndi Igbo* also believe strongly in the *Uhu,* spirit of recognition/charming attitudes; *Ukwu na ije,* spirit of adventure, and, as we stated earlier, *Ikenga,* symbol of achievement. Armed with all these negative and positive attributes, the Igbo are sometimes feared by their neighbours.

Conclusion

In this chapter, an attempt has been made to explore the world view of the *ndi Igbo* in order to expose not only their exemplary traits but also to condemn those traits not conducive to peaceful co-existence with their neighbours. We have pointed out their individualist attributes, zest for industry and adventure, religious and fearless nature. We can draw from all this the conclusion that the *ndi Igbo* are the kind of people they are in Nigeria and elsewhere because of the way they perceive and interpret their cosmology. Just as there is need for them to curtail their so-called avaricious acquisitiveness, there is also need for their neighbours to recognize their versatility, ingenuity, industry and dynamism. The Igbo, like others, should be called to order when they misbehave. But they should also be encouraged when they perform well or achieve tremendously. There is also need for the Igbo neighbours to reduce their discriminatory attitudes to them because they appear, as has been observed by an analyst, more accommodating than any other folk in Nigeria. For example, there are cases of the Igbo abandoning their property in many parts of the country in which they are supposed to live harmoniously and peacefully with other people. The Igbo man's exploitative traits can be used for better ends by channelling them to gainful exploits in foreign lands. Not only that, his ingenuity, innovativeness and technology can be sharpened by government providing industries and factories like PRODA, arms factory and iron works industries, or by encouraging him to establish same, especially in his rural area for better technology in Nigeria. The traditional technological ingenuity of the Igbo rural folks at Awka, Nkwere and Ohafia, for example, cannot be underestimated. In terms of science and technology, in particular, much can be derived from the Igbo rural folk if they are made aware of the resources at their disposal, motivated and energized to collectively utilize such resources for the improvement of their spiritual and material conditions of living. From their cosmology, one can understand that the Igbo folk can blow 'hot' and 'cold,' therefore, the agencies concerned with mobilizing such a folk are advised to deal with them with caution - that foolish but wily folk, the *ndi Igbo*.

Chapter 5

'Once Upon a Kingdom...': Benin in the heroic traditions of Bendel State, Nigeria*

- Isidore Okpewho

Introduction

The name Benin has commanded the attention of students of history and culture for so long that any newcomer hardly stands a chance of treading on territory not already well explored. Yet, part of the appeal of Benin studies lies in the fact that various pieces of evidence thrown up in this field invite further examination; part also derives from the fact that every once in a while we can see gaps in the territory which the earlier explorers have ignored but which yield exciting challenges.

One notable gap may be seen in the life and programme of the Scheme for the Study of Benin History and Culture (generally known as the 'Benin Scheme') inaugurated by Professor K. O. Dike in 1956. The Scheme has a chequered life, due largely to a basic conflict of interests between the main disciplines supporting it. Although art historians and archaeologists were co-opted into it at one stage, the business was primarily in the hands of scholars trained essentially in history on the one hand and anthropology on the other. At a period in humanistic scholarship, when historians and anthropologists debated hotly among themselves as to who was best qualified to study traditional or (more fashionably) 'primitive' societies, Benin was seen as a test field where it was hoped a fruitful collaboration could be achieved. 'The Scheme for the Study of Benin History and Culture,' says Bradbury, the anthropologist and principal researcher of the project, 'is an experiment in interdisciplinary co-operation. Its main aim is to discover how much can be learnt of the history of Benin through

---

* First published in *The Heroic Process: Form, Function and Fantasy in Folk Life* (1988), pp. 613-650

whatever sources and methods are available and practical, and so to lay a foundation for further historical studies in the central area of southern Nigeria.[1]

Obviously it was hoped that this collaboration might result in the publication of a 'cultural history' of Benin. But the collaboration never truly materialized. Bradbury devoted himself to turning out a series of independent studies mostly along anthropological lines, later brought together by Peter Morton-Williams under the title *Benin Studies*.[2] Under an earlier programme, he had produced a quite informative monograph of *The Benin Kingdom*,[3] again basically along anthropological lines and relying considerably on oral evidence. But the historian of the scheme, Alan Ryder, showed little regard for the oral tradition. In his notable book *Benin and the Europeans*,[4] he has relied entirely on evidence derived from European documents on the period and in a few places, treats the claims of the oral evidence a little patronizingly. Other independent contributions were made by the art historian Philip Dark[5] and the archaeologist Graham Connah.[6] Bradbury returned to England in 1961, and even by the time of his death in 1969 there was little hope that the inter-disciplinary history of Benin would take anything like a practical shape.

Although Bradbury, as a professional ethnographer in the tradition of Malinowski and Radcliffe-Brown, did take account of the oral tradition in his studies, his writing reveals a certain underestimation of its usefulness which is only a shade better than Ryder's attitude. 'The limitations in Bradbury's use of the oral tradition may be put down to the narrow functionalism which characterized various shades of social studies at this time. The work of the Benin Scheme in particular was geared towards the specifically pragmatic purposes of historical reconstruction from which aesthetic considerations were largely excluded. This may be seen to some degree in Bradbury's study of the Benin 'cult of the hand,' *ikegobo*.[7] He begins his study by telling us, in relation to the bronze shrine used in the cult, that he 'shall not be concerned with the technical or aesthetic qualities of the casting.' He recognizes that the events depicted in the figurine are narrative in intent, but goes on to reveal a fairly narrow, functionalist appreciation of the nature of the narrative:

> By narrative I mean simply that they were intended to convey some

---

[1] R.E. Bradbury, *Benin Studies*, ed. P. Morton-Williams, London 1973, 17.

[2] This work was published posthumously.

[3] R.E. Bradbury, *The Benin Kingdom and the Edo-speaking Peoples of South-western Nigeria*, London 1957.

[4] A.F.C. Ryder, *Benin and the Europeans, 1485-1897*, London 1969.

[5] P.C. Dark, *Benin Art*, London 1960, .6.

[6] G. Connah, 'Archaeological Research in Benin City, 1961-64' in *Journal of the Historical Society of Nigeria* 2 (1966) and 'New Light on the Benin City Walls' in *Journal of the Historical Society of Nigeria* 3(1967).

[7] Bradbury, *op. cit.* (173), 251-70

information about specific events or particular persons. Provided that they can be properly dated and interpreted such bronzes are potential sources of certain kinds of historical information, but dating and interpretation present many difficulties.

Bradbury also collected and published actual narrative;[8] but in both his editorial and analytical treatment of these tales we can see the functionalist biases once again at play and the aestheticist interest eloquently absent.

This chapter is by no means an attempt to resuscitate the Benin Scheme. It leans, rather, in the direction of more recent Beninologists like Sidahome[9] and Ben-Amos[10] who have explored oral narrative traditions in and about Benin from an interest not so much in historical reconstruction as in the recreative culture of the traditional folk. Specifically, this chapter seeks to probe how Benin, in establishing a political and cultural hegemony over a variety of people, came to loom so large in their mythic imaginations. I will be dealing mostly with heroic narratives, because it was essentially within the context of war and other such confrontations that these peoples formed their images of Benin.

For the study, I am limiting the area of Benin influence to the political boundaries of present-day Bendel State; although Benin was reputed to have controlled an empire that went far beyond this area especially to the west, it is here that its cultural imprint has survived most vividly. Accordingly, I will be making use of a selection of stories recorded from communities in this area by a number of people: by past students of the English Department at the University of Ibadan who did fieldwork, under my supervision, in their villages in the Etsako, Isoko, Kwale and Ijo areas; by the poet-dramatist John Pepper Clark in his classic edition of *The Ozidi Saga* from the Ijo; by Joseph Sidahome in his collection of Ishan tales under the title *Stories of the Benin Empire;* and by me from my own fieldwork among the Bendel Igbo.[11] But first, let us examine the backgrounds of Benin influence over these peoples.

Historical and cultural relations

It is convenient to limit this study, to the political boundaries of present-day Bendel State because - despite the changing political fortunes of Nigeria and the accompanying boundary adjustments designed both to reduce the areas of inter-

---

[8] Ibid., 271-82.

[9] J.E. Sidahome, *Stories of the Ben/n Empire,* London 1964.

[10] D. Ben-Amos, *Sweet Words: Story-telling Events in Benin,* Philadelphia 1971, and 'Two Benin Story-tellers' in *African Folklore,* ed. R. Dorson, Bloomington 1972.

[11] Of the various colleagues who have helped me in this study, I would particularly like to thank Professors Obaro Ikime of the History Department, Onigu Otite of Sociology and Dr Airen Amayo of English. I alone, however, take the blame for whatever shortcomings there are here.

ethnic friction and to evolve a manageable administrative framework for the nation - this area has continued to demonstrate a high degree of cultural uniformity which seems to have compelled successive federal administrations to leave it pretty well intact with its various constituent units. One notable aspect of this uniformity may be seen in language. There are twelve major ethnic units in the state which may be conveniently reclassified into four linguistic groupings: Edo, Igbo, Ijo, and Yoruba (for the Itsekiri), all part of the KWA group of the Niger-Congo language family. Alagoa has pointed out that these four language groups are estimated to have parted ways about 5000 years ago;[12] but in the daily speech of the Bendel peoples the overlaps between them so outweigh the cleavages that 'there can be an argument, at least theoretical, that all the peoples of the Bendel State belong to one social stock.'[13]

Although the fortunes of history and political experience have bred in the various peoples of Bendel State certain sensitivities which must be respected, it may safely be said that for a long time Benin established itself and remained the principal member of that social stock. I am, of course, aware of the implications of such an acknowledgement. This chapter will be concerned with how the various peoples of the old Benin empire so accepted the prominence of Benin (called *Ado, Idu, Aka,* etc., in the folk traditions of the area) that they subordinated their mythic imaginations to the overarching image of the imperial power. But the influence is just as noticeable in contemporary cultural scholarship. Although the Ishan, Etsako, Urhobo, Isoko and other peoples have scarcely been in the habit of calling themselves Edo, scholars have continually imposed that identity on them, presumably as an acknowledgement of the high degree of similarity in social institutions revealed between those peoples and the Bini.

The name itself, Edo, is reported by Egharevba to have originally been that of the slave who helped to save the life of Oba Ewuare in the course of his struggle for the kingship of Benin; on the death of the slave the Oba 'caused the country to be known as Edo after his deified friend.'[14] This may be no more than an eponymous claim, and there is even less justification for the same claim being extended by scholars to peoples who have hardly any illusions about what names to call themselves. In an otherwise stimulating paper, Otite firmly states:

> Just as the Bini are 'the Edo of the Benin Kingdom'...so also the Urhobo are the Edo of their various kingdoms/states and the Ishans the Edo of their various chiefdoms etc. Academically it is currently a non-question to say who is the original or genuine Edo and who is not.[15]

---

[12] E.J. Alagoa, 'Ijo Origins and Migrations I' in *Nigeria Magazine* No. 91 (1966), 282.

[13] O. Otite, 'Historical Aspects of the Sociology of the Bendel State of Nigeria' in *Journal of the Historical Society of Nigeria* 9 (1977), 44.

[14] J.U. Egharevba, *A Short History of Benin*, 3rd edn., Ibadan 1960, 16.

[15] O. Otite, 'Who Are the Edo?' in *Edo Language and its Orthography,* Benin City 1974,19.

Although I recognize the hegemonic menace to which Otite was reacting, I do not consider it particularly urgent that the name Edo should be enthusiastically embraced by people who have perfectly respectable names by which they have been called for as long as anyone can remember.[16]

Still, the power and the position of old Benin within this large social stock can hardly be denied. Whether or not we accept that the visible kinship derives from the impact and imprint of Benin's imperial might, we can at least recognize various shades of cultural similarity between Benin and other groups in this area both Edo and non-Edo. We cannot, of course, expect perfect uniformity across the entire area of the state. However extensive the contacts may have been between Benin and the other groups, the latter have for a long time had historical and other links with communities beyond the present state boundaries - especially across the River Niger to the east and north-east and the creeks of the delta to the south-east - that have inevitably left some imprints on their cultures. But the cultural kinship with Benin is substantial. Perhaps the most noticeable aspect of this is in the pattern of social and political organization. In most areas of the state, it has been found that the basic unit of government is the village or town;[17] even though Ikime has argued for the clan as the large context of village institutions and traditions among the Urhobo and Isoko, he himself acknowledges the fundamental autonomy of the village in the day-to-day government of the two related peoples.[18]

The control of affairs within this unit also reveals a considerable kinship between Benin and the other communities. Casting a broad comparative glance on evidence assembled by various scholars working in the area, Otite has recognized a general pattern of dual or plural organization in the socio-political life of the respective communities, arising partly from the convergence of various streams of migration and partly from the imposition of an alien-derived rulership system on the indigenous village structure.[19] At the bottom of this governmental structure, on the level of indigenous organization, we find that the male population of each village is divided into three age grades - or four, as in

---

[16] There is some gratuitous benevolence in the following statement by Evinma Ogieiriaixi: 'In all my publications, I have consistently maintained that the term *edo* does not exclude the speech-forms of the people of the so-called "*edo* Group of Languages" who live outside the Basin divisions of Midwestern Nigeria (now Bendel State). Accordingly, *edo* for me is not synonymous with *Idu* (Bini). The latter to me, is a variant of *edo,* just as Esan, Ora, Urhobo, Isoko, etc., are variants of *edo'*. See E. Qgieiriaixi, Inconsistencies in the Old *edo* Orthographies,' in *Edo Language and Its Orthography,* Benin City 1974.

[17] Bradbury, *op. cit.* (1957); N. Thomas, Anthropological Report on Ibo-speaking Peoples of Nigeria, Pan 4: Law and Customs of the Ibo of the Asaba District, S. Nigeria, New York 1969 (1914) 6-10.

[18] O. Ikime, *Niger Delta Rivalry,* London 1969, 14-6 and *The Isoko People: A Historical Survey,* Ibadan 1972, 28-42

[19] Otiti, *op. cit.* (1977), 43-53.

the case of the Urhobo-Isoko.[20] On average, the youngest age-set, covering the ages from ten to about twenty-five are responsible for some of the lesser duties needed to keep the environmental, social and cultural life of the community functioning properly: these include the cleaning of the streets of the village, building and maintenance of the premises of the ruler, the digging of graves, and other basic but demanding tasks. The age-set(s) immediately following this represent the main executive class of the society; not only is the first age-set directly answerable to them, but they are generally charged with conducting some of those duties germane to the survival of the community, like (in the past) waging war on other communities with which they may have had scores to settle (boundary disputes, gross assault by citizens of one community on another, refusal to pay mandatory tributes, and so on). The final age-grade is made up of the elders - aged roughly from fifty upwards, who not only superintend the duties of the median age-set(s) but constitute the ultimate authority on the key issues of the cultural and religious life of the community.

This all-pervading structure might leave the impression that the village political organizations in the area is fundamentally gerontocratic in character. But the structure is further complicated, or perhaps enhanced, by a system of titled organization into which male citizens are qualified to enrol on attainment of various kinds of achievement (e.g., killing dangerous animals or, in the past, claiming human heads in war) or, as frequently nowadays, on the payment of usually high fees. So much more highly are these title rated than age in the conferment of status in both the social and political life of the village that a man may suffer some humiliation if he does not take any title. Among the Urhobo, for instance, the final age-set are known as the *ekpako* (sg. *okpako),* and the corresponding titled group into which they could enrol is that of the *edio* or *ehonmwonren* (sg. *odio* and *ohonmwonren);* any *okpako* who did not take the title is excluded from the major deliberations relating to the life of the village and is commonly derided as an *okpako igheghe,* ('ordinary elder,' or 'worthless elder'). In Asaba, a man of forty who has taken the *alo* title could interrupt and supersede a non-titled man of fifty in the course of his speech simply by dropping his goatskin fan on the ground and standing up; the ensuring scene may be uncomfortable and a few objections raised, but the older man would normally have no choice but to let the titled younger man take precedence.

At the top of the village socio-political structure is the ruler of the community. There is no strict uniformity across the area of Bendel State in the method of choice of such a ruler. In many communities the office is traditionally awarded to the oldest man within the titled group in which the old men are qualified to enrol - in effect, a unification of the principal merits of age and title in the village status-system. In Benin, of course, the office of *Oba* is hereditary. Despite the periodic inter-family strife which the monarchy is known to have

---

[20] Ikime, *op. cit.* (1369), 15-6.

undergone throughout its history - due largely to contests over primogeniture[21] - all available evidence indicates that the kingship has stayed within the Oranmiyan-descended line of rulers beginning with Eweka I. Some communities, especially among the Ishan where the earlier rulers *(Enigie)* were appointed by the Oba of Benin from among his sons and top state functionaries, have also observed the hereditary system of rulership.

Both in Benin and in the other communities in this area, the relationship of the titled organization to the monarchy is essentially conciliar. The inherent potential for confrontation between the king and his advisers is perhaps obvious. Benin history shows abundantly how far a monarch could go in satisfying his whims or his emotions - as in the case of Oba Ewuakpe who, grieving the death of his mother, 'ordered a wholesale massacre of his people,'[22] or of Oba Ewuare earlier who, lamenting the death of two of his sons by mutual poisoning, 'made a strict law forbidding anyone in the land of either sex to wash and dress up, or to have carnal intercourse for three years.'[23] Given this likelihood of abuse of power, the titled organizations have traditionally acted as a counterweight to the king's prerogatives, an insurance against having all power concentrated in the hands of one man;[24] indeed in the case of Benin several conflicts have been recorded between the king and his titled advisers centring round the desire of the latter to maintain a balance of power and privilege.[25] In more recent times, however, the benefits of the conciliar relationship of the titled class to the ruler have become equally obvious especially in the more rural communities. Many of the traditional titles are nowadays taken by middle-aged sons of the land who are enlightened by 'modern' education and in the ways of the wider world, and can therefore usefully counsel the less exposed king in his efforts to bring the benefits of technological progress to the people.[26]

From our survey so far it seems clear that Benin shares with most of the present-day Bendel state certain organizational features; at bottom the village or town as the basis of the socio-political structure, marked by a division of the male population into three or four age-sets for the purpose of distribution of labour: superimposed on this is a monarchical system working in studied

---

[21] P. Igbafe, *Benin Under British Administration*, London 1979, 2.

[22] Egharevba, *op. cit.*, 38.

[23] Ibid., 15.

[24] Thomas, *op. cit.*, 7,40; Ikime, *op. cit.* (1969), 25.

[25] Ryder, *op. cit.*, 6-9, 15; Bradbury, *op. cit* (1973), 57.

[26] Far less so, of course, in Benin. Since the late fifteenth century, when the Europeans first came to Benin for trade and other business, the monarchy had led the outreach to the world outside Benin. Egharevba reports *(op. cit.*, 27-8) that Oba Esigie sent one letter by a Portuguese missionary to the King of Portugal (dated 20 October 1516) which reports, among other things, that Esigie 'ordered his son and two of his greatest noblemen...to become Christians, and built a Church in Benin. They learnt how to read and did it very well.' The present *Oba* is a Cambridge graduate and has held some of the topmost administrative offices in the country.

counterpoise with a network of titled organizations into which men of achievement and of means could enrol. A final point of similarity must be mentioned, and that is a marked agnatic or patrilineal bias in the kingship system[27] as against the tendency towards matrilineage found among some eastern Ijo.[28]

Of the 'non-Edo' groups in the Niger Delta, most Ijo clans consider themselves indigenous or autochthonous, tracing their dispersals to only a few 'dispersal centres' within their own area.[29] Still, a few Ijo clans point to roots in Benin. The Mein clan, considered by Alagoa as 'obviously influential over all the Western Delta.'[30] is reported by tradition to have been founded by an ancestor of the same name who left Benin 'because of internal wars' and settled first at Aboh and later at Ogbobiri on the Sagbama-Igbedi Creek. From here some of his descendants dispersed to found other settlements like Kiagbodo under the leader Mgbile, and Akugbene under Kalanama. Once established, each leader sought legitimacy (encouraged no doubt by antecedent Urhobo and Isoko practice) by making contact with the Oba of Benin and receiving political sanction of his title *(pere)* as well as material tokens (bronze insignia, etc.) in return for allegiance to Benin especially in matters of trade.[31] The Tarakiri clan - ancestral home of *The Ozidi Saga* - also looks to Benin origins. Although the eponymous(?) Tara or Tarakiriowei is said to be related to the Kolokuma east of the Sagbama-Igbedi Creek, tradition has it that their father Ondo 'lived at Benin, but left with his three sons because the Oba seized private lands and levied heavy taxes.' Wars with the Mein and other clans caused much dispersal among the Tarakiri, but Orua remains the principal settlement of this clan.[32] As with the Urhobo-Isoko neighbours, the physical presence of Benin here was negligible.

By far the largest 'non-Edo' group in Bendel State are the Igbo communities west of the Niger and embracing the present-day Oshimili, Aniocha, Ndokwa and Ika Local Government areas. Here the sources of derivation are varied, but it is clear that Benin exercised an early influence in the history of the area. In Asaba, for instance, traditions speak mainly of the foundation of the town by Nnebisi from Nteje near Awka east of the Niger. But there were confrontations with Benin, one of which followed an invitation to Benin by an autochthonous

---

[27] Bradbury, *op. cit.* (1957), 15.

[28] E.J. Alagoa, *The Small Brave City State,* Madison 1964, 24-4.

[29] E.J. Alagoa, *A History of the Niger Delta,* Ibadan 1972, 187.

[30] Ibid., 67.

[31] Ibid., 52-3 63-6. On Mgbile's journey to Benin to be ordained as *pere,* see A.O. Edoh, 'The Epic Narrative Tradition in the Torubiri Epic, Kiagbodo Town, Bendel State' (Honours Essay, English Department, University of Ibadan), Ibadan 1979, 2-3. Further on the search for legitimacy, Edoh says: 'Any Ijaw Pere (king) at that time who did not go on a chieftaincy pilgrimage to Benin City was regarded as inferior and generally nicknamed juju priest...Conditions to be satisfied before becoming Pere, my father told me, were difficult. Among them was the producing of a child while in Benin by a Benin woman.

[32] Alagoa, *op. cit.* (1972), 71.

unit (Achala) contending with Nnebisi's descendants. Some of the communities in the Aniocha area also trace their origins to the east, like Ogwashi (= Ogw-Nri or Ogw-Nshi, i.e. meeting-place of the Nri) which looks back to the Igbo civilization of Nri; others claim autochthony, like some of the area around Isele-Uku. Here again, Benin made itself felt early enough. Obior is reported by Egharevba[33] to have been founded by a rich Biniman named Ovio who fell out of grace with the reigning Ogiso and was forced to migrate with his followers. Benin is also said to have attacked and dispersed some elements of the sister communities of Onicha-Ugbo, Onicha-Ukwuu, and Onicha-Olona and forced them to flee across the Niger;[34] in fact, the name Asaba is said to have derived from a Benin statement *A 'i sa ba,* meaning 'we cannot cross,' made by the pursuing imperial troops.

Unlike the delta country, much of the terrain in this area was readily accessible to Benin forces. Benin as usual received regular missions from kings *(obis)* seeking validation of their offices and in addition demanded annual tributes. Any community that proved in any way recalcitrant to the imperial will was instantly visited with a punitive expedition. One of the interesting but by no means exceptional narratives I recorded from an informant, Mr. Ojiudu Okeze of Igbuzo (Ibusa, near Asaba), tells of a curious annual mission from the Oba of Benin demanding a tooth from an old man of the town for a yearly festival in Benin; the Oba and his forces were ultimately destroyed in a confrontation with the man's three sons, one of whom was then installed as Oba! 'An Igbuzo man,' I asked incredulously, 'crowned Oba of Benin?' 'Yes,' he affirmed. 'Don't you see that section over there' - pointing towards one of the town's quarter - 'that was Benin!'[35]

How did Benin come to loom so large in the narrative imagination of these subject peoples that - as in the case of my narrator Ojiudu - it was fabled to be just around the corner? Ikime, discussing Isoko traditions, has stated that 'it is reasonable to expect that those clans which left Benin as refugees would not be anxious to maintain close links.'[36] It might equally be urged that the memory of Benin origins and contacts among these Bendel communities would hardly have been so dramatic and pervasive had that history been a happy one. It is true that some narratives portray the Oba as just and wise (even Solomonic) in his decisions. But a substantial majority of them recall experiences so harsh that the Oba, as Benin in general, frequently emerges as a menace which must be confronted and overcome.

These stories were no doubt inspired by the physical cruelties and generally harsh demands on life in old Benin. It is easy perhaps to dismiss the evidence cited by European scholars as being cobbled together in order to support the

---

[33] Egharevba, op. cit., 4

[34] Thomas, *op. cit.*, 3

[35] For another story of a Benin punitive expedition to Igbuzo, told me by my old teacher Mr. Aniemeka, see Okpewho, *Myth in Africa,* Cambridge 1983, 62-3.

[36] Ikime, *op. cit.,* (1972), 22

larger imperial designs of the European presence there. For instance, one of Vice-Consul Gallwey's reports on a visit to Benin in 1892 speaks of such a proliferation of human sacrifices and of corpses 'strewn about in the most public places' that the city 'might well be called "The City of Skulls."' However, the real aim of the imperial officer emerge clearly enough:

> The rule appears to be one of Terror, and one can only hope that this Treaty may be the foundation of a new order of things throughout the vast territory ruled by the King of Benin.[37]

The oral traditions of various people, however, paint such a vivid picture of terror that one could hardly blame those who fled to save life and limb. According to an Abraka tradition, their founding ancestor 'Avbeka was a son of an Oba of Benin whose birth it had been necessary to keep secret in order to save his life, because the then Oba, his father, had given instructions that all male children born to him should be killed so that there would be no obvious heir to the throne who could become the centre of palace plots.[38]

Other stories point to an equally capricious urge for blood and vengeance on the Oba's part. In the Agboghidi epic from Uzairue, the Oba is shown to have annihilated the people of the town Iyolulu and enslaved the remainder of the population, and on another occasion to have demanded the head of the new-born child of his adversary Agboghidi.[39] In the Ukwuani (Kwale) narrative of 'Onodi Onye-mma' the Oba, incensed that he is losing the favour of a young girl to the hero Gbodumeh, orders that her womb be 'tied' to prevent her ever getting pregnant.[40] Despite Sidahome's dedication of his collection of Ishan tales 'to the Oba of Benin'[41] and the frequently favourable portraiture of the Oba in these stories, standard references to cruelty emerge now and then. For instance, on learning that the hero Elonmo had intruded into the apartment of one of his wives, the Oba 'ordered Elonmo to be executed without delay that very evening, and ordered the execution to be one of shame. That meant that Elonmo was to be hacked to pieces, and the pieces dumped in a special enclosure near the sacred tree which stood opposite the city market. There the pieces would be eaten by

---

[37] See Ryder, *op. cit.*, 347

[38] Ikime, *op. cit.*, (1969), 7.

[39] J. Edemode, 'The Agboghidi Epic' (Project Essay, English Department, University of Ibadan), Ibadan 1977, 10, 12.

[40] F.A. Anene-Boyle, 'The Hero in Ukwuani Heroic Narative' (Honours Essay, English Department, University of Ibadan), Ibadan 1979, 96.

[41] Sidahome may indeed be connected to the Benin monarchy: see Egharevba, *op. cit.,* 84. In his Introduction, Sidahome tells us that his tales 'are Benin stories as told in Ishanland.' It is also interesting to note that unlike some tales I have myself collected from the Bendel Igbo - e.g. at Igbuzo (Ibusa) and Onicha-Ugho - none of the Ishan tales in Sidahome's collection shows a local hero destroying the Oba and ascending the throne of Benin.

dogs, vultures, and night-prowling wild beasts.⁴² In the story of 'Okodan,' we are told that 'the daily prayer of the Oba's subjects was: 'From the anger of the Oba, O God, deliver us' (p. 26).

Such terrors are echoed by no less an authority than the Bini historian Egharevba. Lamenting 'the atrocious hearts of the people'⁴³ as responsible for the numerous migrations from Benin, he documents throughout his *Short History of Benin* the most vivid incidents of horror that had become a mark of the socio-political life of the city and empire, from reckless fratricide (pp. 13, 26, etc.) to the whimsical disregard for the life of the average citizen on the part of the monarchy (pp. 21, 38, etc.). And if anyone would still dispute Gallwey's report, perhaps the following epitaph by Egharevba to the rule of Oba Ovonramwen, who died in Calabar whither the British had exiled him, will prove convincing:

> That the character of the Benin people had sunk very low was shown by the numberless human sacrifices which they offered, and oaths such as *Oba o gha gb-ue* (May the Oba kill you) showed that they feared the Oba more than God or the gods. The old Benin, with its barbarities and horrors, had to fall before the new Benin could rise and take its place.⁴⁴

But perhaps of most dramatic element in the memory of the emigrants, the most solid context with which in their stories they have sought to take their revenge on old Benin, is war. Numerous traditions of origin in this area speak of internal or civil wars in the city state of Benin as the primary cause of migration. Not the least of these were the grim fratricidal contests within the rulership, like the one between the sons of Oba Ozolua or the war over primogeniture between the two eldest sons of Obanosa;⁴⁵ there were also struggles between the Oba and his dignitaries, like the fight between Oba Ehengbuda and the Iyase.⁴⁶ Having left Benin, however, the emigrants and their hosts did not know much peace from it. For war became firmly established as an instrument of Benin policy, ordered by a hierarchy of generals beginning with the Iyase, followed by the Ezomo and then the Ologbosere. Egharevba tells us that 'it usually happened that a king would declare war about three years after his accession to the throne;⁴⁷ the period of utmost war-mongering was perhaps the reign of Oba

---

⁴² Sidahome, *op. cit.*, 133

⁴³ Egharevba, *op. cit.*, 5.

⁴⁴ Egharevba, *op. cit.*, 60. Egharevba may of course have been influenced somewhat by the numerous European authorities on Benin (Ling, Roth, etc.) that he had consulted in compiling his work. But as a member of one of the palace organizations (the House of Iwebo) he must have had independent access to considerable information.

⁴⁵ Egharevba, *op. cit.*, 26, 43.

⁴⁶ Ryder, *op. cit.*, 15.

⁴⁷ J.U. Egharevba, *Benin Law and Custom*, Port Harcourt, 1949, 35.

Ozolua, generally regarded as the most avid devotee of battle.[48] The main purpose of these wars appears to have been the anxiety to secure the widest area of economic control, especially in the face of European commercial activities along the Atlantic seaboard; the Obas must have felt an urgent need to keep alive the transit routes as well as sources of supply of articles within the empire.[49] Thus if any vassal community within the empire did not secure validation from the Oba of the installation of a new ruler (Onogie, Oba, Ovie, etc.) or present yearly tributes to Benin, this was usually taken as an act of apostasy or rebellion and visited with a punitive expedition.

But the military machine soon degenerated to a reckless adventure, to such an extent that the Oba would send soldiers to a community simply 'as a matter of routine. They did not interfere with the local government, but it was customary to entertain them lavishly or face condign punishment like the burning down of an entire village.'[50] The recklessness and arrogance may best be seen in the careers of the Ezomo, who became so much the centre-piece of the war organization that they rivalled the Oba in riches if not in power. 'They delighted in warfare,' Egharevba tells us about them, 'as a hungry man delights in food and if their history could be written it would make a big volume.[51] Is it any wonder then that the subject communities of the empire, living constantly in fear of attack from Benin, developed such a psychology about war that in their narrative imagination they have repeatedly sought to exorcise the bogey of Benin? Let us now turn to a sample survey of the content of these heroic narratives.

Mythological relations

In a sense these stories from outside Benin may have been inspired by stories told within Benin; the emigrants may thus be seen to be striving to recall the archetypes (in some instances at least, notably Ishan) but to have only succeeded in twisting the original imagery and symbolism in the warp of time. Ben-Amos gives us an insight into these archetypes:

> The Benin kingdom was one of the main West African empires and its traditional history is abundant with tales of intra and intertribal warfare, conquests, and victories...The Oba is certainly the political, religious, and social centre of Benin culture. Yet, throughout its folklore, art, beliefs, and

---

[48] Egharevba, *op. cit.,* (1960), 23; Ryder, *op. cit.* 12.
[49] Bradbury, *op. cit.,* (1973), 47-51; Ryder, *op. cit.,* 15.
[50] Ikime, *op. cit.,* (1969), 14.
[51] Egharevba, *op. cit.,* (1969), 81. On the recklessness and arrogance of the Ezomo, see further Okpewho, *'Ezemu:* A Heroic Narrative from Ubulu-Uno, Bendel State' in *Uwa Ndi Igbo; Journal of Igbo Life and Culture,* No. 1 (1984), 70-85

even its political system, there are undertones of tensions between the rural areas and the court.

Ben-Amos goes on later to cite instances of performances by professional Bini story-tellers he has recorded, having to do with contests between the Oba and his nobility.[52] The outcome of these contests is of course obvious, as Ben-Amos elaborates elsewhere in a discussion of Benin folklore and ethnomusicology:

> Finally, in the expressive dimension, the heroes of the professional story-teller are rural magicians and other powerful rural people, or suffering characters on the margins of Benin society. The Oba himself looms in the background as a threatening figure whom the hero cannot combat...[53]

This may well be true of story-tellers within Benin, who could not be expected to put the dreaded Oba in an inferior position. Besides, these storytellers are probably the descendants of those who had faith enough in the nation to remain while others left it. But Ben-Amos' observation is far less true of stories told outside Benin, where the image of the Oba (and the Ogiso of the antecedent dynasty) is frequently a negative one. Even the Ishan, who may be considered the closest to the Bini both geographically and culturally, tell stories in which the will if not the personality of the Oba is successfully combated by local heroes.

Despite his courteous bow to the Benin monarchy in the dedication of his book, Sidahome[54] occasionally portrays heroes who set themselves up in counterpoint to the imperial will. For instance, in the first story titled 'Eneka,' the action of the hero Eneka in interrupting the Ezomo of Uzebu's obeisance to the Oba and later flooring the Oba's champion wrestler Igbadaken has a subtle undertone of revolt to it. In the story titled 'Elonmo,' the hero infiltrates the Oba's palace and abducts one of the harem (an abomination in Benin), overcomes all the grim obstacles put in his way by the imperial machine, and is triumphantly installed Onogie (local king) in place of the incumbent who had aided the Oba against him. 'When the news...was reported to the Oba of Benin as required by custom,' we are told in the closing lines, 'the Oba accepted the fact and confirmed the appointment. He realized that the feud between himself and Elonmo was directed by fate, and decided to end it with good grace.' The Ishan, it is to be understood, were also victims of the obsessive militancy of old Benin; so that even when they tell 'Benin stories' in their homeland, they cannot help giving vent to some of their repressed feelings about the sad old days. Heroes like Eneka and Elonmo are a reification of that resentment.

---

[52] Ben-Amos, *op. cit.,* (1972), 106-7, 110-1.

[53] Ben-Amos, *op. cit.,* (1971), 54.

[54] Sidabome, *op. cit.*

Further away from Benin, however, the revolt is stronger. The stories may hark back nostalgically to Benin backgrounds - as in one Ukwuani (Kwale) tale which starts by recalling 'those times, long before we settled here' and the 'great men - men like the Oba of Idu (Benin), men like Izomo the warrior, Igwara of Idu, Ologbo-selem and Akpe.[55] But there is a progressive reduction of the image of Benin the further we move from the city, such that we can recognize the following general pattern:

First, the principal figures of the imperial organization - the Oba (or Ogiso) and his generals and major warriors - are set up for humiliation if not eventual destruction or at least treated as symbols of the dangers and evils that must be eliminated for the peace and well-being of the community. Secondly, the land of Benin is conjured as a seat of terror that lurks menacingly around and peripheries of the community, attracting other symbols of evil that cannot easily be identified with any known figures in Benin history and society.

Let us make a quick survey of a few of these figures and symbols inspired by the memory of Benin.

Agboghidi

Ben-Amos tells us that story of Agboghidi 'is one of the corner-stones' of professional story-telling performances in Benin and is frequently the piece that opens these:

> The plot concerns rural chiefs, their conflicts with each other, collisions between father and son, and struggles to gain the favours of women . Agboghidi, the rural chief, fights not only against the other country rulers, but also against the chiefs of Benin City, though not against the Oba himself.[56]

Agboghidi is certainly one of the principal figures in Benin oral tradition, and it is arguably from this random source that Egharevba has composed the 'historical' portrait of such a figure. But in Egharevba, Agboghidi is not so much the name of a specific person as a title, a sort of commander or military governor, first appointed by Oba Ehengbuda in the late sixteenth century and stationed at Ugo 'to keep the warlike people of Iyekorhionomwo from attacking Benin City.[57] The better-known Agboghidi of Ugo comes up, however, in the reign of Oba Akengbuda in the eighteenth century, where his real name is given

---

[55] Anene-Boyle, *op. cit.*, 10. Characteristically, most of these figures were imperial warlords. The Ezomo and Ologbosere were members of the supreme military command. Igwara (Benin 'Aruanran') was the governor of Udo who fought Oba Esigie fiercely for a long time until he was finally subdued. He survives in heroic lore as a fierce giant, to be discussed later in this study.
[56] Ben-Amos, *op. cit.*, (1971), 52.
[57] Egharevba, *op. cit.*, (1960), 33.

as Emokpaogbe. Perhaps we should quote the account in full so as to put the personality of the Agboghidi in proper perspective:

> Soon after the accession of Akengbuda, a prince of the house of Oboro-Uku came to Benin City to be invested as Ogie or Obi (king) of Oboro-Uku. While dancing round the city after his investiture, according to custom, he called on the Izeomo at Uzebu, who presented kolanuts to him through his beautiful daughter Adesua who had been betrothed to the Oba. When the Obi caught sight of her he wanted to marry her, but she insulted him, calling him 'Bush Ruler' in derision. The Obi was indignant, and when he got home he used charms to bring Adesua to Oboro-Uku. Against the advice of her servants, she asked leave of her parents to go to Oboro-Uku market to demand a debt owed to her for the sale of goats. When the Obi heard she was there he sent for her, and when she again refused his attentions and insulted him he had her murdered.
>
> When the tidings reached Benin City the Ezomo went to the palace to break the news to the Oba, and to tell him of his intention to make war against Oboro-Uku. The Oba however, said that he would avenge his lover's death himself.
>
> Akengbuda sent troops under the command of Imaran Adiagbon, and another contingent under Emokpaogbe the Agboghidi (Onogie) of Ugo. After severe fighting the town of Oboro-Uku was captured and the head of the Obi was sent by Imaran to the Oba. A dispute then arose between the two generals, each endeavouring to convince the Oba that the victory was due to his special valour, though in fact the credit belonged to Emokpaogbe.
>
> Emokpaogbe was very dissatisfied with the rewards given him by the Oba, and when he returned home to Ugo, acting on the advice of his head slave Arasomwan, and a war drummer, he behaved in such an unbecoming manner that a serious report was made to the Oba against him. The Oba sent for him to come to Benin City, but he refused and had the messengers killed. He then declared war against the Oba, who at first refused to engage in conflict with this general who had distinguished him-self in the Oboro-Uku campaign, and offered to pardon him. But Emokpaogbe would not desist and began to harass the city. The Oba was compelled to despatch three companies of warriors, Obakina, Igbizamete, and Agbobo, dressed in red uniforms, under the command of Ologbose and Imaran. They camped at Ugboko-niro, and fought several battles, and Ugboko-nosote, one of the villages allied to Ugo, and a fierce battle was fought about a mile distant from the town. Emopkaogbe was defeated, but he escaped, and before he could be overtaken he drowned himself in the Jamieson (Igbaghon) river. It is said that Emokpaogbe's wife Emokpolo, who was a sorceress, helped her husband greatly.[58]

Sidahome's Ishan version of this story[59] follows essentially the same lines: as

---

[58] Ibid., 41-2.
[59] Sidahome, *op. cit.*, 45-72.

mentioned earlier, it is entirely possible that it was from the same general pool of performances - spanning the Benin-Ishan region - that Egharevba drew for his historical reconstruction. In Sidahome, however, we get all those details that the empiricist Egharevba must have felt inclined to eliminate, especially because they were of little interest to his monarchically centred history of Benin.

In Sidahome, then, the following details about Agboghidi - reflecting the general pattern of the folk hero's life - emerge. He is born to the Onogie (king) of Ugo and his wife who, following a succession of daughters, are told they will have a son (Emokpaogbe) who will cause great trouble but will be a great warrior. He emerges from his mother's womb with a complete set of teeth and in six months is a fully-grown, formidable but repulsively ugly adult. In an effort to get rid of him, his father the king charms him with an illness which defies all remedy. In the end his mother takes him to 'Obolo,' whose famed magician-king (Ogiobolo) not only cures Emokpaogbe but makes him impervious to all dangers and powers (including those of Ogiobolo himself) as well as weapons; they also enjoin an eternal bond of loyalty on each other. On Emokpaogbe's return, his father makes further plans to kill him, but is killed instead, and Emokpaogbe succeeds him with the name Agboghidi of Ugo.

Fate brings Agboghidi into marriage with the extraordinarily beautiful lady, Emokpolo, born on the same day as him and likewise born with a complete set of teeth. He also acquires a slave from Obolo who plays enchanting music that drives Agboghidi into wild acts of heroism. He gets into all kinds of amorous adventures, acquiring a new wife Udin and falling into a near-fatal love affair with a river-goddess Igbaghon. The rest of Aghoghidi's career echoes essentially Egharevba's account of the confrontation between Benin and Oboro-Uku (Obolo) and Agboghidi's role in it, right down to the treachery of Ima of Ogbelaka (Egharevba's Imaran) and the war between Agboghidi and the forces of the Oba. There are a few interesting twists in Sidahome's version, though. While Egharevba tells us that the Oba sent 'three companies of warriors. . . dressed in red uniforms' against Agboghidi, Sidahome has it that this is an army of little children dressed in red, a combination found to be taboo to Aghoghidi. He continues to flee from this army until in the end he turns into a rope 'although it is also believed by many that Agboghidi drowned himself.' His wife Emokpolo, appropriated by the Oba, later joins Agboghidi in the spirit world, where he continues to threaten that he will destroy the world. The story ends on an anthropological note:

> This explains the great thunderstorms. The lightning flashes are the brandishing of Agboghidi's great sword, Ghoma-Gbesin. The thunder is Agboghidi's showing his rage to the world. The dull echoing which follows the thunder is, of course, his dear wife Emokpolo, soothing and calming him down in order to protect the world she loved.

On 12 October 1980, I recorded the story of the war between Benin and

Ubuku-Uku from my distinguished informant, Mr. Charles Simayi of Ubulu-Uno.[60] Although the figure Agboghidi does not feature at all in this story,[61] the events contained are clearly a variation on those in Egharevba and Sidahome. Whereas in both versions, the Ubulu king goes to Benin to secure validation of his title by the Oba, in Mr. Simayi's version, the leader Ezemu, an expert medicine-man, goes to Benin in response to a general invitation to traditional doctors across the empire to save an incumbent Oba from dying soon after coronation, like successive Obas before him. Having cured the Oba, Ezemu is rewarded with the Oba's first daughter as wife, and her little brother as page. On his way from Benin, he is accosted by the Ezomo who would not let a provincial ruler take a Benin princess away as wife; Ezemu demurs, but on reaching Ubulu draws the princess to him by force of magic. In the ensuing war between Benin and Ubulu, the imperial forces suffer severe losses, losing one contingent after another to a tiny band of seven hunters led by Ezemu I. In the end Benin is forced to sue for peace; as a cardinal part of the settlement, a town (Abudu) halfway between Benin and Ubulu is marked as the boundary between the two peoples, with a firm injunction that the Bini should never again kill the Ubulu.

Besides the disappearance of the Agboghidi figure in this version, there is a significant reduction in the image of Benin: an imperial power is brought to its knees by a small provincial community.[62] Particularly remarkable is the treatment of the Oba of Benin's image. In Egharevba he is shown as being master of his own decisions and actions. In Sidahome the 'peace-loving Oba' continually advises patience against his people's urgent pleas for war with the Obolo. But in the Ubulu version, the Oba is cast alternatively as bloodthirsty (he orders the execution of doctor after doctor who fails the test that will qualify him to treat the sick Oba) and lacking in firmness (he does allow himself to be driven into war with Ubulu, earning the reproof of his soothsayer in the end); in fact, it is the Oba himself that timorously leads the Bini peace party to meet Ezemu and his men at Abudu!

The Agboghidi figure re-emerges in an epic from the 'Edo-speaking' Etsako;[63] here again, in an area sufficiently far from the seat of the empire, the image of Benin and particularly of the Oba suffers a considerable reduction. In this story, Agboghidi is used essentially as a symbol of the revolt of a provincial people against the imperious, high-handed government of the Oba of Benin. Briefly, the Bini annihilate the town of Iyolulu and enslave the remainder of the

---

[60] Okpewho, *op. cit.*, (1984).

[61] I have not encountered the Agboghidi figure so far in the oral traditions of the Bendel Igbo. But I understand that the name appears in the traditional titles of the Obi of Onitsha (eastern Igbo), Ofala Okagbue I.

[62] Ubulu seems to command a certain reputation in the folk traditions of this area: an Ukwuani (Kwale) narrative also tells how Benin was forced to a compromise with her. See Anene-Boyle, *op. cit.*, 85-9.

[63] See Edemode, *op. cit.*

population; the young hero Agboghidi is received into the Oba's household. But he suffers one humiliation after another (e.g., being cheated of the game he has killed) purely on the grounds that he is an outsider, not one of the Oba's children. He continually revolts against this degradation, until one day someone confronts him in a public gathering with the real facts of his background - i.e., what happened to his community. This is the final blow. Agboghidi makes away with a daughter of the Oba, against the latter's protests, and war is effectively declared. Agboghidi returns to his annihilated village Iyolulu, where he is eagerly received by a sorceress Oledo who provides him with magical aid as well as regular warnings of attack from Benin. The Oba sends guards upon guards, and army after army, but Agboghidi exterminates them one after the other until, as we are told, Benin is empty of men...There are only women in Edo now' (Edemode, 'The Agboghidi Epic,' 24). The Oba tries other schemes, working in consultation now with sorcerers who devise magical antidotes to Agboghidi's mystical power. But the war drags on for some more years. In the end the sorcerers discover Agboghidi's real taboo: on one day all the women left in Benin suddenly become 'pregnant without any sexual intercourse;' on the last day of the ninth month they all give birth to male children, who begin to walk and talk that same day; they are then equipped with red uniforms and sent to destroy Agboghidi. Unable to ward off this last danger, Aghoghidi and Oledo decide to take their lives, drowning themselves and the children in the sea.

This Etsako story of Agboghidi reveals its Benin connections in a few places. Apart from the details of red-uniformed warriors and the hero's death by drowning (along with a sorceress) the injustices visited on Agboghidi in the king's household may be seen as a variant on the Benin detail of Agboghidi being cheated of his achievement in the Oboro-Uku war. Besides, Benin and Iyolulu are shown to be so near to each other that the Oba and Agboghidi can see one another from their respective houses (Edemode, *op. cit.*, 12) - an effort, perhaps, to echo the nearness of Benin and Ugo in the 'original' story. However, the revolt against Benin in this provincial tale is just as evident. The Oba is portrayed as powerless and helpless before the humiliating career of the hero; a song which begins 'I threaten, I threaten the king' (ibid., 28) underlines the antimonarchical spirit of the tale; another song urges the hero 'Agboghidi kill Edo!' (ibid., 24) for, after all, 'It's not brutal, It's no waste/That men killed one another in Edo' (ibid., 31); and all through the story the Oba's bloodlust is emphasized by his constantly calling for the head of adult and child alike.

The figure Agboghidi also appears in the Ijo epic entitled *The Ozidi Saga*, edited and translated by the poet-playwright John Pepper Clark. In Bendel State, the Ijo occupy perhaps the furthest reach of the old Benin empire; and though, as seen above, some of the clans invoke Benin roots, this is one of those areas where the political and cultural control of Benin could be said to be the weakest. It is therefore no surprise that the principal figures of Edo folklore do not enjoy quite the same prominence in the traditions of this non-Edo people.

To be sure, Benin continues to be invoked as a large mythical setting for Ijo stories. In his Introduction to *The Ozidi Saga*, Clark makes the following observation on the attitude of the various narrators he has recorded to the setting of the story:

> In the Okabou text the stress is on Orua, or Oruabou, that is, the city seen as a state set in some remote time and place, although within the present boundaries of Tarakiri Clan. Both Afoluwa and Erivini make no such insistence on the Ijo setting of the story, being content to use Ado, the other name for Benin City, the conventional setting of Ijo tales and fables. This, of course, is no evidence that these stories derive from Benin or that the city is the original home of those who own them. Rather, Ado, to the Ijo imagination, is the embodiment of all that is distant and mysterious, the empire of improbable happenings that together with the world of spirits help to explain the events of their own lives. Okabou in fact was always self-conscious when, prodded on by Madam Yakubu of Inekorogha, leader of the recorded session at Ibadan, he toed the clearly patriotic line of preferring the local name to the foreign one of Ado. Beyond this, he retains all other names that are clearly non-Ijo, principal ones like Ozidi, Oreame, Orea, Temugedege, and Ogueren which in all likelihood are Benin, while Odogu is obviously Ibo.[64]

This faintness of the image of Benin is no doubt responsible both for the loss of the standard elements in the Agboghidi canon - dying in a body of water, red-uniformed soldiers, etc. - and indeed for the considerably subordinate position which this character occupies in the Ozidi story. For despite its Benin echoes, this story is thoroughly Ijo in both its ecology and its cultural background, and the various characters in it, whatever their derivations, are subordinated to the superior image which the Ijo oral tradition has created for the local hero Ozidi. Thus, although Agboghidi is one of the few 'human' opponents of the hero and is indeed the first assigned to confront him in the series of battles that Ozidi fights, it takes Ozidi the least time of all to dispose of him (Clark, *op. cit.,* 65-70). In this story, then, we have one of the clearest examples of what happens to images and symbols from Benin a) in an area where Benin political and cultural hegemony was not so strong, and b) when the local tradition asserts itself.

---

[64] J.P. Clark, (ed.), *The Ozidi Saga: From the Ijo of Okabou Ojobolo,* Ibadan 1977, xvii. The Benin derivation of Ozidi is dubious. A variant of the name is Azudu: see Clark, 'The Azudu Saga' in *African Notes* 1(1963), 8-9. There is a Bini word, *Ozudu,* meaning something like 'stout-hearted,' and apt epithet for a hero. Beyond this I have not been able to connect the name Ozidi with any Benin sources. On the problem of the Benin setting of *The Ozidi Saga,* see further Okpewho, 'The Oral Performer and His Audience: A Case Study of *The Ozidi Saga,*' in *The Oral Performance in Africa,* (ed.), I. Okpewho, Spectrum Books, Ibadan, 1990.

Aruanran

A somewhat similar pattern may be seen in the fortunes of the character Aruanran. There is a much larger fabulary shroud covering this figure, it seems, and perhaps for this reason he gets rather short shrift in the empiricist programme of Egharevba. There are basically four references to him in the *Short History*.[65] First, in the war-mongering reign of Oba Ozolua, 'Okhumwu was conquered by Prince Aruanran one of the Oba's sons, who brought a large number of captives to Benin City.' Next, we are told that he was one of the first three sons of Ozolua, the others being Osawe and Ogidogbo; in an effort to find out who was the strongest of the three they were made to pole-vault over a pond in the palace quarter, and while Aruanran and Osawe succeeded, Ogidogbo fell down and was crippled, thus losing the contest for the succession to the obaship. The third reference to Aruanran concerns the contest for the throne between Aruanran and Osawe on the issue of primogeniture. Though he was born first, Aruanran's birth was announced later than Osawe's, and a struggle later ensued during which Aruanran 'went to an old woman at Uroho village who trained him in the art of black magic, which he used after the death of his father in his struggle with Osawe.' The final reference deals with Aruanran's fratricidal war with Osawe, now crowned Oba Esigie. According to Egharevba, Esigie

> ... was greatly worried by his brother Aruanran, chief of Udo, a man of giant stature. At last a punitive expedition was sent against Udo. Many battles were fought, sometimes one side being victorious and sometimes the other. The fiercest went by the name of *Okuo-Ukpoba* (Battle of Blood) in which Onioni, the only son of Aruanran, was killed. To avoid being taken prisoner, Aruanran drowned himself in the lake, Odighi n'Udo.

As we can see, the only concessions Egharevba makes to the folk imagination in these references are to Aruanran being 'a man of giant stature' and to his being equipped with magical skill. In Ben-Amos, however, we get a little more insight into his image in the Benin oral tradition. Ben-Amos sees him as one of the 'folk anti-hero, tragic figure who was part of the king's family but failed to live up to their royal status...a foolhardy giant' who was cheated out of his inheritance and ended his life by drowning in a lake.[66] More pertinently, Ben-Amos tells us that in these Bini stories of Aruanran he is represented as 'a giant who had twenty toes and twenty fingers, and one who could never tell whether he was coming or going.'[67]

There is a rather full treatment of the Aruanran story in Sidahome's an-

---

[65] Egharevba, *op. cit.*, (1960), 24, 25-6.
[66] Ben-Amos, *op. cit.*, (1972), 109
[67] Ben-Amos, op. cit., (1971), 44

thology of 'Benin stories as told in Ishanland.'[68] Again as with the Agboghidi story, there are striking similarities in detail between Sidahome and Egharevba (although the latter is a much abbreviated and selective statement); but there are also striking departures and elaborations. We first meet Arualan (as he is called in Sidahome) in his proto-life as the troublesome and hateful spirit Ekatakpi. The Oba of Benin, Ozolua, and his favourite queen Ohomi are worried about their childlessness and the king sends to the spirit world for a solution; Ekatakpi, after considerable solicitude and violating all injunctions laid on him by the king of the spirit world, is reincarnated in Benin as the child of Ohomi (and named Idobo) but he is born at the same time as another child Esigie (to queen Idia) whose birth is announced first. Robbed of his primogeniture, and hated by the Oba in his early childhood, he withdraws to live with the sorceress queen of Uroho, Iyenuroho, better known as Iyenugholo. Under her this extraordinary child with ten digits on each limb and a mighty head, grows by leaps and bounds to be an over-towering giant. The sorceress renames him Arualan (giant), and equips him with all manner of magical support to ensure total invincibility, including the power to cause her own destruction. Arualan loses no time in putting his powers to the test: he causes Iyenugholo to be turned into a bee and she disappeared forever.

Arualan (in his proto-self Ekatakpi) came into the world destined to become a great warrior. His first military feat after leaving Iyenugholo's palace is his victory over Esohen, king of the remote town Amagba; Arualan destroys the town and brings the head of the intractable Esohen to Oba Ozolua, thus winning the love and attachment of a father who once disowned him. Reinstated with pomp and honour in Benin, Arualan goes on to perform his most endearing feat. The town of Okhumu is ruled by a powerful king (who has continually harassed Benin) and defended by the giant Egbamarhuan who happens to have been fortified with magic by the same Iyenugholo who made Arualan invincible. The war between the Benin and Okhumu forces proves a long and fierce one: but Arualan is able to summon his most infallible tools of sorcery to destroy the enemy and lead a triumphant army and numerous hostages back to Benin.

With the decline in age and wisdom of Oba Ozolua a confrontation between the princes Arualan and Esigie becomes inevitable. By a slip of tongue and contrary to his own eager intent, Ozolua irrevocably names Arualan the king of Udo (instead of Edo); all attempts by the Oba to rectify the situation fail, and Esigie is finally crowned Oba of Benin on Ozolua's death. In the end the two brothers are drawn into a war, which Arualan loses by a tragic error. He orders that his entire possessions be thrown into the lake Odighi if he does not return triumphantly from his march against Benin. Meanwhile the Benin citizens, fully aware they could not withstand Arualan, withdrew from the city to a man. Arualan returns to Udo disappointed but hoping to strike again at Benin some

---

[68] Sidahome, *op. cit.*, 164-96.

day; however, his subjects at Udo, seeing their king returning without the usual sounds of triumph, dump all his possessions into the lake in obedience to his orders. This is the final despair; Arualan jumps into the lake and is lost forever. But he is deified and the point of disappearance 'is regarded as sacred ground to this day.'

The native Benin versions of the Aruanran story, as represented at least by Egharevba and Ben-Amos, are not particularly positive. Egharevba, a palace historian, is patronizing as ever, Ben-Amos is even less charitable in his treatment of the giant. Grouping him with the eighteenth-century Oba Ewuakpe, Ben-Amos says:

> Both were deviant persons within the court, failures within a hierarchical society, rejected by the system because of their own misdoings.[69]

Both Egharevba and Ben-Amos also talk about Aruanran as suffering defeat, with Egharevba specifically suggesting military defeat in which Aruanran took his own life 'to avoid being taken prisoner.'[70] The picture is, however, not quite so bleak in Sidahome's Ishan portrait of the hero. Although in his proto-life in the spirit world he demonstrates considerable recalcitrance and destructiveness, in the human world he shows himself to be a hero very much in control of his stupendous urge for martial action. This is most visibly demonstrated in his treatment of the *agent-provocateurs* from Okhumu: he repeatedly sends them back with a warning to their king to desist from testing the wrath of Benin. On the eve of the Okhumu war, we are told, Oba Ozolua

> prayed that Arualan might strike his enemies hard, but that his enemies should be powerless to strike him.

Arualan objected to this last prayer:

> 'This is to be a battle between men, and
> it should not be one-sided,' he said.
> 'Pray that my enemies should be able to
> strike me, but that I shall emerge victorious.'[71]

And far from suffering any military defeat, he comes to grief only as the victim of a tragic flaw in his massive self-confidence. On the whole, therefore, we could safely consider Sidahome's Ishan portrait of the hero Aruanran as sympathetic. He emerges as a superior factor in the Benin political situation; in the Ishan oral tradition his image has been utilized for the legitimization of revolt

---

[69] Ben-Amos, *op. cit.*, (1971), 44.

[70] Egharevba, *op. cit.*, (1960), 26.

[71] Sidahome, *op. cit.*, 86.

against an overbearing imperial machine.

Much further away from Benin City, in the delta regions to the South, the image of Aruanran undergoes essentially two kinds of transformation. First, he is portrayed as a giant constantly putting his restless energy at the service of the oppressed. In one of the Ukwuani narratives collected by Anene-Boyle, this giant of twenty toes defends his father, the Oba of Idu (Benin), against the men of Atu who have come on the last of the quinquennial missions to pluck the tooth of the Oba for their festival; Igwara (as Aruanran is called among the Ukwuani) kills them all to a man and puts an end to the obnoxious ritual.[72] In another story, Igwara defends his brother's wife, Oyibo, against the seducer Okalimadu and kills the latter in a grim fight, though he goes on later to turn Oyibo into an anthill apparently because he sees her (an exceptional beauty) as a source of more troubles in the future *(op. cit.,* 90-3). Although the giant's old grudge against Benin survives in so far as he sometimes turns around, unprovoked, to slaughter fellow-citizens of Idu *(ibid., 75),* in these Ukwuani stories the emphasis in the portraiture of Igwara seems to be on his using his stupendous energies for the destruction of those who make themselves into a menace to his people though he is often more a menace himself and a dangerous individual.

A second transformation of the Aruanran image puts him in very much the same position in which we saw Agboghidi - in the environment of Ijo folklore, as far away from the seat of the old Benin empire as we could get in this area. Once more, there are clear echoes of the Benin origins of the figure Ogueren or Oguaran, as he is called in *The Ozidi Saga*.[73] He is a giant of unimaginable size, a man 'of twenty hands, twenty feet,' uprooting silk cotton and iroko trees as he tramples along *(op. cit.,* 102).[74] As with Agboghidi, however, this legendary figure from Benin is simply a victim of the urge of a local tradition to assert its own heroes; so that, although he gives Ozidi a great deal more trouble than Agboghidi does, Ogueren crashes to his ruin in the face of Ozidi's irrepressible onslaught.

Other images

Our survey of the major figures in the heroic narratives of communities once dominated by Benin shows that to large extent these narratives - in so far, that is, as Benin is their point of reference - are used for validating the resentment

---

[72] Anene-Boyle, *op. cit.,* 75 ff.
[73] Clark (ed.), *op. cit.,* (1977), 102-26.
[74] Cf. Sidahome, *op. cit.,* 178. In his play *Ozidi* (London 1966), Clark pushes the image of the giant a little further by attributing the huge moat around the old city of Benin to Ogueren's simply walking round the city walls (p. 82).

which the communities felt against the domination.

It will have been observed that, despite their demonstrably rebellious spirit, these narratives featuring the major heroic figures of the Benin oral tradition do make concessions sometimes to Benin, often by way of betraying a certain attachment to the homeland. This is perhaps a manifestation of the nostalgia felt by those emigrants who took the 'Benin' stories to their new places of abode; Bowra made useful observations (albeit in a different context) on this romantic attachment on the part of a people which 'leaves home for some distant land and keeps touch with its past by glorifying it in legends.[75] Hence we find Igwara in Ukwuani narratives principally defending his father the Oba of Benin and its people. An Isoko narrative entitled 'The story of Odugo and his wife Ibakpolo,' which is clearly a variant of the Agboghidi story, also tells of the hero Odugo fighting in defence of the Oba but losing all restraint, until he is brought to grief by an army of red-uniformed children.[76] However, even in such stories it is clear that, however deep the attachment felt for the homeland, there is usually a subtle comment against those who made life impossible whether in that homeland or in the emigrants' new home: usually, the Oba and his generals.

Of the various other images from Old Benin that have received negative treatment in the heroic traditions of subject communities, a particularly interesting one is that of the tooth-plucking Oba, that is, an Oba who every year demands one tooth from the mouth of a prominent man (leader) of a subject community for an annual festival. There is a strange twist to this image among the Ukwuani (Kwale) in 'The Narrative of Oba Nkpeze,[77] for here the Oba is the Oba of Benin who every year must surrender a tooth to envoys from the town Atu for an annual festival, until Igwara (Aruanran) puts an end to the obnoxious order. In other traditions, however, the finger is pointed squarely against Benin. Akegwure discusses one such tale from the Isoko:

> The Omofobhon epic treats the theme of an Oba who would send a band of warriors to 'pluck' the tooth of a particular man to him annually. This tooth he would offer to his personal god as festival offering. This continued for many years until the just God gave this man a hero child Omofobhon who avenged his father's shame by confronting and defeating each successive band of warriors and heroes sent against him by the Oba.[78]

On 13 October 1980, I collected a very similar story from Mr Ojiudu Okeze at Ibusa; in this case, the ensuing war culminates in the killing of the Oba and

---

[75] C.M. Bowra, *Homer*, London 1972, 80.

[76] J.E. Welch, 'The Isoko Clans of the Niger Delta' (PhD Thesis, University of Cambridge), 1935, 409-10.

[77] Anene-Boyle, *op. cit.*, 75-84.

[78] P.O. Akegwure, 'The Hero in Isoko Heroic Narratives' (Honours Essay, English Department, University of Ibadan), Ibadan 1978,4.

the enthronement of the youngest son of the old man (who had annually lost a tooth) as the new Oba of Benin. In the Isoko and Ibusa versions of the tooth-plucking story we have, it would seem, a symbolization of the tributes which Benin exacted annually from these subject communities and the spirit of revolt whereby they sought to throw off forever the yoke of subordination which had been hanging round their necks.

History and fantasy

The variety of evidence so far examined seems to indicate that in a good many cases the oral traditions of a subject community - insofar as they recall Benin whether directly or indirectly - have been employed to highlight one aspect or other of their painful past within the empire. In these tales, Benin may not always be directly identified as a culprit and may indeed be treated with sympathy; but even in such cases a careful analysis will show that the accusing finger is being pointed at Benin albeit obliquely, and that the story only holds up for castigation an evil, set well within the time when Benin had a dominant influence over the life of the community. For instance, in the Ukwuani 'Narrative of Oba Mkpeze,[79] it seems clear that we have an inversion - motivated whether by politics or by art, we cannot really tell - of the system whereby Benin annually imposed tributes that hurt her subjects right down to their eye-teeth. Or perhaps the inversion was psychologically motivated: the Ukwuani would like to see Benin visited, even for a limited time, with the sort of cruelties it practised on other communities!

Did the Ukwuani borrow that tale from their neighbours (e.g., the Isoko) or their ethnic kin (e.g., the Igbuzo) before making that inversion? This question touches the very heart of the limitations in our present study of the history and culture of this area. In the earlier part of this chapter I have done no more than corroborate both oral documentary evidence in establishing the political dominance of Benin over a spread of communities. I started by identifying, again following both forms of evidence, a wide variety of cultural similarities between Benin and these communities. But until we can establish by other methods 'which people are older than which or who drove whom in what direction,[80] it would be difficult, if not pointless, to press any diffusionist claims on these narrative traditions.

In fact, we have to be careful what steps we take in constructing our empiricist histories, and the perspectives from which we assemble our information. I suspect that part of the trouble with the Benin Scheme derived from the fact that the labours of that project were centred to a disproportionate degree on Benin, with the aid no doubt of influential figures like Egharevba. However, a

---

[79] Anene-Boyle, *op. cit.*, 75-84.
[80] Alagoa, *op. cit.*, (1966), 282.

comparison of the evidence of Egharevba and any of the traditions from outside Benin on any historical even - like the Benin-Ubulu war - some reveals that *one man's history is another man's fantasy*. In his dynastic history of Benin, Egharevba seems hardly to have left any room for military failure on the part of any of the Obas: there is, however, reason enough to believe that Ehengbuda, who, according to Egharevba,[81] died in a boat accident, may have in fact suffered a military defeat (given the war-mongering fever of that era) and died in the process.

So, too, with the evidence from the oral traditions of the subject communities: none of them would be expected to tell stories which put them in an inferior position to Benin even though we know that, in terms of organization at least, Benin at the time stood a better chance of winning any military confrontation. And since, given the painful memory of their experiences with Benin, very few of them had reason to love it, the more fantastic the claims they make, the happier they will be to have surmounted, psychologically at least, those 'inaccessible barriers' - to borrow Todorov's phrase[82] - that Benin by its very might and position constituted to their self-realization as well as peace. Benin is evoked as a backdrop even in animal tales that have no human participant,[83] and perhaps there is no greater proof than this of her pervasive influence. But it is mostly in the heroic narratives, set against the background of war and other tests of physical and supernatural strength, that the subject communities have steadily sought to turn the tables against a bogey that loomed so large in their lives.

---

[81] Egharevba, *op. cit.,* (1960), 33.

[82] T. Todorov, *The Fantastic: A Structural Approach to a Literary Genre,* trans. R. Howard, Ithaca 1975, 158. I must point out, however, that while I applaud the recognition by writers like Todorov and Rabkin of the role of the fantastic in all creative literature and especially the narrative, I have little sympathy for the sort of abstract generic taxonomy that they indulge. Their analyses seem to rest entirely on a consideration of the reader of printed narratives (including folktales) as well as the characters of the narrative drama. They cite Propp in their discussion of folktales, and consequently suffer from the basic failure of Proppian taxonomy, which is a lack of consideration of the sociological basis of the tales. For instance, for the Ubulu people to represent themselves as having trounced Benin thoroughly and brought her to knees may be seen as a legitimate manipulation of historical truth for the psychological comfort of the community; but would anyone either in Benin or in Ubulu view the fantastic details of the Ubulu story as 'a direct reversal of ground rules' (E. Rabkins, *The Fantastic In Literature,* Princeton 1976, 14) operating in oral culture, in which notions of magic and the supernatural permeate daily life and thought as deeply as the tales?

[83] See Okpewho,*op. cit.,* (1983), 66 and Ben-Amos, *op. cit.,* (1971), 15.

Chapter 6

Principles of the Igbo oral epic: a study in traditional aesthetic and oral literary criticism [1]

- *Chukwuma Azuonye*

Introduction

During the past few years, there has been a rapid growth of scholarly interest in the investigation of the aesthetic and other principles underlying the composition, performance and public appreciation of the oral literary arts in traditional African societies.[2] With the widespread realization that the oral performer in traditional societies is as much an original and individual artist as his counterparts in literate cultures, scholars have recognized the need not only to study his creative role in the oral performance but also to understand the tastes of the members of the society to whom he addresses his compositions. To understand the tastes of the members of the society in which oral literature flourishes is to understand the principles and expectations which the traditional oral artist aspires to measure up to or even to transcend in his works, for as Parry (1921:1) has correctly observed,

> The literature of every country and every time is understood as it ought to be only by the author and his contemporaries. Between him and them there

---

[1] This paper was originally presented at the Second International Seminar on Igbo Literature organized by the Society for Promoting Igbo Language and Culture at the University of Nigeria, Nsukka, 12-15 August 1981. Based on Chapter 9 of my University of London PhD Thesis (Azuonye, 1979), the principles examined were first discussed at Seminars in the Department of English, University of Nigeria, Nsukka (April 1976) and in the Department of Linguistics and Nigerian Languages, University of Ibadan (May 1979).

[2] See also Dundes (1966) for a global approach to this line of investigation

exists a common stock of experiences which enables the author to mention an object or to express an idea with the certainty that his audience will imagine the same object or will grasp the subtleties of his idea. One aspect of the author's genius is his taking into account at every point the ideas and information of those to whom he is addressing his work. The task, therefore, of one who lives in another age and wants to appreciate the work correctly, consists precisely in rediscovering the varied information and complexes of ideas which the author assumed to be the natural property of his audience.

The need for this kind of rediscovery lies behind the growing interest among students of African oral literature in the investigation of the bases and parameters of audience responses to African oral compositions and performances. Thus, Andrzejwski and Innes (1975:48-49) speculate:

It seems likely that one main aspect of African oral literature with which linguists will be concerned will be that of evaluation, and here is meant not evaluation by foreign scholars, but evaluation by the people themselves of their own oral literature. Of course, evaluation is implicit in the survival of certain tales, etc.; presumably those items which are approved are handed down from generation to generation and others which are less well-regarded cease to be told and are lost. Apart from this, there are two other aspects of evaluation which concern us; the first has to do with the ranking by the people of the various genres of oral literature which they have...The second, and more interesting, kind of evaluation is that which judges one telling of a tale as better than another, or one narrator as more skilled than another.

The purpose of studying the principles of oral literacy evaluation in traditional African societies is not to pursue the phantom of a unique African aesthetic as some pundits would have us believe (see, for example, Chinweizu, Jemie and Madubuike, 1980). Its purpose is rather to ascertain which of the numerous universal and perennial principles of art are most frequently invoked by the members of a particular society in the evaluation of their oral literature as a whole, of a particular genre, or of the compositions and performances of individual artists (see Azuonye 1981a and 1981b). In doing this, we need to pay particular attention to the socio-cultural and historical reference of such evaluative principles, the extent to which they account for the predominance of certain features of theme and style in the works evaluated, and their relevance to the understanding of the society's rating of its oral artists.

Points of this kind emerged in the course of the field investigations (1971-77) on which is based my study of the oral epic songs of the formerly warlike Igbo people of Ohafia, in the Cross River area of south-eastern Nigeria (Azuonye, 1979 and 1981c). The songs, which are performed by non-professional but specialist amateurs on a wide variety of ritual and social occasions, are part of a large corpus of war songs (*abu-aha*)[3], which in turn form part of a much larger complex of heroic music (*iri-aha*) including a well-known type of dramatic war dance and its powerful instrumental accompaniment.[4] Popularly regarded by the Ohafia people as the highest form of literary art in their culture, the songs and other components of *iri-aha* are devoted to the celebration of the doings of illustrious ancestors and heroes in a past heroic age and generally draw a large audience wherever and whenever they are performed.[5] This chapter is based on testimonies recorded from a selection of informants representing both the singers of the songs and their audience. Contained in these testimonies are a number of significant expressions which, in analysis, resolve themselves into four well-defined sets of principles each of which is relevant in its own way to a proper understanding of the social functions of the songs and the poetics of their oral performance.

Before proceeding to the analysis and discussion on these principles, it may be useful to give a brief outline of the kind of situations in which they were enunciated; the social backgrounds, roles, statuses and sensibilities of the evaluators; and the procedure adopted in the field in eliciting the responses.

In any performance of the songs, it is easy to distinguish, among the singer's audience, individuals of various age-grades, both male and female, representing various sections of the locality in which the singer happens to be performing. This is to be expected, in view of the fact that the songs constitute the most important form of literary entertainment in the cultural life of the community. But while the singers' audiences generally represent a cross-section of the community, they are made up (as is usually the case with the audience of all popular forms of literature) of persons whose responses reflect varying depths of critical sensibility. At one end of the pole are the *critics* while at the other end are the *appreciators*. Thompson (1975:23), to whom we owe this distinction between critics and appreciators in African oral literary criticism, defines these two roles as follows:

> Appreciators identify with a work of art; in their vision only the physical facts are in sharp focus, while the aesthetic facets blurred ... Critics both identify (richly reflecting cultural pre-occupations) and criticize (on the basis of relative formal elegance).

The great majority of informants interviewed in the course of my field research at Ohafia seem to belong to the category of *appreciators while the very*

---

[3] See Azuonye 1979: Chapter 2, for a discussion of the characteristic features of two other types of Ohafia war songs (namely, battle songs and invocative war songs) and the nature of their relationship with the epic songs.
[4] The dramatic features of the Ohafia war dance are discussed at some length in Azuonye 1979: Chapter 2.
[5] The key informants include the singers, traditional authorities and local connoisseurs mentioned in the text. See notes 6, 8, 11, 17, 18, 19, 21 and 23 below.

few critics discovered include the singers themselves and other traditional artists.

Hardly anyone of the ordinary villagers interviewed appeared willing or even disposed to delve into matters of "relative formal elegance." They declared their enjoyment of the songs of their favourite singers with the total submission of the kind found among the readership of best-sellers in literate cultures. In the course of the performances witnessed, one could hear them saying with delight: "So this is what actually happened?" "This is very true," and so on.[6] But when disappointed by an incompetent performer, they would respond with weary faces, sighs, mass exeunt, silence or shouts of: "That is not the proper voice," "I wish Okonkwo Oke were alive," and so on.[7] Beyond these, any attempt to bring the ordinary villager to say more provoked lengthy accounts of the various ways in which ceremonies are enlivened by performances of the songs; by reflections on the affective powers of singers who have passed into popular legend; and by patriotic and sometimes, chauvinistic declarations of the superiority of Ohafia singers and their songs to those of neighbouring Cross River Igbo communities. The following dialogue with Mrs. Echeme Ugwu of Ebem, wife of a notable young singer,[8] demonstrates the difficulty of bringing a mere appreciator to specify her standards:

Q. Do you understand what Echeme Ugwu says in his songs?
A. (Instantly) I find it very enjoyable (laughing), I am sure that when you hear him perform, you will give him whatever you have in hand.
Q. Is that so?
A. The things he says are very enjoyable.
Q. Can you tell me why you say that they are enjoyable?
A. They are enjoyable because he says then properly.
Q. How?
A. Properly.
Q. How?
A. Yes, that is why I find them enjoyable.
Q. You spoke about his saying certain things properly. Can you tell me what you mean by that?
A. You mean what I mean by proper?
Q. Yes.
A. There is nothing I do not mean by that.

---

[6] In Igbo: *"Oo ri ife mee nu;" "Qo nne o ji mea!" "O wu ezhiokwu."*
[7] In Igbo: "Ife O awughi olu eji abu ya," "A si Okonkwo Oke no a ndu," etc. N/B: Okonkwo Oke was a leading singer of the late fifties and early sixties whose performances were frequently broadcast over Radio Nigeria. Such was his popularity as a Virtuoso that when he died in 1966, it was rumoured that he had been poisoned by jealous rivals.
[8] Echeme Ugwu of Ebem (Singer E) is widely regarded as Kaalu Igirigiri's son-in-song (see note 13 below); but he has won for himself a special niche among his contemporaries by specializing in the performance of a peculiar repertoire of humorous (often picaresque) tales and moral fables.

Q. What?
A. When I speak of saying these things properly, I mean everything. The point is this: when a person is doing something and I see that it is not good, I say that it is not good. If someone comes and asks you if something you have seen is good or bad, I am sure you can tell him exactly what you saw with your own eyes.
Q. But that has not explained to me what exactly you find proper in his songs?
A. You mean that I should specify it?
Q. Yes, the particular things which you find interesting when you hear them.
A. (Laughing) I cannot. It cannot be specified.
Q. Is that so?
A. O yes. You will have to wait to hear him say these things, then you will be able to see for yourself.
Q. I am not asking you to repeat these things just as he says them.
Q. (Field Assistant): What is it in the songs that *gladdens your heart* when you hear it?
A. There is nothing in them that I do not find interesting. When you hear him sing, you yourself will also see that you will find it all interesting.[9]

Needless to say, Mrs. Echeme Ugwu is here partly playing the role of a dutiful wife, promoting the works of her husband. Nevertheless, her responses do typify the attitudes of the generality of the ordinary folk in the Ohafia society who enjoy the oral epic songs in their organic wholeness rather than in their dissected parts. Nor does Mrs. Echeme Ugwu, like most other people in the community, see the need for or even the possibility of accounting in a specific manner for a kind of aesthetic pleasure which to her is sensual and emotive rather than intellective. At times, her responses during our interview bordered on surprise at our trying so indefatigably to extract a rationale for the appreciation of something which, to her, is entirely beautiful:

A. You will soon get to know the things that make them (the songs) interesting. I say, you will soon get to know the thing that makes them interesting. You will soon get to know these things.
Q. (Field Assistant): But how can we get to know these things if you do not tell us what they are?
A. Ah! (Surprised). You mean I should specify them - the things that I find

---

[9] This and subsequent interviews and testimonies are given in free English translation only for reasons of space; but the original Igbo forms of the significant items of the oral evaluative vocabulary are given, wherever necessary, in the relevant contexts, in the course of the discussion. In this excerpt, the Igbo term glossed as "enjoyable" and "interesting" is *idi utuo* (Being sweet) while *idi mma* (lit. being good) is glossed as "proper" and "good."

interesting in the songs: Ah! But, from where did you people come? Have you ever heard the songs performed? Have you ever heard them performed anywhere?
Q. Yes.
A. Didn't you find them *interesting*?
Q. But is it the same thing you find interesting in the songs that we should also find interesting?
A. Yes, of course.
Q. I don't think so.
A. It is!
Q. I don't think so.
A. It is!!
Q. I believe we find it interesting for different reasons.
A. It all amounts to the same thing.

She was perhaps quite right. We seem to have asked the wrong questions. But the answers are significant. The aesthetic pleasure derived from poetry in the oral performance is the same everywhere no matter how we account for it. Nor can it be specified by a person involved only as an appreciative listener or promotion agent.

The main dividing line between the perceptions of the ordinary folk in the villages and their detribalized counterparts who live in towns and cities outside Ohafia is that while the former at least base their enjoyment on the fact that they know the tales sung by the bards, the latter quite often know nothing about the tales and merely respond to what one traditional authority,[10] Kaalu Olugu of Eziafo,[11] has described as the "outward vibrations" of the performances as opposed to "the bone within the thing itself" (*okpukpu di ya nu n'ime*). Nevertheless, this is Africa cultural nationalism at the local level, a response born of the alienated and expatriate African's sense of identification with the culture of his own native land. A positively valuable kind of response, it had turned the great majority of Ohafia indigenes who live outside the community into patrons and connoisseurs with personal collections of recordings and the predilection to host performances and bestow largesse on the performers whenever there is an occasion for merriment or celebration.

The only category of appreciators whose responses contain profound reflections on the function and social significance of the songs are the traditional authorities (chiefs, priests, elders and other members of the communal establishments). Occasionally, from these, we get flashes of informed criticism,

---

[10] The term, "traditional authority," is used here and elsewhere in this paper to refer to priests, elders, chiefs and others who are well-versed in the customs and traditions of the clan, and whose testimonies are of the order of what Roy Willis (1978) terms "authoritative communication" in his collection of the spoken art of the Fipa of Tanzania.

[11] Kaalu Olugu of Eziafo is a local connoisseur who lives and trades at Umuahia Ibeku. His testimonies were recorded in a taxi, on 24 March, 1976, on the way to Ohafia from Umuahia.

such as the distinction made by Kaalu Olugu of Eziafo, between what he terms the "outward vibration" and the essence ("the bone within the thing itself") in the performances of other singers and that of a singer (Echeme Ugwu of Ebem), who he ranks as the best.

In another testimony, the Chief of Asaga (1976) identifies one aspect of the essence of the songs, namely their value as a means of preserving the culture of the people, in the same way as sculptural images of the heroes of the land are preserved in the *omo-ukwu* shrine[12] and similar halls of ancestral images (*obu nkwa*) elsewhere in Ohafia:

> I think you have just been to the antiquities shrines. Those carved images were carved to depict the times. You'd see quite a number of things there: the founder's wives, soldiers, his children, some criminals among them who were interdicted by the state, the king himself and so on. If you examine them closely, you'd find such people there. That is one way of preserving the culture of the people. And when they begin to *sing it out*, you will remember *what actually happened* (Spoken in English)

But apart from such cultural reflections on "the things which these war songs do for Ohafia" (*ife iri-aha onwa emere nde Ohafia*), traditional authorities tell us little more than just those features of the songs in which they themselves have a vested interest. Thus, the Chief of Asaga (above), in his testimony, concluded by dwelling on the fact that his own father - "the last ruling chief of Asaga" - is mentioned in a composition remembered by him:

> When people begin to sing in praise of the founder, they talk of this and that and then after that, they begin to talk of those who came after him right up to the present ... Even the last ruling paramount chief is mentioned (Spoken in English).

Essentially, therefore, traditional authorities are mostly appreciators who are better-informed about the cultural value of the songs than the ordinary village folk.

The true critics in the Ohafia epic tradition are the singers themselves and other traditional artists. This is hardly surprising. In the first place, all the traditional arts appear to be governed by the same aesthetic principles, which, as we shall see presently, emphasize functionality, authenticity, clarity and creative variety. Thus, artists, other than the bards, can bring insights from their own practice into their discussion of the songs. Secondly, the actual performance of the songs involves the sister arts of instrumental music and dance-drama (see

---

[12] Omo-ukwu is the largest of the numerous local sanctuaries containing wooden images of the heroic ancestors of the clan, the size of each image corresponding to the magnitude of the fame of the ancestor it represents. The sanctuary was declared a national monument by the Federal Department of Antiquities in 1962 (see Nzekwu, 1964).

Azuonye 1979: Chapter 2). Musicians, in particular, provide important insights into the definition of the right kind of voice needed for effective as well as affective vocalization. Their testimonies are also valuable in the explanation of the role of instrumental accompaniment (drumming, trumpeting and percussion) as *aide-memoires* and modulators of the rhythm of the songs. In their own testimonies, the singers themselves provide insights derived from their usually long period of apprenticeship and training (see Azonye 1979: Chapter 3 1981b), the period during which they master the principles by which they will eventually be judged. As committed students of their society, the singers are naturally most able to articulate these standards which underlie audience responses. Thus, while their testimonies, as we shall see, are generally vitiated by their excessive boastfulness, intolerance and feelings of hostility towards rival artists, they ultimately represent the true voice of the tradition.

Because of the depth of insight provided by the singers, I devoted more time to them than to the other categories of informants in the course of my field investigations. In most cases, I interviewed them in three stages, either in the same or in several sittings. In the first stage, the singer was led on to reflect on his own background and training, on the kind of admonitions received from his father or fathers-in-song,[13] on his own career and performance strategy, and on his personal successes, development and current state of maturity. In the second stage, he was led to reflect on the works of other singers, both past and present. He was encouraged to respond to particular compositions played back to him on the tape-recorder - to offer sober criticism and to give vent to animosities. Finally, the singer was given the chance to listen to criticisms of his works by other singers or local connoisseurs and to defend his works against such criticisms.

For the other categories of informants, one interview was usually sufficient to elicit significant reactions. But in these cases, formal recorded interviews were preceded or otherwise complemented by direct observation of the informant's responses as spectators during performances (i.e., whenever it was possible to do so). Such observations were generally followed by informal conversations in which no recording equipment was used and the respondents spoke freely about their likes and dislikes.

All in all, the questions put to the informants in the field were framed to cover four significant areas of evaluation: the merits of individual singers vis-à-vis their predecessors and contemporaries; the quality of particular compositions and their actual performances remembered by the informant or played back on the tape-recorder for his comment; the songs as a literary genre in relation to other genres of oral poetry in Ohafia; and the songs as a cultural heritage of the people vis-à-vis similar types of song elsewhere in the neighbourhood.

---

[13] Father-in-song, *onye-mu-m-ni-n'abal* (lit, person-that-gave-birth-to-me-in-song), is a term commonly used by the Ohafia singers to refer to their masters and mentors (see Azuonye 1979: Chapter 3, and 1981b).

Questions pertaining to the last two aspects served as a check against responses provoked by the first two.[14] To compare singers and their compositions often provoked ethnocentric and similar judgements based on the evaluator's personal knowledge of the singer, his liking of the singer or a member of his troupe, or his clannish preference for a singer from his own hometown. But when reflecting on the songs as a literary genre vis-à-vis other genres in the oral tradition, or as a cultural heritage vis-à-vis the oral epic literature of other communities, most informants did their best to rise above ethnocentric and personal considerations and to enunciate the general principles of the art of the oral epic song in the culture.

Now to the four principles elicited from the testimonies of the informants. They seem, as we shall see in sections 2 to 5 below, to resolve themselves into two broad categories - the functional and the aesthetic. The functional is represented by the principles of functionality (section 2, below) and some aspects of the principle of authenticity (section 3, below) while the aesthetic is represented by the principles of clarity (section 4), creative variation (section 5) and some aspects of the principle of authenticity. While the functional principles are invoked in the appreciation of the dynamic social and psychological functions of the songs, the aesthetic principles constitute the touchstone for the critical evaluation of their formal, stylistic and performance features. Both sets of principles are, however, indivisible components of the same axiological system. Thus, no discussion of the songs in terms of one is complete without reference to the other (see, for example, Azuonye 1981a, 1981b and 1983).

The principle of functionality

By far the most important contexts in which the songs and other components of *iri-aha* (notably the dramatic war dance) are performed are those events and ceremonies in which the traditional heroic ideal of personal success need to be celebrated. Among these are burial and funeral rites, festivals in honour of the ancestors, the celebration of personal achievements in education, business or politics, age-promotion rites, and initiations into title and secret societies. Much grandeur is usually invested on such occasions by implicitly and explicitly comparing the contemporary champion or hero with his forbears as well as by the express recitation of the champion's own praises. According to the singer, Ogbaa Kaalu of Abia:[15]

---

[14] No set questionnaires were used in the interviews. This made it possible for informants to speak at length on points that interested them and to raise issues which were taken up in follow-up questions. But, by and large, it was possible in each interview to cover the four main aspects of evaluation.

[15] Ogbaa Kaalu of Abia (singer D) is a country doctor by profession. He is hardly as prolific and efficient in his performances as his boasts suggest (see Azuonye 1977:301).

Today, head-hunting is out of fashion. But if you grow rich or become highly educated, especially if you go to the white man's land and return with your car and immense knowledge, we would naturally perform for you. By doing such things, you have won your own battle honours. Passing examinations well and bringing home the white man's money: these are the prevailing kinds of war we have today. If you succeed in any of these, it is counted for you as your own battle honour. The same is true of building a big house, one that is truly imposing. People will say (on seeing it): your money is your own battle-trophy. On the day such a house will be opened, we would normally perform for you, for by building it, you have won head in battle, for things of this kind are the only kind of head-hunting that exists in our present-day culture.

Similarly, but with particular reference to traditional ritual ceremonies, another singer, Kaalu Igirigiri of Okon,[16] declares:

The reason why people like these songs very much is that it is customary that when a person dies, these songs should be performed to honour him, to bid him farewell. They are usually performed all through the funeral until the person is buried. That is why people like them very much. In the event of a ceremony, for example, if your father dies and you feel, after a while, that he should be given a befitting second-burial, you will normally come to us and we will perform for you and make it truly interesting. When other people see how interesting it is, they will say: Come and perform for us, come and perform for us - this is truly interesting. That is why people like them very much. When we put up the ceremony known as *igba.ekpe*, various age-sets usually come to us, the particular age-set performing the ceremony would invite us to sing for them, and we would sing for them. In the whole of Ohafia, it is the only form of *iri* (music) which Ohafia people find very interesting, the one which everyone in Ohafia confesses that he appreciates. It is the only form of *iri* which, whenever it is performed, people gather to witness it.

Ogbaa Kaalu of Abia suggests that performances of the kinds described above cannot fail to move their hearers to emulation by awakening dreams of success in their hearts:

Whenever this particular type of *iri* is performed, our hearts brim with joy: because it is the umbilical cord with which we were born. Whenever we hear its rhythm, our hearts swell with joy: we think of the day of our birth and cherish the day of our death; we think of the day we shall raise our heads in pride and rejoice in anticipation of the day we shall grow rich ... So, then, we are most happy to see it performed every time.

---

[16] Kaalu Igirigiri of Okon (Singer B), who died in his late fifties or early sixties (1980) is by far the most versatile of the five singers whose performances were recorded in the course of my field research (1971-1977). A proud, intelligent and highly sensitive artist, his achievements are as impressive as his boasts (see Azuonye, 1981a).

In another testimony, Ogbaa Kaalu speaks specifically of inspiration, the appeal of the songs to these qualities of the spirit generally regarded by the folk as the basis of Ohafia's rise to military power and greatness:

> It is the thing that made us a powerful nation. It is in our blood. It does not matter if your legs and arms are paralysed, nor does it matter if you are crippled and sitting impotent on the ground, but the moment you hear its rhythm, it will surely revive your spirit. The point is that it is bound up with everything we seek, everything we desire in this world, it is the answer to all our needs.

The retired Presbyterian pastor, the late Ukaiwe Maduekwe of Asaga,[17] agrees. In his own testimony, he stresses the affective function of the songs in awakening, especially in the young, what he terms "that old spirit of bravery" which "marks them out from other Igbo people." Maduekwe then refers to a specific modern situation (the Biafran war) in which inspiration from the songs was quickly translated into action. In acknowledgement of the power of the songs to inspire in these and other ways, the Ohafia singer is usually eulogized by his hearers, during performances, a *Okpate-nde-ikom*, "He that awakens the young."

Apart from inspiration or "spiritual awakening" (*ikpate mmuo*), another aspect of the affective function of the songs frequently mentioned in the testimonies of my informants is enlightenment, commonly expressed by the phrases *inye echiche* (lit. giving thought, i.e. intellectual awakening) and *ikpate n'urha* (lit, awakening from sleep, rousing the hearer from his ignorance about traditional custom and myth). In his testimony, Ukaiwe Maduekwe of Asaga describes the way in which a good singer can provoke thoughtless generosity in his over-excited listeners through the revelation of hidden facts about their ancestries:

> He will put you into deep thought about what your great great grandfather was, about your own father, about your father's mother, about the life of your own mother. He will go on and on talking, talking until he wakes you yourself from sleep. Perhaps he will tell you what your father was. As he talks about these things, you will not know when you give him whatever you have in hand. If you have a goat in hand, anything you have in hand, you will give it to him. It awakens your spirit

Audience responses are equally ecstatic when the singer touches upon what, to them, are the hidden secrets of the origins of their own community. Thus, Ogbaa Kaalu of Abia boasts of the effect of such a revelation on his audience at

---

[17] Ukaiwe Maduekwe, a retired Presbyterian pastor, is a keen patron of the performances in whose compound at Asaga the great majority of the songs of Kaalu Igirigiri in my collection were recorded.

Akara (*Isuikwuato*) where he lives and practices traditional medicine:

> There are many people in this village who know nothing about the person that founded it. There are many people in this village who did not know about their founding father until the day I made it the subject of my song and eulogized them ... Afterwards many of them turned round and wondered who told me these things.

But while the ordinary folk are delighted by such revelations, the traditional authorities, for whom communal history is a guarded secret which should not be so publicly declaimed in an uncensored form, are completely shaken and irate. According to Ogbaa Kaalu:

> They were dumbfounded. Some came to me and quietly admonished me never to say such things again. It was a secret, a secret which they hid away from some people. The truth is that there are many people here who have been looking for a way of getting a little bit of historical information - something about the ancestor that founded this village for them, something about their origins and settlement here - but it is hidden away from them. Well, I shut my mouth. Is it of any use to me?

But, in fact, it is. The revelation of the secrets of local history, especially the local history of an enemy or rival community, is one of the ways in which the Ohafia Igbo singer of tales is able to carry his audiences with him in his performances. Quite often, when the facade is torn apart in his profane revelations, one can hear murmurs of excitement and delight spreading through the audience. Such responses can be heard quite distinctly when listening to some of the tape-recordings of the songs. In *Elibe Aja* B3,[18] for example, the singer (Kaalu Igirigiri of Okon) reveals to his audience at Asaga that it is with the skin of the leopardess, killed by their hunter hero, *Elibe Aja*, that the Aro decorate the shrine of their water god till today. As the murmur of excitement spread, the singer consolidated his gains by a short anecdote on the effect of this revelation on the King of Arochukwu himself during a performance he had given before him at Arochukwu:

> I told this to Kamalu Oji
> And he told me not to expose his secrets anymore -
> That was at Aro -
> I had exposed the secret of the great Aro oracle.

Another aspect of the social function of the songs stressed in the testimonies

---

[18] *Elibe Aja* is the story of an Ohafia hunter-hero who, after killing a leopardess which harried Aro country destroying men and livestock, dies while attempting to destroy another beast (a bush-hog) which ravaged crop in the neighbouring community of Amuru. Version B3 of this tale (recorded in 1976) does not contain the account of the death of the hero at Amuru.

of many informants is their value as the embodiment of tradition (*omenaali*) especially the heroic tradition on which the unity and power of the community rests. According to Ogbaa Kaalu of Abia:

> They are the one *òmenaali* which binds together all Ohafia people, right from our very origins - right from the time we came into this world...It is the thing that made us a powerful nation. It is in our blood.

A constant and powerful reminder to the people of their ancestors' unflinching commitment to the ideas of personal achievement and the rewards of honour in life and death, the songs help to ensure the continuance of their heroic spirit from one generation to another. Thus, we are told by the Chief of Asaga (1976):

> When we are reminded of our past, we try to hold our own and wherever we go, we return here to enjoy what our fathers have done to preserve this place for us. People lived here before, but our fathers had to chase them out to inherit here (spoken in English).

The principle of authenticity

For the effective fulfilment of the traditional functions of their songs, Ohafia singers of tales are required to aspire towards a high degree of authenticity in the presentation of the ancestral heroes and their milieu. The testimonies of the critics and appreciators alike are thus full of such phrases as *ife mee eme* (what actually happened) and *eziokwu* (truth). When the singer, Egwu Kaalu of Asaga[19] was asked to explain what he meant by *ife mee ème*, he replied:

> Let me assume that you are a man of deeds - a great wrestler. Assuming that you had wrestled with someone else. Now, let us say that in the contest you, won every bout, throwing your opponent here, there and everywhere. Assuming that everyone knows exactly how you threw your opponent and that I am called upon to sing about it. I will say exactly what happened. If another person comes and says it is your opponent that threw you in the contest, I will rise up and tell that person that he does not know how to sing.

Reality, then, for the Ohafia singer, seems to be verifiable fact: the literal truth of history which is common knowledge, the facts of an event or situation which other witnesses can corroborate. Thus, we are told by Kaalu Igirigiri of

---

[19] Egwu Kaalu of Asaga (Singer C) probably in his mid-forties (1981), is a fine singer who, unfortunately, lost interest in the singing of tales after he secured a job as a bricklayer in a construction firm operating in the neighbourhood of Ohafia, in 1976.

Okon:

> Take yourself, for instance, I can tell you all about your father, his mode of life and the manner of his death, and if you go and ask your kinsmen, they will tell you that your father actually led that kind of life.

Statements of this kind, suggest a higher degree of literal truth in the representation of reality, than is in fact evident in the texts of the songs available to us. See, for example, the text given in the Appendix below. But this apparent discrepancy between theory and practice is explicable in terms of the quality of mid-point mimesis recognized by Thompson in traditional Yoruba sculpture (1975:31). In the Ohafia songs, as in Yoruba sculpture, what is intended is not so much photographic realism as the impression of semblance, something "between abstraction and absolute likeness." We find the same quality in the ancestral images in the *òmò ukwu* and other shrines of ancestral images in Ohafia. The success of these impressions rests almost entirely on the fact that the details are common knowledge. Thus, like the cartoonist, what the singer needs to do in order to win the approval of his audience is to emphasize a dominant feature of a character, object, place or situation by means of a mythopoetic, descriptive or associative epithet or other formula, especially formulas of the particularized category, which, as I have shown elsewhere (Azuonye, 1979. Chapter 5 and 1981d), function in the compositions of the singers as verbal fossils in which the dominant characteristics of individual heroes, localities, etc., are preserved in picturesque and memorable forms.

A singer who commands a rich repertoire of epithets (especially patronymic epithets which refer to the ancestral history, culture and social realm of the most important clans in Ohafia) is thus highly regarded by his audiences as possessing the kind of extensive historical knowledge of which Kaalu Igirigiri boasts in the following testimony:

> I can tell you all about your ancestry, right from the very God that created you, down to the present time; and I can tell you all about the mode of life your kinsmen lead today. None of my rivals knows anything about these things. Even Ohafia as a whole, I can tell you all about our origins - about the place from which we migrated to this place. None of my rivals knows anything about these things. This compound of ours, I can tell you all about its founding father. About other people's compounds, I can tell you all about their founding fathers. When I go to Amaekpu, I can tell them all about their founding fathers. None of my rivals knows anything about these things. As you will know, Amaekpu is not my native village. But I know everything that prevails there. Asaga, I know everything that prevails there, everything about their founding father. Every concealable thing that prevails there. This is what we call *iki-aka* - knowledge of the ancestors, knowledge of the founding father of Asaga, knowledge of the founding father of Akaanu, knowledge of the founding father of Uduma. My rivals know nothing of such things.

Similarly, Ogba Kaalu of Abia boasts:

> I sing my songs in many different styles, in whatever style my audience wants it, right from the very beginning, concerning the origins of Ohafia, how we emigrated from that place from which we came here, right from the beginning concerning the birth of our community, including all the surrounding communities, including Akoli, including even you people that live far out there, I can tell you all about your origins, including even Loori, and Lookpa, and I can tell you about their ways of life, including Bende, up to Alayi, and up to Umuhu, including Abiriba, and up to Igbere and up to Ikwere, and I can tell you how my own people migrated to Abia, how we came to settle at Abia, and I will go on and on and tell you everything about the way of life of various people. All these I learnt from my father. There is a tape-recording mechanism inside my head. I have gone will beyond the stage of apprenticeship.

Armed with "extensive historical knowledge" of this kind, a good singer must be able to rise above ethnocentricism and sing about the heroes of "all the lineages" not just of his own lineage. This criterion is applied to Ukoha Agwunsi of Okon (a musician in Kaalu Igirigiri's troupe) to discredit Echeme Ugwu of Ebem (Singer E) in favour of his master:

> There is someone named Echeme, who sings at Ebem. He only eulogizes his kinsmen, since he knows nothing of heroes that live in all other lineages. He is still a mere apprentice.

This, he says, contrasts with the practice of Kaalu Igirigiri, the master of balanced hero-lists. [20] According to another musician in Kaalu Igiri-giri's troupe, Kaalu Ikpo of Okon,

> The reason why this one (i.e. Kaalu Igirigiri) is such an effective singer is this: he can range over the whole of Nigeria, and when he sings, he will make sure that he calls this person, calls that person and calls that other person. He does not stick to one person. He calls this and that other person - until he calls all of them.

Now to the third level of the meaning of truth and reality in Ohafia literary criticism, i.e. the identification of "truth" and "reality" with objects, places and persons recognized by the hearers of the songs and with the pleasure that comes with this recognition.[21] When, in one of the testimonies quoted above, the Chief of Asaga stresses the fact that "even the last ruling paramount chief is

---

[20] Another master of the balanced hero-list is Poet F (Njoku Mmaju of Uduma Awooke). See Azuonye 1981a and 1983.

[21] Idika Oge, the chief priest of the Omo-ukwu sanctuary at Asaga, mentions two other elements of local colour in a testimony recorded in March 1976: *ife mee ali o*) (what happens in this land) and *nne eji na-arhu orhu* (the way people do their work).

mentioned," he betrays the fact that he is much more concerned with the pleasure of recognizing his own ancestors in the composition than in other literal truth which it embodies. A person who recognizes his ancestor in heroic poetry is, of course, most likely to base his whole response to the rest of the performances on this recognition. Everything also would sound true to him, especially if in subsequent lines he recognizes other "things concerning this land." As we have observed several times in this discussion, every singer knows the magic of appealing to human vanity by paying homage to their hosts through their ancestors, thus preparing them to accept everything else in their songs as true. According to Egwu Kaalu of Asaga,

> I respond to every invitation. Whatever my hosts say I should sing for them, i.e., to suit the occasion for which my services are needed, I will sing that thing for them. If they ask me if I know how to sing it, I will say: yes, I can sing it. If I cannot meet any particular request, I will say so. But, in general, I begin by eulogizing my host after which I tell them about the lives of their own fathers.

Having done this, the singer can proceed to the larger issues of the heroic age, assured that his hosts will agree with him at every point. But apart from the effects of homage, ethnic pride and chauvinism play an important role in determining what audiences accept as authentic. For instance, whereas everyone in Ohafia would normally accept the derogation of the Aro in *Elìbe Àjà* (See Azuonye 1979: 8.2.2), any such presentation of the Ohafia people would be violently rejected. In effect, then, truth amounts to little more than ethnic pride.

On another level, the Ohafia people equate truth with common belief. Thus, no one listening to heroic poetry in Ohafia is disposed to question anything in the songs - no matter how fantastic it might sound to the outsider to the culture - provided it does not contradict widely-accepted beliefs. During my field investigation, I referred Kaalu Igirigiri to one of his versions of the tale of *Nne Àcho, Ùgo*,[22] expecting that he would confirm my own independent interpretation of it as a parable, an interpretation which Ukaiwe Maduekwe of Asaga agrees with completely, but not on my prompting. Surprisingly, Kaalu Igirigiri insisted that the tale is neither fable nor parable but an account of things which actually happened. He says of *Nne Acho Ugo* (a beast) and her children (five birds):

> They are not human beings. It was that mother of theirs that was human, but she gave birth only to birds. That mother of theirs was human, but she gave birth to birds only.

---

[22] The tale of *Nne acho Ugo*, referred to elsewhere in this chapter, is a kind of beast epic. It is the story of a mythical beast abandoned by her five boastful children (Kite, Hawk, Sunbird, Woodpecker and Eagle) on the day of her death. There is no agreement in the testimonies discussed in this paper as to whether the tale is a parable or myth (in the sense of a traditional story pertaining to the origins of phenomena told as true). The conflicting interpretations of the tale are significant because they stress the fact that a traditional story does not always mean one thing to its traditional audiences.

He then goes on to rationalize:

> *Nne Acho Ugo...* behaved very much like what we call *nkita-iyi* (River-dog). Nkita-iyi lives in the river. It isn't human. It isn't fish, this *nkita-iyi*. It isn't beast, this *nkita-iyi*. It isn't a type of fish. It isn't a beast. It has the tail of a mudskipper; it has a beard - mammalian hair. It lives in water and also lives on land. When it gives birth - this *nkita-iyi* - she can produce a beast of the forest. Quite often, when fish see its tall, they gather round it thinking it is one of them. But it eats fish ... Just as it isn't fish and isn't beast, so Nne Acho Ugo Erueghe was. She wasn't human ... She was human as well as bird.

Kaalu Igirigiri goes on to state that Nne Acho Ugo actually lived at Elu - the traditional capital of Ohafia - and that it was on account of this that she came to be widely known throughout the land. This testimony is significant because it demonstrates how easy it is to dismiss as "fantastic" elements such as the above, which in fact constitute part of the widely-accepted beliefs of a society in which oral literature functions. Without the benefit of Kaalu Igirigiri's testimony, it would have been difficult to approach the story in any other way than a parable or myth. But at every stage of the testimony other people supported the views of the bard by side comments and the nodding of heads. It may well be that these people are so used to believing Kaalu Igirigiri's tales that they can no longer challenge anything he says. But it could not be a willing suspension of disbelief. There are times and situations in which people cannot but accept the fantasies of myth and legend as true: i.e. especially when these fantasies answer to their aspirations, prejudices and religious faith.

The higher moral truths of the songs are occasionally stated explicitly at the close of some of the stories. This gives much delight, provoking comments of various kinds which say a lot about the listeners' gratitude for the insights vouchsafed. But equally appealing, is the moral deduced from the underlying allegoric or parabolic meaning of a tale like *Nne Acho Ugo*,[23] in spite of the author's insistence that it is a factual account. Ukaiwe Maduekwe's response is that it is an *ilu* - a parable in which birds have been used to represent genuine historical characters and situations. Here is his exegesis of the tale:

> ...When they (the poets) come to talk in the form of parable (*ilu*), it must be understood that they refer to the actions of particular individuals in the past. About Nne Acho Ugo, it is most probable that the story refers to a real human being - a person who had children - five children. These children boasted among themselves that when their mother died they would do this or that for her. It may be - according to the pattern of life in those days - that, as their mother or father was about to die, one of them went to the wars and got lost there. Another may have gone as well and got lost. Another may have followed and got lost. So only one among the was left. Only one among them was left.

---

[23] See note 22.

The value of this parabolic interpretation of the song is however vitiated by the fact that the informant had been a Presbyterian pastor and that no one else other than him (a western-educated person) offered the same kind of view.

What many informants regard as authentic in the compositions is not always related to any actual features of theme and style in the songs; sometimes it is based only on what they know of the singer's background and training and the degree of fame or popularity he has already attained. Of course, this kind of evaluation is not peculiar to Ohafia. It is a stock-in-trade of the literate book market that a name such as Solzheniskin or Achebe rather than the actual merits of particular new works is often enough to commend the writer to readers, whose assessment might just be: 'A new novel by Achebe? It must be good!'

Not surprisingly, therefore, Ohafia singers and their promoters take every available opportunity to boast to their audiences about their journeys, triumphs, the big events in which they featured as star artists, and, generally, the country-wide popularity they command. Here, for example, is the response of Ogbaa Kaalu of Abia when I asked him if he would sing:

> I am not the one to tell you that, you should ask the people of this town. And when you go to Ohafia you can inquire about my name. When you go to Enugu you will see my name. When you go to Aba, you will see my name. When you go to Umuahia, you will see my name. I am the one called Ogbaa Kaalu. I am a native of Abia.

According to Ogbaa Kaalu, even rivals - for instance, Kaalu Igirigiri of Okon - acknowledge his superiority as a singer:

> You must have noticed that Kaalu Igirigiri is always talking about me - always talking of Ogbaa! Ogbaa! I am the one and only Ogbaa about whom he has talked so much - offspring of the matrician of Ebosi Ego. I am the one and only Ogbaa about whom he has talked so much.

He then alludes to some notable occasions at which his rival allegedly felt so embarrassed by his presence that he was unable to perform at all without first consulting him:

> It is only when occasions involve dignitaries that you can see me singing. I remember the day we went to receive my brother, Eni Njoku,[24] who died in England. We went to receive his remains at the aeroplane field. Kaalu Igirigiri did not sing any song. He kept asking if I had come. He had been looking for me. You see, he always writes to me inviting me to accompany him to other towns to sing, but I have always turned down these invitations, because I have no time to go out singing in other towns. The point is that it is

---

[24] Professor Eni Njoku, Vice-Chancellor of the University of Lagos (1962-66) and of the University of Nigeria, Nsukka (1966-70), died in London in December 1975).

here, where I am settled as a doctor, that my taproot is. But any time
something really momentous crops up, you will certainly see me come to
sing.

These comments reflect a general Igbo dislike for professionalism in song-making. Elsewhere, Ogbaa Kaalu brutally detracts Kaalu Igirigiri for commercializing the tradition of heroic poetry by tending towards sheer professionalism.

On his own part, Kaalu Igirigiri seizes upon every opportunity to tell us about his wide-ranging historical knowledge, and to take glory in the fact that even scholars from the universities have now come to recognize him as the source of authentic information on local history:

There are people who come all the way from Nsukka, where they are
engaged in research. They come, sent by the white man to learn about the
traditions of their native villages, about their origins, about the founding
fathers of their villages. They come to me. Some have just come this month,
and I told them things with which they will do their research. That is why I
am greater than my rivals.

Another point raised by Kaalu Igirigiri and his promoters is that while other singers boast of popularity within Ohafia and elsewhere in Igbo country, Kaalu's fame now extends over the whole of Nigeria. The drummer, Kaalu Ikpo, asserts:

There is no place we have not performed. In Lagos... in Kaduna ... in Calabar.
There is no place we have not performed this iri-aha.

Another extra-textual factor taken into account in evaluating the authenticity and authority of a singer's works is his age. Thus, it is largely on the grounds of age that Egwu Kaalu of Asaga concedes the fact that Kaalu Igirigiri is a better singer than himself:

The fact is that Kaalu Igirigiri is a grand old man. He is an excellent singer.
You see. He is Echeme's father-in-song. Kaalu Igirigiri is now a grand old
man.

The point is clinched by Madam Maduekwe's side comment: "Kaalu Igirigiri is now a graduate of long-standing."

The principle of clarity

This principle is summed up in a phrase from Ogbaa Kaalu of Abia: *imezikwa ka o doo anya nkè oma* (putting things in such a way that they would be clearly perceptible to everyone). In many ways this principle closely resembles the criterion of visibility identified by Thompson in traditional Yoruba art criticism. "Visibility," Thompson (1975:35) write, "refers...to clarity of form and to clarity of the line;" "Carvers seek to express generalized principles of humanity. They carve...nonetheless, with ultimate sharpness of clarity and focus." In the traditional criticism of Ohafia, the notion of clarity, refers primarily to the unity and coherence of narrative form and is offered as a criterion for assessing the triumphs and failures of a truly historical narrative; but in many of the testimonies recorded, we find it applied in many different ways in the evaluation of themes, language and vocalization.

Egwu Kaalu of Asaga is one of the most perceptive exponents of the principle of clarity, so far as it pertains to themes. In the following testimony, in which he acknowledges the fact that Kaalu Igirigiri is a better singer than himself, he rebukes the master for departing from "the plain facts of history" and bringing in "extraneous elements." Any truly historical narrative, he says, is one which deals with the facts in "a straight-forward manner" without bringing in other elements:

> He is a better singer than myself. He is a better singer than myself. But you must understand that we are dealing with 'history'.[25] The thing about our history is that, in relating it, you must do so in a straight-forward manner. The problem with these people (Kaalu Igirigiri and Echeme Ugwu of Ebem) is that when they sing, they bring in extraneous elements which do not contribute to this straight-forward manner of presenting reality.

Elsewhere Egwu Kaalu makes the same point with a slightly different emphasis:

> The poetry of our land is unique. They (the bards) do not get themselves entangled with all sorts of extraneous things. They restrict their narrations to just those things which they know to be the facts of history. They begin by eulogizing, then proceed to talk about just those things they know to have actually happened. You see.

Another way of achieving thematic clarity, as we are told by Ogbaa Kaalu of Abia, is by elaboration rather than ruthless adherence to essential details. By this standard, singers are urged to add as many details as possible so that the listener will never, at any stage, be at a loss in following the plot of the story as a whole or any stage of its development. According to Ogbaa Kaalu, the singer must inform, explain and carry his audience with him, especially by exploiting the full dramatic possibilities of dialogue and the re-enactment of the pathetic as well as the happy utterances of his characters. Thus, for this critic, it is a serious breach of art to involve oneself in any form of abridgement. This is the basis of his

---

[25] Egwu Kaalu's testimony is in Igbo, but he used the English term 'history' for the content of the songs.

criticism of Kaalu Igirigiri's work at Akara, after my field assistant had played back *Amoògu B3*[26] to him:

> There are many things which we spell out clearly by name, which Kaalu Igirigiri does not put into his songs. Thus, he fails to represent things as they really are. He cuts them up into small unrelated bits. But when we, on our part, sing, we explain to you quite clearly how everything went, from the beginning to the end ... He cuts them up into small bits ... There is a person whose story he tells - I mean Amoogu, the person that first fired the gun, with which the short-armed-one of Alike was killed. If you are told how this really happened, from its beginning to the end, tears will roll down from your eyes. But he compresses it far too much.

The pathetic cry of Amoogu's mother, he did not reproduce it properly; yes the pathetic cry of Amoogu's mother, he did not reproduce it properly. That's one thing. The questions asked by Amoogu's mother, he did not reproduce them properly. There was a question which Amoogu's mother asked: "O where is my dear son?" ...She was told her son was on the way.

But at night, her son's head was placed for her on a fence in a bathing enclosure and she was told to go there and take her bath so she would see what was placed there for her. When she got there, she found it was the head of her son. Kaalu Igirigiri did not put this detail into his composition.

Ogbaa Kaalu then goes on to list other details omitted by Kaalu Igirigiri in his composition and concludes:

> When he sings - when Kaalu Igirigiri sings - he does not seem to have the ability to sing in such a way that it will be quite clear to you - so that it will be quite clear to you from what he actually puts into the song, so that you can see it clearly from its beginning to the end. When we, on our part, sing it, we put in even the lament of that woman when her son returned. There is a way in which one can simulate that lament and tears will roil down from your eyes.

Kaalu Igirigiri's response to this criticism appears to be his repeated assertion that complete invocation is a better means of achieving thematic balance, and hence clarity. It is however noticeable that in his more recent compositions (1976 and 1977), he had seen the need to put in many more details than are discernible in his previous works (see Azuonye 1983).

On another level, the principle of clarity applies to the use of language in

---

[26] Amoogu is the tale of the heroism and death of a little-known warrior from the smallest of the twenty-five clans in Ohafia. By sitting naked in he nest of soldier-ants and charging twelve guns - a task which the established heroes of the land are unable to accomplish - he is able to produce he magical weapon, which alone (according to an oracular revelation) can kill the short-armed dwarf of Aliike, an adversary who had inflicted numerous humiliating defeats on the Ohafia. Amoogu is latter killed by jealous comrades-in-arms, but his spirit wreaks vengeance on his assassins.

oral 'historical' poetry. According to Egwu Kaalu of Asaga, any form of poetry which has 'history' as its subject matter, must strive indefatigably towards clarity of expression. Here, the principle of clarity is invoked to repudiate euphemism or the excessively ornate style. For Egwu Kaalu, euphemism occurs when inexperienced singers make excessive use of proverbs and other figurative devices - *ilu* - in their works. Thus, he warns: "excessive use of proverbs is not good" (*itiikari ilu adighi mma*); understandably, he concedes, "proverbs are an essential ingredient of speech" (*eji ilu aka uka*), but they function effectively only in certain types of discourse. In historical poetry, where the most essential elements are "the plain facts," proverbs are not really necessary. They are in fact "extraneous element" (*ife Aduo*). Used excessively, they merely distort the facts and in the end may result in the production of quite a different type of poetry (*abu oduo*):

> If a person repeatedly employs proverbs, it can only be said that he is 'putting in' another kind of poetry, because, if you want to sing a song, in a straightforward manner, about the actual deeds of a particular person - if you really want to articulate the facts clearly, from the beginning to the end - you don't need to put extraneous things into it.

At best, says Egwu Kaalu, "proverbs can function as devices for completing a verse" (*imejuru uka*) or for "remembering what you sing" (*ichete ife I na-agu*). But, he argues:

> If you really wish to articulate the facts clearly ... you simply have to speak directly to your audience. You may say: This is what the particular hero (I will sing about) did. People will pay attention. You will then have to give a clear account of everything, from the beginning to the end.

Egwu Kaalu's observations are, in the end, a reassertion of the universal principle that there is no particular value in the use of *ilu* or any other figurative device unless it contributes to the total meaning of the composition in which it is used. Significantly, he does his best, in his own compositions, to measure up to this principle.

So bare indeed are the songs of proverbs and figurative expressions outside the epithets that, when they occur, they are particularly striking and crucial to the development of the plot. More important to the singers than figurative language is coherence, hence the recurrence of the phrase, "from the beginning to the end" in most critical testimonies. Thus, Ogbaa Kaalu and Egwu Kaalu speak repeatedly of *iza ya isi goruo ali* (taking it from its head and placing it gently on the ground) and also of *ikowakwahu zia ya isi ruo ali* (clearly explaining from the head to the ground). Similarly, when Ogbaa Kaalu accuses Kaalu Igirigiri of engaging in irresponsible abridgement, he refers, as follows, to the standard of formal clarity, which he claims to follow in his own composition: "When we on our part sing the same tale, we clearly explain to you how everything happened, from the very beginning to the end" (*si a mmalite ruo usota ya*). Contrarily, when Kaalu Igirigiri sings the same tale,

> He does not seem to have ability to sing in such a way that it will be quite clear to you - so that it will be quite clear to you from what he actually puts into the song, so that you can see it clearly from its beginning to the end.

Naturally, in an oral tradition, a great deal of attention is paid to the quality of the poet-singer's voice. An inaudible or raucous voice in an oral poem is as bad as an illegible script. Thus many singers frequently boast about the quality of their voices, as in the following testimony from Kaalu Igirigiri of Okon:

> My voice is sweet. But on top of that, I tell them things which gladden their hearts. That is what sustains me in my songs. There are people who insist on singing when they do not have a sweet voice. No one likes what such people sings. As for me, my voice is sweet, and I sing those things which when people hear them, their hearts swell with joy, and they say "These are things that actually happened." But it is the sweetness of the voice that they like above everything else.

This high evaluation of the sweetness of this particular singer's voice has given rise to the standard praise-names for him which I have discussed elsewhere (Azuonye 1979, Chapter 3):

> *Olu nkwa* (musical voice)
> *Olu Ogele* (gong-like voice)
> *Okooku turn nkwa yiri olu* (parrot that built a musical instrument and
>   wears it in his throat)
> *Okooko ,lkam nka* (parrot, the talkative artist)
> *Oji olu ekwu nnu* (He that buys salt with his voice)

From the first two of these praise-names, we can deduce the kind of voice regarded by the people as sweet, i.e. the sonorous and highly pliable voice, the kind described by Okoreaffia (n.d.) as a *sine qua non* for the Igbo story-teller:

> A raucous voice is not good for the purpose of story-telling. A high-pitched voice does not go far. A sweet voice, like Ogele, sounds *kem kem kem* and can also sound *biam-biam-biam* as audiences usually want it.

Referring specifically to the Ohafia situation, Ogbaa Kaalu of Abia denounces poet E (Echeme Ugwu of Ebem) because olu ya na-ada ikike ikike (he sings in a monotonously high-pitched voice). Heroic poetry he says, "does not require a monotonously high-pitched voice" (*O choghu olu ike*); however, there are points in a narrative where the pitch of the voice needs to be raised (*eruo ebe etii olu ike*), i.e. primarily during transitions from the main narrative passages to lyrical or invocative passages.

But the possession of a sweet voice is not a guarantee that one would become a good singer of tales. According to Egwu Kaalu of Asaga, "To sound proper in songs, the voice must have the right kind of modulation" (*olu abu, o nwee Otu esi edowe ya*). This can only be acquired through training under a master-singer. Thus, Kaalu Igirigiri reports:

> If you are a singer and it is recognized that your voice is sweet, Ohafia people will tell you: Go and meet Kaalu Igirigiri. He will teach you how to sing. Your voice is sweet.

From his master, the apprentice will learn, in addition to the art of *iku-aka* (evoking the past), the techniques of "articulating his words in such a way that they would be clearly audible" (*ikapusa ife anu anua nti*). The importance attached to this technique is evident in the frequency with which it is evoked by critics and appreciators alike when ranking one singer against another. For instance, in ranking Kaalu Igirigiri above his son-in-song, Echeme Ugwu, the drummers - Ukaohu Agwunsi and Kaalu Ikpo - stress the fact that *o na akapusa ife anu anua nti* (he articulates his words in such a way that they are clearly audible).

The principle of creative variation

As I have pointed out elsewhere (Azuonye 1979: Chapter 9, and 1981b), Ohafia critics evaluate original and individual talent in terms of the richness of a singer's repertoire of tales, his command of formulas, themes, and other devices of composition, the degree of creative improvisation he is capable of, especially in response to new contexts of situation; further, they judge originality in terms of the singer's ability to increase his repertoire by creating new stories on new and contemporary themes while upholding the inherited heroic ideals; finally, they judge originality, as critics anywhere would, in terms of the singer's ability to recreate stories told him or those borrowed from other poets, so imaginatively, that they become fully identifiable with him. These aspects of creative variation recognized by the traditional aesthetic may be conveniently discussed under the headings:

1) change,
2) growth, and
3) imaginative recreation.

In the following boast, Kaalu Igirigiri of Okon gives us a brief outline of the kind of 'change' (*mgbanwo*) required by tradition in a singer's repertoire of stories:

> I make many changes when I sing my songs. I even make changes in the traditional choric songs (*abu akwukwe*). But more importantly, I can easily switch from the old heroic sings - the one inherited from the ancients - to new songs about the events of today. I can sing newly-created songs - those which nobody in Ohafia has heard before.

To this, Kaalu Ikpo of Okon (who was present at the interview) adds:

> ... our poetry is not of one kind... It is just like we have in a church service. We are all the time changing. We change and say: This one is this, that one is that, this other one is that - like a gramophone record. Doesn't a record have a front and a back? Our poetry is just like that.

In another comment, at the same interview, Ukaoha Agwunsi says of Kaalu Igirigiri:

> Once he has finished singing about a particular hero, he will not mention that hero again in the same performance. Other songs will now be sung in a completely different voice (i.e. form).

The changes wrought by the singers in their compositions is explained, as follows, by Egwu Kaalu of Asaga, by analogy with shifting cultivation:

> It is very much like farming. You clear a piece of land and plant yams in it. After this, you harvest the yams and plant seed yams on the land. Eventually (during the next planting season), you will dig out the seed-yams and leave the land fallow. You then go and clear another piece of land and plant your seed-yams there, followed by another harvest and the plantation of seed yams, after which you will leave the land fallow again. Our poetry is very much like that.

The "seed-yams" are of course the stable devices of composition planted by the singers in a wide variety of new contexts, season after season and year after year. In the course of these shifting cultivation and harvest, says Maduekwe of Asaga, "poetic knowledge increases." Egwu Kaalu agrees using another analogy:

> It grows. It is plentiful. It is somewhat like going through school. After going through one page you turn to another page and after going through that page you turn to another, and so on. The same is true of our poetic practice.

"The pages," he explains "are the stories told by old men."
Despite increases in poetic knowledge, the form of the songs remains

"essentially unchanged." Thus, in spite of his earlier testimony regarding his capacity to make changes in his songs, Kaalu Igirigiri is able to say:

> I don't sing my songs, at Okon, in a form different from that in which I sing them at Asaga. The thing I sing at Okon is what I sing at Asaga, it is also what I sing at Ebem ... That is why Ohafia people all agree that I am the best of all the poets.

In a similar vein, Egwu Kaalu asserts:

> Nothing extraneous is put into the songs. By that I mean that it is exactly what I sang in 1972 that I will sing today.

(See Azuonye 1983 for an attempt to resolve the apparent inconsistency between these statements).

I now turn to the third aspect of the principle of creative variation in which the emphasis is on the imaginative recreation of reality. In his Principles of Literary Criticism (1924: 188-191), I.A. Richards distinguishes "six distinct senses" of the word, "imagination," namely:

1. The production of vivid images, usually visual images ...
2. The use of figurative language ...
3. Sympathetic reproducing of other people's states of mind, particularly emotional states.
4. Inventiveness, the bringing together of elements that are not ordinarily connected ...
5. ... an ordering of experience in definite ways and for definite ends or purposes, not necessarily deliberate and conscious, but limited to a given field of phenomena. The technical triumphs of the arts are instances of this kind of imagination.

In stating the sixth and last sense of the word, Richards quotes a well-known definition offered by Coleridge in *Biographia Literaria*:

> The synthetic and magical power, to which we have exclusively appropriated the name of imagination...reveals itself in the balance or reconciliation of opposite or discordant qualities...the sense of novelty and freshness, with old and familiar objects; a more than usual order; judgement ever awake and steady self-possession with enthusiasm and feeling profound or vehement... The sense of musical delight...effects, and modifying a series of thoughts by some one predominant thought and feeling (Richards 1924: 190-191).

A closer examination of the testimonies quoted above will show that "the sense of novelty and freshness, with old and familiar objects" is one of the most recurrent themes in traditional Ohafia literary criticism. We find it expressed in statements such as the following, in which Kaalu Igirigiri boasts of the ability to recreate any story told him, so imaginatively that even the original narrator will respond to it with a "sense of novelty and freshness:"

> You have just told me that you are a native of Isuikwuato. Well, then, let us say that before leaving my house now you told me all about the way of life of your own people. When I come to sing about it, sometime in the future, I will do it in such a way that even you yourself will have to learn it all over again. That is why I say I am a better singer of tales than all my rivals.

Application and conclusion

I have, in three recent studies (Azuonye 1979, 1981b and 1983) demonstrated the value of the foregoing principles as touchstones for the criticism of the Ohafia Igbo oral epic songs: first, in a primary analysis of their characteristic features in relation to their social functions (Azuonye 1979); secondly, in the study of the artistic career and performance of an individual singer (Azuonye 198 ib); and, finally, in the discussion of those elements of the songs which remain stable in the midst of the changes wrought by individual singers in their renderings of various tales on different occasions (Azuonye 1983). On the whole, we have seen that these principles enable us to better appreciate why certain features are dominant in the songs. Take the question of their compact structural brevity and the plainness of their language, two qualities which stand out clearly in various texts of the songs available at the moment.[27] An outsider who knows nothing about the principles of clarity and creative variation in the Ohafia tradition of oral literary criticism can easily invoke evolutionist theories and interpret these as elements of the "primitive epic," the so-called ancestors of the epic, much discussed in the writings of European classicists and comparatists (see de Vries, 1962 and Kirk, 1972). Such an investigator will fail to recognize the fact that this quality of the songs is essentially a concomitant of aesthetic principles (shared in common by the singers of the songs and their hearers) which demand that they should possess such qualities. Keeping close to the narrative line without digression, avoiding "extraneous elements" so as to remain faithful to what the community regards as the "authentic" components of the historical tradition - these and other consequences of the principles of clarity (section 5 above) cannot but result in short, straight-forward and homogenous narratives.

Because of this quality of the songs and by reason of the principle of creative variation, each singer possesses a larger repertoire of tales and is expected to be able to render as many of these as possible on each occasion of performance (see section 5 above). Clearly, it is the briefer type of oral epic verse that is best

---

[27] See Azuonye, 1979, 1981a, 1981c and 1983.

suited to fulfil these principles; for the briefer the song, the more variety there will be in the repertoire of each singer and the larger the number of songs he can render on each occasion. Other points of special interest pertaining to the orality of the songs and their social functions have also emerged from the discussion.

But all these notwithstanding, it would be wrong to regard the four principles of evaluation identified and discussed as a special preserve of the Ohafia culture. "In discussions...with several Mandinka," writes Innes (1978:11), "it became clear that a bard is judged on a range of different factors such as his musicianship, historical knowledge, clarity of diction, use of language, fluency and coherence of narration." These are essentially a selection of principles which are, to all intents and purposes, congruent with some if not all the four principles noted in the axiological system of the Ohafia Igbo. Nor is there anything uniquely African in these principles, as the apologists for a unique African aesthetic would have us presume. Of Peig Sayers, the "queen of Gaelic story-teller" (1873-1958), the Gaelic student, Robin Flower, has written: "...she has so clean and finished a style of speech that you can follow all the nicest articulations of the language on her lips without any effort" (Dorson, 1975: xxii). This, clearly, is another way of putting the demand, in Ohafia oral traditional aesthetic, for "putting things in such a way that they will be clearly audible" - an aspect of the principle of clarity. By the same token, other aspects of the principles of the Ohafia Igbo oral epic are discernible in the testimonies of singers, critics and appreciators from other cultures, outside Africa. For example, the testimony of Egwu Kaalu of Asaga, quoted in our discussion of the principle of authenticity, is reminiscent of what Lord (1964:19) says of the practice of the Yugoslav bard, Stjepan Majstorovie: "He sang his songs according to the company he was in, since he had to please his audience or else expect no reward. Thus, when he was with Turks he sang Moslem songs or his own songs in such a way that the Moslems won the battles" etc.

The principles of oral literary evaluation in the Ohafia Igbo oral epic tradition are a particular selection of universal and perennial principles of art relevant to the evaluation of a particular genre, in a particular oral tradition, against the background of a particular historical and social situation.

Bibliography

Andrzejwski, B.W. and Innes, G. 1975. "Reflections on African Oral Literature." *African Languages* 1: 5-57.
d' Azevedo, Warren L. ed. 1975. *The Traditional Artist in African Societies*. Bloomington: Indiana University Press.
Azuonye, Chukwuma. 1975. "The Narrative War Songs of the Ohafia Igbo: A Critical analysis of their characteristic features in relation to their social functions." PhD thesis, University of London.

Azuonye, Chukwuma. 1981a. "Kaalu Igirigiri, an Ohafia Igbo Singer of Tales." Presented at the 6th Ibadan Annual African Literature Conference, July27 - August 1, 1981. Forthcoming in *The Oral Performance in Africa* (ed.) Isidore Okpewho, Ibadan: Spectrum Books Ltd.

Azuonye, Chukwuma. 198 lb. "The Collection, Transcription and Preservation of Igbo Oral Literature: Problems and Methodology." 6th Ibadan Annual African Literature Conference, July 27 - August 1, 1981. Forthcoming in *Kiabara: Journal of the Humanities* (University of Port Harcourt).

Azuonye, Chukwuma. 1981c. "The Traditional Epithet in Igbo Epic Poetry: Its Meaning and Cultural Significance." Presented at the Second International Seminar on Igbo Literature, University of Nigeria, Nsukka, August 12-15, 1981. Forthcoming in Igbo: Journal of the Society for Promoting Igbo Language and Culture, No.2.

Azuonye, Chukwuma. 1983. "Stability and Change in the Performances of Ohafia Igbo Singers of Tales." *Research in African Literatures*, Vol. 14, No. 3 (Special Issue on "Epic and Panegyric Poetry in Africa"): 332-380.

Bowra, C.M. 1957. *The Meaning of the Heroic Age*. Earl Grey Memorial Lecture, 37, Newcastle-upon-Tyne: Andrew Reid and Co.

Chinweizu, Jemie, Onwuchekwa, and Madubuike, Ihechukwu, 1980. *Towards the Decolonization of African Literature*. Enugu: Fourth Dimension Publishers.

Dundes, Alan. "Metafolklore and Oral Literary Criticism." *The Monist*, 50: 505-516.

Dorson, Richard M. (ed). 1975. *Folktales Told Around the World*. Chicago and London: The University of Chicago Press.

Ebeogu, Afam. 1981. "The Poetic Dynamics of the Proverbs: A Tradition for Western Igbo Poetry." Presented at the 2nd International Seminar on Igbo Literature, University of Nigeria, Nsukka, August 12-15.

Innes, Gordon. 1978. *Kelefa Saane: His Career as Recounted By Two Mandinka Bards*. London: School of Oriental and African Studies.

Kirk, G.S. 1972. *The Songs of Homer*. London: Cambridge University Press.

Lord, Albert B. 1968. *The Singer of Tales*. New York: Athenaeum.

Macebuh, Stanley. 1974. "African Aesthetics in Traditional African Mt." Okike, 5:13-25.

Nzekwu, Onuora. 1964. "Gino Ukwu Temple." Nigeria, 80: 117-126.

Okoreaffia, C.O. n.d. Elements of Igbo Language Studies. Nsukka/Onitsha: Published by the Author.

Okpewho, Isidore. 1979. *The Epic in Africa: Towards a Poetics of the Oral Performance*. New York: Columbia University Press.

Parry, Milman. 1928. The Traditional Epithet in Homer. In: Adam Parry (ed.) The Making of Homeric Verse: The Collected papers of Milman Parry. Oxford: Clarendon Press, 1-190.

Richards, I. A. 1924. Principles of Literary Criticism. London: Kegan Paul.

Thompson, Robert Parris. 1975. "Yoruba Art Criticism." In: d'Azevedo, 1975.
Vries, Jan de. 1963. *Heroic Song and Heroic Legend*. London: Oxford University Press.
Willis, Roy. 1978. *There was a Certain Man: Spoken Art of the Fipa*. Oxford: Clarendon Press.

Chapter 7

Poetry of the Urhobo Dance Udje[1]

- J. P. Clark

For us raised in the tradition of English poetry, especially that of the Romantics and Victorians, poetry is words moving across and down the page in precise line formation, all in well measured feet, falling to recurrent echoing sounds. Such poetry, composed in the head, after much magic inspiration, is set down by hand on paper, and directed at the eye that reads it. Perhaps, more than ever before, it has become a phenomenon determined by punctuation and stress, so that a passage that was prose before, by careful typographical re-arrangement and manipulation of stops and points of stress, emerges a glorious poem. A recent famous case that immediately comes to mind is that of the veteran Scottish poet Hugh MacDiarrmid creating his poem *Perfect* by uncannily chopping up a prose passage from the collection of short stories *The Blue Bed* by the comparatively unknown Glyn Jones. In case you think I am teasing, let me quote the piece that for over twenty years has been praised by professors and critics as the perfect Imagist poem Ezra Pound and others did not write but which in fact is a prose passage taken word for word from a short story:

> I found a pigeon's skull on the machair
> All the bones pure white and dry, and chalky,
> But perfect
> Without a crack or a flaw anywhere.
> At the back rising out of the beak,
> Were twin domes like bubbles of thin bone,
> Almost transparent, where the brain had been
> That fixed the tilt of the wings.

Poetry like this belongs to what we may call the 'literate tradition'. We have it on the joint authority of T. S. Eliot, the All Souls College scholar John Sparrow and the editor of the *Times Literary Supplement* that its chief props consist of the following: (i) 'A system of punctuation', (ii) 'A convention of stress's, and (iii) 'A convention of typographical arrangement'. Together these form even more than imagery, assonance and alliteration, the main mechanics of English poetry. Thus the *Time Literary Supplement* says 'our tendency to look for an underlying 'best' or rhythm in words arranged in verse form is a convention learnt from experience. It is because there exists this convention that any words arranged in verse form will at once set the trained reader of poetry, searching for a rhythm in them'. Which is all very fair, except that it is not all the fare.

There is also poetry of another convention. It does not go by lines drilled across and down the page; it does not follow any regular beat or metre as we know it in English poetry; nor does it sport repetitive patterns of echoes called rhymes. This poetry, also composed in the head with its due share of demonic possession, is not written down; nor is it directed at the eye. In other words, it is a poetry that does not depend on some celebrated system of calligraphics known as an alphabet, that magnificent cleric set-up without which no people, from the times of the Pharaohs to the present, can lay claim to any high civilization having for its chief shrine and repository a revelatory religion and a great body of writings or literature.

From the engendering of the word to its rendering as a poem, this is poetry that is delivered by mouth and aimed at the ear to move the whole body. In place of paper, it relies for its propagation and preservation on performance and memory. In other words, it is poetry that derives from a tradition quite different from that in which we have all been steeped from the first day either of our hands could reach over our heads to touch our ears on the far side, thus confirming us old enough to be entered by the teacher into his blue register and led into the ABC class. Its tradition is the aural or oral, as it is better known. Oral tradition then by our definition is no simple stock of fables or body of unsophisticated literary forms and works fit only for adolescent consumption. It is the convention of composition and delivery practised by pre-literate people as distinct from the 'literate tradition'.

With one, the phenomenon of word is auditory; with the other it has become conditioned to the visual. This is not to say in the 'literate tradition' readers of poetry do not at all apply their mouths and ears. But as the *Time Literary Supplement* again puts it magisterially, 'the effect will of course be 'visual' if we are reading silently, but it will be a mental reproduction of an auditory experience, and it will of course derive from a visual response to a spatial convention'. This is quite some gymnastics for the senses! "

We can liken this convention to that of classical music with its tonic notes, scales and keys. To be able to make sense of a score, not to talk of rendering it, one has first to acquire the necessary technique–which is a visual experience. Afterwards, one may perform the piece by hand or mouth for pleasure of the ear, another kind of experience entirely. Poetry of the literate tradition', although not written in any occult alphabet, seems to me therefore to demand and produce this special skill and experience generally accepted with classical music. And since this can come only by mental effort, it is a convention that has become associated with the intellectual class or so-called elite, indeed to such an extent as to turn poetry in literate societies into a rite for a cult increasingly on the decline.

In contrast, the effect of our kind of poetry is a direct audible one of words issuing from the mouth to delight the ear and stir the entire human frame in interplay with others in a close audience. In other words, ours is poetry that is spoken and sung by mouth or rendered to and on musical instrument. Today there are attempts to record it on tape and paper either in the original or in translations. *Yoruba Poetry* by Bakare Gbadamosi and Ulli Beier belongs to this, similarly *Akan Poetry* of Professor Kwabena Nketia and *Ewe Poetry* of Geormbeeyi Adali-Mortti. The new Oxford Library of African Literature offers from the Swahili, Somali and Ankole further evidence, irrefutable if often tongue-tied. And if I may mention my own effort in this field, *The Ozidi of Atazi*, a seven-day Ijaw saga now in process of publication in both the original and English version. The range then in 'oral tradition' as with the 'literate tradition' includes rhetoric, drama, lyric and epic–a living repertory for performance by the living people.

The poetry we are going to examine here happens in fact to be one that is sung, recited and spoken by mouth and with music. Accordingly, I shall call the three specimens I have managed to transcribe pure song-poems. By that I mean pieces dependent as much on melody as on word content. They are taken from the Urhobo of the Niger Delta, and all three derive from the dance *Udje*.

A word about this dance. Practised principally by male members of an Urhobo community, the *Udje* is straight entertainment. That is, it is all art and little or no ritual and religion. Unless you take into account the preternatural exercises to stop rain and provide fine weather for play, or the protective charms sometimes sported by leading players against rivals irate over uncomplimentary compositions made of their lives. As a matter of fact, feelings can on occasions run so high as to result in popular belief in crippling illness or loss of life for the *obo-ile* or doctor of songs. Such was the fate of my uncle. For many clans and towns among the Urhobo, *Udje* is the premier dance form, providing the peak of personal and collective display at seasons of festival. Performance is by age groups, wards and towns, each using the other as subject for its songs. While the dance steps and overall movements as well as the drumming are fairly uniform and standard among all dancers of *Udje*, its song-poems are diverse in form and material; it is these that spell out the identity of the individual artist, group or place. Therefore, a song-poem must be singular, telling and beautiful for one person, one ward or town to sing another to a fall, as the local saying goes. This then is topical poetry of social comment and inter-community competition composed by the season. But it is topical poetry saved from obscurity and turned into common currency for its immediate public as well as for the stranger from the outside by reason of its having been masterfully minted from particular ores to an alloy of fluid meaning and function.

Let us now listen to three examples of this poetry. They are only translations done in a rush and therefore still very much in a raw and rough state. As you very well know, all translations of poetry from one language to another can only be at best approximations to the fact, I mean the artefact that is the original. Remember that and you have leapt the immense gulf existing between the originals and my hurried translations.

The is the song-poem *Koyoyo*, a second one called *Akalaudo* and finally one composed by my mother's younger brother Debesi, dead some ten years ago. If only because charity begins at home and as Confucius enjoins us, we must begin by doing good nearer home, I shall offer you first my uncle's composition, *The Death of Okrika:*

1st Solo:

> Illness that struck Okrika,
>   gods of the sea all migrated to land,
> Illness that struck Okrika, gods of the sea all
>   migrated to land.
> Ikwinini cried to Abraham: What shall we so
>   water will turn into broth?
> So hob of fire will fall off our neck?
> Agbranran opening mouth replied
> They go at once for a healer,
> And a healer by name Itomu they called in
> Although healer's invitation fees they found no
>   money to pay.

2nd Solo:

> Money of Idolo so much rumoured about,
>   many thought it a great fortune–
>   this was what they dug up.
> But though drug after drug was administered,
>   the disease would not go.
> O tumour that attacked the rich,
> Lanced as for a pauper, was what brought the
>   patient death!

Duet:

Death that killed Okrika,

  dope of it dazed a whole city;
Death that killed Okrika,
  dope of it dazed a whole city;
Ofigo, on hearing at Umolo, with naked shift,
  answered the cry of death
O sister dead, I am caught with cold!

Solo:

And now see what spectacle!

Group:

Most painful to me are earrings of hers
  Nwachukwu minted
Similarly, the trinkets, the bangles Okrika wore in
  pageant to her groom–now what becomes them all?
                                            (Repeat)
Garters and anklets of Okrika have fallen on days of
  black; so too her silken scarves of card patterns.
Silver of Okrika from which she ate her bridal fare,
Ofigo in fury has smashed and broken them all.
When a District Officer goes home on leave,
  his servants seek fresh service.
Okrika was dead not three days
  when her bridesmaids rushed off to Ipipa,
And there resumed their rubbing of cam.
Okrika, arriving dead at the gateway of Urhoro,
  put finger to mouth:
Who killed her, she wept, with her also will go
Thus she took Edegware in tow.
A bat screamed past by night;
At break of day, if a mother loses a child,
Who would you say has taken life?
Ikwinini spoke boastfully of herbs;
Three days after Okrika fell dead:
God is it has eaten sasswood!
As I see Okrika's death, it is like a housewife
  who goes to the well,
Suddenly, rope breaks in two, and pot has
  fallen deep down the well.
Ukuujere swept straight from home,
With loud lament bewailed her lot:
I let children slip through my hands,
I let money slip through my hands,

> I let husband slip through my hands
> All life has frittered through my hands.
> Those of you going to Umolo, look, will you
> tell my brother Ofigo,
> Tell him to find the refund on my head so
> I'll return home and we two can set up keep.
> O sister who saved me from care,
> My sister who filled my solitude,
> Whatever tree sheds leaves, it is God has struck it.
> Greetings then, you at our spectacle!
> Ofigo gives alarm voice you run this way:
> And you of wards of Iroko, really you excel
> at singular deeds!
> Who goes by the name Okrika that passes away
> and you fall to feasting?
>
> Tray of reed with which Okrika displayed wares,
> lies now she's dead in front of some shrine
> Agbranran as administrator passed to Ipipa the tray;
> But Ipipa declining, swore he bears the burden who
> taps unripe palm.
> Children from deep down the district,
> surely you take death as a game of raffle
> At any time the lot falls ill
> Swiftly you shift it on to another.
> Yes, death that killed Okrika,
> migratory parrots going to roost,
> have broken their flight home
> For Agbranran with Kwinini, we hear,
> has clean killed their ward.
> Now Ofigo flings down himself that death of youth
> should pass one by
> But oh, do not weep!
> Had followers of the gods not done wrong
> Death had not come our way.

Next comes the much older poem *Akalaudo:*

> I am the tree akalaudo, and never shall shave head to the flood.
> Where I chose my talents I myself know
> It was up in heaven I chose my own lot
> Oh Urhoro, passage for them going and coming,
> God Osolobruwhe it is who gives man his blessing
> Which is enough to live by.
> Come then forswear yourselves
> Come then forswear yourselves
> I sing of my life, and all orphans of the earth

weep blind their eyes
Weep themselves weary and dry.
Of myself first I will sing before going outside
So the world may see and well assess.
This therefore is a song of home:
Now we have arrived, who delights in riddle let him remember
Did the rich show continence the poor had not taken offence.
Another year is up, and since wine there must be
 for festivity, the family descends on Akalaudo, on
 Akalaudo that they fled before –
Indeed talk of money is no small matter!
Day is child of God *Oghene*,
And nigh the child of God *Osolobruwhe*;
Therefore are they fruits of one womb.
But what Day did by Night that Night sulks till now
Clearly they remain daggers drawn.
One year now I have left home
My foes falling over themselves in joy
Our district has become theirs at last.
An orphan, if weak of tongue,
 will turn a servant to the family,
Will become slave to the community at large.
But they very well know, really they ought to know
 I am the tree akalaudo
And never shall shave my head to the flood.
Whatever fortune I chose to come with
I already know
It is in heaven I said I will set out thus
Oh Urhoro, passage of all going and coming,
It is God Osolobruwhe who does man his honours,
And this should be enough to live by.

And now finally, *Koyoyo* a song-poem also some generations back:

Leader:

Koyoyo is the name of the half-brother of Dogho
Sharks there are in water yet a small fish splashes
 all over the place
Koyoyo the never-do-well it is who now parades
 himself about town!
Staggered his thighs as a scarecrow's
 set up on a farm,
Thick blunt his teeth gums like the
 love-mound of Onoshete---

Hear me, I greet you all!

Group:

Koyoyo, here we come again,
   so get yourself prepared;
Your mouth scarlet like that of a kola-nut eater
Visitors to your mouth have all returned home,
   Koyoyo,
What is it befits man can be found on you?
Seen in his outfit on the wings of dance,
His head shows stuffed like a miner's with mud:
His mouth broken into many windows as is the
   African Church on the road to Amede.
Now, who is ugly can behave awkward.
Going to Fekunu, the fellow proposed to her
   they bear children together
Children they did not find, and Koyoyo has led
   the woman a merry dance to bed!
In shame Fekunu abused the man:
Look at his hook of a nose looped like the
   handle to a bucket,
His ugly parts a hundredfold:
Full drained he stands though people may not
   know it.
Possessed of a head huge as Egbebunu's
Observe his mouth eaten in half like the
   kitchen knife at a boarding house.
Truly, life of the fool is what fills the
   whiteman's purse with gold of the land!
Money on one banana bunch with that of a
   puncheon now stands at par,
Still Koyoyo brags and belabours himself.
Seizing a climber's rig, loudly he set off palm-nuts
   collecting at Ogidi
But price of one kerosene-tin of oil
   stands only at tu'pence!
On account of this the man will sweep
   and soak himself in early morning dew;
Indeed Koyoyo little minds what work he does.
So next he moves camp to the bank of River Ogu:
He cut *elala* and took them for *esa*
He cut *ilogen* and took them for *irhuaro*,
Vowing with these to dope the river of all fish!
Baits however did not catch and with every fish
   filtered through,

Go home, man, and thereafter live on water
undiluted!
Seeing Koyoyo eat, fear of fate all of a sudden
gripped me:
His nostrils dilating like a hare housewives have
drenched with kitchen-wash
Whoever saw him blossom in youth before age and
decay set hands on the wretch?
Thus Erhiurhere would cry:
Mother, I am gone adrift and lost.
Koyoyo to whom I was given in marriage,
Smell from his mouth will not let me eat my food.
Had I my own fortune, I'd leave his house;
Thanks to money I really would be gone by now.

Each piece above rides a theme that followed to the end reveals to the attendant spectator and listener a whole terrain of thought and life as intensely lived today by Urhobo people. The first explores the question of premature death, the second the problem of survival of the single man in face of rivalries, often unhealthy, that bedevil a polygamous household, and the last underscores with invective and humour the contempt and ridicule to which the poor and ugly stand exposed in society.

Let us, however tentatively, chart the course of this poetry. As you would have observed already, all three specimens I have given do not abide by the audio-visual aids and rules of poetry as you know them: lines, metre, and rhymes that you can follow with the eye across and down the page. No doubt this is an absence that many of us will consider a grave sin of omission! The rhythm here is one of common speech, common speech that drawing on special vocabulary tends in all the clans and settlements towards the twin dialects of Udu and Ujẹvben or Jeremi, dialects that many Urhobo regard as the most musical and ornate version of their tongue.

This leads us to another aspect of the quality of common speech in forming the poetry of Udje: its impregnation all the way by the melody line of the song that is at the same time the poem. So, that a piece comes to be loved as much for its melody as for the content of its words. Our concern however is with the words. It is because, even when forced apart from their twin companion of melody as we have tried to do in our poor medium of translation, they stand on their own feet and command appreciation that they constitute for us genuine examples of poetry.

In the Urhobo the language texture of each teems with tonal clusters and vowel harmonies. There are flights of phraseology and semantic glides that simply take the breath away. And elision and assimilation as well as assonance and alliteration occur in plenty. All these are verbal features and felicities calculated to charm like magic or medicine. You will remember the man who makes them is called '*obo-ile*,' that is the 'doctor of songs' much in the same way as another is 'doctor of herbs or medicine'. The latter in fact, like his Biblical compeer, knows all too well the potency and efficacy of the word. And the word, in all its manifestations in these song-poems, is what cannot be transferred wholesale and successfully from Urhobo to English, more so as one language is tonal and the other inflected.

Furthermore, there is in the one the use of words and concepts for which equivalents are hard to find in the other. An example is the Urhobo expression 'visitors to your mouth' which I could not resist retaining in my English rendering of Koyoyo. All it means in straight English is 'teeth'; but translated baldly like that, we miss the transitory nature of characters coming and going conveyed in the image of 'visitors'. As against this, I have had to replace, most reluctantly, the Urhobo deep expression 'birds of the dead' in *Akalaudo* by using the simple word 'orphan' which is what it means. A more common incidence of failure is that arising from the inadequate and cock-eyed education many of us have had. While we can toss off names like nightingales, deer and oaks, we do not know the names of our own birds, our animals nor of the trees in the forests and savannah that surround us. Because of this handicap I am still trying to make good, I have had to retain the Urhobo originals for the trees *akalaudo, elala, esa* and *ilogen* in my English translations.

But it is not all despair. I can here and now give you some idea of other elements vital to the structuring of each song-poem. The language of each works by images, metaphors, similes, proverbs and a whole gamut of figures of speech. *Koyoyo,* for instance, is a running stairway built on such literary devices. As the song says, the man's 'bad parts number a hundredfold'. He is an insignificant fish in the sea trying to pass for a shark; he is a scarecrow; his lips, worn down like a kitchen knife used by too many cooks, are red as with eating too much kola-nut; his mouth sports a row of windows as a church; he proposes marriage when he has not the means to keep a wife; he labours in the morning dew only to get a few pennies from European produce buyers; indeed there is nothing he handles with his crooked bands that does not become cursed, turning, unlike with Midas of the golden touch, everything into ash.

In the second piece *Akalaudo,* all is built around and insulated in one symbol and parable, that of a tree that remains evergreen come flood, come drought. The subject is the self that suffers yet survives in face of the most relentless persecution and opposition. And in these beautiful lines–

> Day is child of God Oghene,
> And Night the child of God Osolobruwhe
> Therefore are they fruits of the same womb.
> What Day did by Night that Night sulks till now
> Clearly they remain daggers drawn–

the antipathetic relation, that is, the close bond of blood and the bitter conflict existing at one and the same time between the protagonist of our poem and his own people, leaps to life before us.

With *The Death of Okrika* the structuring and devices show even more developed and complex. It is death that drove sea-gods to land; it carried dope that 'dazed a whole city'; and migratory parrots going home to roost, on hearing it, turned in their flight, running helter-skelter. Dope here, by the way, is the poison from the raw fruit of the piassava palm, wine from which brews our famous 'illicit gin'. Bailed from boats into the river at its source, it summons up all fish, making them die with the ebbing tide. And that was the effect the death of the girl Okrika had on the town Iyara. This is hyperbole pure and simple, but very telling indeed, and to the Urhobo poet and composer like my late uncle a ready tool. Single items of wear and wares like coral beads and crockery left behind by the dead are held up to highlight the loss that is the bride. The transfer of her fickle maids to another is seen in terms of cooks and steward to the white man on leave moving without feeling to serve and wait on another master. Incidentally, there is passage here which in its use of imagery always takes me to Gerald Manley Hopkins' fourth stanza of his famous dirge *The Wreck of the Deutschland*.

> I am soft sift
> In an hourglass at the wall
> Fast, but mined with a motion, a drift,
> And it crowds and it combs to the fall;
> I steady as a water in a well, to a poise, to a pane,
> But roped with, always, all the way down from
>   the tall
> Fells of flanks of the voel, a vein
> Of the gospel proffer, a pressure, a principle,
>   Christ's gift.

Now listen to this passage:

> As I see Okrika's death, it is like a housewife who
>   goes to the well;
> Suddenly, rope breaks in two, and pot has fallen
>   deep down the well.

Very likely you do not see any similarity between both verses, and probably there exists none: what with one so Christian and the other patently pagan! But in my mind's eye the abrupt end of the bride of Christ drowning in her ill-fated passage and pilgrimage coalesces with that of the bride Okrika dying suddenly in her pageant taken with other maids of her clan, all freshly dedicated to the fertility god Ogbaurhie. And their manner of coming and going combines for me this somewhat metaphysical picture of time running out on the wall and life spilling or collecting as a pool in the bottom and dark of a well.

Since time for us is also running out, let us touch upon one or two points more and we shall be finished. One is the remarkable use made of indirection, parallel statements, and innuendo in these poems. Everybody in the neighbourhood knew the young bride Okrika did not die naturally; nor was her death from the wound of her circumcision— which is abomination enough. She died before her time in her fullest flush at the instance of somebody's witchcraft and magic powers. But for almost through the whole narrative no guilty names are mentioned directly except by hints, suggestions and parallels as in this passage:

> A bat screamed past by night:
> At break of day, if a mother loses a child,
> Who would you say has taken life?
> Ikwinini spoke boastfully of herbs;
> Three days after, Okrika fell dead:
> God it is has eaten sasswood!

Secondly, the use of the accumulative utterance, often juxtaposed in quick transition and without connectives, as well as the use of repetition, a device that is organic to the song character of the poem. Ukejere lamenting the loss of her younger sister, states this in terms of the full inventory of her own life. It all amounts to precious little. Indeed with her sister's dead, the account shows irretrievably red. Thus she sings of herself—

> I let children slip through my hands
> I let money slip through my hands
> I let husband slip through my hands
> All life has frittered through my hands.

These are terrible things to happen to a person in Urhobo society and I suppose in human society anywhere. In these poem-songs sung at *Udje* we see them all terrifyingly set out.

In fact, the whole system of values, the entire social structure with its mores, its beliefs and practices stands revealed with skill in these songs, perhaps fuller and more convincing than any anthropologist can supply in several volumes of treatise. Incidentally, public morality here appears almost puritanic: love of good husbandry, of industry with profit and no loss, and condemnation at the same time of poverty, ugliness, and sloth. Indeed, between *Akalaudo* and *The Death of Okrika* there issues forth a strong shaft of religion lighting up all the way of life after death. The orphan Akalaudo declares that all his talents derive from God in the sky. As he carried them safely into the world through Urhoro, the passage for those unborn and dying, so will he tend them in this life in spite of fierce family jealousies and hostility. Predestination then is the thing, although unlike the Calvinist kind and more like the Catholic belief of free-will for the soul, fate or predestination for the Urhobo is the choice of talents a man makes himself when setting out on life's journey. If another, by supernatural means, like witchcraft, seeks to reverse the course and order as with the bride Okrika, then justice, as the victim demands and obtains at the passage to the other world, is *Osolobruwhe*'s the God Almighty. But this is another subject entirely, one for further investigation as I collect more specimens of the poetry of the Urhobo dance *Udje*.

Chapter 8

Egalitarian ethos in Tiv folktales

- *Tar Ahura*

In this chapter we argue that the Tiv folktales, usually transmitted through extemporization, function as a powerful mass medium which expresses the socio-cosmological rationalizations of the people. An egalitarian and republican people, the Tiv use their folktales to celebrate and uphold this spirit. Indeed, the folktales represent the most positive, life-affirming forces and values in Tivland. The tales and other fictive experiences serve the revolutionary ends of creating an alternative world in which those who use their powers and influence recklessly are exposed and brought under control. The medium of the folktale offers an additional avenue for denouncing class privileges and proclaiming the values of egalitarianism.

"Revolutionary consciousness" is used in the context of this discussion to refer to the awareness of human potentialities which help one to rationalize and to understand a social environment such that it can be transformed to advance a society to a higher level of achievement and fulfilment. The term "folktale" denotes a literary form in the oral traditions in which stories are told and performed to the home or village audience for the purposes of transmitting cultural education and counselling the members of that community.

Introduction

As introduction, an attempt will be made to discuss the Tiv people and their world-view which will help to illuminate the discussion of the Tiv folktales later.

Rupert East's description of the Tiv captures much of the essential qualities of the people. According to him, the Tiv

> are a stockily built, virile race of farmers whose two great aims in life are to fill their yam stores and granaries with food, theft homes with children; an

independent people, who have little respect for princes, and have never felt the need for cohesion, or obedience to a central authority, or unifying code. Cheerful, and on the whole contented, they are not afraid of tangible forces or misfortunes, though always on their guard against the great unseen army of evil forces and the occult machinations of their fellow men.[1]

This general portrait of the Tiv reveals the distinctive features of Tiv life in which everybody is assumed to be equal. This egalitarian ethos explains the violent resistance to the appointment of chiefs during the colonial era. The Tiv saw that such an appointment would automatically place one person in an undue advantage over others, thus making it possible for the person so elevated to use his position to exploit the other members of the community. Thus, even though the Tiv were reasonably large in number they never had a paramount political leader until 1946 when the first *Tor Tiv* (King) was crowned by the colonial administration. Authority to Tiv, as Eugene Rubingh has accurately observed,

> resided intrinsically in the very personality of the leader; he cannot be clothed with it artificially simply by an appointment. Furthermore, the authority is valid for those who are organically bound through their kinship to the holder of the authority.[2]

In other words, for the Tiv, kinship means quite a lot in social organization as will as in artistic discourse. For the individual to attain the status of leadership, such a person must have qualities that can endear him to his kin. These qualities include strength of will, rich witchcraft potential and, above all, the ability to set the *tar* (land) right. This last attribute is crucial since it is one that tests the individual's ability to contribute to the general good of the community.

As an egalitarian group of people the inter-personal relationship that is cherished by the Tiv is the one based on co-operation rather than individualism. It is everybody's duty to see that no member of the society unduly, towers above the others because to the Tiv, to be unique is tantamount to being evil. Thus the individual must remain one with the society and the universe. Everybody must be seen to be working in co-operation with one another for the good of the community. Individualism is detested because of its tendency to break social harmony as well as the cosmic order. Rubingh's view on this matter deserves to be quoted:

> Anyone who expressed unusual individualism, anyone who tended to move out from the time-honoured form of maintaining the serenity of the totality, was potentially dangerous to everyone. He was moving on untested pathways and might commit any number of unpropitious acts and upset the carefully

---

[1] Rupert East, *AKIGA's Story*, London: Oxford University Press, 1939, p. 13.
[2] Eugene Rubingh: *Sons of Tiv*, Michigan: Baker Books House, 1969, p. 64.

structured balance of the world.[3]

It is the desire for stability that results in Tiv's deep-rooted love for egalitarianism. If all things are equal, they reason, happiness will be achieved by all since all of them have similar expectations in life. These include: a home teeming with children, granaries and stores bursting with foodstuff and, above all, good health for all. It is only when people move outside these basic concerns and seek for other worldly things for self-aggrandizement that they begin to pose a serious danger to the well-being of the community as a cohesive whole.

Prior to the intervention of colonial values in marital affairs, the Tiv made sure that no one in the marriage covenant was cheated by another. That is why marriage by exchange was the most favoured system among the Tiv. The system offered an opportunity for continuity and balance in the social organization. In this system if man 'A' wanted to marry, he would get hold of his marriageable ward *(Ingyol)* and exchange her with 'B' marriageable ward. Physical beauty was never a priority in these exchanges because, to the Tiv, beauty is not only aesthetic but more often than not, also material. A woman who could produce many children was automatically beautiful especially if there were male children among them. In this arrangement, "A" would not ill-treat his wife because, if he did, "B" could equally mete out similar punishment to his wife ('A's ward) in retaliation. Similarly if 'A's ward produced five children for "B" while "B's" ward produced eight children for "A," for example, there was an obvious imbalance. The man, "B" had the right to demand a squaring up with "A" so that "A" could either give 'B' another ward to produce the requisite 'balance children, or give "B" his daughter (by "B's" ward). "B" would then give out the said daughter in marriage by exchange to his ward. This system ensured stability in the homes. It also encouraged filial respect as well as group unity.

It can thus be seen that the Tiv have a delicate and intricate social organization which is aimed principally at maintaining social equilibrium or balance. In this way exploitation of one person or group by another is made very difficult. The Tiv folktales help greatly in upholding the Tiv world-view and keeping down the urge by individual members of the community, to grow larger than the community.

Tiv and their Arts

Basically Tiv arts are symbolic and metaphoric projections of the Tiv worldview as examined above. Tiv folktales are a good example of this fictivization process. There is a robust tradition of all art forms in Tivland chief among which is the dance, which is the most popular form of entertainment and recreation. The importance of the dance to the Tiv has been well commented upon by

---

[3] Rubingh, *op. cit.*, p. 69.

Peggy Harper as follows:

> Dance has traditionally been an integral part of Tiv culture as an essential element in the ceremonies and rites that mark the significant events of a man's life.[4]

Dance, in fact, permeates all the Tiv performing arts, including folktale rendition and performance. The Tiv demonstrate such high creativity in dance and music that each historical occasion is one for a new dance idiom which captures the dynamic reality of the Tiv experience. Thus many Tiv dances are historical documentation of events as well as trends in Tiv history. Charles Keil is thus right in his observation that, among the Tiv, dance affirms life, negates death and the evil aspect of *Tsav* (witchcraft), demonstrates strength, the discipline, the power of its young men and women.[5] In fact, for the Tiv song, dance and tale-telling constitute the most positive, life- and value-affirming forces. That is why almost every compound tries to have one or two good drummers and an oral performer. Apart from providing entertainment for the community, Tiv songs and folktales are also veritable political tools when viewed from a materialist perspective. Many folktales and the accompanying songs are indeed rehearsals for a 'revolution' in that they provide performances in which powerful members of the community are usually ridiculed and disgraced by the less powerful, thus offering a moral lesson that in human life reckless display of power and influence to the disadvantage of the less fortunate is wrong and that society will not condone such acts. It is for this reason that, in settling a given dispute, song usually comes in handy as a tool that is wielded by the weaker party. Song is constantly used to lower or raise the personality of people in a dispute, to cry against oppression and to detract an enemy. In the world of Keil, the Tiv see and hear, know and understand the great value of song, drama and dance in the struggle for justice and equality.[6] Generally the Tiv are farmers who love their arts very much. Farm work nurtures the body while the arts nourish the intellectual and spiritual aspects of man. Both functions are almost equally important to the Tiv, hence separate periods are set aside for each of them. The arts flourish between the end of harvest and the beginning of rains. There is less farm work at this time and so there is ample time for artistic pursuits. Secondly, after harvest the stories and the granaries are full and since there is no material want, the artistic spirit can be let loose.

---

[4] Peggy Harper, "Tsough: A Tiv dance," in *African Notes*, Vol. 6, No. 1, Third Term, 1969-1970 Session.
[5] Charles Keil, *Tiv Song: The Sociology of Art in a Classless Society*, Chicago and London: The University of Chicago Press, 1979, p. 248.
[6] Keil, *op. cit.*, p. 258.

Tiv Folktales

Performance of tales is usually done after the evening meal. Initially they were told by the adult members of the household to the young, growing children as part of traditional education and counselling necessary for the upbringing of the youths. But in art the Tiv seem to be restless, always trying out new forms or variations from the existing ones so as to provide renewed interest in the arts. This is because the Tiv are generally very proud of their creative dynamism. This experimentation encouraged the Tiv to move tale-telling from the home to the village arena or square and made the rendition of these tales a competitive business amongst village bands, and sometime amongst villages or lineages. This dynamic adaptability is recognized by Harper, when she says that the "Tiv are remarkable for their ability to adapt old forms to new conditions and for their delight in inventing style."[7] The extension from the home to the village square did not, however, mean the end of tale-telling to children in the home. It was just an extension of the practice to a higher and finer level of performance within the popular culture because for the Tiv, art has always been a popular event which should satisfy the aesthetic needs of the collective. The Mexican Marxist aesthetician, Adolfo Vasquez, expresses a similar view to Harper's when he observes that:

> the destiny of art as popular collective creation is, therefore, connected to the destiny of man as a creative being...The restoration of the aesthetic or creative principle of human labour...creates favourable conditions for the development of the creative capacity of the people in arts.[8]

As stated earlier, the Tiv folktales are an expression of the Tiv's social, political, cultural and economic values. They also express communal hopes, aspirations, frustrations and general world-view. Because of this thematic amplitude, the stories are a common stock of each community's oral memory. However, the rendition of each tale provides for stylistic innovation and meaning. Philip Noss has remarked this feature In Gbaya story-telling events:

> The tale that is received from the father is a kind of common denominator of the literary creativity of a people, the most viable genius being the creativity displayed by the narrator as he tells and reinterprets the ancient plot and theme.[9]

---

[7] Harper, *op. cit.*, p. 54.
[8] Adolfo Sanchez Vazquez: *Art and Society: Essays in Marxist Aesthetics,* London: Merlin Press, 1973, p. 279.
[9] Philip A. Noss, "Creation and the Gbaya Tale," in *Artist and Audience: African Literature as Shared Experience* (eds.) R.K. Priebe and T.A. Hale, (eds.), Washington D.C.: Three Continents Press, 1979, p. 3.

Part of the narrator's creativity is seen in the ability to recreate historical experiences so as to be able to bring to awareness the need for the attainment of certain objectives. Some performance events are deliberately cued for the purpose of enriching the utopian dreams of the community so that it can envision, in artistic terms, self-redeeming projects. The Tiv folktales really argue against those who contend that tradition is a static phenomenon. The tales present tradition as a pattern of growth or dialectic. This is because, to the Tiv, nothing is static and the Tiv indeed love to see change. That is why the narrator of the tales usually falls back on his genius to give the tales new forms, expressions and interpretation.

As has been pointed out earlier, the central function of the tales is to help in ensuring egalitarianism and fair play in the society. People who try to move away from the communal norms in order to assert their individuality are roundly chastised and corrected through examples of similar characters in the folktales while those who work for the good of the community are valorized. That is why many Tiv tales are structured on a binary scale of struggle between vice and virtue, with virtue triumphing over vice.

For example, there is a tale about the Hare and his family during a famine that spread through the entire land. The hare, being unequal to the challenges of the famine, decides on a very selfish policy. He calls his wife and tells her that from now on it is everyone to himself or herself. If he, the husband, finds food, he will eat it alone. If his wife finds food she should eat it with her children. In this way the Hare disclaims all responsibility to his family. His wife sends for food from her mother who lives in a different country. In response the mother sends the daughter plenty of beans. The wife cooks and eats the beans with her children whilst the Hare watches, hungry. One day the wife cooks a delicious meal of beans, leaves it on the fire and together with her children, goes to the stream for water. In their absence the Hare consumes all the beans. On their return from the stream they find no beans in the basin. The hare denies any knowledge of the theft. In frustration his wife sends to her mother who dispatches a drummer to her daughter to detect the thief. A big gathering of the animals is called and the search for the thief begins. The drummer beats the drum and sings a song to the effect that if it is the Hare that has stolen the beans his stomach should distend abnormally. If, however, it is the Hare's son (whom the hare has implicated in the theft) who is the culprit, his stomach should distend slightly. As the dancing progresses the hare's stomach distends abnormally causing him tremendous pain until finally he confesses to the theft and is consequently relieved. Meanwhile, the hare however, has been disgraced before the entire animal world.

The moral message in this tale is that selfishness does not pay. The Hare, unable to perform his family and social responsibilities, decides that the best course lies in a selfish policy of each to himself and possibly, God for all. It is a policy which capitalist societies, especially in the developing nations, have pursued to the detriment of the less privileged. The hare thinks that as a man in a male-dominated society, he could afford to sacrifice his family in times of difficulty in the hope that he would always get a new wife and children if he survived the famine. But his efforts vitiate the Tiv's concept of social justice and public good. As noted earlier, the Tiv abhor individualism and the hare's tricks here indicate an attempt to move out from the time-honoured framework for maintaining group harmony. For this he has to be disgraced before the entire animal kingdom. As can be deduced from the tale, it is the pursuit of personal gains that is responsible for many social ills in the society. We are, therefore, called upon to shun social ills occasioned by individualism so that members of the society can come together and work for the good of all.

The belief in the general good is central to the Tiv sense of justice and agrees, in a large measure, with the Tiv world-view. Generally the Tiv conceive of themselves as a series of concentric circles arranged with the smallest circle in the middle aiding the large ones surrounding it until the largest circle is reached. The individual is this smallest circle while Tiv, the progenitor in the race, is the largest circle. In between the two circles, that is, the smallest and the largest, are the people, animals, the land, ancestors and the spirits. The smallest circle represents the individual because to the Tiv the individual is inconsequential, if not dangerous, and is surrounded by forces much superior to him while Tiv, the group, is superior to all. These concentric circles emphasize the continuity of Tiv in which every member of the community, including the tangible and intangible elements, is conceived as forming an important element in the continuum. Within this continuum, every human being, animal, spirit, etceteras, is as important as the other in bringing about peace, good health and fertility of the land as well as of the women.

The revolutionary import of Tiv folktales, it would be recalled, is to warn against the emergence of social or economic classes whose members can use their unearned influence to the detriment of the other members of the society. One is thus surprised when Hagher asks the question as to "whether it is possible to observe a link between the composite nature of Tiv art and its so-called egalitarianism.[10] Tiv arts, as we have said again and again, are a reflection of the Tiv world-view, and egalitarianism, as we have also emphasized, is a composite part of the Tiv world-view. The Tiv folktales, in particular, serve this purpose the most. The following tale will serve as a useful illustration:

One day, the king of all the animals called a general meeting of the animals to discuss ways of maintaining peace between the animals. He suggested that to achieve the desired peace, no animal should engage in an argument with the other since it is such arguments that usually cause brawls among the animals. The animals accepted this and enacted a law prescribing the death penalty for

---

[10] Iyorwuese Hagher, "Performance in Tiv Oral Poetry" in *Oral Poetry in Nigeria,* U. N. Abalogu, Garba Ashiwaju and Regina Amadi-Tshiwala, (eds.) Lagos: Nigeria Magazine, 1981, p. 38.

any offender. One afternoon Mosquito came into Hare's hut and told the Hare how Zebra had annoyed him on the way by stepping on his wings. In anger, Mosquito continued, he kicked Zebra with his leg and Zebra fell over. Hare broke into laughter, wanting to know how Mosquito with his tiny legs could kick Zebra to a fall. Thereupon Mosquito called out to the other animals to come and hear how Hare had started an argument with him. Hare was pronounced guilty and was to be executed. Hare pleaded that he be killed across the river and the request was accepted since that was his last wish. Elephant was so excited at the prospect of Hare's imminent death that he suggested Giraffe should carry Hare on his head so that Hare would not pull off a fast one and escape. Halfway through the river Hare shouted on Giraffe to stop: he had just stepped on a large fish and would like to carry it along. Elephant burst out laughing, asking how possible it was for Hare seated far up there on Giraffe head to step on a fish in the river. Hare called the attention of the other animals to the most recent crime committed by Elephant and asked that since Elephant's crime was the latest, Elephant should be hanged first. The animals agreed that Elephant too should die. However, the animals decided to abolish the law without killing anybody.

This story raises many fundamental issues that touch on social inequalities. Central to these issues is the question of law and order. Should separate sets of law be made for the poor and the rich as we witness in our society today? When this tale is told in detail it reveals a folk knowledge about how the elephant, representing the rich and mighty, actually encouraged the enactment of this law as a tool against the Hare, who has been his traditional enemy, and in this context, the underdog. The Elephant, by virtue of his size and power, regards himself as the king of the animal kingdom. But the Hare, relying on his brainwork, always undoes the Elephant. For this the Elephant has mortal hatred for the Hare and uses every opportunity to do away the Hare. That is why Elephant is in favour of this law. He knows that the Hare will never take any unsatisfactory explanation or happening without questioning it. There is a dim possibility that the Elephant even had a hand in the planning of the Mosquito's story. The Elephant thus proposes the law not knowing that the same law would apply to him. Consistent with Tiv egalitarianism, when the Elephant also commits the offence, the animals agree that he too should be hanged since the law is made for all members of the society. Yet what is more fundamental in this story is the realization by the animals that law is made for man and not man for law; so when a particular law becomes inimical to the interests of the people it is supposed to serve, it should be dispensed with. The lesson from the tale is that one should never use opportunities or privileges to maltreat the less fortunate members of the society for, as the Tiv say, when you throw out ashes the wind brings them back to you, that is, whatever bad you plan for another will come back to you. The tale thus tries to create an alternative society in which the mighty are undone; in which those who want to create classes based on privileges are made to abandon such intentions for they have no place within the traditional Tiv society. We can, therefore, see that Tiv folktales are serious political tools when analysed from a materialist point of view. What we find in this tale and many others of its type is a rehearsal for a revolution. The performances in the tale create exemplary situations in which powerful members are ridiculed and brought to disgrace by the less powerful. As stated earlier, this offers as moral that in human life reckless display of power to the disadvantage of the less fortunate is abhorrent to the traditional Tiv society and the society will always meet the challenges and prevent abuses and set the larger society on the path of human dignity.

The traditional Tiv society is conscious of the fact that folktales, as a form of art, help to mould people's convictions and character through the aesthetic experiences that the tales evoke. Thus the folktale sessions offer opportunities for experiences rather than illusions. Most of the folktales are historical but the histories are usually interpreted positively to give the people hope. The folktales constitute creative social criticism and they function as powerful means of raising people's hopes so that they can continue to struggle for social justice. Their overall effect is to convert the audience from passive recipients of received truth to active protagonists in creating an artistic experience. The following tale illustrates the struggle against social injustice and how this struggle is aimed at giving the downtrodden confidence in their abilities to overcome injustice.

One hot afternoon, the Lion lay sleeping under a shade on the foot of a mountain. A big stone chipped off from the mountain and rested firmly on the Lion. After struggling unsuccessfully for three days to extricate himself, he finally begged the Pig that was passing by to help, for besides the weight of the stone, he was almost dying of hunger. The Pig agreed to help lift the stone after getting assurance of safety from the Lion. When the Lion got his freedom he decided that he was too hungry to allow the Pig to go uneaten. The Pig pleaded and reminded the Lion of his earlier promise. As the argument continued the Hare arrived at the scene and after listening to both sides, decided to adjudicate in the matter. He told the Lion that before he could say anything he wanted to see the position in which the Lion was before the Pig arrived so that he would be able to ascertain his claims justly. The Lion lay down where he was and the stone was placed on him. The Pig and the Hare then moved away, leaving the Lion with his problems which finally killed him.

Here the Lion represents the powerful and rich members of the society for whom the less privileged members of the society represented by the Pig and the Hare exist to satisfy their gluttonous appetites. It is the fate of the less privileged to sweat for the Lions of the society and the payment for their sweat is death or disregard at the whims of the Lions of the society. To the latter the less privileged should exist only when the Lions of the world allow them. However, the intervention by the Hare suggests that the survival and safety of the downtrodden depends on their solidarity as a class.

Conclusion

The egalitarian traits in Tiv tales testify to the strong residues of socialist thinking in pre-capitalist societies in Nigeria. As in most art forms of other African peoples, the universe fictionalized in the tales predates the present era in which individualism has supplanted communal well-being, at least at the level of national politics. It does appear that in the world of the remote past, which the tales recreate, there were already faint signs of social differentiation. However, the resolution of the conflicts of tales that explore this theme shows that, at all times, the display of privilege was considered an anti-social behaviour which attracted penalties. Thanks to colonialism and capitalism, Tivland remains a rural and underdeveloped backwoods of modern Nigeria. As a consequence, the ethos of a peasant society has survived into the modern era and thus given a contemporaneous relevance to the themes of the folktales. As borne out in Tiv wars of resistance against feudal and colonial hegemony, there is a large reservoir of communalistic thinking in Tiv tales which can be creatively unitized by agents of revolutionary change.

Chapter 9

Social and ethical values of story-telling among the Berom of Plateau State

- Abu Abarry

Though some scholarship has been carried out on the history, geography and ethnology of the Berom of Plateau State of Nigeria, not much seems to have been done on their rich and interesting oral literature.[1] The neglect and relative obscurity suffered by their literature and those of their neighbours on the Plateau seem to emanate largely from the pre-occupation of many earlier collectors of oral literatures in the former northern Nigeria with the culture of the major ethnic/linguistic group like the Hausa/Fulani, the Kanuri and Nupe. So while the literatures of these latter groups are well-known, those of the minority groups like the Berom remain virtually unnoticed and unexplored.[2] Thus the conception of oral literature in northern Nigeria created in the public mind would seem to derive mainly from the perception of the major groups. This approach gives only a partial picture of the region's cultural complexity and its total verbal artistic resources. For example, the status of tales *(Tatsanuyoyi)* among the Hausawa is lower than that of stories in many African societies, including the Berom.[3] There

---

The research on which this chapter is based was partly funded by the Research Grants Committee, University of Jos (Faculty of Arts), 1983/84.

1. The Berom are one of the major ethnic groups in Plateau State of Nigeria; and the largest single ethnic entity in the capital, Jos. Traditionally they are "animists" and ancestralogists but in recent times many of them have embraced Christianity. In the past their chief occupations were farming, hunting and working in the tin mines. However, today they are found in virtually every sphere of public and private business. See J. G. Davies, *The Berom - A study of a Nigerian Tribe, 1942-49*, Jos, pp. 40-49. H.D. Gun, *People of Jos Area of Northern Nigeria*, London, International African Institute, 1953. T. M. Baker, *The Social Organization of the Birom*, unpublished thesis, University College, London, 1954, and Kiyoshi Shimuzu, *The Language of Jos Division*, Centre for the Study of Nigerian Languages. Ahmadu Bello University, Zaria, 1975.
2. Neil Skinner, *An Anthology of Hausa Literature*, Zaria, Northern Nigerian Publishing Company, 1980, pp. 1-7.
3. L. Bouquaux, *Les Instruments de Musique Birom*, Paris: Societe D'Edition, Les Belles Lettres,

is, therefore, a critical need for a more vigorous, objective and systematic collection, analysis and publication of the oral traditions of the ethic minorities on the Plateau in a way reflect their culture, their unique social outlook and traditional aesthetics.

The Berom have a thriving tradition of oral literature which, among other forms, consists of tales, songs, chants, legends and myths. But to attempt to consider all such poetic and literary formulations here would be both premature and presumptuous. What follows, then, is a modest attempt to highlight only one of the above named genres, namely, the folktale which will be critically analysed for its social and ethnical values. This would logically lead us into an examination of its context, themes, generic features and performance techniques. Because we are also interested in the impact of the form on its audience, a consideration of its sources of appeal and influence in Berom society seems clearly in place, in the examination.

Story telling is a delightful social drama among the peoples of the Plateau. Despite developments in formal education and a marked increase in literacy rate, this traditional art is still vibrant today. Its recreational uses apart, it is a powerful communicative medium that reflects the people's historical origins, social organization, religions beliefs and ancestral wisdoms.[4] Being a repository of their values and worldview, the stories clarify social attitudes and promote national pride, group cohesion, and cultural continuity. They also reflect the people's fears, hopes and aspirations. Moreover, the participation of the narrator and his audience in story-telling sessions also serves as a vent through which pent-up feelings, whether aroused by unfulfilled dreams, fear, hatred or aggression, may be ventilated.

The Berom perform their tales usually at night, preferably on a moonlight night, and in a compound or an open space adjoining a number of houses or huts. Depending on the type of tale, the audience may consist of adults and children of both sexes who sit around the fire in a relaxed atmosphere. The performance may be accompanied by a traditional six-stringed Berom harp called "dohem," the two stringed "Yom," or the reed flute "molo."[5] A session begins with a peculiar opening formula consisting of a "signature tune", chanted in monotone. This is immediately followed with a warning from the narrator that what he says, thereafter, should be regarded as basically fiction or fantasies with a tinge of realism. The audience's suspension of disbelief is thus secured till the end of the stories when the narrator "returns to earth."

1982, p. 17.
[4] This is typical of tales in traditional societies. See S. Vansina, *Oral Traditional*, London, Routledge and Kegan Paul Ltd., 1965, pp. 154-159.
[5] See O. N. Ihekole, *Birom Folktales,* Jos: The National Museum, 1980, pp. 17-81.
S.B. Fom *Folktales Among the Berom of Plateau State,* unpublished Long Essay, University of Jos, 1984, Appendix, and *Ya Berom: Berom Folkstories,* Jos: Berom Language Committee, 1975 pp. 25-29.

Typological and thematic dimensions of Berom tales are both interesting and instructive.[6] There are basically two main tale types, the fictitious/didactic tales *(Ya)* and the "true" tales *(Ha)*. 'Ya' tales may be either fictions or didactic, with entertainment and pleasure being the main objective. As such they are more popular, and their performances are more frequent and open in the society. In the main, they are mildly satirical but devoid of strong and deliberate moral sentiments. The stories are dominated by animal characters with the Hare as the stereotyped hero. He is the master trickster, cunning, agile, resourceful and naughty. He exploits his craftiness and wit to subdue stronger, bigger and more ferocious creatures. Comparable to the Spider among the Hausawa, and the Tortoise in Yoruba and Igbo tales, the Hare occasionally over-reaches himself, and gets worsted or even ruined in his schemes.[7] The didactic aspects of 'Ya' tales are meant to promote certain models of behavioural conduct, emphasize the observance of social custom, and instill healthy moral principles in the audience. It may be light-hearted or solemn, and the characterization may consist exclusively of animals or humans and occasionally of both. The Hare is nearly always the central character.

The "Ha" tales are, however, quite different both in content and status from those described above. They are generally regarded as "true" or "real" stories and the characterization consists exclusively of humans. The tales usually seek to explain past historical events or enable the people to comprehend serious philosophical problems of life pertinent to the Berom worldview, history, and customs.[8] They are serious tales which seek to probe the origin and nature of things, both tangible and intangible. As such they reflect the philosophical and religious outlook of the people, their value system and attitude to basic human issues.

The sessions at which such tales are performed are neither festive nor public. They are usually more seclusive and solemn. The audience is select, and the performance never takes place before "strangers," nor can its Content be carelessly divulged. This publishing restriction emanates from the assumed affinity of the tales with the ancestral and supernatural worlds. The recurrent themes of the 'Ya' and didactic tales include the quest for survival, eternal conflicts between good and evil forces, the Berom notion of justice, and their powers of patience and endurance. Some tales comment on significant episodes in the life cycle such as birth, adolescence, courtship, marriage and death. Those relating to the latter describe the elaborate obstacles deliberately placed in the path of a man who wishes to marry a woman he loves. Such a suitor may be required to undergo a series of ordeals or even magical tests before he can

---

[6] B. K. and S. W. Walker, *Nigerian Folktales*, New Brunswick, University Press, 1961, pp. 15-17; H.A.S. Johnston, *A Selection of Hausa Stories*, London, Oxford University Press, 1966, pp. 7-21.
[7] Mariede-Paul Neirs, "The Peoples of the Jos Plateau, Their Philosophy," See also L. Bouquianux, *Textes Birom*, Paris, Societe D'Edition, Les Belles Lettres, 1970, pp. 342-355.
[8] Ruth Finnegan, *Oral Literature in Africa*, London, Oxford University Press, 1970, pp. 342-355.

qualify for his bride's hand. He may also be required to sow and harvest crops or even cultivate a large farm in a day. All these stringent measures are meant to test the sincerity of the suitor's professed love, his courage, industry and general readiness for leadership of a marital home. Other themes explored in the teles are vanity and pre-occupation with beauty for its own sake. Beautiful girls are often portrayed as being morally weak, deceitful or malevolent, who sow discord among intimate friends, kinsmen or even communities. The tales emphasize grace, modesty, moral principles and industriousness as desirable and permanent values to seek in a prospective spouse. Other ethical and moral qualities highlighted include love, trust, friendship, loyalty as opposed to deceit, guilt, escape, and punishment.

The animal characters that feature in the tales are similar to those found in other parts of Tropical Africa.[9] The more recurrent of these are the Hare, Tortoise, Spider and their larger dupes such as the Hyena and the Elephant. The Hare is once again the stock hero. He is small but has a wit or wisdom far beyond that of the other animals. Opposition to societal hierarchy in the normal world or a perversion of its values are expressed in this trickster and his adventures. But tales may also be spun around ordinary and extraordinary beings who may be named (Davou, Chu) identified by type (a man, an old woman, a ghost, a devil). Some relate to personified objects such as parts of the body, vegetables or even abstractions like hunger, truth, or death. And in all cases, both human and animal characters are shown to be fallible irrespective of their reputation, status, family background or special attributes.

However, apart from the central animal figures, other creatures play a secondary role. Some of these have already been noted. Others and their stock attributes are described below. The Lion is royal, strong, powerful but not particularly intelligent; the Elephant is heavy and ponderous but rather slow; the Hyena has brute force though stupid; the Leopard is untrustworthy and vicious, and is often tricked in spite of his cunning. The Antelope is portrayed as clever, the Deer is stupid. With a few exceptions these animals are generally represented as humanoids operating in essentially human settings.

All such interesting themes and ideas are communicated to the audience in such a manner as to persuade and influence them. The tales show forthright realism which tends to see life as it is. There is no sentimentality or wishful thinking. But such projections of stark reality are balanced by the use of an aesthetically patterned language, splendid characterization, narrator-audience rapport and creative spontaneity. The Berom story-teller knows that his skill and artistry are determined by his imagination and relations with his audience, and he strives not merely to actualize a tale but also to transform it into a unique

---

[9] This is reminiscent of story-telling among The Ga of Ghana, though the Ga's is more dramatic and stylized. See Abu Abarry, "Oral Rhetoric And Poetics: Story-Telling Among the Gas of Ghana," in S.O. Asein, ed., *Comparative Approaches To Modern African Literature,* Ibadan: Ibadan University Press, 1982, pp. 24-37.

experience. He brings his intellect, skill, and experience to transform general outlines and themes sanctioned by tradition. This facilitates the rendition of a tale in a much more delightful manner than he had imbibed it. He skilfully manipulates core-clichés episodic patterns, oratory, narrator-audience dynamics, drama, songs, and his own mood to ensure a successful performance with a lasting impact on his audiences. His deliberate exploitation of the "Signature tune" and opening formula to awaken interest and establish rapport and a suspension of belief in the audience has already been noted.

The narrator normally uses any of the following stock expressions as introduction to the tales: "One day Dog met Hare on the way to the river, "Once there lived a beautiful girl...,a farmer...or a hunter...;" "Dog and Hen went farming in the bush." Sometimes, he prefaces the narration with a moral precept or a philosophical statement or question: "Don't depend on too much beauty ...;" "Many people feel that quietness is a sign of quilt. What they do not realize is that it can also be a sign of innocence ," "Hard work is always rewarding ...," "How do you think Death came into the world?..." and so on. The quest motif technique may also be used: "One day Dog went to the forest to fetch firewood. While he was chopping the wood, the axe-head came off and fell into a stream. Dog began to cry..." The plot may also begin with a dramatic dialogue: "The wife of Weasel bore a child, and then called the husband and said, 'Go and get the kind of clothes which I like and bring them!' The husband listened to his wife's words, and said, 'What kind of clothes do you like?' The wife replied her husband 'I like the hide of an Elephant'..." A few stories begin with a direct ethnic identification tag: "We Berom also have tales. This tale is about Hare and Sea Elephant ..."

Once the tale is underway, additional strategies are introduced and skilfully orchestrated for maximum impact. For example, the narrator does not indulge in any elaborate description of scene, action or character. But traditional practice has established conventions by which such literary outlines are fleshed out and embellished, leading to greater understanding and heightened effect. Another effective technique is the exploitation of the associational power of words, symbols and images from human, natural and supernatural worlds. For instance, through the narrator's imaginative use of mythical and animal characters lessons are drawn from nature, a satirical point is driven home, wisdom and human folly are exposed, and the inner working of the mind is explored.

By skilful voice modulation, appropriate theme, mood and character are captured by the narrator. He may also induce abrupt breaks and pauses in narratorial flow for special effect. Through tonal variation, dialogue and gestures, he dramatizes the action to highlight the significance of the roles of the various characters. Structural and phonological repetitions are imaginatively deployed to suggest duration of an act, length of time or space. They may also be utilized to stress the dramatic importance of certain episodes. Onomatopoeia is freely used to capture the sound or movement of objects while ideophones lend vividness and elegance to the narrative discourse. For example: Hare threw his sac into the water "Poss," and his stick, "trass;" the Canoe capsized "Wuu rip..." and the Hare runs "reng...reng...reng;" an egg breaks "puss... puss...," and a dove soars in anger *"pwa ... pwa ...pwa."*

The pronoun "We" is exploited to emphasize ethnic affinity and to stimulate joint participation with the audience in the experience of the tales. This device enhances plausibility, endowing the tales with an air of actual occurrence. Audience participation is effected also through the songs that are intermittently sung by both the narrator and the audience; the songs reflect theme, mood, characterization, climatic movement, and the moral of a tale. Moreover, members of the audience interrupt with comments, exclamations of amazement or terror, and show empathy with sympathetic and intelligent nods in the course of the performance. And after taking the audience through a number of episodes that move inexorably toward a climax and a resolution, the story-teller may end with an implied or stated moral thus: "This is why we should not depend too much on beauty..." or "This is the end of the story about the Lion and the Hare ..." or "That was how Death came into being..." There are no elaborate, stylized closing formulas typical of Hausa and Yoruba tales, for example.[10]

As we have seen, story-telling is indeed a serious and dynamic art form among the Berom. It is replete with interesting themes, ideas and concepts which contain the social, cultural and philosophical values of the people. It is educative, integrative, recreational and therapeutic. It validates and criticizes conduct and strengthens social institutions that promote cohesion in the society.

---

[10] Hausa tales end with "Kurungus Kan Kuzu." meaning "If not for Kuzu, I would have lied. But they are lies any way," and the Yoruba, "That was the point to which I followed the action and returned," and the audience responds, "Welcome."

Chapter 10

Feminism and oral literature: the example of Igbo birth-songs

- Afam Ebeogu

Introduction

Any discussion of the dominant forms, types or generic categories of oral poetry among the Igbo of Nigeria that omits the birth-songs would be neglecting a significant feature in the dynamics of oral creativity.[1] For these birth-songs are the product of a particular biological class or group in the society and, as scholars of the sociology of literature have recognized, the theme and form of a piece of literary work may bear witness to the origin and production of that literature.[2] It is the intention of this essay to examine these songs, first, from the point of view of their possible typlogical classifications, and then to show how, no matter how classified, these birth-songs are an extremely convenient avenue for Igbo womenfolk to express their understanding of the norms and values of the Igbo society, and to comment on some of these norms and values.

---

1 It is instructive that two fairly serious recent collections of Igbo oral poems devote considerable space to birth-songs. (See F.C. Ogbalu: *Igbo Poems and Songs*, Onitsha: University Press n.d., pp. 14-62 - this edition was later to re-appear in a revised form as Mbem Na Egwu Igbo. Macmillan Nig. Publishers 1978, pp. 19-62 Nnabuenyi Ugonna: *Abu na Egwuregwu Odinala Igbo*. Longman Nigeria 1980, pp. 105-117).

2 This has been the persistent argument of Marxist literary critics, as is illustrated in Terry Eagleton's *Marxism and Literary Criticism*, London: Methuen 1976. But non-Marxists, like Richard Dorson, also recognize this fact, particularly in the area of folk literature which, argues Dorson, was originally class-motivated. (See Richard Dorson: "Africa and the Folklorists:" *African Folklore*. (ed) Richard Dorson, Bloomington: Indian University Press 1972, p. 3). The "sociology of literature" is the focus of Rene Wellek and Austin Warren in chapter 9 ("Literature and Society") of their book: *Theory of Literature* (Harmondsworth: Penguin 1976, p. 94-109) in which the issue of treated from the point of view of an apparently non-partisan ideological perspective.

The word "feminism" here is not being used in the rather restricted sense of female protest and campaign for emancipation in a situation of male domination and chauvinism in the society.[3] Rather "feminism" is expanded to mean "women's point of view" expressed in an uncensored medium. The issue is not necessarily whether what the women say is radically opposed to established conventions, but that what they say represents their own honest, realistic and constructive perception of order and stability in the society. In handling our argument, we do not lose sight of the fact that what we are discussing is literature; that the medium of the women's feminism is literary, and that the stylistic demands of the literary genre provide the structural framework for the feminist message.

Igbo birth-songs: a typology of situations

A classification of any piece of oral literature by situation is intended to mean that kind of taxonomic exercise that relies on the occasion of the performance of the literature. Many authoritative treatments of oral literature in Africa have been based on this kind of typology,[4] and with justification. For it would appeal as if it is the occasion of performance of a piece of oral literature that determines its form and structure, and even if one insists on a typology of form and structure, as is normally required for written literature, one would ultimately be drawn back to considering how relevant the form and structure are to the occasion of performance. Our concern is not to prefer any one type to the other, but to recognize all possible typologies as they relate to Igbo birth-songs.[5]

---

3 This brand of feminism as an organized ideological movement is the subject of Maren Lockwood Carden's *The New Feminist Movement* (New York: Russell Sage Foundations 1974). It is true that feminist movements probably enjoy the greatest tempo in the United States of America and Europe, but this phenomenon has become the subject of serious discussion all over Africa. In Nigeria, the existence of women liberation and women rights movements is reflected in the formation of modern exclusive women organizations, such as the National Council for Women Societies, the Women in Nigeria and other professional women organizations, whose major objective is raising the consciousness of women to their rights as individuals operating outside the framework of female stereo-typing institutionalized over the ages by an essentially male-dominated ethic. See Nina Mba: *Nigerian Women Mobilized: Women's Political Activity in Nigeria, 1900-1965* (Berkeley: Institute of International Studies; University of California 1982). For a literary perspective of the phenomenon of feminism, see Lloyd Brown: *Women Writers in Black Africa* (Connecticut: Greenwood Press 1981; Maggie Humm: *Feminist Criticism*. Sussex: The Harvester Press 1986; Carole Davies & Adams Graves (eds): *Ngambika: Studies of Women in African Literature*, Trenton, New Jersey, African World Press Inc., 1984).
4 This is Ruth Finnegan's major approach in her book: *Oral Literature in Africa* (London: OUP. 1970). It is not surprising that three major collections of oral poems of the Igbo are faithful to Ruth Finnegan's pattern. (See Ogbalu *op. cit.,* Ugonna *op. cit.,* and Nwoga & Egudu: *Poetic Heritage* (Igho Traditional Verse) (Enugu: Nwankwo-Ifejika & Co., 1971).
5 The sixty or so birth-songs studied for the purpose of this essay were collected by me and my

Birth songs are surely situation-bound and, in all cases, there is a relevance of the occasion to child-birth. The most common situation is the birth of a child. When the event takes place, other women raise a jubilant alarm called *oro*, which instantly brings every woman to the scene of the birth. A good example of an *oro* runs thus:[6]

Hia hia hia eeee!
Hia hia hia eeee!
Oe oe oe eeeee!
Oe oe oe eeeee!

Onye ji ego bia nga o o o!	Whosoever has money let the person come here!
o mura gini e e e!	Did she give birth to what?
Nwa nwoke o o of	A male child!
Nwa nwayi a a a!	A female child!
Oe oe oe ooo!	Oe oe oe ooo!
Chineke I mee Ia o o o!	God you have done well!

This initial song, which is half-sung and half-chanted in a high-pitched tone by as many women as are present, usually has an instant effect. Every woman in the community leaves whatever she is doing and runs to the direction of the song. Immediately, the women form a circular dancing formation, and begin to perform as many birth-songs as are possible during the period. The duration of performance differs from occasion to occasion, depending, for instance, on the ability of "the man of the house" to provide impromptu entertainment for the performers, and in the number of women present. The duration, however, could last for one or two hours, and as the earliest callers leave, they tend to be replaced by new arrivals.

But there are other occasions for the birth-songs. These include all the major landmarks in the chain of rituals of thanksgiving and purification involving childbirth, in which groups outside the nuclear family are involved. These occasions include: the 'naming' ceremony of the child which takes place twenty-eight days after the birth of the child (in Christian homes, the tendency is for the ritual of baptism to replace this occasion); the first "outing" ceremony of the mother of the child after childbirth - *i puta n'omugwu* - which takes her to the

---

1983/84 students of African Oral Literature. Whereas my collections were from only one Local Government Area of Anambra State of Nigeria, those of my students were from various areas of Igboland. The similarity in all the songs is very obvious, so much so that, in most cases, the words used are the same, except for dialectal differences. There are however cases of modifications of songs-in-performance, as we shall illustrate later.

6 "One mystical trait of the Ibo(sic) woman," says Sylvia Leith-Ross, "is the connection between the vertility of the soil and the fertility of their bodies." (*African Women*, London: Faber & Faber 1939, p. 234). Nina Mba echoes the above when she says that "in most Igboland, women were concerned with fertility rites and child birth ritual   (Nina Mba, *op. cit*., p. 32).

communal market where she fraternizes and frolics with her fellow women in the open, rubbing camwood and powder on them and receiving gifts in return; the presentation of "maternity meal" *(nri omugwo)* to the maternal grandmother of the new-born child, and, in some areas of Igboland, during puberty rites for girls who would soon be initiated into womanhood. The rationale for performing the birth-song in the last-mentioned occasion stems from the belief that such a rite is a fertility rite in which the girl's primary value as a "bearer of children" is affirmed.[7]

Our typology of situation thus shows that birth-songs are a women's affair; they are occasioned by a women's event - the delivery of a child and other activities ancillary to births. The performance of the songs is almost exclusive to women. There is only one known occasion in which men take part in the actual performance of birth-songs, and this is when the women, through the medium of their songs, invite the father of the child to come out and demonstrate his own role in the whole affair of "making a child." The following song illustrates such an occasion, and the reference to mat, or wrapper in modern versions of the song, echoes the sexual act that results in the pregnancy.[8]

Olee nwoke mere iha a!	Where is the man who has done this?
Olee nwoke mere iha a?	Where is the man who has done this?
Nwoke mere ihe a	The man who has done this
Ya were akwa o ji aru ala	Come out with his sneaky wrapper
Bia gbara ayi egwu	Come and dance for us.

Even from such a song as above, it is clear that the performance is a woman's affair, and that the women's invitation to the man to dance for them is a way of ridiculing men's tendency to pretend to be aloof in the midst of the excitement over a successful childbirth.

A typology of medium

---

7 In modern times, women's dancing groups usually include well-known birth-songs in their choral repertoire. These songs are however contemporary forms of hymn-based songs or traditionally-based, carefully composed, rehearsed and adapted choral formats, at times structured into well-choreographed dances. Because of this restructuring of the forms of such originally pure birth-songs, we hesitate to include the miscellaneous occasions of their performance in our situational typology.

8 An Igbo Proverb says that "you do not get a wife for a man and at the same time provide him with a mat" (*a gaghi alunye nwoke nwayi zutaraya ute*). This is usually used to remain a man that there is a limit to which he can rely on the benevolence of other people. Even if the "bride-price" for his wife had been provided by another, a man is, at least, expected to perform the sexual act himself.

We have tried to establish the occasion for most birth-songs among the Igbo, and a logical follow-up is the medium. "Medium" here suggests "the how" of the performance of these songs; the manner in which they are realized. These songs are essentially vocal performances[9] accompanied by dance and, but not always, improvised musical instrumentation. They are mostly "songs' in the actual sense of their being sung, rather than in the general sense of "poetry-as-song which Preminger talks about.[10] The only occasion in which a birth-song acquires some chant-like quality is during the *oro,* which we have mentioned earlier on.

Usually the women dance in a circular formation as they sing the song, and the performance is accompanied by abundant histrionics, the degree depending on the content of the song. For example, in the songs in which they make allusions to the sexual act as being a glorious one, (since it results in pregnancy and childbirth), the women make very suggestive gestures which some people might consider obscene, indicating the location of the organs, and sometimes providing a gestural description of such organs that are involved in the procreative act, and the nature of the physiological movement that has precipitated the occasion. The following is an example of such a song whose total effect depends greatly on histrionic accompaniment:

Ndoghari ukwu lee e e e	The twisting of the waist
Ndoghari ukwu	The twisting of the waist.
Ndoghari ukwu lee e e e	The twisting of the waist
Ndoghari ukwu	The twisting of the waist.
Ebe ndoghari ukwu turu ime	The place the twisting of the waist results to pregnancy
Ndoghari ukwu	The twisting of the waist.
o bughi ebe udoghari ukwu muru nnwa	Is not the place of twisting of the waist results to childbirth.
Ndoghari ukwu	The twisting of the waist.
Ihe ndoghari ukwu e mee la	A twisting-of-the-waist event has taken place
Ndoghari ukwu.	The twisting of the waist.

As the women dance to this song in a circular formation, they take measured leaps towards the right, during which they hold their hands on both sides of their waists, twist the waist, expand the gap between their legs, and point at the position of their genitals, all in rhythm with the song and the dance. Every

---

9 Some scholars of oral literature would use the vocal performances of poetry as yardsticks for a model classification of oral poetry. (See Ulli Beier & B. Gbadamasi: *Yoruba Poetry.* Ibadan: Government Printers 1959).

10 Alex Preminger (ed): *Princeton Encyclopedia of Poetry and Poetics.* (London: Macmillan, 1974, p. 780).

woman in the group joins in the demonstration, no matter how reserved or shy she might be considered to be in her private life. The performance is, therefore, understood by all as a special event in which song and the rhythm of dance combine with symbolic action to maximize communication. It is a medium that affords the women an opportunity to express a group consciousness, for, as Ernst Fischer has observed, "rhythmical movement assists work, co-ordinates effort, and connects the individual with a social group."[11]

There is a general air of hilarity during the performance, and this attracts an appreciable number of audience as the time of day and the nature of the season would allow. Most members of the audience are men and children, for even where there are women, who for reasons of old age or ill-health, cannot join in the performance, they throw in occasional phrases of praise and promptings to the performers, thus affirming their spiritual identification with the essence and mood of the performance.

A few men could make uncomplimentary and humorous remarks about the immodesty" of the women, but this is usually done in the spirit of the satiric and the overall comic mode of the performance. For no one ever forgets what has occasioned the performance: somewhere inside the house - or in the maternity or hospital in modern times - a child is lying in the cradle. Thus the moment is one of demonstration of divine blessing. An Igbo proper name ("Ifeyinwa") says that "there is nothing as valuable as a child," an expression which most of the songs repeat, echo or imply. Any anger or gesture of disapproval during the performance would be construed by the community as ingratitude directed against the mystical force in charge of fecundity - in the case of the traditional Igbo society, the Earth goddess, Ala.

Forms of Igbo birth-songs

Because these birth-songs are realized through the medium of vocal music and dance, there is a heavy reliance on the time-line, repetition of segments, adhesive markers and the lengthening of vowel sounds. Igbo birth-songs confirm John Nketia's conclusion that "the use of time-line (a recurring rhythmic pattern of fixed duration or time span), which clarifies the regulative beat, is a common feature of rhythmic organization in some African traditions."[12] It does not matter whether the line contains essentially only a word or whether there are up to ten words. What is important is that the duration in time in all the lines in the stanza is the same. What happens is that where the line has very few words, as in a refrain which could be a repetition of just one word, the word is lengthened through the use of significant, ululating vowel sounds so as to make the line have

---

[11] Ernst Fischer: *The Necessity of Art*. (London: Penguin 1963) p. 35.
12 J.H.N. Nketia: *The Music of Africa*. (New York: W.W. Holt 1974, pp. 131-132.

the same length as when many words are used in the same breath-period. While the lengthening process through the use of breath is on, the rhythm of the dance is of course maintained, so that in the end, all the lines have the same number of beats determined by the rhythm of the music.[13]

In our formal analysis of Igbo birth-songs, we identify three categories. The first category is that group of songs where the song is made up of only one stanza, and no line of the stanza, possibly other than the last, is a total segmental repeat of the other. The second category is that where the song is again made up of only one stanza, but where alternate line of the stanza are merely repeats of one syntactical segment. The third category is where the song is made up of more than one stanza, each stanza having either the form of the first category or that of the second. We all examine these formal categories more closely, with a view to identifying their rhythmic structure.

In the first category, the song is made up of only one stanza, each line of the stanza, possibly other than the last, not exactly the same syntactical unit as any other. The stanza is repeated as often as possible in the course of the performance, until the women decide to move over to another song. All the women in the group sing the song in unison; there is no solo as distinct from the chorus. The following is an illustration:

Unu no n'ulo eme gini e e e?	Are you in the house doing what?
Ayi no n'ulo amuga nnwa o.	We are in the house delivering children.
Ka mgbe ututu, ka mgbe anyasi	Since morning, since night
Ayi a muola nnwa o o o	We have delivered a child.
Obi a dila ayi mma o o o	We are now happy.
Ayi no n'ulo amu nnwa.	We are in the house delivering children.

In this six-line stanza, the last line is a repeat of the second. It is a significant repeat, because it is an affirmation of the central idea of the song - that the primary duty of the women is to give birth. Our study of many of the songs in our collection reveals that there is nothing fixed about the number of lines in the stanza: there are mainly four-line, five-line, six-line, seven-line and eight-line stanzas, the four-line stanza being the most common. Where the number of lines is even, the last may or may not be a repeat of one of the lines, but where the number is odd, the last line is usually a repeat of one of the lines which embody the central idea of the song. It is easy to determine what constitutes a line in the stanzas if one is able to listen to the song *in performance*. This is because the

---

13 O.R. Dethorne uses the "breath-pause" as the criterion for determining the constituents of a line in African oral poetry. (See Dathorne: *The Black Mind: A History of African Literature*. Minneapolis 1974, p. 63). 5. Babalola's treatment of the forms of the Yoruba *Ijala* admits the validity of such an approach. (Adeboye S. Babalola: "The characteristic features of outer forms of Yoruba Ijala chants:" *Odu* 2 (July 1964), p. 34.

line, in performance, is identifiable as one syntactical unit constituting a breath-groups, *and it is determined by one complex unit of dance steps*. In other words, the line-metre of the song is determined by the rhythm of the dance accompanying the song. Where, therefore, there are fewer words in some lines than in others, all the singers have to do is lengthen either the last vowel sound of the song, or add a vowel sound different from the last but easily assimilable by it.

The second category of form of the birth-songs is that in which the song is made up of only one stanza, but the alternate lines of the stanza are repeats and also refrains. The following song illustrates this category:

Onye n'onye kuru omumu?	Who and who have carried the child?
Omumu ka-mma o o o	Childbirth is better.
Onye n'onye kuru omumu?	Who and who have carried the child?
Omumu ka-mma o o o	Childbirth is better.
Ihe no ngaa kuru omumu.	Everybody here has carried the child.
Omumu ka-mma o o o	Childbirth is better.
I kuru omumu i muta omumu.	Carry the child and get a child.
Omumu ka-mma o o o.	Childbirth is better.

Most often, all the women in the group sing all the lines of the song, but at times there is a solo-and-chorus identification where only one singer in the group - the one who usually beats the improvised musical instrument - renders the major lines, while the chorus sings the refrain. Where this happens, the tendency is for the length of the stanza to be determined at the discretion of the solo performer, who could create more of the major lines.

The third category is the one featuring more than one stanza. We find, however, that each stanza is of the form of the first category, and it would therefore be unnecessary to illustrate this type. What needs to be added is that this form of more-than-one stanza song is not as dominant as the single-stanza forms, and that of the two single-stanza forms, the second, which features many repeats, whether as refrains or not, is the most prevalent.

The issue that arises from our discussion of the forms of Igbo birth-songs is that of composition. There is no doubt that the nature of the situation of these songs gives them a great communal significance. Like most forms of folklore, the songs are "due to the collective action of the multitude and could not be traced to one individual influence."[14] This conclusion is justified by the fact that the songs do not seem to "rely on fixed texts that performers memorize."[15] The songs are communal creations of the women as one group, and the unpredictable nature of pregnancies and births makes it impossible for the womenfolk to have

---

14 J. Frazer: *Folklore in Old Testament*. (London: Macmillan 1919). Vol. 1, p. 9.
15 Robert Kellog: "Oral Literature:" *New Literary History*, 1:1, 1973, p.57.

any specific "trial version"[16] of the songs before they are publicly performed. It is rather the repeated performances of these wrongs, and the fairly standard typology established by the occasion of their performance, that give the forms and words of the songs some fixed pattern. This fixedness is however fragile, and Albert Lord's theory of "themes" and "formulas"[17] of oral epic composition would seem to apply very much to Igbo birth-songs. To that extent then, the songs have "fixed texts," but there is no doubt that at any single performance, there is evidence of some kind of creation-in-performance, often aided by the factor of liberties associated with solo performance. It is significant that the many cases of repeats of expressions in the songs are usually associated with a chorus, who cannot take the liberties of textual variation. The songs examined in this study come from various parts of Igboland, and are both very traditional and at the same time fairly modern in origin. But there is no doubt that they belong to the same genre of oral poetry. Where there are some differences in two or more versions of the same song from different areas of the culture, and performed by groups with different religious orientations, the differences have been in the area of dialect and lexical items.

For an illustration: in a popular birth-song, the women argue that the birth of a child is an opportunity for them to receive all kinds of gifts from their husbands. The gifts mentioned in some versions of the song include cloth (of unspecified nature), meat (of unspecified nature), yam, rice and motor car; while in some other versions of the same song the gifts listed include beef, salad, "Etorika" (a kind of very expensive georgette material in modern times), Mercedes Benz car and *ntu oyi* (air-conditioned car). There is no doubt that the former version would be performed by women whose values have a traditional orientation, whose demands are modest and congruent with the material circumstances of the community, while the latter version would be performed by fairly young wives of our contemporary times, who are in a position to expect from their husbands such expensive gifts as *utu oyi* and Mercedes Benz cars!

But their form is the same: both are the one-stanza song of our second category, where the major lines constitute a list of the gifts expected at childbirth, while the repeated lines, in one way or the other, denote "the act of giving." In one of such songs, the modern version expresses the positive act of possessing *(a gan enwe* - "I will have") in place of that of expecting *(dim ga-enyem* - "my husband will give me") which the more traditional version expresses. These versions indicate different marital attitudes: the first perceives obligations from a husband as mandatory, whereas the second sees such obligations from the point of view of benevolence.

Our examination of the forms of Igbo birth-songs establishes that the songs belong to women entirely, and afford them exclusive opportunity to make any

---

16 G.S. Kirk: *The Songs of Homer* (Cambridge: Cambridge University Press) 1962, p. 55.
17 Albert Lord: *The Singer of Tales*. (Cambridge: Mass.) 1960.

comments they are inclined to.

Themes of the birth-songs

We shall proceed to examine the content of these songs in order to be able to classify them as birth-songs solely from the evidence of their content.[18]

One of the most pervading themes in the songs is the idea of the child being the primary justification for marriages. These songs emphasize this idea unambiguously. The refrain for one of the most popular songs insists that the beauty of womanhood lies in children *(mma nwayi bu nnwa);* and another song wants to know whether there is any woman who has any greater priority than children *(A nam aju gi si/Mkap gi odi ole/Na-abughi nnwa?).* The best way to satisfy a husband is to bear children for him *(Nwayi muo nnwa, obi aloo diya o);* and it is only the child that gives a woman a sense of belonging in her husband's place *(Onye muru nnwa nodu na be di ya ribe ngwodongwo).* Childbirth preserves a marriage, for no matter what a woman does, she is safe as long as she has children *(Ihe omega, ihe omege/Gbaghara ya na-omuru nnwa ohuru);* childbearing justifies a woman's womanhood *(Onye nwunye ya na-amutaghi nnwa/Odi ka o lutaa nwoke ibe ya n'ulo -* "when a man's wife fails to get a child, it appears as if the man has married a fellow man"). Getting a child is a duty a woman must perform *(Ezigbo dim e wela iwe na-agam amutara gi nnwa -* "My good husband, do not be annoyed for I must get you a child"), while a barren woman is a thing of ridicule in the community *(Dedem i meela mou nnwa/Asi na-imutaghi nnwa/Ha gara ime gi ihe ochi -*"My dede, you did well to get a child/Had it been that you had no child/They would be laughing at you").

It is easy to see from these songs that the Igbo woman does not regard childbearing as an evil, but rather, a thing of joy as well as an obligation. This is to be appreciated in the context of a society that believes strongly in reincarnation, in this kind of society, consequently, the woman is regarded as an important link in this recurrent cycle of human existence.[19] Not to bear children is to create a weak link in the chain of human regeneration; and this would amount to a disaster for the family, the clan and the community.

This probably explains why the woman in the society, as is expressed in these

---

18 For an anthropological discussion of this view, see R.N. Henderson: *The King-In-Every Man: Evolutionary Trend in Onitsha-Ibo Speaking Society and Culture.* (New Haven: Yale University Press 1972, p.214; C.K. Meek: *Law and Authority in a Nigerian Tribe,* London: OUP. 1937, pp. 7'71; A.E. Afigbo: "Culture and Fertility Among the Igbo of Nigeria: a Historical Investigation:" Igbo Standardization Seminars, 1974-75 (mimeo). F. Arinze couches his view in a biblical language when he says that "the Ibo woman could well say with Rachel: 'Thou must need give me children, or it will be my death,' Genesis 30:1" is *Sacrifice in Ibo Religion.* (Ibadan: Ibadan University Press 1970) p. 40.

19 See P.A. Talbot: *Some Nigerian Fertility Cults.* (London: O.U.P. 1927), pp. 6-89.

songs, sees her role as a bearer of children as heroic. The woman really makes the world what it is *(Ala mara nna/Ala joro njo/Obu nwayi na-edozi ya* - "If the land is good/If the land is bad/It is the woman who is responsible"), and no matter what a man is, he is the product of the woman, as this defiant piece illustrates:

O si n'ole?	Where did he come from?
O si n'ikpu.	He came from the vagina.
O si n'ole?	Where did he come from?
o si n'ikpu	He came from the vagina.
Ma nnwa beke?	The white man?
O si n'ikpu.	He came from the vagina.
Profeso?	The Professor?
O si n'ikpu.	He came from the vagina.
Presidenti?	The President?
O si n'ikpu.	He came from the vagina.
Govano?	The Governor?
O si n'ikpu.	He came from the vagina.
O si n'ole?	Where did he come from?
o si n'ikpu.	He came from the vagina.

And in a gesture of strong protest and complaint, the women accuse the man of indolence. For the women do not only go through the rigours of childbirth, but they are also always busy, while the men deliberately subjugate them: The rigours of childbirth then become a metaphor for the suffering and endurance of the womenfolk:

Kpuru kpuru bu na ngbe mbu	Hardship is a primordial thing.
Kpuru kpuru nnwa.	The hardship of childbirth.
Umu nwoke na-eje ozi soso otu onwa,	The men do real work only once in the month
Ma a muchaa nnwa	For after the birth of the child
Emechaa ha ewere anyi dowe n'azu.	Again they relegate us to the background.

One is not surprised that their songs go to the length of trumpeting the hazards and heroism of pregnancy and childbirth. The pregnant woman bears the greatest suffering in the world, living on the edge of fear and uncertainty, and yet the people think she is in a period of glory *(Nwayi d'ime taga afufu n'uwa/Umu uwa si na o riwe la/Ebe oji obi n'abo a gariga)*. The many birth-songs that plead with death not to "kill a woman in her pregnancy" *(onwu e gbula nwayi n'afo ime)* compare pregnancy to a journey to the brink of death. Elsewhere it is described as being similar to climbing the precarious top of the giant iroko tree

(Ekele diri Chineke/Onye mere ka o ritue n'udo/N'ihe na ya bu elu oji/A dighi ofere - "Thanks be to God/Who made her climb down safely/For that iroko top/Is not a plaything"). Many of the songs present the whole business of pregnancy and childbirth as being akin to the uncertainties of investment in the market, in which one stands as much chance of losing terribly (dying) as of gaining (delivering safely). In these songs there is constant reference to the "market of the night" *(ahia abali),* "the market of the bed" *(ahia bedi),* and the enviable risky business like the climbing of a hill *(Ugwu nnwa di ebube/Onye na-adighi ike/A gaghi ari ugwa nnwa* - "The hill of childbirth is glorious/Whosoever is not strong/Cannot climb the hill of childbirth"). And the songs often ridicule men for being party to a venture the risk of which only the woman bears (Ihe ayi diri abuo me/Ahia mgbaji ukwu/Emerega a si otu onye bute ibuya - "The thing two of us did/The market of the breaking of the waist/Later only one person was asked to carry the load").

Perhaps one of the most thematic characteristics of these songs is their unapologetic sexual overtones and innuendoes. Ordinarily these women are uncommonly modest, even to the point of prudishness. But their performance of the birth-songs suggests that the songs provide them with an opportunity to exhibit a surprising degree of 'obscenity' both in words and gestures. But constant reference to the sexual act in the songs is not frivolous, for the women seem to argue that the sexual act is a creative act which leads to the generation and regeneration of the human species.

The sexual content of the birth-songs includes not only the obscene gestures earlier described, but also brazen references to the female genital organs as the proud "road" through which the child emerges into the world from the dark, mysterious recesses of the womb. Thus, the woman is happy that the final points of the transition which a child traverses before it becomes human are the organs around the pelvis *(ikpu).* The sexual organs are therefore very useful organs because they bring out riches into the world. One of the songs can therefore frown at the prostitute, because she is misusing her organs for mere satisfaction of the sexual urge (ideophonically described in one of the songs as *in nwanchoronwu).* The sexual dance *(egwu ukwu)* which results in child-birth is a dance of beauty *(egwu oma),* and the joy of sex is not a frivolous one, but one of suffering *(o di uto n'afufu).* The noise made by couples in the sexual act (all ideophonically described as *biam biam,* or *biribiri,* or *ngwodongwo)* is the best of noises, because it leads to pregnancy and childbirth. As one of the songs put it very unashamedly:

Shaka shaka   *Shaka shaka*
Ihe anyi gbatara n'ute   The agony we won on the mat.
Piom piom   *Piom piom*
Ihe anyi mitara n'onu   The game we won from kissing.
Kiri kiri   *Kiri kiri*

Ihe anyi chitara n'ochi   What we gained from laughter.
Uru bedi, uru bedi wu nnwa. The benefit of the bed, the benefit of
                         the bed is the child.
These sexual overtones and innuendoes, expressed through gestures of the sexual act, through the liberal mention of the sexual organs, and through the use of ideophones, seem to indicate that the women see the occasion of their performance as a moment of liberty and freedom from societal restrictions. Mircea Eliade discusses this phenomenon of "sexual liberties" on a universal, mythic dimension when he argues that

> the secret behind it is the revelation of fecundity . . . (they) are nor erotic, but of a ritual character: they represent vestiges of forgotten mystery and not profane enjoyments. we cannot otherwise explain the fact that in societies where modesty and chastity are obligatory, the girls and the women behave on certain sacred occasions ... in a manner that terribly shocked the observers ... This complete reversal of behaviour - from modesty to exhibitionism - serves a ritual purpose, and is therefore in the interests of the whole community. The orgiastic character of this feminine mystery is explained by the need for a periodic abolition of the norms that govern profane existence, in other words, the necessity of suspending the law that bears like deed weight upon the customary, and of re-entering into a state of spontaneity.[20]

We cannot improve on Eliade's observation, except to add that we find it applicable to the performance of Igbo birth-songs.

An off-shoot of the sexual licence which some of these birth-songs reveal is the occasional affirmation in the songs that the occasion of childbirth is an opportunity for the expression of the solidarity of the women. A good number of these songs actually mention the community where the childbirth has occurred, and, in all cases, what follows is a call to all the women to assemble, for one of them is on a maternity outing and therefore needs comradeship. One song affirms that the event of one childbirth by one woman is a thing of glory and concern for all womanhood, and each second line of the three of the four stanzas of the song expresses this idea in a different way - *o churu ndi ibe ayi ura* ("she has kept all our colleagues awake"), *o kwara mum mwayi ibe ya oru* ("she has stopped all her fellow women from going to work"), and *okwara umu nwayi ibe ya ahia* ("she has stopped all her female colleagues from going to the market"). Indeed, a good number of these songs express some degree of group defiance by the women, like the one that calls on all women in the homes to come out and celebrate a birth, for no matter what they do as a consequence, nobody can penalize them *(ife anyi mere n'okwu a diro ya).* A similar song asserts that they - the women - are out (during the performance) solely for the purpose of exhibiting their pride and importance, for which reason they would not tolerate

---

20 Mircea Eliade: *Myths, Dreams and Mysteries.* (New York: Colophon Books 1959), pp. 212-219.

any trouble *(Anyi biara ebea ikpa nganga/Onye enye n'anyi torobulu)*.

While the women express their non-conformist views; however, they never keep their focus for long off the primary value of the event: the value of the child. It is for this that a good number of the songs emphasize that it is not enough to have a child; it is equally important to give the child much adequate training as would enable it to be useful in life. The most popular expression in many of these songs is that whoever gets a child has the responsibility of training that child *(o muru nnwa zua nnwa ya)*, an observation which many early scholars in Igbo studies have made.[21] No amount of suffering is too great in the training of a child, and one of the songs expresses delight in the women collecting firewood, fetching water, going to the market, all for the joy of not only making sure that the child survives but also that he or she is well-trained. Another song in the same vein, lists some inconvenient sources from which women eke out some livelihood for the benefit of training their children: the picking of palm nuts, having to go without supper, doing all types of odd jobs, keeping sleepless nights, and ignoring sickness. Another song includes the expenditure on books, school fees, school uniforms and bags as part of the sacrifices of bringing up a child.

But the women do believe that the effort is worth the trouble, because they will eventually reap the fruits of their labour. The child, after all, is being trained so that it can become an adult and then take care of the mother. No wonder that a song says that the joy of having a child is best experienced at old age *(mma nnwa bu na nka)*. As one of the recurrent phrases in the Igbo kolanut prayer puts it, "we bring up our children so that they can look after us" *(Anyi zua nnwa, nnwa a zua anyi)*. It is not surprising that a good number of these songs go to the extent of listing all imaginable good things of life which a mother expects from her children in future, and the unmistakable impression is that this expectation helps to sustain her hope in life.

While these songs emphasize the need to give a child adequate training, some of them do not fail to mention that, eventually, the child in fact belongs to the community as a whole, for which reason the business of training him is a communal responsibility. Thus many of the songs insist that whosoever shall hear the cry of a child must respond immediately, for it is not only one person that owns the child *(O nuru akwa nnwa gbata/Na o bughi otu onye nwe nnwa)*. Some of the songs mention and praise the community "which owns the child." One song says, specifically, that whoever undertakes the training of a child alone will never recover from the fatigue *(Onye naani ya na-azu nnwa/Ike gwuru ya)*. The last line of the first stanza of a three-stanza birth-song in answer to a question as to "who owns the child," affirms that it is the *Ama ala*, the highest legislative body in the typical Igbo village group and thus a symbol for the conscience of the whole community *(Ama ala nwe nnwa!)*.

---

21 Leith-Ross op. cit, p. 181 & G.T. Basden: *Niger Ibos*. (London: Frank Cass, 1966), pp. 189-90.

Conclusion

In this chapter, we have tried, using four classificatory typologies - of situation, medium, form and theme - to establish that Igbo birth-songs qualify as respectable and distinctive folk poetry in its own right. We have tried to show how this poetry is an all-women affair, which makes it a convenient medium for the women to express certain views and attitudes without inhibition. This lends this form to some feminist possibilities, with the degree of feminism expressed depending entirely on the women's sense of responsibility and obligation to their community.

It is generally agreed that the Igbo society, like most other African societies, evinces a great degree of male chauvinism. As Ada Mere puts it, "because she is stereo-typed as physically weak, fickle-minded, highly emotional and because she, traditionally, is involved in patrilocal marriage an does not perpetuate family name, (the women's) status in the Igbo traditional society is low."[22] But it is also known that, even in the past, Igbo women had some fairly well-organized social mechanism for making their feelings over any matter of public concern known. Sylvia Leith-Ross found these women "possessing startling energy, great powers of organization and leadership...practical common sense and quick apprehension of reality,"[23] and that Igbo women are in theory dependent upon men, but in practice independent of them."[24] F.A. Arinze, substantiating this view, believes that among the Igbo,

> women have more power than was generally recognized by earlier authors. They can hold their own not only by means of public demonstrations, group strikes, ridicule, and refusal to cook for their husbands but also by their inherent vitality, courage, self-reliance and uncommon organizational ability. In this connection the Aba riots of 1929 were an eye-opener.[25]

It would therefore appear as if the feminist tendencies in Igbo birth-songs are congruent with the activities of Igbo women in other spheres of life. What indeed is surprising on the surface is that these women do not use the occasion of these songs, as they well might do, for a kind of very strong protest that would resemble the modern day patterns of feminist emancipation. Rather, what these songs project is a kind of mature, positive and benign feminism that could

---

22 Ada Mere: "Social Values Heritage in the Igbo:" *Ikenga* 2:1, Jan. 1973, p. 3. For similar views, see Ezeanya: "Women in Traditional Religion:" *Orita* x/2. Dec. 1976, p. 106, and Phoebe Ottenberg: "Marriage Relationship in the Double Descent System of Afikpo of South Eastern Nigeria." University Microfilm Inc. D. Dissertation, North-Western University 1958, p. 237.
23 Leith-Ross *op. cit.*, p. 337.
24 Ibid., p. 20.
25 Arinze, *op. cit.*, p. 4. For similar views, see Ottenberg, *op. cit.*, p. iii; D. Forde & G.I. Jones: *Ibi and Ibibio-Speaking Peoples of South-Eastern Nigeria*. (London: International African Institute 1950), p. 14; M.M. Green: *Igbo Village Affairs*. London: Frank Cass. 1964), p. 113.

fearlessly ask relevant questions about, and make significant comments on, the nature of the society without seeking to undermine or otherwise subvert cherished traditional values.

One possible reason for the low-keyed feminism in these songs is the nature of the occasion of the songs. It is an occasion that is, of course, traceable to marriage, and, as Jordan has aptly observed, "marriage was an excellent sign of the fundamental sanity of Ibo (sic) view of life, for nothing reflects the sanity or insanity of any society better than its attitude towards marriage."[26] But a more appealing explanation of the nature of the feminism in these songs is that the medium of the feminist view-point is literary, for which reason a great deal of subtlety is demanded. These women performers of Igbo birth-songs seem to realize not only this need for literary subtlety, but also the fact that the occasion for their performance is one of joy. In other words, they are operating within the framework of art, and as George Devereux points out, "art ... prescribes polite ways of saying impolite things; it provides ways of expressing the inexpressible."[27]

There is a great deal that modern-day champions of the female cause can learn from the realistic but shrewd posture of the female performances of Igbo birth-songs. These performances no doubt recognize the need for the society to shed off its male chauvinistic excesses and recognize the right of the woman to a fuller realization of her potentials as an individual. They seem to ask that the truth about female contributions to the society be acknowledged, and the performance of the birth-songs is an opportunity for them to demand for a change of attitude on the part of the menfolk, while at the same time the women refrain from being iconoclasts. The women strike the impression of realists, who recognize that the subjugation of women in the society is the product of many years of entrenched male chauvinism, for which reason it would be unrealistic to expect to precipitate an immediate, revolutionary change of attitude on the part of the men. Urbanity, wit and group confidence seem to be the preferred alternative, and here the suggestive subtleties of the literary medium - the performance of the birth-songs - easily provide an appropriate framework. The women want a change, it would appear, but not the kind of change that would topple in one fell swoop the essential values that sustain the culture to which they are part. The brazen confrontational attitude that often characterizes some modern forms of the feminist movement, thereby undermining the degree of seriousness which their cause certainly demands from society, would seem to be out of place in the world of the women who perform the Igbo birth-songs.

---

26 Jordan, *op. cit.*, p. 221.
27 George Devereux: "Art and Mythology: A General Theory" in Carol Joplin (ed.): *Art And Aesthetics in Primitive Societies*. (New York: E.P. Dutton & Co. Inc. 1971), pp. 193-224.

Chapter 11

Children's oral literature and socialization in Yoruba

- Akinwumi Isola

The apparent neglect of children's literature in African languages by creative writers and critics alike raises fundamental questions about our conception of the role literature plays in the socialization of the child. Whereas the adult Yoruba has a good number of literature texts - many of them well-written - to choose from, the child hardly has any respectable choice. The unbelievably poor content quality and low literary standard of the few that exist (some of them are poor translations from dubious originals) cannot fail to embarrass anyone who cares about what our children read.

I am painfully aware of being out of my depth in the area of current theories on educational methodology, but with the growing global recognition of the powers of literature, I find it necessary to publicly lament our inability to liberate ourselves from the cobwebs of colonial and neo-colonial delusion that are preventing us from giving to our children a body of written literature that can equip them adequately for the future struggles ahead.

What I intend to do in this essay, therefore, is first to discuss what used to be readily available as oral literature for children among the Yoruba but which is fast disappearing, then to review the present situation with an attempt to explain what went wrong and, finally, to suggest possible guidelines for remedial action that may lead to an improvement of written literature for children.

Language is the abiding place of culture and literature provides its illumination. Culture, according to Clifford Geertz, donates an historically transmitted pattern of meanings embodied in symbols, a system of inherited conceptions expressed in symbolic forms by means of which men communicate, perpetuate and develop their knowledge about, and attitudes towards life.[1]

In a society where orality is dominant, the potent tool usually used for communicating, perpetuating and developing knowledge is oral literature. The socialization of children into Yoruba culture is through poetic language where

---

[1] *The Interpretation of Cultures,* Hutchinson of London, 1975, p. 89.

rhythm is deliberately foregrounded. In fact, at the very beginning, it is all rhythmic sound and movement with no intention of any verbal communication. Any patterned sound or movement would do. Although the intention here is often to pacify the crying child, the action indirectly sensitizes the child to rhythm in sound and movement. This may be the origin of the observation that the African race, than most other races is more sensitive to rhythm (in poetry and dance).

A little later in the child's education, real words are introduced. Although the child does not yet understand any speech, he is now getting accustomed to the sound patterns of the language in addition to the rhythm in popular lullabies like:

Iya re o o	Mother,
Waa gbe o!	Come and carry your child.
Taa lo na an o!	Who beat this child!
Iya e ni	It's the mother
O gbomu rodo,	She has gone to the river with her breasts
O fere de!	She'll soon be back
Ogburo o, ko roko,	Ogburo (name of child) he goes to no farm
Ogburo o, ko rodo	Ogburo, he goes to no river
Bo ba ji a gbobe kana	He wakes up and warms the stew,
Jeba tan a sekan rondo.	He eats *eba*, his belly becomes extended.
Omo oloro tii jeyin awo.	It's the rich man's son who eats guinea fowl's eggs.

or

Dele nko o!	Where is Dele!
o wa nile o,	He's at home
o sun jabura si yara o.	He's fast asleep in the room.

There are numerous other examples which can be a rich source of material for a writer of literature for children who wants highly patterned poetry in which content is not at a premiums.[2]

The content of the poems gradually changes when the child has started to speak. To facilitate language acquisition, tongue-twisters are available to drill the child in the pronunciation of certain consonant combinations. For example:

Agbon n gbagbon gagbon
A coconut fruit is carrying a coconut fruit and climbing a coconut palm *Adie funfun ma funfun nifunfunkufunfun mo*
White hen, stop being white in such an objectionably white fashion
Opobo gbobo bogbe
The monkey killer hides the monkey in the bush.
Boo. ba tete gbobo bogbe
If you don't quickly throw the monkey into the bush

---

[2] See, for example, Shaba Laide, *Orin Aremo Ni Aarin Ife ati Ijesa,* M.A. Thesis, Obafemi Awolowo University, Ile-Ife, 1988.

Obo o gbe o bogbe.
The monkey will throw you into the bush.

Strictly speaking, the tongue-twisting is untranslatable. The consonants are arranged in such a way as to make pronunciation difficult.

Similar to tongue-twisters, but serving as aide-memoire for counting, are certain unmemonics. They are composed in a way to help the child remember counting from one to ten. Couched in poetic language, they are easier to recall than dry numbers. Here are some examples:

Eni bi eni (1) *Eji bi eji* (2) *Eta n tagba* (3) *Erin woroko* (4) *Arun n gbodo* (5) *Efa ti ele* (6) *Boro n boro* (7) *Aro ni bata* (8) *Mo jalakesan* (9) *Gbangba lewa* (10)

The following one serves both as aide-memoire and as practice in long-breathing. It is a poem to be recited from line one to ten in one long breath. If you stop to breathe you have to start all over again:

Ka mugba lamu ka fi damu, o dent,
Ka mugba Iamu ka fi damu, o deji,
Ka mugba lamu ka fi damu, o deta,
Ka mugba lamu ka fi damu, o derin,
Ka mugba lamu ka fi damu, o darun,
Ka mugba lamu ka fi damu, o defa,
Ka mugba lamu ka fi damu, o deje,
Ka mugba lamu ka fi damu, o dejo,
Ka mugba Iamu ka fi damu, o desan,
Ka mugba Iamu ka fi damu, o dewa.

(Lift the calabash off the water-pot and cover it back, one, to ten). These poems provide solid foundations in language acquisition and the fruits of the experience are reaped throughout life.

Some of the poems actually introduce the child to the first rudiments of language analysis. There are short poems that describe points of articulation for certain sounds, and others that describe body position or body movement for certain activities. The following poem describes various positions of the lips when particular sounds are pronounced:

Eni ti oo pe toro a senu toosin
Agba ti yoo pe sisi a fe erigi
Apewuuke la a p A waawu.
Apeforisopo legbeedogbon.
To say *toro* your lips protrude
To say *sisi* the lips must spread
To say *Awaawu,* your cheeks are blown.
Egbeedogbon is said as If' you would knock your head against a post.

The child enjoys the poem, but the embers of the future linguist in him are being stoked.

A special bodily posture, assumed in some daily activities, is the subject of the following poem:

> Baa nudi ikun laa mu,
> Eni ti yoo le tiroo, a te pepe enu.
> Osuku-n-suku,
> Ori eni ti n lota ko nii gbe bikan.
> To clean your anus, your knees knock each other,
> To put antimony on your eye lashes, you spread and flat- ten your lips.
> Up-and-down
> The head of one who grinds pepper cannot be stable.

Although these are common, everyday activities, the humorous poem will induce the child to pay special attention when next he sees any one engaged in any of the activities mentioned.

Although proverbs are the special preserve of elders, the fact that they are used ever so often in the presence of children sometimes sets the child thinking. Proverbs arise from close observation of phenomena, are like axioms, widely accepted for their intrinsic value and self-evident truth. So, when adults want to present any information as universal truth, they do so through a proverb. The value of proverbs to the child, however, is that some of them are amazing summaries of empirical observations, the veracity of which the child may want to investigate later in life. For example the proverb:

> Bile ba ka akoni mo A jedo ekun
> When the valiant is about to be humiliated, he eats tiger liver (, i.e. takes poison.)

I had wondered from the first day I heard this proverb, some forty years ago, Whether tiger liver is indeed poisonous. There is another proverb that says:

> Bi sobia yoo ba degbo, Oluganbe la a ke si.
> "When a guinea-worm attack leaves a sore, you should seek the help of the Oluganbe plant."

The proverb may be used to illustrate relevant points, but the direct observation it contains points to a remedy for guinea-worm sore, which may have a general application for other stubborn sores. Proverbs like the above keep the child wondering. They keep him asking whether statements contained in them are true, and they may trigger off future investigations and important discoveries.

Of the literary genres for children, folktales are of great value for indirectly introducing the child to the socio-political problems of the society because the folktales of a people tend to serve as commentaries on their fears and aspirations. A community of poor people will invariably create in their folktales desirable reversals of roles: the poor miraculously becoming rich. A rich community will prefer folktales where rogues and other criminals are punished. So, in the Yoruba society folktales are woven around two important themes (among others):

Ala Oso (dreams of prosperity - for the poor) and
Ala ise (nightmares of bad fortune - for the rich).

By listening to these folktales, therefore, the child may begin to have a feeling of some of the social and economic relations that exist in the society. Through the 'why-tales,' the child acquires some of the humorous explanations for certain phenomena. And because they contain allegorical fantasy, folktales generally tend to awaken the child's creative interest and ability, and he gets ample practice when he takes his turn at story-telling sessions. Serious efforts to adapt folktales for written children's literature will be very rewarding. Riddles are also another source of practice for decoding metaphors.

The various songs that normally accompany many activities in the community also provide good source materials for written literature. Appropriate songs accompany wrestling matches, moonlight games and some simple social ceremonies.

In the Yoruba society of not too long ago, the literary practices described above were robustly evident. Today the picture is embarrassingly very different.

Culture, is behaviour typical of a group or class. But since that group or class is of living people with a history, culture cannot escape the effects of the course of history. This dynamic nature of culture explains the present cultural confusion in the Yoruba society. Colonialism intervened and we now have significantly different social and economic relations of production which now determine our social order. The old social institutions that ensured the continuity of certain cultural practices have become irrelevant and the discontinuation of ceremonies connected with them has caused the death of the literature they engendered.

The rude intervention of two foreign religions of Islam and Christianity (active companions of colonialism) has dealt devastating blows on many major aspects of Yoruba culture. The effects of the foreign religious disaster have led to the virtual disappearance of Yoruba oral poetry for children. What we now have in its place is a pitiable parody of Euro-American nursery rhymes taught by half-baked local teachers in senile repetition. Even illiterate women hardly now remember good nursery rhymes in Yoruba.

An illiterate wife of a semi-illiterate worker composed a rhyme that utterly embarrassed her husband and friends. Because the husband was fond of calling everybody "bastard," the wife grew to like the sound of the word and started singing the rhyme to pacify her crying child:

Taju bastard

Taju bastard
Baba e bastard.

All important social ceremonies have completely been taken over by semi-illiterate men of God who continually apply the form of faith, predicting eschatology as if religion and orality were happy couples.

The explanation for all this, of course, is that religion is produced by real-life economic conditions and that is why it has such a strong hold on men. It is the result of a continuation of what Cliff Slaughter describes as "s social order in which men's destiny escapes their control."[3] They have to look for succour somewhere, anywhere. Some oppressed Nigerians move rapidly from one religion to another looking for salvation from a problem created by the oppressive economic conditions.

The Islamic belief of man-as-slave and God as ruthlessly revengeful on the one hand, and the Christian notion of the ineradicable sin of man and the horrible punishment prepared for the unbelieving, on the other hand, have sufficiently battered the new generation into a state of near mindlessness that precludes thought, let alone creative analysis. With such fatal lack of dialogue with the natural environment, men now rely on religious teachings to supply their songs and poetry, ignoring the substance of reality for the chloroform of religion.

The average Yoruba child today has not learnt many Yoruba nursery rhymes. They all chant "bah bah black sheep" in a country where the sheep hardly produces any wool. The child cannot tell any Yoruba folktales. He has never heard any tongue-twisters repeated. He cannot remember any proverbs. The most popular Yoruba song he loves is "*O se o Jesu*" (Thank you Jesus). He does not know his natural environment. And because he has not mastered the Yoruba language, he has no access to information about Yoruba culture. It is not his fault. He is a victim of an oppressive socio-economic condition which has attacked the very source of cultural information.

In spite of the fact that the foreign religious drug is being advocated with such hysterical enthusiasm, our society remains evidently not yet redeemed. So, we have the urgent task of vigorously struggling against these redemptive creeds that have deformed our culture.

IV

Before discussing possible guidelines for remedial action, it is necessary to emphasize that any political struggle that does not have a strong cultural revival policy, is ignorantly cutting off a rich area of our possible contributions to world civilization. I would like to quote Terry Eagleton here:

---

[3] *Marxism, Ideology and Literature*, Macmillan, London, 1980, p. 31.

Imperialism is not only the exploitation of cheap labour power, raw materials and easy markets, but the uprooting of languages and customs - not just the imposition of foreign armies, but of alien ways of experiencing it. It manifests itself not only in company balance sheets and in air-bases, but can be traced to the most intimate roots of speech and signification. In such situations (which are right here with us) culture is so vitally bound up with one's common identity that there is no need to argue for its relation to political struggle. It is arguing against it which would seem incomprehensible.[4]

Although the 'new cultural policy' for Nigeria provides for the revival of re aspects of our culture, it is clear that we cannot bring back that era of a glorious traditional Yoruba culture. It is gone for ever. In fact, the belief that if you went deep enough into the villages in the areas you would still find authentic aspects of our culture is erroneous. Christian and Islamic songs have virtually replaced Yoruba traditional songs at marriage, funeral and other ceremonies.

In the present circumstances, the first urgent step to take is the launching of a massive programme for the collection of all extant genres of oral children's literature - lullabies; nursery rhymes; tongue-twisters; counting nmemonics; language games/codes; moonlight game songs; wrestling songs; riddles and jokes; proverbs; folktales and others. These should be extensively collected, preserved, translated and analysed.

Since our goal is the generation of written literature for children, the second step will be to encourage gifted creative artists to use such collected materials as a base for writing literature books for children. In writing such books, however, writers should do the selection of material and the creative presentation in the best way to get the relevant progressive message across to the children. There should be an improvement the traditional, oral mode of presentation in order to suit the modern system of formal education and reading. It is also important to use annotations to explain the contradictions in the texts that are due to changes in culture and social perception.

There are poems, for example, which glorify the cruel exploitation of the poor by the rich and which are joyfully repeated even by the poor themselves probably because of the beautiful poetry or the melodious tune. Some examples are:

>Ada lenu talika
>Igbo la ofi san.
>*A poor men's mouth is a mere cutlass,*
>*We'll use it to clear the bush.*
>Ada lenu talika
>Igbo la ofi san.
>*A poor man's ink is a mere cutlass,*
>*We'll use it to clear the bush.*

---

[4] *Literary Theory: An Introduction,* University of Minnesota Press, 1983, p. 215.

or
*Ejo olowo ko
Bi talika ba po o.* a
*Bolowo ii se bebe
Otosi a roko igi.*
It is not the rich man's fault
That there are many wretched people
When the rich has celebration
The poor will fetch firewood.

When such poems are used, they should be put in such contexts as will clearly show the contradictions, they should be placed side by side with such other poems as would present a correct assessment of the conditions. Poems with progressive content should be preferred to those with reactionary content. An example of a positive poem is:

*Iwo ko lo da mi,
O se n soro bi Olodumare
Iwo ko lo da mi.*
You are not my creator
Why are you talking like God the almighty.
You are not my creator.
or
*Aitowoo rin ejo lo n seku pa won,
Boka ba saaju, ti paramole tle e,
Ti ojola n wo ruru bo leyin,
Taa lo le duro!*
It is because snakes do not move about together that they are easily killed.
If the python takes the 1ead, followed by the viper,
And the boa-constrictor brings up the rear,
Who would wait?

Folktales that teach the values of team-work and dedicated struggle against oppression should be preferred to those that present the condition of the poor as hopeless and unchangeable.

We are not advocating here, a naked presentation of any ideology at this level. That kind of approach may be counter-productive. What we are saying is that these stories or poems themselves should be such that can help children get a correct understanding of their society. There is plenty of room for good-natured fantasy and creative imagination, but care should be taken that education is not tarred with the same brush as religion.

Bibliography

Awoniyi, Adedeji (1986) *Okediran ati Okele Iyan* Vantage Publishers, Ibadan.
 - *Opolo ati Omolewa* Vantage Publishers, Ibadan.
 - *Ogbon Agbonju* Vantage Publishers, Ibadan.
 - *ObaAgbaraganmi* Vantage Publishers, Ibadan.
Akinlade, Kola (1986) *Yemi Dabira* Vantage Publishers, Ibadan.
Tunde Ati, Awon *Ore Re* Vantage Publishers, Ibadan
Graham, Phillis (1972) *The Jesus Hoax,* Leslie Frewin, London.
Okediji, Oladejo (1972) *Ogani Bukola,* Macmillan, Ibadan.
Seldan, Raman (1985) *A Reader's Guide To Contemporary Literary Theory,* The University Press of Kentucky.

Chapter 12

Literature and society in Lagos (late 19th to early 20th century)·

- Samuel Omo Asein

One of the historical events of the last century which had profound influence on the life-patterns and values of the peoples of Nigeria was the introduction of Christianity and western form of education. That was not, however, the first of such contacts between Europe and Nigeria. As early as 1515, we are told, there were contacts between the Portuguese and the *oba* and chiefs of Benin. It is on record, too, that the Portuguese did in fact attempt to establish a base for the propagation of Christian ideas and principles of education.[1] Then, as was to be the case in the nineteenth century, there was a collusion between the civil and the ecclesiastical authorities in a single-minded effort to bring 'light to the unrighteous'. About a quarter of a century after the arrival of the Portuguese in 1515, sufficient interest in education had been built up and not surprisingly, a mission which arrived in Benin in 1539, found among the new converts 'a Christian Negro, teaching boys to read.'[2]

This is probably the farthest we can go in tracing the origins and growth of western education in Nigeria. The initial success in the introduction of this form of education was short-lived, and although there was some degree of enthusiasm in the Benin court as well as among the chiefs, the influence of the Portuguese, and the impact of their way of life on that of the indigenous peoples were negligible. That contact left no form of written tradition, and to the best of our knowledge, no form of written literature grew from that experience of the scribal tradition of the West.

It was a later contact with Europe in the nineteenth century which left a per-

---

* * Reprinted *from Nigeria Magazine*, No. 117-118, 1975, pp. 22-32.
[1] For a more detailed account of this early missionary effort and its significance in regard to the development of education in Nigeria, see L.J. Lewis, *Society, Schools and Progress in Nigeria*, London, Pergamon Press, 1965, Chapter III, pp. 23-37.
[2] Ibid., p. 23.

manent mark on the society in Nigeria, altering it were certain fundamental values which Nigerians, especially the new-literates of that period, had held on to.

The missionary adventure in Nigeria in the nineteenth century began with the arrival of the Wesleyan Methodist Mission (1842), followed a few years after by the Church Missionary Society of England. By 1849, the latter had made significant progress in its proselytizing enterprise along the coast and in the adjoining areas, and had established stations in Badagry, Lagos, Abeokuta and Ibadan. This missionary zeal was not confined to Nigeria. Indeed, it was part of the movement in the nineteenth century by various European bodies to 'civilize' those whom they considered the primitive peoples of the world and was intended to be a practical demonstration by these missionaries of their professed humanitarianism. Ironically, it went to confirm the belief current at that time that there was a difference between the natural endowment and capabilities of the civilized (synonymous with Europe) and the primitive. The latter, invariably included Africans. The nineteenth century also saw a rush for overseas colonies by such major European powers as Britain, France and Germany. It was this great 'Scramble for Africa' that brought the British as colonizers to Nigeria.

What we now know as Nigeria did not come under colonial rule until the second half of the nineteenth century. The secession of Lagos in 1861, the 'conquest' of the so-called 'warring tribes' in the hinterland and the consequent establishment of protectorates in the north and the south prepared the way for the amalgamation of the two 'protectorates' into a single political entity under the governorship of Sir Fredrick Lugard. For the next four and a half decades, Nigeria remained a colony of Britain before it was granted independent status in October, 1960.

For several reasons, the hundred odd years which elapsed between 1861 and 1960 marked a distinctive phase in our national history. It was a period of 'revolutionary' changes which had far-reaching consequences in terms of values, traditions and modes of thoughts, all of which kept changing according to the intensity of the clashes of Nigerian indigenous culture and the foreign culture of the colonizers.

Although the introduction of Christianity antedated the establishment of colonial rule in Nigeria, the former was made a tool, in subsequent years, for pacifying the converts and ensuring a firmer and more permanent grip on the minds of the colonized peoples. Of special significance in this respect were the mission schools and the supplementary Sunday school classes which produced the first batch of locally educated, but disoriented and detribalized natives. The manner and frequency of exposure of this group to western civilization and culture has been described in detail by Mrs. Hinderer in her *Memorials*.

Writing about the school children and adults who attended Sunday School classes, Mrs. Hinderer commented on the enthusiasm of the initiates who on hearing the sound of the second bell, 'would run to the school with their nice English bags of coloured prints or their grass bags on their heads, containing their books'.³ She went further to give details of their equipage:

> ...some with only the English Primer, others more advanced in the new art of reading with various portions of the word of God. St. Luke, the Psalms, Proverbs and Genesis, being among the great favourites.⁴

She recalled that the less receptive ones in the group were made to repeat parts of the Catechism, and that 'sometimes for a change the whole school came together to go over the creed, the Lord's Prayer, and the Ten Commandments, to make sure they have not forgotten.⁵ It was from this first generation of converts that the missions got some of the indigenous advocates who in turn helped to further the cause of the new Faith, while at the same time laying the foundations for an institutionalized religious education in the century.

In later years, Henry Carr, whose one 'consuming interest was education',⁶ turned out to be the most influential of the lot. Assistant Director of Education in the early part of the twentieth century, Henry Carr, like many of his contemporaries who had gone through the mission school system, advocated an educational system which had a firm Christian base. For him, religion, by which he meant Christian religion, 'was the most effectual of the sanctions for the practice of virtue, the right conduct of life, and manners, the science of improving the temper and for making the heart better.'⁷ He spoke spiritedly of its benefits and enjoined the policy makers to aim 'at something higher and more practical than mere knowledge of some of the facts of Bible history.' 'We should allot', he reasoned, 'sufficient time to religious instruction in our schools and should endeavour to train boys and girls systematically in practical morality based on religious sanctions.'⁸

Colonial education in Nigeria in the nineteenth century was, therefore, as a matter of policy, geared to meet specific ecclesiastical and secular needs. The authorities made no bones about this narrow view of the purpose and relevance of education in society. One of the oldest secondary grammar schools in the country stressed in its prospectus that the motive behind the establishment of the school was:

---

³ Cited by L.J. Lewis, ibid., p. 25.
⁴ Ibid., p. 26.
⁵ Ibid.
⁶ L.C. Gwam, "Dr. Henry Carr," in *The Requirements of Education at Lagos*, Ibadan, June 1966, p. 22.
⁷ Henry Carr, *Lectures and Speeches* collected by L.C. Gwam and edited with introduction by C.O. Taiwo, Ibadan, Oxford University Press, 1969, p. 47.
⁸ Ibid., p.30.

to help meet the requirements of the present state of this colony, by furnishing the young people with a sound, practical *English education*. We recognize this among the essential wants of the country, and not so much a proficiency' in the classics. Hence particular attention will be given throughout the course to correct enunciation and accurate diction.[9]

While catering to the interest of the administration, the mission schools were not oblivious of the proselytizing role which had been entrusted to them. Thus, in addition to providing the necessary manpower for the administration, they made sure that their products had sufficient 'moral and religious training'. In doing this they believed they were serving their own interests as well as those of the parents of such students. The Catholic Mission, for instance, pointed out that St. Gregory Grammar School was founded in the hope that the school might provide for "members of their congregation an opportunity of giving their children a thorough secular education as well as sound religious instruction".[10]

These statements of objectives by the missions represented the rule rather than the exception. In fact, in official circles a similar view was taken of the end of education in a colonial context. No less a figure than Sir Frederick Lugard, the first colonial governor of Nigeria, gave approval to the policy which he had himself championed in his dealings in the northern parts of the country. Sir Frederick asserted that "the chief function of government primary and secondary schools among primitive communities should be to train the more promising boys from the village schools as teachers for those schools, as clerks for the local native courts, and as interpreters".[11] In the process, he urged that particular attention should be given to the secure hold of the colonial power on the colonized through indoctrination. Unfortunately, like many other over-praised colonial administrators, Sir Frederick hid his racial prejudice under the cloak of English patriotic zeal. No wonder he dared to suggest a system in which each primary school was headed by a Briton, while each secondary school had, as a rule at least two British teachers on its staff. By such an arrangement he hoped that the aliens "by the stimulus of living example, will set the standard of the school. For it is their influence", he insisted, "which will form the character and ideals of the boys, and introduce the English Public School code of honour".[12]

It was obvious then that the pupils were being groomed to be native Englishmen rather than Nigerians. A typical list of subject offerings in most of these secondary schools included "reading English prose and poetry, Geometry, Rhetoric and Composition, Logic, Moral Science, Greek, Latin, French, History and Book-keeping". As more and more people got the basic elements of the

---

[9] *The Lagos Observer*, 4 December, 1886.
[10] *The Lagos Standard*, 12 February, 1896.
[11] Quoted by Otonti Nduka in *Western Education and the Nigerian Cultural Background*, Ibadan, Oxford University Press, 1965, p. 21.
[12] Cited by Otonti Nduka, *op. cit.*, p. 35.

English language which was later adopted as a *lingua franca* in the country, there was a corresponding anxiety to ensure correct usage. Less formal methods of transmission of new knowledge were adopted.

Apart from the formal training which new literates acquired in the various institutions, there were added incentives in the form of essay competitions and literary contests. The organizers of one of such competitions which was advertised in *The Lagos Observer* of 6 and 18 November 1884 offered a prize of £5 for the best essay on a specific subject. The main idea according to that advertisement was "to encourage the study of English composition in Lagos". A similar concern for good usage and respectable style of writing prompted doggerels like 'Boil it Down', *The Lagos Observer,* 12 August, 1883 and 'How to Write a Letter', *The Lagos Observer,* 11 October, 1883. The main aim of these and like verses was to teach the refinements of style to the new literates and the emphasis was on correctness of diction and, especially in the theatre, on 'pronunciation and articulation'.

It did not take long, however, before the shortcomings of the system became apparent. The indiscriminate acquisition of foreign values and norms by the native peoples caused considerable concern in the colony and aroused a storm of protest and criticism in certain sections of the community. As early as 1883, an anonymous correspondent had criticized the classical foundation of liberal arts education in the colony. The critic saw the 'vigorous and strenuous efforts ... to Romanize and Hellenize the youth, [making] their poor brains the vain receptacles of ... scrapes of Greek and Latin'[13] as a supreme example of a systematized deculturalization of the African. He was dismayed to note the harsh truth about the false bases of the elite culture of the time:

> An enlightened stranger, seeing the almost purposeless exertion put forth in this direction to the neglect of studies of more practical utility, would hardly deny that our youth are being trained to enter the gate of Capena, tread on the Flaminian way, and there musing apostrophize the ashes of the descendants of Romulus; or to undertake a journey to Athens, and under a modern Leonidas defend a new Therinopylae.[14]

Some of the critics recognized quite early the dangerous trend in societal habits as more and more literates made strenuous efforts to deny their Africanity engaging in what a critic aptly described as a mad gamble in which they bartered away their individualities. Apart from this early manifestation of a desire to assert and preserve the African personality and what in our time is tantamount to a negritadist consciousness, there were other grounds for criticism of the colonial educational system in so far as it tended to encourage Africans to deny their traditional value-system. Sir Alan Burns, a well-known authority on

---

[13] *The Lagos Observer*, 8 November, 1883.
[14] Ibid.

colonial Nigerian history summed up this trend when he observed that while it was true that 'the pupils of most of these schools were lacking in book-learning and still worse off as regards character and discipline; these semi-educated youths in their attempt 'to break away completely from any tribal control',[15] ended up as imitators of European instead of being good Africans.[16]

The significance of the foregoing lies in the fact that the system helped to build up a class of 'native literates' who after passing through the elementary and secondary stages of colonial education considered themselves as belonging to a higher level of culture. These 'black Victorians', as Dr. Obiechina once described them, showed a startling willingness to discard all vestiges of traditional African culture. This trend was manifested in virtually all aspects of life in nineteenth century Nigeria, especially in the emergent urban society in Lagos and environs. The prevalent avidity for foreign values and the simultaneous tendency towards self-effacement and rejection of one's essential personality had to do with the tacit acceptance by Lagosians of current notions of racial superiority/inferiority in the nineteenth century. Otonti Nduka's comments on this self-effacing tendency as symptomatic of the impact of western culture on Nigerian society during the period of colonialism are pertinent and most revealing. According to him:

> [the] myth of European racial superiority was for all practical purposes accepted by the Nigerians themselves, as well as by most other dependent peoples, [and] was one of the saddest of the consequences of the contact between Nigeria and the West. The natural pride of the Nigerian peoples in their own cultures and their self-confidence were [sic] dealt serious blows ... The myth, coupled with the exigencies of the colonial relationship, accounts more than anything else for the pathetic and often ludicrous attempt to copy every possible culture trait of the European, from his religion and education to his two-or-three piece woollen suit, and the adoption of the more fanciful new comer 's names ... Not only his virtues but also his vices were equally grist for the mill of uncritical imitation.[17]

It was this class of culturally disorientated Nigerians which produced the earliest forms of creative literature in English in Nigeria. Their writings show evidence of the influence of the kind of education which the writers had received and the religious background which informed their thought.

Perhaps it would have been impossible for the educated elite of this period to sustain its newly acquired literary interest if there had not been an effective and influential newspaper industry. In a sense the Nigerian press during the late

---

[15] *The Lagos Observer*, 2 and 16 April, 1887.

[16] Alan Burns, *History of Nigeria*, 4th Edn., London, George Allen & Unwin Ltd., 1951, p. 243.

[17] Otonti Nduka, *op. cit.*, pp. 5 - 6.

nineteenth century and early twentieth century helped in consolidating the newly acquired knowledge and ushered in Lagos and environs what one might call an age of public enlightenment. It was a transitional period as attention began to shift from the oral tradition of the preceding centuries to the written tradition. Right from its inception in 1862, the Nigerian press catered for the literary taste of the colony and encouraged creative expression by the new literates. Many of them had their poems published in the newspapers and whenever there was a theatrical performance, it was not unusual to read in the dailies critiques and reviews of such performances. Thus, in a way, the newspapers provided for the literate society in Nigeria in the late nineteenth and early twentieth centuries the same kind of base for general knowledge which the English press created for the English reading public in the early part of the eighteenth century.

Furthermore, it served as the watchdog of public morality, upholding virtue and chastening vice. It registered the varying levels of social and public consciousness at a time when it was almost sacrilegious to speak against the colonial administration. To a large extent, the press assumed a guiding role in the community and many of the papers emphasized this role in their various editorials. Mr. J.A. Savage probably spoke for many when in a toast for the press on the occasion of the jubilee celebration of the birth of the Queen, he described the Nigerian press as 'the mainspring of intellectual, spiritual and moral growth which had had the unique power to check abuses and uphold virtue'.[18] The moral bias of the newspapers was understandable especially as many of the leading papers were owned by African churchmen who were anxious to protect their religious interest, as well as give the masses a broad knowledge of contemporary events. However that may be, some of these papers gave some space to literary reviews, occasional verses and stories. Some other, like *The African Times,* were less included towards matters of literary interest, and did not for that reason have 'much room for poetry' and like subjects. They may very well have learnt a lesson from the experience of Robert Campbell with *The Anglo-African.*[19]

If the proliferation of newspaper and the consequent dissemination of ideas, and public enlightenment helped to whet the appetite of the literate public in Nigeria in the nineteenth century, it was the establishment of libraries and the

---

[18] *The Lagos Observer*, 22 June, 1887.

[19] Robert Campbell had established *The Anglo-African* in the hope that a paper which catered for the literary tastes of a society where "the desire for education and enlightenment was widespread," would succeed. Dr. Omu shows in his study that the maiden issue contained among other things "a serial story culled from a novel." The literary content of *The Anglo-African was its undoing.* Dr. Omu explains that *"in spite of the efforts of The Anglo-African* to positively promote general enlightenment and encourage the growth of literary ... the newspaper could hardly pay its way ... Campbell's hopes that the growing demand for education could be reflected in the patronage of his newspaper were disappointed. In playing down local political squabbles and feeding the reading public on a diet of serial stories, the paper forfeited the support of many people." "The Anglo-African, 1863-1865," *Nigeria Magazine*, No. 90, September 1966, pp. 206-212.

availability of 'popular' literature in the local bookstores which sustained the interest in reading which had already been aroused, and further encouraged such avid and more adventurous readers as wished to go beyond the ordinary level of public knowledge. As was to be expected, this kind of literature conditioned the tone and level of attainment of the literate members of the society, and the models and literary preferences of those who aspired to become writers.

The various self-improvement societies and literary clubs also contributed immensely to this general awareness. Many of the dramatic activities of the late nineteenth century were an integral part of the programmes of the clubs and societies, which numbered over a dozen during the period under review. They included such performing groups as the Brazilian Dramatic Company, the Melodramatic Society, the Aurora Club, the Faji School Entertainment Society, the Young Abstainers Club, the Young Men's Literary Association and the Entertainment Societies of St. Gregory Grammar School, The Lagos Grammar School and Wesley High School. Many of these societies had patrons of the arts whom they honoured from time to time with special presentations. The most influential of these patrons was Dr. M. Agbebi, on whom the Young Men's Literary Association conferred honorary presidency, for this 'literary generosity and acknowledged patriotic spirit' and his 'many liberal actions in the dispensation on those advantages with which God has intellectually blessed [him] ...'[20]

Apart from dramatic productions which the literary clubs organized from time to time, there were also programmes of lectures and debates as well as impromptu speeches. A typical club of that period was the Aurora Literary Club which sought to express and encourage 'sound views upon all questions of general, intellectual and moral importance by means of lectures, essays, debates, impromptu speeches and other useful agencies as may be determined from time to time by [its] members...'[21] It organized fortnightly meetings at which addresses and papers were read. One of such papers which has a direct bearing on the subject of this essay was that given by Mr. Highmore 'a Welsh national and an employee of John Holt.'[22] Highmore stressed in his paper the need to educate the masses through the establishment of literary clubs which, it was hoped, would place within reach of the individual adequate facilities for self-improvement. The following extract from a reviewer s summary emphasizes Highmore's pertinent comments on the nature and quality of literary activity in the colony and his recommendations for further improvement.

> Speaking of reading, Mr. Highmore said that in these days of many books, in these times when within a month, over a hundred books are published, it is

---

[20] An address presented to Dr. M. Agbebi, by the members of "The Young Men's Literary Association," *The Lagos Standard*, 20 November, 1895.

[21] *The Lagos Standard*, 1 May, 1895.

[22] *The Lagos Standard*, 20 November, 1895.

difficult for one of to make his choice. He would advise the members to read whatever is worth reading and be careful of authors they keep company with.

Of ancient writers, if the members would have an insight into the origin of literature, he would recommend, Homer, Aeschilus [sic] and Plato. Of modern writers, those with whom he had been strongly impressed are Shakespeare, Dante, Spencer, Scott, Burns and Tennyson; and from these he would like members to make their choice.

Novel reading, Mr. Highmore said, seems to him to be underrated in Lagos. He said that to know the customs and manner of people, whose countries they have not visited or may never visit; that to be quite conversant with the ways of the true Englishman, the members must learn from books which instruct on these subjects, and these books are novels.

Poets he need not tell them are the law-givers of the world, the teachers of mankind. And, therefore, it behoves every member to pay as much attention to poetry as he can. Mr. Highmore's closing remarks were directed to the necessity of self-sacrifice. He says that if the members would all raise up their country; if it is their desire to bring their now despised land to its pristine state, they must sacrifice themselves'.[23]

The most popular form of entertainment in the late nineteenth century were concerts an entertainment which started with the arrival of missionaries and school masters and administrative officers. Concert programmes were arranged primarily for their entertainment value. But quite often, concerts formed the main part of a fund-raising exercise Sometimes, too, the concerts gave the participants a sense of achievement and responsibility.[24] The important fact, however, is that in organizing these concerts, the producers were in fact helping to develop in the community an interest in dramatic literature and to acquaint the audience with that genre. Before the formal presentation of these dramatic entertainments, elaborate press publicity was given, stating the occasion of production, purpose and details of the side shows. Public interest was further enlisted by the mention of the patrons and by the special emphasis placed on the musical aspect if there was any. A typical advertisement of the concerts which newspapers helped to bring to the notice of the public was that of a production of a play entitled *'Laurence and Xystus'*.

> Notice. *A* Grand Evening ENTERTAINMENT UNDER THE PATRONAGE OF HIS EXCELLENCY FRED EVANS, C.M.C. ACTING ADMINISTRATOR, Will be given on Friday, the 10th December, BY THE PUPILS OF ST. GREGORY'S GRAMMER SCHOOL, AT THE ROMAN CATHOLIC SCHOOL-ROOM, IGROSHERE STREET, WHEN A CELEBRATED DRAMA IN FIVE ACTS 'LAURENCE AND XYSTUS' WILL BE PERFORMED. The Programme will be interspersed with songs,

---

[23] Ibid.

[24] See M.J.C. Echeruo, "Concert and Theatre in late Nineteenth Century Lagos," *Nigeria Magazine*, No. 74, September 1962, pp. 68-74.

Glees and Recitations, DOORS OPEN AT 7 P.M., PERFORMANCE TO COMMENCE AT 8 PRECISELY, ADMISSION BY TICKETS ONLY: FIRST CLASS 4s. SECOND CLASS, 2s. TICKETS CAN BE HAD AT THE CATHOLIC BOOKSHOP IGBOSHERE STREET, AND FROM MRS. W. W. LEWIS, Kakawa Street, MR. J. D. FAIRLEY, Marina, MR. J. A. CAMPOS, Hamburg Street, MR. J. J. DA COSTA, Marina and at The Office of *The Lagos Observer,* BISHOP STREET. BY KIND PERMISSION THE COLONIAL BAND WILL BE IN ATTENDANCE. THE PROCEEDS OF THE ENTERTAINMENT WILL BE APPLIED TO THE REPAIRING OF THE SCHOOLS. N.B. Programmes at 3d. each, can be had seance tenante.[25]

These productions showed a conscious effort to imitate such styles and mannerisms as were current in Europe; so were the critical reviews that followed. The criteria for critical judgement were those which were considered acceptable to public taste in the mother country. Nevertheless, there is evidence of the immense popularity of these entertainments in the record of attendance. There was, for instance, the case of the 'creditable performance in 1886, by the Baptist Academy dramatic group. The record attendance was attributed to the reputation of the group for its high-quality productions. A reviewer of the performance explained that:

> Encouraged by the fair moon, light evening...and induced by the fame of the performances of the pupils of this school, it was not surprising to observe that long before the hour of opening approached, a large and respectable gathering had wended their way through the confines of the town to the school-room, so that even the most rigidly punctual could scarcely find resting ground anywhere within the school-room upon entering.[26]

For the same reason, the public entertainments were also occasion for an open demonstration of hooliganism which provoked a lot of press criticisms from time to time. A review published in 1883 condemned lawless and disorderly behaviour of the audience in unmistakable terms:

> Nothing could be more reprehensible than the ill-manners exhibited by the occupants of the back benches at the recent Concert at the Breadfruit Schoolroom. There are certain class of irresponsibles who take a special delight on such occasions in making themselves ridiculous by exhibiting their low-breeding and ill-manners. It is very difficult to deal with this class of canaille, they bring entirely destitute of every sense of shame, and the only effectual way of reaching them is the summary method which the Superintendent of Police was obliged to resort to last Friday night. The feeling is now becoming very general that it is time that our public entertainments were rid of the intolerable nuisance; and the only practicable means suggested for doing so is

---

[25] *The Lagos Observer*, 4 December, 1886.
[26] *The Lagos Observer*, 14 December, 1886.

by abolishing the system of back seat tickets altogether. As a rule the returns obtained from this plan of cheap seating are by no means large, and in no measure compensate for the disorder which is introduced, and which not only produces immediate trouble but tends to disincline persons for [sic] taking part in such undertakings, thereby incurring the risk of exposing themselves to *the senseless looting of a brawling mob.* While the abolition, therefore, of the back seat system will not involve much pecuniary loss, it will enhance such projects by enabling them to be better appreciated, and by removing all objection to capable persons taking part in them. We could recommend the suggestion to the consideration of the promoters of the next public entertainment.[27]

Although they very often came under the attack of the missionary groups for allegedly corrupting public moral, the concerts and other dramatic performances in the nineteenth century were intended to inculcate in the populace a sense of good taste and to discourage moral turpitude in whatever form. Accordingly, producers were often enjoined to 'elevate the moral and intellectual tone of the masses rather than pander to low and vulgar tastes.'[28] In spite of attacks, however, the entertainment groups managed to survive, and there is no doubt that they helped in a large measure to stir up interest in dramatic literature in colonial Nigeria.

In the choice of plays for production, one could see a certain preference for didactic and doctrinaire plays, such as 'the sacred drama *Absalom*'[29] which were intended to complement direct missionary proselytizing exercises among the natives and to further encourage the converts in their new faith. As the records of plays performed in Lagos during the period will show, the sources were as varied as the influence, ranging from the comic delight of Moliere in *He Would be a Lord,* to the tragic history of *Sir Thomas More*. Although the ultimate aim might have been to instruct the materials were often far from being orthodoxy religious.

It is one of the homes of Nigerian literary history that the most significant literate achievement is in the realm of fictional prose. Surprisingly creative fiction was not a major literary form in the nineteenth century; a few short stories and portions of serial 'novels' appeared in some of the newspapers. The *Anglo-African* was among the few papers that devoted much space to fictional prose and other literary subjects. An early attempt in the novel form appeared in *The Lagos Standard* of 13 February, 1985 in the form of an opening chapter of a projected novel entitled *Theodora*. Only the opening chapter of that novel by Lola ever appeared and neither the book nor the author was mentioned in subsequent issues of the paper. A close examination of this surviving chapter

---

[27] *Editorial, Lagos Weekly Record,* 3 June, 1893.

[28] *The Lagos Observer,* 2 March, 1882.

[29] "The Melodramatic Entertainment of the 4th Instant," *The Lagos Standard,* 9 October, 1895.

gives us a clear indication of the influence of travel literature. The semi-biographical opening paragraph reminds us of the kind of experience which Equiano, the eighteenth century Nigerian writer, immortalized in his travelogue; the close attention to minute details of operation of the closing paragraph; the conscious appeal to the visual sense in the succinct description of the landscape and the protagonist's resigned acceptance of his fate recall some of the great fictional creations of life in a rural setting. *Theodora* touches on the opposition between the bustling urban life of Lagos and the quiet rusticity of the country far removed, from *the madding crowd* - the city versus the country - a theme which Hardy, Balzac and other European novelist had popularized in the nineteenth century. Although the same theme recurs in some of the novels of the sixties, there is none of the elaborate presentation of character and setting which Lola gives us in this stylized opening chapter of *Theodora*. The surviving chapter has in addition a strong religious flavour, and there is no doubt that the moral and religious purpose may have been influenced by developments at the time.

Of the three main literary forms poetry was the most popular. The permanence of poetry as a literary form in Nigeria is understandable in an age in which the new literates were beginning to master the techniques of the English language poetry seemed to them the 'easiest' literary form to try their hands on. It was possible, they imagined, to express the thought unit in a poem without undue involvement in technicalities which a sustained use of the language would lead the prose writer into. More challenging was the dramatic form which demands a mastery of the language as well as a genuine acquaintance with the techniques of the stage. Dramatic literature was represented in the form of theatrical performances rather than actual dramas for the stage. In the light of this, it can be argued that although there were theatrical productions and theatre reviews in the nineteenth century, there was no evident tradition of written drama in Nigeria. There may have been some plays written by 'natives' but such plays were by and large insignificant in terms of helping to establish a dramatic tradition. Ultimately one is left with the body of poems which appeared in the weeklies and dailies as our main literary inheritance from the last century.

With the kind of religious and educational background such as we have outlined above, it was no surprise that most of the writers of the late nineteenth century emphasized the content of their works more than anything else. A strong religious and narrow-minded outlook dictated the tone of the didactic poetry of the period.

Many of the poems appeared in Nigeria newspapers during the period under review belong to that class of writing which in the absence of any spectacular imaginative depth relies on the cleverness of the writer in the twist which he gives to familiar themes. With the possible exception of the visual and ornate, poems in the nineteenth century were *functional*. Whether it was a consciously didactic composition, a moral tale in verse, a devotional verse, an elegaic celebration of a lost relation, friend or lover the poet attempted to make his verse a functional vehicle. There were occasional, albeit unsuccessful, experiments with the satirical mode especially in the parodic poem 'Her Ten Commandments', But the 'satires' strike one as being clever in a derogatory sense. A close examination of other poems in this category confirms this view. While it was obvious that these versifiers had something to say they lacked the subtlety to transform the ordinary into a permanent poetic statement. There was a general lack of profundity. Only in the more personal elegaic compositions do we find some degree of emotional involvement; but such poems were regrettably bedevilled by trivial biographical details, posturing and false academism.

These weaknesses confirm the view that the literature was a product of late nineteenth and early twentieth century Nigerian society and it would have been a miracle, judging by the models and the level of their educational attainment, for the writers to have written differently.

In the twenties and after, especially in such influential papers as *The Lagos Weekly Record,* the dominant socio-political thought came from the United States. With Lawrence Dunbar as 'the first Negro poet' and the growth of the UKIA, people became increasingly aware of their racial identity and destiny. It is easy to trace in the sentimental prose of the late nineteenth century and later years the influence of such writers as Marie Corelli, Bertha Clay and Rider Haggard who were widely read in Nigeria during the period under consideration. In this respect also, the Bible had considerable influence on the early writers. Epigraphs to poems and the actual content of most of the verses published in the newspapers illustrate the point. With the religious and secular interest in public morality the inevitable tradition was one of didactic literature to which belong such works as *Segilola* by Isaac Thomas and *A Daughter of the Pharaohs* by Mohammed Duse, both of which appeared serially in the late 1920s and early 1930s respectively.

Chapter 13

Ideological orphanage: the intelligentsia and literary development in Colonial Nigeria

- *G. G. Darah*

All Nigeria ethnic groups had thriving traditions of oral literature before they came in contact with Arabs and Europeans. But by the end of formal colonialism in 1960 many of these traditions had become marginalized in favour of written forms of literature. This state of cultural decline was a logical outcome of a process set in motion by the advent of colonialism. The introduction of colonial administration was a legal sanction of the economic and military subjugation of the peoples who now make up the country. The central objective of colonialism was to secure control over the forces of production for the extraction of surplus. To justify its predatory presence, therefore, colonialism needed a programme of cultural orientation for the indigenous population or, at least, a strategic section of it. This aim was achieved mainly through formal education and religious indoctrination. The establishment of colonial and religious institutions profoundly affected the concept and practice of literature. This essay will attempt a survey of the institutional and ideological stimuli that shaped the development of written literature during the colonial period.

The year 1900 is a convenient point from which to begin. It is to be noted, however, that European cultural influence dates back to the fifteenth century. This was particularly noticeable in coastal settlements such as Calabar, Warri, and Lagos, thanks to the activities of traders and missionaries.[1] Between 1861

An earlier version of this chapter was first published in the *Ife Monographs on Literature and Criticism*, No. 1, 1984.

[1] In some parts of the Niger Delta this influence was so deep that there were Nigerians who were literate in Portuguese, Spanish and English. For example, Don Domingo, a prince in the Warri Kingdom, obtained a university degree in Portugal. He married a Portuguese wife and later

(the year the British acquired Lagos) and 1900 when the Protectorate of Southern Nigeria was proclaimed, western European influence was fairly widespread in most of southern Nigeria. Lugard's military conquest of the northern parts was completed by the first decade of this century. In 1914 the Northern and Southern Provinces were amalgamated into one administrative unit, although the hoisting of the British flag at Lokoja in January 1900 is regarded as a formal declaration of the conquest of Nigeria. Thenceforth, the economic and ideological subordination of the various peoples became more formal and deliberate.

The nineteenth century background

Literature and the Jihadist movement

Although Islamic religious influence in the north began as far back as the eleventh century, a literary tradition in Arabic did not become noticeable until some seven hundred years later. According to Mahmud, it was "during the eighteenth century that a cultural blossoming occurred which prepared the path for the full bloom of Arabic literature...in the early nineteenth century under the leadership of the Sokoto revivalists."[2] This development was a consequence of the Jihad (Holy War) led by Uthman Dan Fodio. The Jihad was both a religious and intellectual movement and it brought in its wake radical reform tendencies which gave impetus to the popularization of literature as both a medium of religious instruction as well as a weapon for criticizing the powers-that-be. According to Mervyn Hisket, the triumph of the Jihad movement and the subsequent establishment of a caliphate in the north opened up new opportunities for the jihadists and their supporters to continue to "use verse to express their responses to the social, political and religious forces set in motion by the event."[3]

By the end of the nineteenth century, Islamic cultural imperialism had become a *fait accompli* in the north. As the Middle East became the main source of the region's spiritual inspiration, all intellectual activity among the dominant classes was validated on the basis of its patrimony with Arabic and Islam. Effort was made to indigenize the Arabic script and this produced a combination of Arabic and Hausa known as *Ajami* which was used widely for literary purposes. Despite this nationalist attempt in the area of language development, the literary tradition up to the twentieth century "remained essentially Islamic and continued to be modelled on classical Arabic prototypes."[4]

---

became a king.
[2] K. Mahmud, "The Arabic Literacy Tradition in Nigeria," *Nigerian Magazine*, No. 145, 1983, p.41.
[3] Mervyn Hisket, *History of Hausa Islamic Verse*, London; University of London, *1975*, p. 19.
[4] I owe this point to Dan Scharfe and Yahaya Aliyu. See their "Hausa Poetry" in *Introduction to*

The Black Victorians

Just as literacy in the north was brought about through the agency of Islam, so was literacy in the south the product of Christian "fishers of men". But unlike in the north where the spread of Arabic and Islam went through some whirlwind phases, the spread of Christianity and education was relatively slow in the south. As has already been mentioned, European influence had been felt on the coast for centuries; but it was not until the mid-nineteenth century that educational opportunities became available to a sizeable number of people. The main concentration of educational facilities was Lagos and its environs which, after 1861, became the beach-head for British penetration of the coastal regions. The pioneering efforts were made by missionaries who, according to Asein, used the Church and schools in "the service of God and Empire." As Asein further remarks in his study of the period, Christianity "was made a tool...for pacifying the converts and ensuring a firmer and more permanent grip on the minds of the colonized people."[5]

The curriculum of most schools consisted of reading and writing, but attention was also paid to the study of the scriptures. Since the ideological objective of the missionaries was to wean the Africans away from the indigenous culture, the pedagogical process was geared towards moulding the minds of the "natives" to accept the superiority of the white race. Thus, the products of the schools saw themselves as "black Europeans" or "Black Victorians" (Queen Victoria was the British monarch during the second half of the nineteenth century). As Ayandele has cogently put the point, the educated elite of the time were "deluded hybrids" who, regardless of their political instincts,

> "were...mentally, religiously and culturally part of the British empire. They...all...accepted...the western version of Christianity...adopted European names in favour of (sic) African ones, donned European dress, and regarded with reverence...the language that Shakespeare spoke as the only one worth speaking."[6]

Besides the school system, a flourishing indigenous newspaper industry encouraged the readership to develop interest in literary matters. Among the papers that popularized literary tastes were the *Anglo-African, The Lagos Observer, Lagos Standard,* and *Lagos Weekly Record.* By the close of the nineteenth century social clubs and societies offered additional opportunities for the expression of literary talents through patronage of the arts in general and drama

---

African Literature: An Anthology of Critical Writing, Ulli Beier (ed.), London: Longman Group Ltd., New Edition, 1980, p. 36.

[5] S.O. Asein, "Literature and Society in Lagos: Late 19th - early 20th Century," *Nigerian Magazine,* Nos. 117-118, 1975, p. 23.

[6] E.A. Ayandele, *The Educated Elite in Nigeria Society,* Ibadan: Ibadan University Press, 1974, p. 19.

in particular. In Lagos alone there were over half a dozen of such groups which organized periodic concerts. Nor surprisingly, the literary heritage favoured by the clubs was a combination of Anglo-Saxon and Graeco-Roman traditions. The model authors whose works featured regularly were Homer and Aeschylus (Greek), Dante (Italian), Shakespeare, Spencer and Tennyson (English). A few members of the elite who attempted to write literary works produced only poor imitations of the European classics. Much of the writing was moralistic and didactic like the Biblical scriptures which informed the choice of themes and authors' perspective.[7]

It has been found necessary to review these developments in the nineteenth century because they have causal significance for what happened during the colonial era. From the account given so far, some basic features can be remarked. First, Islamic and Christian education in the north and south respectively was the main tool for effecting the ideological subordination of the people under these religions. Thus, the products of the educational institutions served as the agencies through which the spiritual disarming of the indigenous peoples was achieved. Second, the notion of literature and culture fostered by either Islam or Christianity regarded the subject peoples as incapable of creating or appreciating literature. Third, the religious, and later, colonial institutions encouraged the growth of a small elite group in each of the country's nationalists. The main cultural credentials of this elite were writing and reading skills. The emergence of this culturally alienated elite, therefore, radically altered the notion of, and attitude to literary creativity and criticism as practised in the context of the oral tradition.

The early twentieth century

At the dawn of the twentieth century, the belief that Europe was synonymous with civilization was already firmly entrenched in the consciousness of the educated elite in the south. Their counterparts in the Islamized north also looked towards the Middle East for spiritual and intellectual inspiration. Thus, by the time the British imperialists finally conquered the country in the early decades of the century, the elite in both parts of the country had their souls already "mortgaged" to foreign lands.

In the post-Jihad period literature in the Islamized parts of the north continued to be used to expose the inadequacies of the political reformers who had superseded the rulers of the old dynasties. In the early years of the century, the most important event to influence literature was the military conquest of the

---

[7] Details of these developments are available in Asein, *op. cit.* For a fuller discussion on the place of the concert performances in Lagos cultural life of the time, see M.J.C. Echeruo, "Concert and Theatre in late 19th Century Lagos" in Yemi Ogunbiyi (ed.), *Drama and Theatre in Nigeria: A Critical Source Book*, Lagos: *Nigeria Magazine*, 1981, pp. 357-369.

north by the British forces led by Frederick Lugard. The occupation of the region engendered both military and cultural reactions. The tone of the reactions in literary form varied from area to area. Some scholars of the period maintain that the literature protesting the British occupation lacked vigour owing largely to the belief among the Hausa that the occupation was an apocalyptic signal of the birth of a new era of peace.[8] However, recent studies of extant works on the period indicated that the protest was quite vehement.[9]

Verse remained the popular form during the period. One of the surviving works titled *"Wakar Narasa"* by Umaru Salaga deals with the coming of Christianity to northern Nigerian following the end of Lugard's military campaigns. Among the patriotic poets produced by the anti-British resistance was Aliyu Dan Sidi, the Emir of Zaria, who wrote a long poem which combined eulogy of his reign with criticism of British rule. Lugard penalized the Emir by deposing and exiling him to Lokoja. According to Scharfe and Aliyu, to whom we are indebted for this account, Dan Sidi's poetic career was also significant because it established *"Ajami* as a major literary form" and replaced "the Arabic that had dominated the nineteenth century.[10] Shehu na Salga, a contemporary of Dan Sidi, also wrote epics with a strong nationalist flavour. One such work is *"Bagauda"* composed as a tribute to the first Habe (Hausa) ruler of the dynasty of Kano.[11]

There was no tradition of literature by indigenous authors in English or any other European language in the north at the time. The development of the English language was slow owing to the delay in the establishment of western-type schools. Whereas by the year of the amalgamation in 1914 there were about 20,000 Koranic schools with an estimated population of 250,000 pupils, the first colonial education officer (Hans Vischer) was appointed only in 1912. Despite Lugard's so-called concerted efforts "to bring the educational systems of Nigeria together in equality of opportunity,"[12] the colonial government insisted that missionaries (the main agencies of western education), should confine their stations and schools in the north to predominantly non-Muslim areas, save where Emirs were willing to accept their presence.[13] It is worth noting, in contrast, that by the 1860s a vigorous press in English was already in existence

---

[8] Mervyn Hisket, *op. cit.,* p. 103.
[9] See Mohammed Sokoto's account in chapter 10 of this volume.
[10] Dan Scharfe and Yahaya Aliyu, *op. cit.,* p. 37.
[11] Ibid., p.37.
[12] A.H.M. Kirk-Green, "Introduction" to Sonia Graham's *Government and Mission Education in Northern Nigeria: 1900-1919,* Ibadan: Ibadan University Press, 1966, p. ix.
[13] Ibid., p. xxiii. For a more detailed account of the place of the English language in the educational development of Northern Nigeria during this period, see Abiodun Adetugbo. "The Development of English Language in Nigeria Up to 1914: A Socio-Historical Appraisal," *Journal of the Historical Society of Nigeria,* Vol. 9, No. 2, 1978, pp. 89-103, and Adekunle Adeniran, "Personalities and Politics in the Establishment of English in Northern Nigeria During the British Colonial Administration, 1900-1943," ibid., pp. 105-126.

in Lagos and Abeokuta. The absence of such an intellectual institution in the north considerably slowed down the spread of European cultural influence, including the English language.

However, European scholars showed an active interest in the study of literature and related subjects in the north of the country in the early decades of the country. The following titles reveal the enthusiasm with which the endeavour was pursued: Charlton, L.A. *Hausa Reading Book* (Oxford, 1908), Edgar, Frank *Tatsuniyoyi Na Hausa* (Vols. I & II, 1911 and Vol. III, 1913), Fletcher, R.S. *Hausa Sayings & Folklore* (London, 1912), Rattery, R.S. *Hausa Folklore* (Oxford, 1913), Tremearne, A.J.N. *Hausa Superstitions and Customs* (London, 1913). These studies brought Hausa literature and culture to the notice of European readers. From the point of view of literary history, however, Frank Edgar's three-volume *Tatsuniyoyi Na Hausa* was the most important. The volumes consist of fictional narratives and other cultural miscellanea totalling 683 items. They were collected and compiled by Edgar while he was political officer in the north from 1905 to 1927. Most of the entries in H.A.S. Johnson's *A Selection of Hausa Stories* (Oxford, 1966) are taken from Edgar's three-volumes which have now been reissued by Frank Cass (1969) under the title *Hausa Tales and Traditions*. They were translated and edited by Neil Skinner who was for many years an editorial superintendent to the North Regional Literature Agency established in 1953.

Literature in indigenous languages

Writing in indigenous languages gained in impetus as a result of the development of orthographies for some of the major Nigerian languages such as Hausa, Igbo, Yoruba, Efik, Tiv, and Nupe. The effort was sponsored by missionaries who needed the facility for evangelical work. Writing in Yoruba started in the early decades of the nineteenth century, thanks to the initiative by Christian institutions and the patriotism of ex-slaves. Bishop Ajayi Crowther, one of such returnees, translated the Christian Bible into Yoruba by the middle of the nineteenth century. His translation of the entire work was published in 1900 as *Bibeli Mimo*. In the opinion of Adeboye Babalola and Albert Gerard, the Bible "set a particular style of the Yoruba language as a standard for all Yoruba-speaking people to use..."[14] A newspaper in Yoruba and English *Iwe Irohin* was started by Reverend Henry Townsend in Abeokuta in 1859. Another missionary worker, David Hinderer, translated John Bunyan's *Pilgrim's Progress* into Yoruba as *Ilosiwaju ero-mimo* in 1866. Babalola and Gerard agree that the book "proved as popular as *Bibeli Mimo* and was to exert considerable influence on

---

[14] See their "A Brief Survey of Creative Writing in Yoruba," *Review of National Literature*, Vol.11, No..2, 1971, p. 189.

Yoruba prose fiction in the middle of the twentieth century."[15]

As the number of mission schools grew the demand for reading material also increased. Between 1909 and 1915, for example, the Church Missionary Society (CMS) published anthologies of prose and poetry to meet this demand. From the beginning of the twentieth century, therefore, creative writing in Yoruba had become virtually an extension of the theological discourse promoted by the missionaries. This ideological orientation left an indelible mark on Yoruba written literature for about a century. Among Yoruba writers not directly linked to the work of the churches are Sobowale Sowande (1858-1936), Kolawole Ajisafe (1870-1940), Adetinikan Obasa (1878-1948). Obasa published three anthologies of Yoruba folklore and oral narratives between 1927 and 1945. Other notable writers in Yoruba are Akintunde Akintan, Oluwole Delano, Folayan Odunju, Ibitoye Ojo and Adeboye Babalola who with Odunjo are regarded as pioneer dramatists.

The exploration of gnomic lore and folk traditions begun by Obasa and was developed to its fullest potential by Daniel Olorunfemi Fagunwa (1903-1963). In most of his writings, Fagunwa leaves no one in doubt that he was a devout Christian.[16] As Karin Barber demonstrates in chapter 14, below Fagunwa established his reputation as a master story-teller and has remained for decades a fertile source of intellectual and aesthetic influence for the Yoruba-speaking areas of West Africa.

Abubakar Imam was the most prolific writer to emerge in the north in the period under review. In many important respects his literary career compares with that of Fagunwa. Imam was a teacher, an inspector of education and an editor of the Hausa language newspaper, *Gaskiya Ta Fi Kwabo* "Truth Is Worth More Than a Penny". His place in the development of written literature in the north is important in another respect. As our review of the nineteenth century bears out, a radical outlook dominated the literary scene for about a hundred years after the Jihad. The writings of Imam show a clear shift in ideological orientation. On the evidence provided by some scholars of Imam, it does seem that he is typical of the writer as a pedagogue of the *status quo* which, in the period between 1930 and 1960, meant support for colonialism as well as the institution of Islamic aristocracy and conformism.[17]

In spite of the enormous official support given to the tradition represented by Imam's writings, the radical streak in the region's letters survived into the second half of the twentieth century. This was more noticeable in the written poetry where the most distinguished voices were those of Mu'azu Hadejia, Aminu Kano, Sa'ad Zungur, Aliyu Akilu and Na'ibi Wali. Aliyu Na-Mangi, who also belonged to this generation, was in a class by himself. Though blind,

---

[15] Ibid., pp. 189-190.
[16] See, for instance, Afolabi Olabimtan's "Religion as a Theme in Fagunwa's Novels" in *Odu* (Journal of West African Studies), University of Ife, New Series, No. 11, 1975, pp. 101-114.
[17] A fuller portrait of Abubakar Imam is available in chapter 12 below.

he nevertheless produced one of the most ambitious works; *Wakar Imfiraji* a narrative in twelve books, which remains a classic example of the creative fusion of Arabic and Hausa traditions of poetry. The politics of decolonization which matured in the late forties helped to delineate the ideological contours of the writings. To the Northern Peoples Congress (NPC), which represented the conservative voice in politics, belonged writers like Abubakar Imam and Nigeria's first prime minister, Abubakar Tafawa Balewa. Aminu Kano and Sa'ad Zungur were of the Northern Elements Progressive Union (NEPU) which contested political space with the NPC by advocating the emancipation and empowerment of the oppressed masses *talakawa*.[18]

Although Christian missionaries did work in Igbo-speaking areas in the nineteenth century, the first primer based on Igbo orthography did not appear until 1927. Thus, the use of Igbo language for creative writing did not get the type of encouragement that Yoruba, for example, received. However, Peter Nwana blazed the trail in novel-writing in Igbo when Longmans of London published his *Omenuko* in 1933. According to Ernest Emenyonu, the novel "won an all-African literary contest in indigenous African languages organized by the International Institute of African Languages and Cultures."[19] Based on the experiences of an émigré by name Omenuko, the book explores the theme of the "fate of the alienated individual in a situation where identification with the group seems the only way to keep alive."[20] As the works of Chinua Achebe, John Munonye and Nkem Nwankwo have shown the tension between individual privilege and group solidarity has been an enduring theme of the creative writing by Igbo intellectuals since the colonial rupture of their indigenous culture.

Itinerant theatre: the Ogunde tradition

It is somewhat ironical that the Christian Church which worked to stifle indigenous cultural practice ultimately set in motion a cultural movement that gave birth to one of the most vibrant artistic developments in Africa: the travelling theatre.[21] According to Yemi Ogunbiyi's insightful reconstruction of the origin of contemporary Nigerian professional theatre practice,[22] the secessionist moves within the Protestant Church in Lagos in the 1890s created an avenue for the use of indigenous music and dance to propagate the gospels. By the mid-thirties, the innovative combination of church plays, music and dance

---

[18] For details on the interface between radical politics and the vocation of poetry during the period, see Dandatti Abdulkadir in chapter 13 below.
[19] Ernest Emenyonu, "Early Fiction in Igbo" in Bernth Linfors (ed.), *Critical Remarks on Nigerian Literatures*, London: Heinemann Educational Books, 1979, p. 85.
[20] Ibid.,p.87.
[21] A detailed study of this tradition is available in Biodun Jeyifo, *The Yoruba Travelling Theatre of Nigeria*, Lagos, *Nigeria Magazine*, 1984.
[22] Yemi Ogunbiyi, *op. cit.*, pp. 17-24.

became known as 'Native Air Opera'. Through the efforts of people like A.K. Ajisafe, E.A. Dawodu, Ajibola Layeni and others, the operas were already a popular cultural diet when, in 1944, Ogunde became the organist and composer of sacred songs for the Church of the Lord at Ebute-Metta in Lagos.

Ogunde's performances freed the opera from the strict confines of the Church and monotonous Church rhythms and imbued it with a sprinkling of Yoruba music and dances. Thus began an eventful career which has made Ogunde the undisputed leader and teacher of the popular theatre in Nigeria.

In order to understand the enormous cultural and political influence that Ogunde wielded from 1944 to 1960 a brief account of his career is in order. His first opera was in 1944 and was titled "The Garden of Eden and the Throne of God." This was followed by "Africa and God," Nebuchadnezzar's Reign and Belshazzar's Feast" and "Journey to Heaven." This list shows the strong Christian background of Ogunde's "African Music Research Party," as his group was the called. The name has undergone several changes since then. It was "Ogunde Theatre Party" in 1947, "Ogunde Concert Party" in the fifties and has been "Ogunde Theatre" since the sixties. Ogunde's first non-theological play, "Worse Than Crime," was a subtle criticism of colonialism. This moved Ogunde into the mainstream of the anti-colonial struggle which was then growing in intensity. For staging "Worse Than Crime," the colonial authorities detained him and his assistant, G.B. Kuyinu, for two days. Thenceforth, the exploration of political themes became a fairly regular pre-occupation of the group as the following titles attest: "Strike and Hunger" (1945), "Tiger's Empire" (1946), "Herbert Macaulay" (1946), "Towards Liberty" (1947), "Breed and Bullet" (1950), "Song of Unity" (1960).

For lending his theatrical talent to the nationalist struggles, Ogunde was constantly harassed by the police. "Strike and Hunger" was a tribute to the proletarian power of the Nigerian workers during the first ever nation-wide general strike in 1945. A performance of the play in Jos was stopped midway by the police and Ogunde and five others in his group were subsequently fined ₦250.00. "Breed and Bullet," based on the massacre of coal miners at Iva Valley, Enugu, was first staged in 1950. During a performance tour of northern cities in 1951, the colonial authorities banned scheduled appearances in Kano, Kaduna, and Makurdi. The British colonialists reacted to Ogunde's plays because they feared that he was using the medium to introduce anti-colonial politics into the north of the country.

Cultural nationalism as exemplified by drama was vigorously supported by the indigenous press, which formed part of the intellectual vanguard of the anti-colonial crusade. To a large extent, it can be said that between 1945 and 1960. politics and the arts mutually influenced each other. Other theatre groups that were part of the cultural front of the nationalist movement were those of Ajibola Layeni, Miss Adunni Oluwole (founder of the Commoners' Liberal Party in 1945), and to a limited extent, Kola Ogunmola.

It is worth remarking in passing that the mutual collaboration between politics of nationalism and the theatre did not survive long into the post-independence era. For example, during the inter-factional squabbles among the Yoruba elite in the early sixties, Ogunde's "Yoruba Ronu" (a play denouncing tyranny and calling for Yoruba solidarity) aroused the ire of premier Akintola's government. Consequently, Ogunde's Concert Party was banned in 1964 from performing throughout the Western Region.[23]

As a titan of the theatre, Ogunde inaugurated and nurtured a rich heritage of professional and semi-professional theatre practice embracing some one hundred groups. Among the great names influenced by him are Kola Ogunmola, Duro Ladipo, Moses Olaiya, Oyin Adejobi, and Ade Afolayan.

The Onitsha literary renaissance: twilight in the East?

The general ferment of ideas and broadening of ideological perspectives which accompanied the immediate post-World War II years constitute a watershed in the intellectual development in Nigeria. Almost contemporaneous with the emergence of Ogunde and Sa'adu Zungur on Nigeria's literary horizon was what it now known by literary historians as the Onitsha Market Literature. It was a literary renaissance involving a whole range of writers, readers, journalists, traders, booksellers, printers, and teenage school children.

The emergence of this first Nigerian popular literature in English coincided with the rise of Onitsha as the commercial centre of Eastern Nigeria. The town witnessed a tremendous spurt in the growth of literacy, population of young people, printing facilities, and a certain level of leisure life conducive to reading. As Achebe describes the literary revolution of the time, Onitsha "was a place of day schools and night schools, mission schools/and private schools, grammar schools, of one-room academies and backyard colleges."[24] More significantly, Onitsha "was a self-confident place where a man could not be deterred even by insufficient education from aspiring..."[25] Further intellectual influences came from India and Far Eastern countries from where returning soldiers brought ideas, information, and printing skills.

Between 1947 and 1966 the Onitsha tradition had produced over two hundred titles spanning fiction, ethics, manuals on financial management, sales promotion, catechisms on love and conjugal affairs, biography, and politics (domestic and international). The most popular theme was that of love and *Veronica My Daughter* by A. Ogali, one of the titles exploring this theme, sold

---

[23] For much of this profile I am indebted to Ebun Clark's *Hubert Ogunde: The Making of Nigerian Theatre*, London: Oxford University Press, 1979, esp. pp. 3-93.
[24] In "Foreword" to Emmanuel Obiechina's *Literature for the Masses: An Analytical Study of Popular Pamphleteering in Nigeria,* Enugu: Nwakwo-Ifejika & Co. Publishers, 1971, p. x.
[25] Ibid., p. x.

over 60,000 copies within a few years of publication. Like Ogunde's dramatic fair, and the concert party tradition in the nineteenth century, most of the Onitsha titles announced their hortatory intentions. Examples were *Why Boys Never Trust Money-Monger Girls, Beware of Women, Money is Hard to Get but Easy to Spend, The Game of Love, The Chains of Love,* etc.[26]

Besides the three characteristics of simplicity of language and technique, brevity of form, and low pricing mentioned by Obiechina, the Onitsha pamphlets endeared themselves to a wide reading public because they appeared in virtually all genres of literature and related fields. Of special significance were the drama sketches which now offer theatre historians and critics "clues towards understanding the earliest forms of contemporary Nigerian literary drama."[27] The dramatized biographies of figures such as Nkrumah, Lumumba, Azikiwe, Jomo Kenyatta, Nyerere, etc., bear testimony to the influence of international politics on popular consciousness at the time.

Obiechina's bibliography already referred to lists some seventy authors who participated in the tradition between 1947 and 1966. The most prolific among them were Thomas Orlando Iguh, O.A. Ogali (author of *Veronica My Daughter),* O. Olisa, and F.N. Stephen. With the exception of Cyprian Ekwensi whose *When Love Whispers* and *Ikolo the Wrestler and Other Igbo Tales* appeared in 1947, no Nigerian writer of note was nurtured at Onitsha. This certainly must be a matter of interest for literary historians.

The overall impact of the Onitsha phenomenon on later Nigerian fiction in English is difficult to measure. However, from the point of view of literary development, the epoch is of great significance. It demonstrated our capacity to domesticate foreign-influenced literary themes and techniques. It also proved how the English language, which in the hands of university-trained writers screens most people from the nation's literary culture, can be adapted to the needs of the majority. The Onitsha tradition also throws into bolder relief the tragic magnitude of the ideological homelessness of our literary muses since imperialism, working mainly through the University of Ibadan, hijacked the nation's right to determine the direction of its literary growth. This feature will be discussed in some detail below.

Seen from the perspective of literary ideology, there is some close affinity between Onitsha tradition and the drama of James Ene Henshaw. This is especially so in regard to the theme of clash between urban (foreign) and rural life, and also his tendency to bend the plays to a didactic end. Undoubtedly, Henshaw was a more accomplished playwright than the Onitsha authors, but his concentration on comedies links him, however remotely, with the concert plays of the nineteenth century, the Onitsha genial spirit, and the Yoruba travelling

---

[26] A comprehensive bibliography of the titles is in Emmanuel Obiechina, *Onitsha Market Literature,* Heinemann Educational Books, 1972, pp. 177-182.
[27] Yemi Ogunbiyi, "Nigerian Theatre and Drama: A Critical Profile" in Yemi Ogunbiyi (ed.), *op. cit.,* p. 26.

theatre.

While the young Onitsha authors were creating a literary language out of English, Amos Tutuola with a comparative educational background was embarking on a similar career. With his first work, *The Palm wine Drinkard*, appearing in 1952, Tutuola inaugurated a tradition of fiction in English which has remained unique and almost impossible to imitate. Popularly regarded as the pioneer Nigerian novelist in English, Tutuola, like Fagunwa, is reputed for his uncanny facility to create an extremely visual or magistic language, one that attempts to capture the vividness of a situation or object through the power of description. Like Fagunwa, Ogunde and Soyinka, Tutuola draws heavily on the Yoruba folkloric world of gods, demons, myths, legends, and magic. His other works. appearing before 1960 are *My Life in the Bush of Ghosts* (1954), *Simbi and the Satyr of the Dark Jungle* (1955) and *The Brave African Huntress* (1958). Two years after Tutuola's *Drinkard*, Ekwensi's *People of the City* was published. Between this and his *When Love Whispers* (1947) he published *The Leopard's Claw* (1950). T.M. Aluko's *One Man One Wife* and Achebe's *Things Fall Apart* (1958), complete the fiction fare before 1960.

Worthy to mention is the impact of novels by fantasy-hunting Europeans which were in free circulation in the fifties. Among the widely read authors were Rider Haggard, Edgar Wallace and Evelyn Waugh. Haggard's *She, King, Solomon's Mines,* and *Allan Quartermain* were certainly best-sellers, especially since one or the other of them appeared regularly in the reading list of literature courses in the secondary, modern, and grammar schools, in the then Western Region. Graham Greene's *Heart of the Matter* (1948) and Elspeth Huxley's *The Walled City,* based largely on Margery Perham's accounts of colonial rule in Northern Nigeria, and Joyce Cary's *African Witch* and *Mister Johnson* also found space in many shelves. It was the obviously false views and racial snobbery in these works that prompted people like Achebe to embark on novelwriting.

Towards 1960: Ibadan and the homeless muses

The University College of Ibadan established in 1948 did not begin to play a significant role in the development of literature until the second half of the fifties. As a Nigerian campus of the University of London, its literature curriculum emphasized European classics from Greece to the British Isles. For the students at the time, culture began and ended in the Graeco-Roman world. This intellectual alienation was later to leave an indelible mark on the conception and complexion of written literature in Nigeria.

Some Nigerian poets, Ulli Beier tells us, had had their works published in British journals between 1949 and 1954. Among these were Keia Epelle, Enitan Brown, Dennis Osadebay and Adeboye Babalola. Osadebay was the first to publish an entire volume *African Sings* in 1951. Good poetry, however, had to await the intellectual ferment on the eve of political independence. Olumbe Bassir's *An Anthology of West African Verse* (1957) is devoted almost entirely to francophone poets and does not include any Nigerian poet of note except the pioneering Osadebay. Although Osadebay's entries share in the general mood of expectations of a post-colonial dawn, the poems, in the words of Adrian Roscoe, "tell vividly enough of tutelage, cultural uncertainty, and imitation of metropolitan tradition."[28] The negritude poets in Bassir's anthology - David Diop, Birago Diop, Leopold Senghor - being clearly inspired by patriotic political passions produced works whose themes and techniques inevitably exhibited a definite anti-imperialist posture. In contrast, Osadebay's effort, despite its obvious gesture to an African world, was undoubtedly an embarrassing apology to imperialism. The timidity of tone shown in Osadebay's poems has remained a national trade mark of Nigerian poetry in English since the fifties.[29]

After Osadebay came the generation educated at the University College Ibadan. The students admitted were from the elite secondary schools in the country - Government Colleges at Ibadan, Umuahia, Ughelli, King's College Lagos, Barewa College, Zaria - to name a few. Out of this selection emerged the voices that were to shape the future of Nigerian literature in English.

Poetry was the form in which the young writers first distinguished themselves. Output was facilitated by the establishment in the late fifties of two journals - *Black Orpheus* and *The Horn*. The latter was founded and run by the students of the English Department of the University through the encouragement of Martin Banham, an English lecturer. J.P. Clark was its first editor. Others who made appearance in it were Wole Soyinka, Abiola Irele, Mac Akpoyoware, Pius Oleghe, Aig Higo, Christopher Okigbo, and Bridget Akwada. Later contributions came from Nelson Olawaiye (Ahmadu Bello University) and Glory Nwanodi (University of Nigeria, Nsukka). Obi Esli, Dapo Adelugba, and Omolara Ogundipe-Leslie were also part of *The Horn* team in the early sixties. Among the significant female voices to come out of the period was Mabel Imoukhuede whose verse was noted for its Negritude energy. But as a literary ideology Negritude did not find a favourable climate in Nigeria.

The harvest of poetry at the university was helped by the teaching of African literature in the late fifties. This offered the opportunity for cultural self-

---

[28] Adrian Roscoe, *Mother is Gold: A Study in West African Literature,* Cambridge: The University Press, 1971, p. 15.

[29] This is evident in the works of Christopher Okigbo, John Pepper Clark and Wole Soyinka who together make up the "three-personnel great tradition" of Nigerian poetry in English. Each of them has written on political events in Nigeria but their poetry is remarkably silent on the atrocities committed against the Nigerian people by the combined forces of colonialism and imperialism. An elaborate treatment of this matter for the whole of African literature in European languages may be found in Omafume Onoge, "The Crisis of Consciousness in Modern African Literature; A Survey," *Canadian Journal of African Studies,* Vol. VIII, No. 2, 1974.

discovery for many talented students. Gabriel Okara, the only one not nurtured at the University College, was part of this harvest. He made his first appearance in *Black Orpheus* in 1957. Edited selections from *The Horn* were published as *Nigerian Student Verse* by the University College Press in 1960. The selection as well as many of the entries in *The Horn* and *Black Orpheus* showed strong influence of English Romantic poetry which was compulsory at Ibadan for decades. As Beier remarks of these poems, they "fail to give one the feeling that they were written in Nigeria."[30] Adeboye Babalola's translation of *Ijala* (Yoruba hunters' verse) appeared in some issues of *African Affairs* before 1954, and in the first number of *Black Orpheus* in 1957. These specimens of oral poetic heritage drew some attention to a tradition that six decades of British colonialism had suppressed. Although Gbadamosi and Beier followed up the pioneering example of Babalola with their *Yoruba Poetry* (1959), interest in oral poetry was very minimal until the early seventies. As Chinweizu has recently pointed out, the poetic tradition that crystallized at Ibadan and later Nsukka was technically and philosophically a modern, bourgeois European one written by Europeanized sensibilities in Nigerian skin."[31]

The creative outburst which the University atmosphere and the heightened political consciousness in the country offered manifested itself in drama too. Courses in drama and theatre were introduced at the University in 1957. By 1959 three amateur drama groups were in existence which between them treated the Ibadan audience to a wide variety of plays taken from Greek, English and Nigerian dramatic repertories. Soyinka's *The Swamp Dwellers* and *The Lion and the Jewel* were staged in 1958. Soyinka had, in his three years stay at Leeds, England, given a promise of himself as a man of the theatre. His arrival in Nigeria in 1960 gave great impetus to the enthusiastic theatrical experiment then going on at Ibadan. Buoyed up by a spirit of nationalism and discovery, the young actors grouped into "The 1960 Masks." This was the first and most ambitious theatre formation up till that time and it comprised Yemi Lijadu, Ralph Opara, Segun Olusola, Funlayo Asekun, Olga Adeniyi-Jones, Tola Soares, and Francesca Pereira. The group was later joined by Patrick Osie, Femi Euba, Elsie Olusola, Jimi Johnson, Tunji Oyelana, and Wale Ogunyemi. Thus began what has been described as the nucleus of a truly Nigerian theatre in conception and design.[32]

This period also witnessed great creative experimentation in production techniques, especially in adaptation of texts. Shakespeare's *The Taming of the*

---

[30] Ulli Beier, "Some Nigerian Poets," *Presence Africaine*, Vols. 4/5, Nos. 32/33. 1960, p. 62.
[31] See his "Prodigals, Come Home!" *Okike* (An African Journal of New Writing), No. 4, December 1973, p. 6. A more spirited critique of the disease of European bourgeois anomie in written African literature is in Chinweizu, Madubuike and Jemie, *Toward the Decolonization of African Literature*, vol. I, Enugu: Fourth Dimension Publishers, 1980.
[32] I owe this point to Yemi Ogunbiyi on whom I have relied for much of the information on this period. See especially pp. 27-31 of his book cited above. See also, Gerald Moore, *Wole Soyinka*, London: Evans Brothers Ltd., 1971, pp. 3-9.

Shrew and Nkem Nwankwo's *Danda* were adapted and produced. Spurred on by the euphoria of an emergent independent nation, the staff and students in Ibadan hoped to break the barrier between "gown" and "town" by embarking on countrywide tours during which town halls, cinema centres, and school dining halls were converted to theatres.

The numerous attempts to give a national character to drama in particular and the arts in general received institutional validation with the founding of the Mbari Club in 1961. Deriving its name from the Owerri Mbari houses built in honour of *Ala* (Mother Earth), the Club was part of the patriotic urge to free artists and the arts from the direct influence of colonial institutions such as the British Council which had since 1945 played some "midwifery" role in the sphere of culture. The founding members of the Club were Wole Soyinka, Amos Tutuola, Yetunde Esan, Frances Ademola, D.O. Fagunwa, Mabel Aig-Imoukhuede, and Ulli Beier (German). The group later included J.P. Clark, Demas Nwoko, and Ezekiel Mphahlele (South African). Mbari's manifesto was to promote "understanding and appreciation of permanent values of new trends in art, literature, music and theatre" and to seek "complete integration of these values into our stream of life."[33] Although less endowed financially than the British Council, and later, the Unites States Information Service Centres, the Mbari Club saw itself as a national alternative to these imperialist-sponsored agencies. In fulfilment of these aims, the Mbari Centre, opened in July 1961, was a cultural complex "comprising a gallery for exhibition, a library for research and information and a court-yard used as an open-air theatre."[34] The Mbari phenomenon manifested itself in Osogbo in 1962 and Mbari Mbayo, thanks to Duro Ladipo's foresight. It offered inspiration and venue for developments in Yoruba operatic theatre which Ogunde had made a national institution in the fifties. Moving farther afield from Ibadan, the Mbari spirit settled at Enugu in 1963 when John Ekwere opened a centre there.

It must be mentioned that despite the enthusiasm of the Ibadan-inspired artists to give a national identity to their works, many of them could not totally free themselves from the entranced world of Western European literature, especially its decadent phase. Much of the poetry, as we have observed, continued to be inspired by the dying energies of Anglo-Saxon tradition as evidenced in mature Soyinka and early Okigbo's[35] output in which obscurity of ideas and diction seems to constitute a literary ideology. Whereas Fagunwa and Tutuola's heroes emerge from the demon-ruled world with the self-knowledge

---

[33] From "Forward," *Brochure: Mbari*, quoted by J.A. Adedeji, "A Profile of Nigerian Theatre, 1960-70," *Nigerian Magazine*, Nos. 107-109, Dec. 1970-Aug. 1971, p. 5.
[34] Ibid.,p.5.
[35] From the point of view of understanding of meaning by the average reader, there is a definite progression in textual density as one moves from Soyinka's early prose and poetry to the phase of his writings which Professor Eldred Jones chooses to refer to as "essential Soyinka." Conversely, Okigbo's poetry becomes increasingly less alienating as one moves from the myth-infested world of "Heavensgate" to the more secular one of "Paths of Thunder."

of a "culturally-earthed" people, Achebe's counterparts for instance, seem doomed to what Femi Osofisan recently referred to as a tragic catharsis whose literary ancestry is traceable to Thomas Hardy and George Eliot. Despite courageous experimentation in dramatic techniques, the spirit of criticism remained indebted for a long time to perspectives derived from the Euro-American world of letters. It is instructive, for instance, that when J.P. Clark produced a dramatic manifesto in book form later, he conceded the inspiration to England with the revealing title of *The Example of Shakespeare.**

One final aspect to consider concerns the role of foreign critics and publishing houses during the period. The criticism of the then emergent African literature has its theoretical anchorage in the conservative camp of Euro-American scholarship. The University College at Ibadan offered the best climate for criticism; but the College was at best a peripheral extension of London University. Critical thinking in the English Department was influenced by the expatriate staff among whom were Molly Mahood and Martin Banham. In fact, the first black head of the department, Professor M.J.C. Echeruo, was appointed only in 1974. He too was a product of the period when colonial ideology reigned supreme in the department. The other known voices of criticism at the time were Ulli Beier (German) and Gerald Moore (English). Their opinions further entrenched the imperialist bias of the criticism.

As cultural institutions, the foreign publishing houses probably did more than any other force to subvert the emergence of a truly national literature. Among the leading publishing concerns were Frank Cass, Oxford, Cambridge, Heinemann, Thomas Nelson, and Longman. We recall the critical role of publishers during the Onitsha literary revolution.[36] It is certainly an index of our neo-colonial thraldom that the bulk of the literature created in Nigeria since 1952 has been published by foreign firms. Given the overall cultural agenda of imperialism, the publishing houses must have exercised strong ideological control over the material sent in by authors. It is highly probable that in the name of a "tiger does not shout its tigritude" many anti-imperialist works were killed at the desks of reactionary foreign editors.

As George Plekhanov remarked long ago, to appreciate the literature of a people, one must understand their history or social life. As we have tried to show in the survey, the character of a written tradition of literature is determined largely by the world outlook of the literati. We have pointed to the fact that the two imperialist religions of Islam and Christianity used their schools and places of worship to nurse an ideologically fettered intelligentsia. That intelligentsia has grown in size and power during the three decades since independence. Through its management of secular and religious institutions in the country the intelligentsia has continued to perpetuate the legacy of servility to foreign

---

* Longman, 1970.
[36] See Don Dodson's "The Role of the Publisher in Onitsha Market Literature," Bernth Lindfors (ed.), *op. cit.*, pp. 191-207.

cultural influences. This partly explains why much of the literature produced by the educated elite is shot through with ideas and sentiments expressive of cultural insecurity. If, as has been suggested by Ogunba, no people which depends on foreign sources for its literacy models can hope to attain spiritual fulfilment,[37] then there is need to question the nationality of some of the literature that has been produced since 1900. Although the debate about the criteria making for the emergence of a national literature cannot be fully entered into here, those who are genuinely concerned about the moral, spiritual and ideological health of Nigerian literature ought to heed Chinweizu's call for a deliberate effort to go beyond European realism;[38] and, we hasten to add, Islamic mysticism, too.

---

[37] Oyin Ogunba, "Literary Art and Literary Creativity in Contemporary Africa," inaugural lecture, University of Ife Press, 1979, p. 1.

[38] See his "Beyond European Realism," *Okike*, No. 14, 1978, pp. 1-3. A similar conclusion is reached by Gene H. Bell in his "The Rise of the Latin American Novel," ibid., pp. 4-24. A more thorough treatment of the matter is in Gordon Brotherston, *The Emergence of the Latin American Novel*, Cambridge: Cambridge University Press, paperback edition, 1979.

Chapter 14

The songs and poems of the Satiru Revolt c. 1894-1906*

- Abubakar Sokoto Mohammed

Introduction

I hope that the songs and poems will be of some interest to our colleagues, especially in the area of literature. I also wish to use the songs and poems to demonstrate to our colleagues in the social sciences an untapped source of valuable date particularly with regards to historical investigation.

In order to provide a framework within which to properly comprehend the songs and poems that I am going to present I think that it is necessary to briefly explain what the Satiru revolt was all about and to lay out a chronology of the events. This will enable the readers to locate the timing and significance of the songs and poems within the context of the revolt itself.

The Satiru revolt was the social movement which began around 1898 in the Sokoto Caliphate and reached its climax with the battles against British colonial forces in 1906 in the Sokoto Province.

There have been various interpretations of this rebellion by different scholars. Some have labelled the Satirawa as religious fanatics, others see it as an ethnic conflict. My own interpretation, which is based on available evidence, is that the rebellion was a manifestation of a continuing class struggle from the Sokoto Caliphate to the conquest of the society by British colonialism. Hence, it was an uprising of slaves and peasants which was initially directed against the aristocrats of the Sokoto Caliphate and later, with the imposition of British imperialism on the society, was aimed at overthrowing British colonial rule.

The settlement of Satiru was located about 20 kilometres south of the city of Sokoto. The ruins of the village are now marked by a forest reserve in Danchadi district which is in the Bodinga local government area of Sokoto State. The Satiru forest reserve lies about 8 kilometres to the west of Dange on a laterite

---

* The objective of this chapter is to specifically present the songs and poems that were related to the Satiru revolt which I came across in the course of my MSc research.

road linking Dange with Danchadi. The actual site of the destroyed settlement of Satiru is on the northern edge of the forest reserve.

The events leading to the Satiru revolt of 1906 began towards the end of the nineteenth century in the Sokoto Caliphate. From available evidence, the revolt was led by poor Islamic scholars whose aim was to overthrow the Sokoto Caliphate. They attracted followers, mainly poor peasants and slaves who escaped from their masters, by making use of the Mahdist ideology to articulate their struggles against their major enemies.

The consequences of the imposition of the colonial policies of British imperialism on the Sokoto Caliphate at the beginning of the twentieth century contributed to the development and character of the revolt which exploded in 1906. This added an anti-colonial dimension to the original outlook of the struggles of the Satiru community.

The initial defeat of the British forces and the troops of the *Sarakuna* by the Satirawa (people from Satiru) in 1906 was a significant military and political feat in both the history of the Caliphate and that of British colonialism in Northern Nigeria.

On the surface, the Satiru revolt may look like any of the Mahdist, anti-colonial revolts which took place in the region in this period. But the uniqueness of Satiru lies in its historical location and objective.

The establishment of the Satiru community and he manifestation of its rebellious tendency was historically located in a period of transition from the tribute-paying (feudal) social formation of the Sokoto Caliphate to the British colonial formation. Most scholars who have studied Satiru have failed to grips this very important fact. It was the class struggle between the slaves, peasants and other exploited classes and the aristocracy and their allies such as wealthy merchants and bureaucrats within the 'feudal' formation of the Caliphate that gave rise to the revolt.

The main objective of the Satiru revolt makes it a special case among peasant revolts. While most peasant revolts tended to be reformist or even backward-looking, the Satiru revolt was revolutionary and forward-looking. Other peasant revolts merely made economic demands but that of Satiru was aimed at seizing the political power of the Sokoto Caliphate, struck a compromise with the rulers of the erstwhile Caliphate, the Satirawa launched a struggle against the British imperialists and their local allies. This was, of course, as a result of the oppressive and exploitative policies that were imposed by the British and which they implemented jointly with the *Sarakuna*, e.g., taxes, conscription, compulsory labour, etc.

The militant reaction of the slaves and poor peasants to the exploitation and oppression of both the Sokoto Caliphate and British colonialism gave rise to a series of battles in which the Satirawa initially emerged as a formidable and serious threat. But these battles culminated in the annihilation of the Satirawa and the complete destruction of their settlement on 10 March, 1906.

A chronology of the Satiru Revolt C. 1894-1906

C. 1894 - The village of Satiru was established by a group of poor mallams led by Mallam Siba. Escaped slaves and peasants flocked to Satiru in large numbers. The village had an estimated population of about 10,000 by 1906.

The slaves gained their freedom in Satiru and the peasants neither paid taxes nor supplied compulsory labour to the state and the rich classes.

The poor scholars who led the community utilized the Mahdist ideology in their struggles against the Sokoto Caliphate and British colonialism. Main occupations of the Satiru people were farming, crafts, banditry and *Takkai* dancing.

Defeat of the Sokoto Caliphate by the British forces.

C 1903 - 1903   The newly appointed Sarkin Musulmi informed the British of the existence of the Satiru rebels. Mallam Maikaho, one of the leaders of Satiru declared himself a Mahdi. He was arrested by the Sarkin Musulmi and died in prison while awaiting trial.

1904 Mallam Isa Dan Maikaho, son of M. Maikaho took over the leadership of Satiru.

13 February, 1906   The Satirawa attacked Tsomau, a neighbouring village, apparently for refusing to support them. The satirawa killed 12 people.

- This incident was reported to the Acting Resident of Sokoto, Mr. Hillary, by the Sarkin Musulmi.

14 February, 1906   The Acting Resident, Mr. Hillary went out with the Sokoto Garrison to arrest M. Isa, headman of Satiru who had proclaimed himself Prophet Isa (Jesus Christ).

- Mr. Hillary went along with Mr. Scott, Assistant Resident, Dr. Ellis, Medical Officer, Lt. Blackwood, the only Military Officer in the station. Sergeant Gosling and 69 native rank and file and two enlisted labourers all Mounted Infantry.

- On their arrival at Satiru, the Satirawa attacked the British force. Lt. Blackwood, Mr. Hillary, Mr. Scott and 27 native soldiers were killed; Dr. Ellis and three native were wounded and the Maxim gun was captured. It was reported that this was the first reverse sustained by the West African Frontier Force (WAFF) since its formation by Lugard in 1897.

- The Satirawa lost 30-40 killed and wounded.

- Mallam Siba escaped from the battle and fled.

15 February, 1906   The Resident of Sokoto Province, Major Burdon, who was proceeding on leave, returned to Sokoto to organize the defence of the Front with the aid of Sarkin Musulmi and loyal chiefs.

16 February, 1906   Mallam Isa Dan Maikaho died of wounds sustained in the battle of 14 February, 1906.
17 February, 1906   On hearing of the disaster of 13 February, the Sarkin Musulmi called in all his chiefs and fiefholders to attack Satiru.
-   The Marafan Gwadabawa, Maiturare, the military commander of Sarkin Musulmi collected all headmen and all Sokoto and neighbouring chiefs and attacked Satiru in full force, with about 3,000 foot and horse men.
-   The Sokoto forces were woefully defeated by the Satirawa and forced to withdraw. There were heavy casualties among the Sokoto forces which included some important chiefs. The Marafa himself narrowly escaped falling into the hands of the Satirawa.
*Alfa Saybou (Dan Maikaho) and supporters seemed have arrived at Satiru from Kobkitanda in the Zaberma territory to the west after the defeat of his own anti-colonialist, Mahdist revolt against the French about this time. His movement had also killed two French military officers.

C. 17 February -
10 March, 1906   The success recorded by Satiru and the efforts to draw more supporters to their fold must have led to the numerous raids that were carried out against neighbouring towns and villages between about 17 February, 1906 and 10 March, 1906.
-   For example, Danchadi was reported to have been burnt by the Satirawa on 6 March, 1906.
-   Dange was burnt by the Satirawa on 8 March, 1906.
-   Other settlements that were burnt by the Satirawa included Runjin Kwarai, Runjin Gawo, Redu Makera, Jaredi, Dandin Mahe, Zangalawa, Bunazawa, Hausawan Maiwa and Kindiru.
-   Shuni, Bodinga and Sifawa were said to have been deserted because of the fear of the possible attacks of the Satirawa.
10 March, 1906   In view of the serious threat that the Satiru rebellion posed to British colonialism in Northern Nigeria, the High Commissioner, F.D. Lugard, undertook a mass mobilization and concentration of the British forces in order to launch a punitive expedition against the Satirawa who have so far remained undefeated by all enemies.

Hence, Lugard mobilized 573 troops and 70 police with a total of about 44 white men including civilians. This force was drawn from Sokoto, Kontogora, Kano, Lokoja and Zungeru. It was reported that both Lagos and Tiv expedition troops had arrived in Zungeru too late to take part in the action against Satiru. This massive concentration of troops in Sokoto against the village of Satiru was larger than all other expeditions in the history of the British conquest of the Caliphate, with the exception of the main expedition which conquered Kano and Sokoto in 1903.

At 2.00 a.m. on 10 March 1906, the concentrated British forces including a large number of local horsemen marched out of Sokoto under the command of Major R.H. Godwin. The objective was that " so dangerous a body of fanatics should not merely be defeated but annihilated." Lugard also agreed with this objectives of the commander of the expeditionary force and asserted that " with the force and weapons at their command they should annihilate them and it is necessary for the recovery of our prestige that the victory should be a signal one."

The Satirawa were attacked by the British force and they put up a very brave and strong resistance. Owing to superior fire power the British force killed thousands of the Satiru militants. Driven from the village the Satirawa were pursued by the mounted infantry and the native horsemen in all directions. The hot pursuit was reported to have continued for two days.

Apart from the thousands of casualties that were inflicted on the Satirawa, many were arrested and imprisoned or executed. The village was razed to the ground with no wall or tree left standing. In fact the Satirawa were reported to have been practically exterminated. Some 3,000 women and children were said to have been handed over to the Sultan for disposal. Resident Burdon ordered the Sultan to prohibit anybody from making a farm in Satiru forever. The Sultan was also reported to have pronounced a curse on anyone building or farming on the site of Satiru. Long after the annihilation of the Satirawa the British continued to keep a watch on Satiru through the patrols of the Mounted Infantry. Today the site of Satiru is marked by a forest reserve in the Bodinga local government of Sokoto State.

Lugard justified the massacre by pointing out that " the military situation demanded a signal and overwhelming victory for the restoration of British prestige, and prevention of any such rising in the future."

12 March, 1906	A great durbar was held with the Sarkin Musulmi and all chiefs engaged on the side of the British. At this gathering Lugard's message of thanks for the loyalty of the *Sarkuna* and the confidence that he had throughout that they would prove loyal was read to the Sultan before a vast assembly and received with liveliest satisfaction.
3 July, 1906	Sarkin Musulmi received an Honorary Companionship of the most distinguished Order of St. Michael and St. George (CMG) for his loyal conduct during the Satiru rebellion. Thus, the British rewarded loyalty and punished disloyalty accordingly.

Songs and poems of Satiru

Nine songs and poems of the Satiru revolt will be presented along with some comments here.

The Praise - Song (Kirari) of Satiru
Satiru,
Sa turu - turu da idanu,
 Ta Mallam Siba.

> **English Translation**
> Satiru, The one that makes eyes to bulge,
> Mallam Siba's (town).

This poem tells us the name of the founder of the settlement of Satiru, i.e., Mallam Siba. It also informs us about the rebellions reputation of the community. Thus, it makes the eyes of its enemies literally bulge out of hardship. This seems to be a reference to the defeat which the Satirawa initially inflicted on the forces the Caliphate and the British.

(ii)   Song of the Takkai Dance
Marafa ka dade ba ka zaka ba,
Dan Modoma ka dade ba ka Zaka ba,
Belle Nasara mat dan wando,
Babban Mutun da rigay yara,
Sabara kina son lihidi?

> **English Translation**
> Marafa we challenge you to come,
> Dan Modama we challenge you to come,
> More so the white man who wears shorts,
> The great one who wears children's clothes,
> Sabara, do you want some *lihidi?*

One of the major preoccupations of the members of the Satiru community was said to be their practice of the *takkat* dance in the evenings. This is a martial art which also affords the singers a chance to express their criticisms against some authorities or persons.

This song was likely to have been made after the initial defeat of the British forces by the Satirawa or after the attack on Tsomau. The song is challenging the two major enemies or the Satirawa, i.e., the Sokoto aristocrats and the British. Marafa was the military commander of the Sokoto forces and Dan Modoma was the fiefholder of Danchaid under whose jurisdiction Satiru was supposed to fall. Their contemptuous reference to the British is also indicative of their vehement opposition of the colonialists.

The state of military preparedness of the Satirawa is also expressed in the last line of the songs. The *Sabara* is a wild shrub. *Lihidi* is a quilted protection for horses. The Satirawa were reported to adorn the wild shrubs with the quilted protection of the horses of their opponents after killing the horse and the rider.

(iii)   Song of the Danchadi Men
Mazan Danchadi Kara Zube,
Mazan Danchadi Kara suka sha,
Ba su motsi.

English Translation
Men of Danchadi, heap of stalks,
Men of Danchadi, chewers of sugar cane,
They are not agile.

This was also one of the songs that were sung by the Satirawa during their sessions of *takkai* dance. This song portrays the contempt of the Satiru community for their immediate political over-lords because Danchadi was the seat of the fiefholder who was nearest to them. The militancy of the Satiru community as opposed to the docility of their neighbours can also be seen in this song.

(iv)   Isa Dan Maikaho's Song
Isa Bajinin Maikaho,
In don tsoron mutuwa, tashi mu tai fada,
Dan Waire ya mutu Ruma, ba a yi kom ba,
Kaura Hasau ya mutu Maradi, ba a yi komiba,
Gobe kaiton Danchadi!

English Translation
Isa, the hero of Maikaho,
Shun fear of death, let's go to war,
Dan Waire died at Ruma and nothing happened,
Kaura Hasau died at Maradi and nothing happened,
Tomorrow woe unto Danchadi!

This song confirms the fact that Isa took over the leadership of the Satiru community after the death of his father in 1904. The song was made by 'Yar Kundus, a female musician of the Satirawa. The song seemed to have been intended to instigate and embolden Isa to go to war. The song makes references to famous warriors (Dan Waire and Kaura Hasau) in the history of Katsina and Maradi to fire Isa's militancy. Hence, in 1906 Satiru started launching attacks on its opponents and neighbours.

(v) Mallam Siba's Song

Mallam Siba in damo na a jawo gogi nai,
In ba a ba da gogi a ba da kafab baya.

English Translation
If Mallam Siba is a *damo*[1] pull out his tail,
If the tail cannot be released then hand over the hind leg.

This song was reported to have been sung for Mallam Siba (the founder of Satiru) by the youths of Dange, a neighbouring settlement which was attacked and burnt by the Satirawa.

The tendency of the Satirawa to attack neighbouring settlements didn't seem to endear them to such communities. This song pointed to the concern of such communities about the violent activities of the Satirawa. It was satirical and a call for curbing the excesses of the Satirawa, particularly their leaders.

(vi) Song of Satiru by Mallam Dan Sa'a Mai Mai Wa'azu of Gyarabshi Village (in Wamakko District) of Sokoto State.

In zani na Dabagare ban bi ta Satiru,
Ina bi ta Dan Ttkkau,
Ina bi ta Zanzaro,
Tsakanin Gyarabshi da Shuni sai an yi rakiya?
A bin ga na Satiru ya bace muna da lissahi!

English Translation
On my way to Dabagare I will not pass through Satiru,
I could go through Dan *Takkau*,
I could go through Zanzaro,
So between Gyarabshi and Shuni one has to be escorted?
This affair of Satiru is beyond our comprehension!

This poem indicates how much Satiru was a terror in the whole region in view of its focal location between may fields. Thus, it became an obstacle, which had to be avoided on the way of travellers across the region.

(vii) The Song of Satiru by Mallam Muhamman of Rumbuki

1. *Mun gode Allah zahirinmu da badini*
   Ga shirin da mun ka yi za mu wakas Satiru.
2. *Don sun bide ka bide' aminci duk kiya,*
   Kowas shigesu makogwaro nai a shi jiya,

---

[1] *damo* is an iguana lizard, and is a symbol of stoicism in Hausa philosophy.

3. Don sun difa ka ba su duk ba ka tsira ba,
   Marini Yahaya sara yai tara,
4. Dubi 'yan dakarun ga maciya rama,
   Wadanda ba su gadi bunga ba ga uwa da uba duka,
5. Nufinsu su samu mulkin duniya,
   Wai su sa bargo da sakata Satiru,

6. Maciya amana na wadanda ba su da gaskiya,
   Kowa ka keta da zamba sai shi bi Satiru,
7. Da nit Mallam Labbo sai nayi zullumi,
   kane ga su Dan Modoma babu tukabbiri,
   Ya baka bayani babu wanda ka kwanta tai
8. Ku dubi ana kadin mutane awa gada!
   Ka ce dai gada ta an ka tayas Satiru,
9. Ka dubi anafafin mutane awa duma!
   Ka ce dai duma na an ka fafe Satiru,
10. Ka dubi gari ja-wur yana Kaskasniya!
    Ka ce alhaarini an ka shanya Satiru,
11. Dubi gari na dwai awa daudawab batso!
    Ka ce dai batso na an ka shanya ga Satiru,
12. Ka dubi garin sheggu har ya zan gari!
    Ga yau sai su yanyawa ka kuka Satiru.

English Translation

1. We thank Allah with our lips and hearts,
   On our intention to compose a song of Satiru,
2. If they seek your trust, reject them,
   Whoever encroaches upon them,
   his throat shall bear the brunt,
3. Granting their request will not guarantee your safety,
   Yahaya,[2] the dyer, bore up a nine cuts,
4. Look at these belligerent eaters of *rama*[3],
   Who have never inherited farms from both the
   mother's side and the father's side,
   Their intention was to acquire worldly power,
   In order to install *bargo*[4] and *sakata*[5] at Satiru,

---

[2] M. Yahaya who was killed in the clash between Tsomau and Satiru was reported to have married out a daughter of his to the Satirawa
[3] Leaves
[4] Blanket. These seem to have some symbolic meaning of luxury and could also be associated with the ruling class.
[5] Latch

> Violators of trust who are short of truth,
> Those who are wicked and cheats should follow Satiru,
> Whenever I remember Mallam Labbo I regret,
> The youngest brother of Dan Modoma[6] and co.,
> Who was no braggart,
> He furnishes you with knowledge with all seriousness,
> He furnishes you with knowledge which is unsurpassed.
> Look at how people are being hunted like antelopes!
> As if it were antelopes being hunted in Satiru,
> Look at how people are being *slit* like gourds!
> As if it were gourds being *slit* in Satiru,
> Look at how a whole town is so red and glistening!
> As if it were *alharini*[7] spread out in Satiru,
> Look at a whole town stinking like *daudawab batso*[8]!
> As if it were *batso* spread out in Satiru,
> Look at how the settlement of bastards developed into a town!
> Today only foxes are waiting in Satiru.

This poem gives a vivid description (probably an eye-witness account), written, in the aftermath of the massacre of the Satirawa. This can be seen from how the Satirawa were callously killed (like antelopes). We are also told of how the village turned red from the blood of the massacred community. The offensive odour of the environment from the corpses of the Satiru people is also described.

Another important information that is contained in this poem concerns the objectives of the Satiru revolt, i.e., " Their intention was to acquire worldly power." This confirms the uniqueness of the Satiru rebellion when compared to similar peasant movements.

The poem also contains an attempt to discredit the Satiru community at the ideological level by presenting the members as murderers, distrustful and untruthful.

(viii) Song of Satiru War by Magaji Mai Bodinga (of the Waziri's Household)

> Bismillahir Rahmanir Rahimi. Sallal-Lahu ala man la Nabiyi ba'adahu.
> 1. Mun gode Allah da a kadiri
>   Da ya ba da ikon baje Satiru,
> 2. Da ya ba da ikon baje masu karya,
>   Ga tasamma addin da Addahiru,
> 3. Dashe ya ki kamu dashen Mai kaho,
>   Da sun yi taronsu ya tattaru,

---

[6] Title of the fiefholder of Danchadi
[7] Arabic – a cloth made of brilliant blue-red colour silk.
[8] A variety of locust bean which has a very offensive odour.

4. Da Siba musiba da aj ja-gaba,
   Idan sun yi taronsu ya tattaru,
5. Su dauko hatsi har da man kone-kone,
   Hatsaitsan Musulmim mazan Satiru!
6. Ga ran assibit babu kodai garesu,
   Muharramu Yadin an baje Satiru,
7. Ga tashinsu biyu babu har sha hudu,
   Kahin sun ka zamma cikan Satiru,
8. Musulmi fari yai farar zuciya,
   Baki yai baki an baje Satiru,
9. Akwai wasu warwatse ban san su ba,
   Idan ta yi girma su zo Satiru,
10. Karatu da dufu rashin hankali,
    A kwai shi ga manyan da sa Satiru,
11. Zama mun ji babansu can yai ishara,
    Bikinsa shina zakkuwa Satiru,
12. Idan ya taho bisa kowa shi shirya,
    Ku kammai ku damre shi nan Satiru,
13. Ku turke shi daki, fadi ya zaka,
    Ku kama da kowa cikan Satiru,
Kaho ya bace an ka komo ga sa,
    Ashe dai dabara baje Satiru,
Ku ce gardi ya kullu bashe sun tun nan,
    Balle gobe can inda ba Satiru.
Mun gode ma Allah ga warke kasa,
    Na kadon da ke sun biya Satiru.
Mu gode ma Allah da ya shafe taron-,
    Miyagun da an nan cikin Satiru.
Mu zan addu'a in da Allah shi Karba,
    Shi bar muna Sarkinmu Addahiru.
Shi yo jinkiri arziki daukaka,
    Mu taru ga Sarkinmu Addahiru.
Shi kore bala'i diyan jarraba,
    Waba'i da yunwa, zaman Dahiru.
Cikin hakan nan wanda duk ya mutu,
    Musulmi, Cika mai da ke ga fara.
Ina gode Allah, ina yin Salati,
    Ga Annabi sunansa Addahiru.
    Tammat, tammat, tammat bi hamdil Lahi.

English Translation
In the name of Allah, the Most Merciful and the Beneficent, Peace be upon he whom there is not Prophet after.
Thanks be unto Allah the Omnipotent,

Who made it possible to sack Satiru.
Who made it possible to disband the liars,
Who rose against the Religion and Addahiru.
The plant of Maikaho failed to sprout,
Formerly they were up to 3,000 at Satiru.
4. And Siba, the terror that was their leader,
Whenever they had gathered together.
5. They would carry millet, and even oil for arson,
The millet of Muslims, men of Satiru!
6. By Saturday there was none of them,
By the Inviolable Hand, Satiru was levelled.
They started with less than two and grew up to fourteen,
Before they were settled in Satiru.
A good Muslim will be happy,
A bad Muslim sad, Satiru had been sacked.
There are others here and there that I know not of,
When it is ripe let them come to Satiru.
Unorthodox knowledge is insane,
Which was typical of the leaders of Satiru.
For we heard that their leader made a prophecy,
That his off-spring shall come to Satiru.
If he comes from above let all be ready,
Catch him and tie him up in Satiru.
Confine him to the room, the prophecy is complete,
And arrest all that are in Satiru.
The horn disappeared and they turned to the Ox,
Thus, the best strategy was the destruction of Satiru.
Say, the scholars plot did mislead them here,
More, so the next day where there will be no Satiru.
Thanks be unto Allah for cleansing the land,
of the kado that lived in Satiru.
Thanks be unto Allah for wiping the clique,
of the devilish dwellers of Satiru.
We should pray for Allah to answer,
And let live our *Sarki* Addahiru.
To give longevity, prosperity, majesty,
We should rally round our *Sarki* Addahiru.
Let Him repel the catastrophe of the unworthy beings,
Plague and famine in the reign of Dahiru.
Under the circumstances whoever dies,
A Muslim, Grant him pardon.
I am thanking Allah, and showering praise
On the Prophet whose name is Addahiru.
The end, the end, the end with praise of Allah.

This poem was written after the annihilation of the Satirawa. Hence, it was a continuation of the armed class struggle at the ideological level. The poem speaks for itself.

But it is important to point out that it served the interests of both the *Sara kuna* and the British equally well. The poem discredited the learned leaders of the Satirawa and condemned the Satiru community. It justified the massacre of the Satirawa and the destruction of their settlement from both a religious and political perspective by pointing out that they rose against the Religion and the *Sarkin Musulmi*.

(ix) Kirari (Praise-Song) for the Satirawa

Satirawa!
Arnan fako madauka magana,
ko an kashe kum kun kashe Hilliri.

English Translation
Satirawa!
Heathens of the hard plains,
Despite your annihilation, you have killed Hilliri[9]

This poem seems like an epitaph for the Satirawa after their annihilation. Hence even though they were wiped out, they had waged an anti-colonial struggle!

Conclusion

The major point that I wish to underscore is that songs and poems can be a valuable source of qualitative data for social science research, the trend towards statistical mechanisation notwithstanding. These poems could be valuable especially in historical researches either as eye-witness accounts of events or reflections of contemporary opinions on various burning issues.

Another important suggestion that one can make is for the encouragement of the collection of data in our national languages either in the form of published materials, or oral tradition in our research activities.

Finally, I would like to appeal to our colleagues in literature to always try to situate songs and poems and other works within their social context in order for these works to be more meaningful. This presumes providing appropriate historical, social, political and economic background to whatever researches or

---

[9] Hilliri - refers to Acting Resident H.R.P. Hillary who led the British force to Satiru and was killed in the action of 14 February, 1906. I wish to acknowledge the assistance that I received from B.S.Y. Alhassan of the Department of Nigerian and African Languages, A.B.U., Zaira in translating the poems from Hausa into English.

works they are carrying out in the area of languages and literature.

It is only through this type of interaction between the arts and the social sciences in our research endeavours that some co-operation can be forged amongst us and our researches made more fruitful.

Chapter 15

Style and ideology in Fagunwa and Okediji

- Karin Barber

All literature is ideological. Whether the author is aware of it or not, every work of literature reveals a configuration of beliefs and assumptions about the nature of the world which is never neutral. It serves particular social interests by legitimizing, tacitly or explicitly, certain social structures. In a society where class is developed or developing, world views tend to express class interests, and the world view of the ruling class tends to be the dominant one.[1] Obviously, however, this does not mean that all the works of literature produced by members of the same class express an identical configuration of beliefs. In many respects they may differ and even oppose each other. This is the case with the works of the two most important Yoruba novelists, D.O. Fagunwa and Oladejo Okediji. Both of them belong to the nascent 'proto-bourgeoisie' that had been forming in Nigeria since the middle of the nineteenth century.[2] Both belong to the same segment of this elite, the segment which gained its status through education and the acquisition of a teaching post. Both share the same broad ideological framework. They subscribe to a humanitarian ethnic enjoining consideration and care for others, personal modesty and moderation, and belief in virtue as its own reward. This is in marked contrast with some strands in the

---

[1] The term "world view" or "world vision" as applied to class beliefs and attitudes was first used by Lucien Goldmann in *The Hidden God* (trans. Philip Thody, London, Routledge and Kegan Paul, 1964). The theory that the world view of the ruling class is the dominant one is well expressed in Christopher Caudwell's *Illusion and Reality* (1937, reprint, New York: International Publishers, 1973).

[2] "Proto-bourgeoisie" is the term used by Philip Ehrenasft in 'The Rise of a Protobourgeoisie in Yorubaland,' in *African Social Studies*, (eds.) Peter C.W. Gutkind and Peter Waterman, (London, Heinemann, 1977), pp. 116-124. Ebrensaft is concerned mainly with the group of returned ex-slaves from Sierra Leone and elsewhere who formed the core of a new, principally commercial elite based in Lagos in the period before colonial rule was imposed. But by Fagunwa's time the nascent bourgeoisie had not developed into a true class, and the term "proto-bourgeoisie" still seems appropriate.

ethics of pre-Christian Yorubaland: those expressed, for instance, in *oriki* genre of poetry, where might is right and outrageous, self-serving behaviour is applauded as a sign of power.³ However, within this broad common framework there is a very great difference between Fagunwa's stance and Okediji's, revealed not only in the content of their works but also in the form and the language. Fagunwa is solidly conservative, upholding with eulogistic fervour the established authority structure and the values that maintain it. Okediji is relatively radical, expressing disgust with the state of the society and calling for action from the underprivileged to put things right. Okediji, unlike Fagunwa, is able to transcend the values of his own interest-group (the elite) to ally in sympathy with the rest of society.

It is not good enough to attribute these differences to the individuality of creative genius. Individuality is an important and undeniable factor, but it works within particular social and historical conditions which demarcate its scope and form. When Marx asserted that it was possible for certain people to transcend their own class viewpoint and ally with another, his point was precisely that only a certain social group, located at a particular historical juncture, would be in a position to achieve this. There were definite circumstances that *enabled* the more far-sighted members of one group (the intellectual section of the bourgeoisie) to perceive the validity of the world view of another group (the proletariat).⁴ Okediji is a writer of exceptional sensitivity and sympathies; but one must also ask if there were not social-historical circumstances, absent in Fagunwa's time, which enabled Okediji's individual talent to express itself in the way it did. Fagunwa was writing in the 1940s and 1950s; Okediji's two novels were published in 1969 and 1971. Two changes that took place in the intervening period seem relevant here.

First, the composition, size, and general role of the class they both belonged to underwent significant changes. For most members of the class, these changes would be perceived as deterioration, and the ills of society would be far more glaringly apparent in 1970 than in 1950. Second, the particular segment of the proto-bourgeoisie that they both belonged to - educators and academics - lost status within the class during that period. With the take-over by Nigerians of government and its economic controls, the boom in business that was experienced in the 1950s and 1960s, and especially the sudden upsurge of oil money at the end of that period, business men and entrepreneurs became more

---

³ The values expressed in *oriki*, of course, were only one aspect of the world view of pre-Christian Yorubaland. Since one purpose of *oriki* is the aggrandisement of individual 'Big Men' through encomia, it is likely that they exaggerate the values relating to power and individual glory at the expense of other values (such as those of group solidarity, helping one's fellow men, etc.) See Karin Barber, 'Oriki in Okuku Town,' unpublished Ph.D. thesis, University of Ife, 1979.

⁴ This position is stated in Marx and Engel's *Communist Manifesto*, (1848), and was subsequently elaborated by Lenin in *What is to be Done?* (1902).

conspicuously successful than ever, while salaried workers lost relatively in prestige and income. The teacher of 1970 had a similar stake in the *status quo*.

The following analysis attempts to show, first, what social circumstances made possible, or reinforced, the divergence in Fagunwa's and Okediji's philosophies; and second, how these ideological differences are revealed in the smallest details as well as in the overall design of the works.

II

In the 1940s and 1950s, the commercial segment of the proto-bourgeoisie was in the majority, but tremendous prestige attached to the segment of administrative and educational salaried workers. At that period the requirements of indirect rule and especially the policy that it should be self-supporting meant that the whole administrative and educational structure was very slight.[5] Nigerians employed in it were rare and privileged, and were associated with the colonial rulers whom they served.[6] They belonged to a hierarchy which, even during nationalist preparations for independence, was generally presumed to be stable and more or less permanent. The only passport to the coveted posts in this hierarchy was education, and the only acceptable education in Southern Nigeria was, very largely, controlled and dispensed by the missionaries. Education and Christianity were still identified together. Educated people were Christians: Christians got education. The missionaries regarded education as a means to conversion, while the colonial administration regarded it as a source of personnel; but their interests coincided because the values that were emphasized by the missionaries were those that served to maintain the *status quo* and promote the smooth running of the colonial machinery. Prominent among these values were obedience, respect for authority, thrift, temperance, reliability, punctuality, honesty, patience in adversity, and personal zeal for progress through hard work. Hierarchical values, already present in traditional Yoruba society, were selectively reinforced by the colonial-missionary authorities for their own ends.

Fagunwa endorsed those values whole-heartedly. O.B. Yai has summarized, most succinctly, Fagunwa's principal moral precepts as beliefs in; (1) social immobilism, viz., that an individual should know his place and keep to it. "It is a sin to question the existing social order or try to change it." (2) meritocracy, viz.,

---

[5] See A.G. Hopkins, *An Economic History of West Africa,* (London: Longman, 1973) pp. 167-171, 187-192, and P.C. Lloyd, 'Power and Independence: Urban Africans,' *Perception of Social Inequality*, (London: Routledge and Kegan Paul, 1974), pp. 60-63.

[6] This does not mean, of course, that the colonial rulers themselves regarded their Nigerian employees as belonging to the same group as themselves. Compared with the pre-colonial period of imperialism in the late 19th century, the Nigerian elite of the colonial period were of relatively junior status in relation to the British colonial officers, and were never accepted by them as colleagues. See Lloyd, *op. cit.*

the erroneous belief of people in capitalist societies that "every poor man can become a millionaire in future. Therefore, every citizen should be content with the current social order with the hope that he may be the next millionaire." (3) patience and hard work as the most important qualities a man can possess, for it is by employing them that he will make it in the world.[7]

But Fagunwa did not merely espouse these values; he identified himself so closely with them that he took on something of the role of a missionary himself. His stories are full of sermons; their tone is pervasively didactic. As a very small and select elite, scarcely established as a class, it was natural for the educated few of Fagunwa's time to regard themselves as spokesmen for, and interpreters of, the authorities who had given them their privileges. But Fagunwa does this with an enthusiasm that becomes at times absurd; and, as we shall see, his didacticism, far from being a mere incidental appendage to his writing, is actually its structural mainstay, albeit an unsatisfactory one. And, conversely, Fagunwa also regards himself as the representative of Yoruba culture and tradition to the colonial authorities and to the rest of the elite. Thus, we find in his work an extensive use, or misuse, of traditional oral materials and themes which are nevertheless constantly heavily edited and "interpreted" to make them acceptable to an elite Christian audience. This is done in a tone of rather muted and subservient nationalism; his work is an example of what *"awa enia dudu"* 'we Africans' can do under the auspices of the colonial authorities, of course, and his final prayer in *Ogboju Ode Ninu Igbo Irunmale* is *"orile ede nyin yio tubo ma po si i ni ogbon ati ni agbara, awa enia dudu ko ni ire ehin mo lailai"* "your nation will still increase in strength and wisdom, we Africans will not lag behind ever again." Thus, placed in the narrow channel of the elite, between the colonial authorities and the Yoruba masses, Fagunwa passes idealized images both ways. He presents an image of ideal missionary virtues to aspirants from the masses; and he presents an image of an idealized and "improved" traditional culture to the colonial authorities and to the elite. Fagunwa's air of self-appointed authority, his self-confident, unabashed moralizing, were only possible because he and his kind were at that time so rare and so privileged.

The situation of the elite was very different thirty years later, when Okediji began publishing. With the establishment, first, of regional elected governments and, then in 1960, of the national federal government, the administrative and educational services were greatly expanded. Political parties made provision of social services one of their first priorities. In the Western Region the Action Group government introduced a scheme for universal free primary education in 1955, and also tried to increase secondary education and provide much more extensive health care. The civil service expanded correspondingly. The administrative and service sector was Nigerianized almost completely by the

---

[7] O.B. Yai, 'Ideas for a Political Reading of Fagunwa', unpublished seminar paper presented at conference on Radical Perspectives on African Literature and Society, University of Ibadan, December, 1977.

early '60s, so that African teachers, headmasters, doctors, civil servants at all levels, and other authority figures, were the norm and no longer the privileged exception. Government itself, moreover, was no longer a "given," imposed from outside and presumed able to run smoothly for an indefinite period. In the hands of the elite it had already, by the time Okediji published his first novel, disintegrated into civil war and been taken over by the military. The government was the principal accumulator of capital, and increasingly the main road to profit lay in acquisition of government contracts, loans and licences. Politicians allied with businessmen were the big men of the day; patronage and corruption, therefore, became more and more the hallmarks of success.[8] This development reached its climax with the immense inflow of oil money at the end of the 1960s. Fortunes were made overnight; conscious displays of wealth, often by half-educated men, were the order of the day. The spectacle of crooks making their pile and retiring to enjoy it made it impossible to believe in the patience-and-hard-work ethic with quite the same enthusiasm as before. Indeed, the whole missionary morality began to lose its immediate relevance when education was no longer the passport to the highest prestige, and when the missionaries no longer controlled education. Instead of the clear-cut precepts of Fagunwa's time, a confusion of values seems to have prevailed.

This confusion can be seen in the Yoruba novelists who came after Fagunwa. Nostalgia for the good rural life was combined with a determination to make it in the bad modern world. Thus, T.A. Awoniyi's *Aiye Kooto* (1973) paints an affectionate portrait of village life with its solid and stable moral values, but makes it clear that the hero is to become a wealthy commercial farmer not content with the "simple" and "humble" life the author praises. Femi Jeboda's *Olowolaiyemo* (1963), on the other hand, follows with glee the adventures of a ruffian on the make, only to reform him and set him up as an honest and contented farmer at the end; it is noteworthy, however, that this "reform" is the book's weak point - it does not ring true, and so both sets of values (clever ruthless trickery; honesty thrift) are undermined.

In the absence of any strong and acceptable communal code, the rise of the lone hero is inevitable. Fagunwa, it is true, portrays lone individuals on their adventures, but in his case the individuals inhabit a stable social world which they temporarily leave, and always return to (in *Ogboju Ode* we even find a *party* of heroes, sent on their mission by the *Oba* and with the blessings of the whole community). The modern lone hero, by contrast, inhabits an unstable and hostile social environment. He can trust no one but himself. He suspects traps and betrayals at every step. The obvious model for such a hero is in the western detective novel and crime thriller. Kola Akinlade uses the former, Okediji the latter. Built into the conventions of the plots of these genres is the loneliness and isolation of the hero; he *has* to suspect everyone (to do otherwise would be

---

[8] See, Lloyd, *op. cit.*

unprofessional); and the excitement of the story depends on the unexpected attack, the nasty surprise, the betrayal. These conventions are apt vehicles for expression of a world view which sees society as a competitive jungle through which the individual has to pick a dangerous path.

Okediji makes this an explicit theme in his two novels. Lapade, the hero of both of them, is a loner who trusts no one except his faithful strong-arm man Tafa. The background is a society getting out of control. Armed robbery, burglary, hemp-peddling and child-stealing are all rife and on the increase, and society is unable to do anything to check them. The police force is not only incompetent and stupid, but also puts more effort into checking Lapade's activities than into catching the criminals. Lapade is always pitted at least as much against his old colleague and rival, the Police Chief, Audu Karimu, as he is against the criminals. Lapade always stands uncompromisingly for honesty, loyalty, justice and fair-dealing; but it is significant that the world in which he operates is confused and compromised. The police force, i.e., the administrative system, plays a role in the story not very different from the role of the law-breakers who flout that system. Tafa is an ex-criminal. There are no hard-and-fast distinctions and Lapade himself is sometimes found in highly compromising situations; when he gloats over the money he has taken from the robbers, for instance, or when he orders his henchman to knock out a captured criminal's teeth, his own mentality does not seem so very different from theirs.

Lapade relies only on his own wit and determination to bring the criminals to book, outwit the police and collar the booty for himself. But it is Okediji's strength that he makes Lapade stand for more than just the individual struggling against a dangerous world and succeeding. Lapade espouses the cause of the victims of society, the ordinary people who are neither in the administrative system nor making their living by flouting it. These people suffer at the hands of the criminals and are let down or fobbed off by the police. Okediji emphasizes the helplessness of such people by making them innocent children (Tolani in *Aja L'o L'eru*) or appealing young girls (Seli and Angelina in *Aja L'o L'eru*), Femi in *Agbalagba Akan,* or amiable young men attempting to help him (Dele and Kunle in *Agbalagba Akan).* The untold wealth which Lapade wrests from the criminals and conceals from the police is distributed, if only in part, to these victims. In *Agbalagba Akan,* for instance, he gives some of it to the families of the murdered Dele and Kunle, and some to Femi to replace her stolen belongings. The rather naively romantic Robin Hood-ish tone of these activities is offset by the fact that Lapade is very definitely a man of the people himself. He is placed at a definite social level (unlike Fagunwa's literate hunters!), and this level is a modest one. He is a farmer, having left the police force on the death of his father; he rides a bicycle, while the criminals and police have cars at their disposal; he reads the newspapers and listens to the radio, but has no pretensions to the life of the educated elite; much is made of his enjoyment of the simple pleasures of life, like sending out for a good plate of *amala* with *gbegiri* soup, or smoking a cigarette in a deck-chair.

III

The differences between Fagunwa's outlook and Okediji's are revealed in the form of their works and also in the language. Let us take Fagunwa first.

We have seen that Fagunwa took upon himself the role of teacher. He wanted to present colonial-missionary values to people preparing to join the educated elite. At the same time he wanted to present "Yoruba tradition," censored and interpreted by himself, to the colonial authorities and the Nigerian elite, to foster a sense of modest national pride which would spur them on to greater achievements. So, he used themes and stories drawn from the Yoruba oral tradition to put across a colonial version of a Christian moral message. This two-way didacticism and the resulting mixture of thematic tendencies is really the key to the form and style of the two books I want examine: *Igbo Olodumare* and *Ogboju Ode Ninu Igbo Irunmale*.[9]

One major feature of the form of these novels is their construction from numerous self-contained incidents which are strung together one after another without any strong narrative links. This is especially noticeable in *Ogboju Ode*. The story is about not one but three separate journeys made into the forest by the hero. There is nothing to link them except occasional casual references, during the later journeys, to incidents that occurred or characters that were encountered during the earlier ones. Each of the journeys, similarly, is made up of a series of separate episodes. Some of these are mere brief encounters with different kinds of *iwin* (spirits), others are quite long self-contained stories as, for instance, the tale of the various attempts on the life of the *Oba* in one town where the hero stays. The episodes are joined only by the theme of the journey; the hero extricates himself from one adventure, goes a little further, and gets involved in another.

The story lacks not only the internal cement of causal sequence, but also any definite linear sense of direction. The hero has no goal, he wanders from situation to situation; and has a tendency to settle down in different spots (often with a lady *iwin*) until something else happens to uproot him.[10] The story, then, is a

---

[9] D.O. Fagunwa, *Igbo Olodumare*, (Lagos: Nelson, 1949) and *Ogboju Ode Ninu Igbo Irunmale*, (Lagos: Nelson, 1950). All quotations will be from these editions. These were Fagunwa's first two novels, *Ogboju Ode* having orginally been published by CMS Bookshop, Lagos in 1938. Later works include *Ireke Onibudo*, (1949), *Irinkerindo Ninu Igbo Elegbeje*, (1954) and Adiitu Olodumare, (1961). Fagunwa's productive life extended from 1936, when he wrote Ogboju Ode until his death in 1963. His major works, however, were composed in the 1940s and early 1950s. For details see Ayo Bamgbose, *The Novels of D.O. Fagunwa*, (Benin: Ethiope Publishing Corporation, 1974).

[10] In the third journey in Ogboju Ode the heroes seem to have a more definite goal - their mission is to reach Oke Langbodo and bring something back for their Oba. But their reason for going does not seem sufficiently pressing to justify all the hardships they endure. It seems

collection of episodes rather than a purposive sequence. It is as if the story were fundamentally static, it fills in a space rather than moving along a trajectory. This makes the ending very appropriate: everything comes to a complete standstill in the house of Iragbeje at Oke Langbodo, and for seven days the hunters sit and listen to stories told by their host. Here we see in their most developed form the two characteristics just mentioned: lack of linear movement (the hunters are immobilized) and composition from separate self-contained incidents (each story told by Iragbeje is an independent traditional tale).

These formal characteristics could be seen as simply the result of Fagunwa's attempt to use traditional oral narrative materials to string together, that is, a lot of stories that were originally independent in attempt to meet the externally-imposed requirement of the *length* suitable to a book. But Fagunwa had another reason for using this form, as we can see from the fact that his treatment actually *exaggerates* those characteristics. He used this form because it was well-suited to his didactic purpose. His strong and consistent aim, which gives the stories a kind of artificial unity, is to draw a moral from every encounter and every incident. A leisurely, inconsequential plot is ideal, for it allows him to pause and deliver a sermon whenever the fancy takes him. There is no need to hurry on, for he and his hero are not going anywhere in particular.

Fagunwa uses every means at his disposal to present his moral ideas. Not only the narrator but the characters themselves frequently offer a little sermon as comment on some incident. Some of the characters even seem to have been introduced for the sole purpose of acting as a mouth-piece for Fagunwa's moral discourse. As well as Iragbeje and Baba Onirungbon Yeuke, the wise old men of *Ogboju Ode* and *Igbo Olodumare* respectively, we have characters like the hero's mother in *Igbo Olodumare* who appears to him in mysterious circumstances only to lecture him for the space of four pages on such topics as the virtues of determination, honesty, and caring for one's wife! Themes, too, are sometimes introduced gratuitously, for the sake of the opportunity they offer of sermonizing. In the introduction to *Igbo Olodumare,* for example, the first narrator, who plays no significant part in the subsequent story, merely acting as a scribe to the narrator proper, is presented as brooding on his father's death. His extensive meditations on the subject give him the opportunity to make moral points, first, that children should show gratitude for, and attempt to repay, their parents' kindness, and second, that one must be resigned to God's will. These examples suggest that for Fagunwa it is the moral which is important; the story is a vehicle to carry the moral.

---

rather to be a mere excuse for another journey into the forest. And the novel as a whole does not hang together on the strength of the structure of a single episode. In a more general sense, all Fagunwa's heroes have a kind of goal in so far as they set off into the forest in order to practise their craft of hunting in the most courageous and glorious way possible. But again this aim is not specific enough to impel the hero in any particular direction. One episode follows another almost without the hero's volition.

The constant tendency in Fagunwa's writing is to move away from the immediate narrative situation to more general themes. This happens even in the middle of the most dramatic scenes. In the mortal combat between the hero and the fearsome *iwin* Anjonnu-Iberu in *Igbo Olodumare,* for example, there is a pause while the wives of the two combatants bring food and water for them. This leads Fagunwa to reflect on the importance of wifely duty, and from there he moves on to more and more general considerations:

> Bayi ni awon mejeji se ti nwon toju oko won, nitori itoju oko nipataki ise obirin t'o ni oko. Igbati inu tokotaya ba dun ni nwon to le gbadun omo won. Suru ni baba ati iya anfani, omugo enia ni nwipe suru on po ju nitori suru ko ni opin. Ki tokotaya mope bi suru ti awon ba mu fun ara won loni ba ju ti ana lo, awon yio ni owo, awon yio ni omo, awon yio si ni alafia ni ise olubori owo ati omo. Jeki awon enia ma re o je, mu suru fun won, se iwo mo ninu ara re pe, nwon bere isubu ni eleyini. Bi enia ba re o je, ti iwo si se bi enipe iwo ko tile mo, iwo ti gbe eleyini si inu ikoko gbigbona, eri okan re yio si ma ko ina mo o. Sugbon bi iwo ko ba mu suru to, ti iwo nba oloriburuku enia binu po, on o ko iwa omugo ran o, on a si mo pe ohun ti on se dun o, on a gbe ewu igberaga wo si ejika, beni on ko ni ireti ati lo si iwaju mo nitire, nigbati on ba si ko ibanuje ba o loni, a se be di o lowo ilosiwaju ehin ola. *(Igbo Olodumare, p. 32)*.

This is how both of them ministered to their husbands, because ministering to her husband is a wife's chief task. Only when husband and wife are both contented can they enjoy their children. Patience is the father and mother of benefits, only an idiot says his patience has been excessive, because patience has no limit. Let husbands and wives realize that if the forbearance they show each other today is greater than yesterday's, they will have money, they will have children, and they will have the blessing of good health which is superior to both money and children. Let people cheat you, bear with them, for you know inside you that this means they have begun their downfall. If someone cheats you and you take no notice, you have put that person into a boiling cooking-pot, and his bad conscience will be heaping fire on him. But if you are not patient enough, if you get angry with the wicked man, he will use you with contempt, and he will know that what he did pained you, he will put on the garment of pride, and though he has no ambition to make progress himself, when he has afflicted you with wretchedness today, he will go on to hinder your advancement in the future.

Notice how each idea gives rise to another one, still more remote from the original topic. Thinking about wifely duty leads him to think about the quality most necessary to a happy marriage - patience; thinking about patience leads to a lengthy consideration of this quality as the path to all the good things of life, of situations where patience is most needed and of the consequences of *not* having patience in such situations. Meanwhile, the reader has forgotten all about the fight, the outcome of which still hangs in the balance. Carrying through a tense and dramatic scene is less important in Fagunwa than the presentation of the moral reflections that arise from it. The constant drift from the immediate narrative situation to general moral considerations is too important to be called digression. The hunter wandering through the bush making strange encounters is an apt vehicle for the moralist, wandering through the incidents of his plots and hanging a sermon on each one.

The ending of both books shows how well the discontinuous, quasi-static form suits Fagunwa's didactic purpose. We have already noted that the storytelling sessions at Iragbeje's and Baba Onirungbon Yeuke's houses bring the formal characteristics of the books to their logical conclusion, providing a kind of structural climax. This is also true from a thematic point of view. When the action is finally immobilized a veritable feast of moralizing sets in; the wise men are given a free hand, unimpeded by any narrative constraints, to talk as much as they like. All the stories they tell are to illustrate (not always very appositely) some moral theme or other. As well as stories there are straightforward sermons and exhortations. We feel that here Fagunwa is really in his element; this is the thematic consummation of the book. That it should coincide with the structural climax shows clearly how well the aimless, non-sequential episodic narrative style works as a vehicle for Fagunwa's moral purpose.

It must be said, however, that Fagunwa's moralizing is not a success. It is self-indulgent and opportunistic. The presentation of his moral stance does not follow a consistent schematic organization but is simply a series of sermons on any topic that happens to arise. The most trivial points of etiquette are given the same weight as the most serious moral issues. The vehicle that he hangs the assorted sermons on is not consistently used. The world of traditional oral tales is not in itself a bad setting for the modern pilgrim's progress through life (and Fagunwa says explicitly in both books that this is how he intends it to be read); but in Fagunwa we find the Christian "interpretation" so crude and heavy-handed, and yet, so patchy that the stories do not work either as traditional tales or as moral allegories. One might cite as an example, the uneven treatment of the denizens of the forest. Some of the *iwin* are left untampered with - fearsome an unpredictable beings to be avoided or overcome by the hero, and nothing more. Others are interpreted as being fallen angels undergoing punishment for their disobedience to God. In *Ogboju Ode,* Aroni, Kurembete, Were-orun and all the inhabitants of the "sinful town" are treated like this. Still, others are given a strong emblematic significance in the manner of Bunyan's *Pilgrim's Progress* or English morality plays. One *iwin* is named *Eru* (fear), and is a terrifying monster which is only overpowered by the singing of a sweet song about God's goodness to man (illustrating, presumably, the moral that perfect love casteth out fear). Others of this type are *Iranlowo* (Succour) *and Iwapele* (Gentleness) who represent what their names suggest. None of these styles of interpretation is carried through.

A similar inconsistency is found in the mechanisms of narrative movement.

Sometimes Fagunwa goes out of his way to insist that it is God's direct intervention alone - through an agent such as *Iranlowo* or through the efficacy of the hero's prayer - that can change the situation. At other times the hero is saved by *egbe* medicine[11] and by magical pepper pods, and strengthened by a potion given to him by his wife-to-be, a witch. Although these two mechanisms are similar in the sense that they both represent the unexpected incursion of an external, inexplicable force they are incompatible because God's intervention implies an overall Divine Plan (which is not followed up) whereas *egbe* medicine implies human self-help. Occasionally, Fagunwa seems to feel embarrassment at the incongruity of these two modes of explanation and hastens to paper over the cracks - as, for instance, when the hunters in *Ogboju Ode* perform a sacrifice to get out of a tight spot, and Fagunwa has to explain:

> *Gegebi asa ile wa, a mu eiye yi a la inu re a bu epo si i a si gbe e sinu apadi kekere kan bayi a gbe e lo si idi igi nla kan ti mbe leba odo wa. Inu Olorun dun pe a ronu-piwada- ki ise nitori ebo ti a ru - sugbon nitori o mo pe ibasepe a ni oye jube lo ni, a ba sin on ni ona ti o dara ju eyini lo.*
> (*Ogboju Ode Ninu Igbo Irunmale*, p. 58-9).

> In accordance with the custom of our land, we slit open this bird and poured palm oil onto it, and we put it in a little potsherd, we took it to the foot of a big tree nearby us. God was glad that we had repented - not because of the sacrifice that we offered - but because he knew that if we had been more enlightened we would have found a better way of serving him (i.e., we did our best according to our lights).

Fagunwa has fallen between two stools. If one compares him with Tutuola one sees how much better Tutuola's stories succeed as tales of the folk imagination, because the non-causal sequences, the random and unexplained happenings, the brief encounters without consequences all help to create the peculiar ambience of Tutuola's stories, the ambience of the terrible and the marvellous. Fagunwa, by tampering with this world, by explaining some things and not others, by giving some an allegorical interpretation and leaving others, has robbed it of its authentic thrill. But if one compares him on the other hand with Bunyan, one sees how much better Bunyan succeeds in creating a convincing moral allegory, because he is *consistently* allegorical and because he has a total conceptual scheme, a comprehensive view of the moral difficulties and dangers that the pilgrim through life has to encounter.

If the form of Fagunwa's stories is both determined, and vitiated, by his desire to moralize, one can say the same of his language, the tendency to drift away from the concrete issue onto the most diverse moral themes is repeated in the tendency of his prose style to drift from the point through association and

---

[11] *Egbe* medicine: a charm believed to have the power of transporting its owner instantaneously to another place.

sheer rhetorical momentum. As with his plots, there is a lack of forward movement; a tendency to elaborate in a leisurely and expansive fashion on any given point rather than move on directly to a new point. This elaboration sometimes takes the form of simple repetitive variation on a theme:

> ... *igbana ni baba mi pa oju de, ti o rekoja oke odo, ti o ki aiye pe o digbose, ti akuko ko lehin okunrin. (Igbo Olodumare, p. 2).*
>
> at that time my father closed his eyes (for the last time) and crossed the river of life, and bid the world farewell, and the cock crowed behind the man.

All four clauses mean the same thing - the man died. The sentence is the static embroidery of a single point. The leisurely, drifting tendency of his prose can also be seen in his great predilection for simile. Hardly anything is mentioned without being compared with something else:

> *Ibiti mo ti nronu bayi ni okunrin na ti kigbe lairotele, ohun re si dabi igbati... jagidijagan aa mi bi iyawo eniti o lo si oju ogun, mo si nwariri bi igbati alupupu ti o baje ba ngun ori oke, nitori igbe okunrin na lagbara bi ti kiniun, o rin ile dodo bi ti ajanaku, o gba igbo kankan bi igbati reluwe ba nsunmo eti ilu ti o nfon fere kikankikan. (Igbo Olodumare, p. 4).*
>
> As I was brooding thus, the man suddenly gave a great shout, and his voice sounded like a hooligan messenger throwing something down from a height, I was as frightened as the wife of a man gone to the battle-front, and I was shaking like a defective motorbike going uphill, because the man's shout was as powerful as a lion's, it was as heavy as an elephant's, it shook the bush as violently as a train approaching the edge of a town with its whistle blasting.

These similes have a certain charm in their own right; but they do not build up a vivid, frightening picture of the approaching man because there are too many diverse images involved. The man's voice is like the thud of a falling object, the roar of a lion, the trumpeting of an elephant, and also an approaching train; the narrator in his terror is like a wife whose husband is going to war but also like a defective motorbike going uphill! The disparity of all these images means that they cancel each other out and the total picture is diffuse and blurred. It is as if the similes were being included for their own sake rather than to illuminate a particular idea. This impression is reinforced by the frequent instances of a simile taking on a life of its own and generating its own string of qualifying clauses, and even further similes of its own to describe it:

> *Sugbon bi mo fe bi mo ko okunrin na yo si mi dandan, inu bi mi gidigidi, mo fa oju ro bi eniti ebi npa, mo npose bi eniti iya nje, mo di enu dudu bi omo odo ti o fo awo onje, ti ko le so fun ni, ti o nrin kakiri egbe ogiri, ti inu omo na si daru bi igedegede idi emu inu sago. (Igbo Olodumare, p. 3).*

But whether I liked it or not the man approached me determinedly, I was furious, I frowned like someone gnawed by hunger, I sighed like an afflicted man, I screwed up my face like a house-boy who has broken a plate and can't bring himself to own up, but creeps around against the wall and feels as disturbed as the lees at the bottom of the palm wine in the flagon.

The *omo odo ti o fo awo onje* is first introduced as a simile to illustrate the sullen attitude of the narrator, but Fagunwa gets carried away by the idea and goes on to describe the behaviour of the *omo odo* in detail; even introducing a further simile - *bi igedegede idi emu inu sago* - to embellish the description. The image of the house-boy has taken over, and now engages our attention more than the original subject, i.e., the narrator's mood. This type of displacement of attention occurs constantly in Fagunwa's prose and it suggests that the writer is in no hurry to nail down any particular idea or image. Instead he is content to elaborate whatever idea happens to be before him. This kind of writing is decorative more than purposive - and has, indeed, been much commended for this quality.[12] Like the plots of his books, his prose seems to be filling in a given space as attractively as possible.

Another characteristic of Fagunwa's style which seems to derive from his didactic intention is its rhetorical monotony. Sentences are composed of long strings of structurally identical clauses, as can be seen from the excerpts above. Monotony is characteristic not only of individual sentences but of the books' style as a whole; the same type of sentence is repeated again and again. The tone never changes. We find the same repetitiousness, the same redundancy of simile, the same elaborate biblical formulations whether it is a fight that is being described or a sermon that is being delivered. There is no variation even when dialogue is introduced. The hero answers a challenge from the enraged *Esu-kekere-ode* like this:

> *Bayi ni iwin na so si baba mi baba mi na si fesi bi o ti ye ki alagbara fesi fun alagbara. O wo Esu-kekere-ode bi igbati janduku obirin ba fi oju ibaje wo oko re; o wipe: "Eniti ofi ase gbe oju o tan ara re je; eniti o duro de reluwe yio ba ara re ni orun alakeji; agba ti o ri ejo ti ko sa ara iku l'o nya a; eranko ti o ba nfi oju di ode ehin aro ni yio sun, eniti o gboju le ogun fi ara re fun osi ta; ebora ti o ba fi oju di mi yio ma ti orun de orun ni, emi okunrin ni mo wi be, oni ni ngo so fun enyin ebora Igbo Olodumare pe, nigbati Eleda da ohun gbogbo ti mbe ninu aiye tan, o fi enia se olori gbogbo won ...*
> *(Igbo Olodumare, p. 16).*

Thus, spoke the spirit to my father, and my father replied as one mighty man ought to reply to another. He looked at *Esu-kekere-ode* like a shrewish wife

---

[12] See, for example, Bamgbose, *The Novels of D.O. Fagunwa*. Fagunwa's 'fine style' is here presented as his chief merit.

glowering at her husband, and said: "Anyone who tries to carry rainwater in a sieve is deceiving himself; anyone who stands in the path of a train will find himself in heaven; an elder who sees a snake and doesn't run is hastening the day of his own death; a wild animal that scoffs at the hunter will end up sleeping behind the fireplace (i.e. will be killed and hung up to smoke), anyone who depends on what he hopes to inherit gives himself over to wretchedness; a spirit that is disrespectful to me will certainly wander eternally from heaven to heaven, I, a man, say so, today I shall make it clear to you spirits of Igbo Olodumare that when the Creator had created everything in the world, he made human beings the lords of all...

The style used for speech is not different in any way from the style of the straight narrative; neither is even remotely like natural speech. Much has been made of Fagunwa's technique of "narrative distancing", i.e., setting the story at several removes from actuality by means of narrators.[13] For example, *Igbo Olodumare* opens with the voice of one narrator who is then called upon to write down a story dictated by someone else, who in turn is not telling his own story but his father's, and who, half-way through, stops narrating and begins to read aloud the story as written down by his father; and towards the end we get still another layer when one of the characters, Baba Onirungbon Yeuke, temporarily takes over the role of story-teller. It has been said that the story is presented like this because the narrative material is incongruous with present-day reality. This is true; but while one is reading the story one soon forgets how many layers of narration there are - it is as if the entire story were being told by the same voice. The reason for this is that the style is so uniform that it makes no difference *who* is speaking. All of them use the same stately and artificial rhetoric - and all of them moralize. However many narrators and characters Fagunwa introduces, they are all mouthpieces speaking with the same voice; the parsonical voice of Fagunwa. The monotony of the language reveals more than anything else that the real *raison d'etre* of the stories is to deliver a sermon.

IV

Okediji, on the other hand, plots his novels so that there is always a task of great urgency for the hero to perform. In *Aja L'o L'eru*[14] it is literally a matter of life and death; the criminals abduct a little girl and Lapade has to trace her and rescue her before she comes to any harm. In *Agbalagba Akan*[15] the action is given an initial impetus by the murder of Lapade's friend and assistant Dele, which has to be avenged. Once involved, he is driven on by the need to avoid

---

[13] The question is extensively discussed by Omolara Ogundipe-Leslie in 'The Poetics of Fiction by Yoruba Writers: the case of *Ogboju Ode Ninu Igbo Irunmale* by D.O. Fagunwa,' seminar paper presented at Ife University Conference on Yoruba Civilization, 1976.

[14] Oladejo Okediji, *Aja L'o L'eru*, (London: Longman 1969).

[15] Oladejo Okediji, *Agbalagba Akan*, (London: Longman, 1971).

crises as they pile up. Throughout the story his house is surrounded by the police, so there is always extra pressure on him to get back inside the house before his absence is noticed.

The urgency and necessity of his actions is highlighted in both books by his initial reluctance to get involved; he is anxious to get back to his farm, and only his public-spiritedness and the real urgency of the case prevent him. The hectic and exhausting nature of his activities is emphasized by the short rests that he snatches - rests that he luxuriates in, only to have them rudely interrupted by a new development in the unfolding crisis. He is also given to reflecting on the awful pace of his adventures and recapitulating all that has happened - another way of emphasizing the speed of the action:

> ... O wo aago, o si ya a lenu pe aago kan ko tii lu. O tun fi okan wo ohun ti o ti sele laarin wakati marun sehin. Bi iru re sele ni ogota odun, enia fere le so pe o po ju. Iru re ki i sele si opolopo enia titi nwon ofi lo je Olodumare nipe. Isele ojoojumo ni fun Lapade.
>
> Tafa l'o si koko de laaaro nibiti oun ti nreti oloka. Ibi ti oun ti nmura oko lowo, lati sa jinna si jjongbon, ni Kunle ta biobio wole de. Sule Alayimo, ayimo ki i p'oloko. Bawo Ladeji lona Iwo lohun. Oku Dele ninu papa. Baba ode, baba onibaba. Moto oniburedi Jaiyeola, abikokolori. Audu Karimu. Audu Karimu... (Agbalagba Akan, p. 35).

He looked at his watch, and was surprised to find that it was not yet one o'clock. He went over all the things that had happened in the last five hours. Even if they had been spread over sixty years, it would be almost too much. Many people don't experience the like in an entire lifetime. It was an everyday occurrence for Lapade.

It was Tafa who had turned up first in the morning while he was waiting for the *oka* seller. As he was getting ready to go to the farm, to get well away from trouble, Kunle had come hurtling in. Sule Alayimo, "Turning doesn't kill the driver." Ladeji's palm-wine factory on the Iwo road, Dele's body in the field. The old hunter, that fine old man. The bread van. Jaiyeola, with the lump on his head. Audu Karimu. Audu Karimu. Audu Karimu ...

Lapade always has a very definite objective: to defeat the criminals, outwit the police, and save the victims; and the stories move at break-neck speed as he pursues these objectives, brief pauses for rest and reflection merely accentuating the narrative's headlong pace.

But although the stories are fast and full of action (at times they seem overcrowded with fights, kidnappings, sudden journeys to remote hideouts) they never become a monotonous recital of violence. It is Okediji's great merit that he keeps his hero human even in the most extreme circumstances. Despite his popular-hero attributes of immense strength, powerful intelligence, and so on, he is no mere superman. We are allowed to see him in moments of doubt and vulnerability. This is achieved largely through the use of interior monologue, which brings the events of the story to us as if experienced by him. The narrative moves casually from ordinary third-person narrative to interior monologue and back:

> *Oju iho kokoro ni Lapade ti wa nyo Adegun wo lehin ilekun ninu yara lohun. O ranju, o garun garun, ko ri nkankan. O pada lo si koro igun ile ti o ti duro tele ri. Ki oun mu suuru, nitori suuru le se okuta jinna. O ti pada si igun ile naa ki Femi too wa fowoto o. Femi. Nwon ko se ankasifi ku sinu yara re. Awon ole atunisihooho yen. Afi ki Olorun tuna asiri awon naa.*
> *(Agbalagba Akan, p. 152).*

> Lapade had been secretly watching Adegun on the other side of the door in that room, through the keyhole. Peer and crane his neck as he would, he could see nothing. He went back into the corner of the house where he had been standing before. He would have to be patient, for with patience even a stone can be cooked till it's done. He had reached the corner of the house when Femi touched him. Femi. They hadn't left so much as a handkerchief in her room. Those were 'Strip-you-naked' thieves. Just let God strip their own evil secrets bare in turn.

The first three sentences of this excerpt are in ordinary third-person narrative, but with *Ki oun mu suuru* we begin to hear the words that Lapade is thinking or saying to himself. These thoughts are presented vividly in the way that they would really occur to someone - i.e., slightly disjointed, moving forward swiftly and then pausing over a particularly arresting thought: *Femi. Nwon ko se ankasifi ku sinu yara re...*

Interior monologue also allows flashbacks which provide necessary background information to the story. Thus, the information that Lapade was formerly a policeman, that he left the force when his father died, and that his old colleagues have since been promoted above their merits, is all provided at the beginning of *Aja L'o L'eru* in the form of memories passing through Lapade's mind as he cycles along the road to Ibadan. This is a highly economical and effective way of putting the reader in the picture.

Okediji adopts conventions that make possible an absorbing and fast-moving story. This is requisite in a thriller; but Okediji also turns these characteristics to moral and critical account. Just as Fagunwa used the form most suited to his purpose of sermonizing, so Okediji chooses a form which best allows him to express his conception of society's moral crisis. The story moves fast because innocent people are threatened, as much by corruption within the system as by criminals who evade that system. Lapade has to save them, striking a blow for individual integrity in the face of moral chaos. The theme is the efficacy of action, in direct contrast to Fagunwa's ethic of "social immobilism." The narrative technique of interior monologue, which does so much to make Lapade human and accessible to us, has the effect of engaging us intimately with Lapade's own moral stand. Seeing things through his eyes, our viewpoint is coloured with his humanity, and his moral outlook is the one we most naturally adopt.

The language, even more than the form, of Okediji's novels reveals his moral sympathies. While Fagunwa erects an imposing artificial facade of style which keeps the reader at a distance, Okediji is a master of the colloquial. He has an extraordinary capacity to catch the rhythms and style of ordinary speech and make it live on the printed page, so that one hears it rather than merely reading it:

> *"Iya o! Iya!" Eni kan dahun lati inu ile, o ni "Oooo, kini o? O o*
> *... o kojusi aba, o ni "Iya o! Iya!" Eni kan dahun lati inu ile, o ni "Oooo, kini o? O o fee pakuo mo ko? S'o ti yaa re o nu-un? Moo bo nile bo ba tire o o. B'o d'aaro o pa yoku. Ee t'o-o pa un naa nii j'oun."*
>   *Omobinrin t'o wa nita ni, "T'ekuo ko o. Awon alejo kan l'o de o."*
>   *"Tani nwon l'awon mbeere?"*
>   *"Emi o bi won o. Emi tie seb'awon ara'-a*
>   *'Badan l'o de tele ni.*
> *Af'igba 'm'mo w'oju-u won ti mo ri ip'awon ko."*
> *Onitohun yoju sita. Iya agbalagba ni, o gbon kujokujo ...*
> *(Aja L'o L'eru, pp. 105-6).*

> ... she turned to the hut and said "Ma'am! am!"
> Someone answered from inside, saying "Yes, what is it? You don't want to shell palmnuts any more, is that it? So you're tired already, are you? Come on in if you're tired. You can shell the rest tomorrow. You haven't done so bad already.
> The girl outside said, "It is not the palm-nuts. Some visitors have arrived,"
> "Who do they say they want to see?"
> I didn't ask them. Actually I thought they were the Ibadan people at first. It was only when I saw their faces I realized it wasn't them."
> The other speaker came out. It was an old woman, decrepit with age...

This is more than a beautifully faithful reproduction of a local dialect. Even before the old woman emerges from the hut, we have a vivid impression of her from her speech alone. The deep accent suggests a rural, uneducated and probably elderly person. She is garrulous and lively; jumping to the conclusion that Seli is calling because she is tired of shelling palm-nuts, she chatters away on this theme until the girl stops her. Her tone is a mixture of kindness and asperity; the touch of scorn in *S'o ti yaa re o nu-un?* is immediately softened by the indulgence and concern in *Moo bo nile b'o ba ti re o o.* The accurately-captured tone of the voice - the garrulity, the asperity, the indulgence - presents her whole character to us before she even appears on the scene. Okediji's fine ear for the nuances of ordinary speech reveals a profound familiarity with, and understanding of, the kind of people he portrays. This does not preclude satire, and the speech of some characters (notably Audu Karimu, in both books, and Doogo in *Agbalagba Akan*) is irresistibly comic.
All the dialogue, satirical or otherwise, is quite evidently drawn from continuous creative contact with the real environment.

It is not only the dialogue which captures colloquial speech patterns. The use of interior monologue means that much of the story can be told in a speech-like way. Language can be used as the thought or words of Lapade which would not be appropriate coming from an impersonal author - like such biting comments as *Audu naa ni nwon wa ti fi je inspekto agba yi. Sio!* (And they went and made that same Audu into Chief Inspector. Ugh! (*Aja L'o L'eru*, p. 2). Throughout, the style is simple, flexible, lively and colloquial. It could be described as heightened speech. For while it has all the nuances, the changes of tone and tempo, the pithy directness of real speech, these qualities are shaped to the requirements of the narrative - to arouse anticipation, create tension, suggest a mood - with a skill which is beyond the scope of ordinary speakers. This can be seen in the way that proverbs are woven in. Proverbs are part of speech; they are the ordinary person's verbal art, learnt by being heard in everyday conversation. But Okediji uses them far more frequently and effectively than they are used in real speech. (And it must be added that by "real speech" we here mean the speech only of those people whose way of life has allowed them to remain in touch with *ijinle Yoruba* - "deep Yoruba.")

Any passage taken at random from either novel will illustrate these points, as well as suggesting far more. This is the opening of *Agbalagba Akan:*

> *O pe ti Lapade ti ji. O ti rorin, o si ti we. O wa joko, o si fehinti lori aga alaso kan ni palo re. Timutimu alawo kan ti awon onisona fi aworan orisirisi dara si lara wa niwaju re, o gbe ese mejeeje le e. O diju. O lo aso aran alarabara kan bayii modi; ko wewu beeni ko bo sokoto. Ojo ti a o ba sonu, gagaaga l'are eni i ya. O njobi o nmu siga re, laiyaju. A ki i tanna mo on ofun.*
>
> *Ko yasi iwe-irohin gbogbo ti o wa lori tabili nitosi odo re. Ko fokansi redio ti nke tantan lara ogiri; o sa nfa eefln siga satari, b'o ba yo nimu, a tun tu u jade lenu. Beeni o njobi wuyanwuyan lenu bi eni njesu. Sugbon ko yaju.*
>
> *Eni kan wole de .....*

Lapade had woken up long ago. He had cleaned his teeth and washed. Then he had sat down, and he was reclining in a deck-chair in his parlour. A leather cushion decorated with all kinds of designs lay in front of him, and he rested both his feet on it. His eyes were closed. He had wrapped a many-coloured velvet cloth around his waist; he had no shirt or trousers on. On the day of one's downfall one starts off feeling on top of the world. He was eating kola, he was smoking his cigarette, without opening his eyes. There is no need to light a lamp to see the way down one's throat.

He didn't glance at all the newspapers that lay on the table next to him. He paid no attention to the radio that was playing from the wall; he just kept inhaling the cigarette smoke and emitting it from nose and mouth alike. At the same time he was munching kola as if he were eating yams. But he didn't open his eyes.

Someone came in ...

With a simple sentence that is highly effective, we are plunged at once into the first scene. There is no introduction, no explanation of who Lapade is, and the sense of being immediately in the thick of things is heightened by the statement that Lapade has *already* been awake for some time - i.e., before the story began. The scene is set in a few sentences. Notice how effective a very simple construction can be when juxtaposed with longer and more elaborate sentences *O diju*. Constant variations of this type engage the reader's attention and make him ready for any sudden changes the story may bring; the reader is on his toes (mentally speaking) from the very first sentence. The picture being painted is of Lapade at ease. The details about the chair he is reclining in, the cloth he is wearing, his relaxed posture, and so on, all help to build up a convincing image of someone enjoying complete rest. But then comes the proverb, *Ojo ti a o ba sonu, gagaaga l'ara eni i ya*. This proverb both encapsulates the preceding description, and rouses apprehensions about what is to come. The phrase *gagaaga l'ara eni i ya* sums up Lapade's state of comfort, enjoyment and well-being, so far conveyed only through concrete details. But *Ojo ti a o ba sonu* sounds a strong note of warning. It is only on a day of calamity that one feels so good to start with. After this suggestion of impending disaster, the description of Lapade's pleasure continues, but there is now a kind of tension, an expectation that something will happen to disturb him; and the emphasis is now on his *obliviousness* to the world; he ignores both radio and papers and doesn't even open his eyes. Thus, we are prepared for the whole chain of events that begins to unfold with the first entrant, *Eni kan wole de*.

This, then, is highly skilled and carefully judged writing. It makes its effects unobtrusively. It sounds completely natural, but it is beautifully composed. This illusion of natural speech is maintained, and the verbal skill of the work is rarely put on display. Conspicuous rhetoric is occasionally used for chosen effects - see, for example, the description of Lapade and Tafa fleeing through the bush in *Agbalagba Akan* (p. 21). The normal style, however, is a concealed rhetoric which even deliberately repudiates "fine-sounding" prose. Tafa, the great word-spinner, the tireless verbal artist, is always getting them into trouble with his endless verbosity. He listens to his own voice too much and is too involved in his own verbal fantasies to pay proper attention to the outside world. Lapade on the other hand, knows that *Eni ti kofohun ki isiwi* - "One who says nothing never speaks wrongly" *(Agbalagba Akan,* p. 108). Lapade is presented as someone who watches and thinks but is impatient of too much talk. The apparently natural, speech-like style does more than reveal understanding of, and sympathy with, the common man; it makes a specific moral point. Lapade, the man of unaffected colloquial speech (which can be eloquent, despite his own disclaimer) is the good man. The pompous elaborations of Audu Karimu, the ludicrous rhetorical vehemence of Doogo, imply a kind of moral opacity and deviousness; the effusions of Tafa are, at best, a loveable weakness. The brilliance of Okediji's novels lies in the way this adherence to the cause of ordinariness is maintained by means of - and not in spite of - his own exuberant, endless, astonishing verbal creativity and skill.

V

It has been argued in this chapter that the striking difference in style and structure of the two writers' novels is best approached from the point of view of the differences in their ideologies; and that the difference in their ideologies, in turn, are best understood in terms of what the changing social-historical circumstances permitted or encouraged them, as members of an emerging social class, to see. Neither writer can be described as merely "reflecting" a prevailing class attitude, and Okediji was actually able to reach a position that was quite a typical of the group to which he objectively belonged. This was taken even further in his play *Rere Run* (1973). Here he discards the romantic individualism of the novels (where the hero, single-handed, redresses social wrongs in thrilling and often rather bloodthirsty style) and, in a naturalistic study of worker-employer confrontation, shows his awareness of the need for united action from the exploited - though he does doubt whether it can be achieved. Here he has come out more clearly in a political attitude alien to his class.

It was emphasized, also, that the "class" being discussed was, and still is, nascent - in the process of formation - and peripheral - a by-product of the world capitalist economy. Such a social formation, it should be stressed, cannot be said to have a completely distinctive, coherent, "class" view of the world. Even in the fully-formed classes of an advanced capitalist society, no class ideology is separate and impermeable; many ideas are shared by all classes and many are passed down from rulers to ruled. This is even more the case in a society where class is nascent. While Fagunwa's ideas undoubtedly had their origin in the colonial-missionary nexus, they cannot be claimed to belong solely and specifically to the elite. Missionary morality was pervasive and was quickly absorbed into the thinking of masses of converts who remained peasants and workers. This can be seen in the themes and attitudes continually enacted in the common man's most popular entertainment, the Yoruba travelling theatre. Fagunwa's distinction was that he realized so clearly - and with such fervent approval - how that morality served to uphold structures of authority and privilege.

If Fagunwa's ideology extends, at least in some of its aspects, far beyond the bounds of his "class," Okediji's has hardly been attained, except in partial and scattered groups, even within the one "class" whose interests it represents, the peasants and workers. Current social and political developments, however, suggest that this will not remain the case.

Chapter 16

Abubakar Imam and the conservative conscience

- Abba Aliyu Sani

Alhaji Abubakar Imam is probably the earliest and most famous modern Hausa writer to emerge from the northern states of Nigeria. Imam was a teacher, journalist, editor, novelist, and politician. The focus of discussion in this chapter is the contribution of Abubakar Imam to the evolution of a conservative conscience, particularly among the pioneer elites in Northern Nigeria. In fact, John Paden, author of *Ahmadu Bello, Sardauna of Sokoto*, has confidently asserted that: 'Abubakar Imam is still regarded as one of the founding fathers of Northern consciousness.'[1]

The emphasis in this discussion will be on Imam's writings in the Hausa newspaper *Gaskiya Ta Fi Kwabo* (Truth is worth more than a penny) and his three-volume stories, *Magana Jari Ce* (The craft of story telling is a valuable asset) published in the period 1937-1939.

Born in 1911 in Kagara in the former Kontagora Province in the present Niger State to Shehu Usman (the first judge of Kagara), Abubakar Imam had his primary education at the Katsina Provincial School from where he preceded to the famous Katsina Teachers' College from 1927 to 1930.[2] In 1931 he joined the Katsina Native Authority as a teacher of English at the Katsina Middle School. It was at this time that Imam's creative abilities became apparent. In 1933, his *Ruwan Bagala* (The Search for the Water of Cure) won the first prize in a Hausa

---

[1] John N. Paden, *Ahmadu Bello, Sardauna of Sokoto: Values and Leadership in Nigeria*, Zaria, Hudahuda Publishing Company Ltd., 1986, p. 143.

[2] Founded in 1921-22 by the British, Katsina College has produced and moulded virtually all the first generation elite of Northern Nigeria. Among other prominent leaders trained in the College are Isa Kaita, Ahmadu Bello, Abubakar Tafawa Balewa, Kashim Ibrahim and Aminu Kano. As Paden has pointed out at pp. 96-100 of his book, the concern of the British was to use Katsina College to groom the character and consciousness of the future leaders of Nigeria in the image of the colonizer. Abubakar Imam was, therefore, among other things, a beneficiary of the education system at Katsina which encouraged Northerners to think in terms of "regional" rather than "provincial" loyalties as Paden attests to in his study.

language writing competition organized by the British-sponsored Zaria Translation Bureau, then headed by Dr. Rupert East.[3]

In 1934 he was appointed the first honorary secretary of the Katsina Provincial Board, which was a local parliament of District heads. In view of the immense contribution the Bureau expected from him, Imam was seconded to the Bureau from 1935-1939, during which time he produced the three-volume book, *Magana Jari Ce*. Meanwhile the Bureau had had to move headquarters to Katsina to effectively exploit Imam's writing skills. In 1939 he moved to Zaria to become the Hausa editor in the Zaria Translation Bureau (ZTB). He was promoted Hausa editor of *Gaskiya Ta Fi Kwabo* (GTK) in 1948, and according to John Paden, Imam thus became the first Northerner to occupy a senior civil service appointment in Northern Nigeria. Imam was still editor of the paper until 1951 when he was elected to serve in the Northern Region House of Assembly in Kaduna and the House of Representatives in Lagos. He represented Zaria City. John Paden further acknowledges that Imam was one of the founders of the Northern People's Congress whose general secretary he was. He had also co-founded the Northern Peoples Union (Jamiyar Mutanen Arewa or JMA) with Dr. R.A.B. Dikko, the first medical doctor and university graduate of northern Nigeria origin.

In 1943, while serving as editor of *Gaskiya*, Imam joined the first Anglophone West African Press Delegation to the United Kingdom which was sponsored by the British Council.[4]

In 1954, Imam resigned from active politics to head the Book Section of the Gaskiya Corporation, Zaria, and subsequently became the first Superintendent of the Northern Regional Literature Agency (NORLA) when it was created. In 1955, he was appointed a member of the Public Service Commission of the Northern Region and in 1957 he rose to the status of a full-time Commissioner of that commission. In 1962, Imam won the Margaret Wrong Memorial Fund Scholarship of the University of London for his "distinguished editorial services as Hausa editor of *Gaskiya Ta Fi Kwabo,* editorial superintendent of NORLA

---

[3] Much of the background leading to the inception of the Translation Bureau and its successors - the Zaria Literature Bureau and the Northern Regional Literature Agency (NORLA) - is examined in my "Cultural Imperialism and Publishing in Northern Nigeria: 1903-1960" in chapter 19 of this volume. Other winning titles in the 1933 competition were *Gandoki* (The Adventures of Warrior Gandoki) by Imam's elder brother, Bello Kagara, *Shehu Umar* by Abubakar Tafawa Balewa, Nigeria's first Prime Minister, *Idon Matambayi* (The Eye of the Questioner) by Muhammadu Gwarzo, and *Jiki Magayi* (It is the Body which Tells) co-authored by John Tafida Wusasa and Dr. Rupert East, the brain behind the project.

[4] On the delegation from Nigeria along with Abubakar Imam were Dr. Nnamdi Azikiwe, editor of the *West African Pilot*, and Isaac B. Thomas, editor of *Akeke EKO*. From the Gold Coast were R.B. Wuta-Ofei, editor of the Gold Coast Spectator and Daniel U. Sackie, editor of *The Independent*; from Sierra Leone was Dephon Thompson, editor of the *Sierra Leone Standard*, while C.W. Downes Thomas, editor of the *Gambia Echo* represented The Gambia.

and his authorship of fiction, history and miscellaneous writings in Hausa."[5]

Imam died as a result of injuries sustained in a road accident along Kaduna-Zaria road in 1981. He was the author of seventeen books in Hausa, ranging from creative works, travelogue, religion, history to science, biography and journalism.

Established in 1939 in the heat of the second Great European War (World War II) and first edited by Imam, the Hausa newspaper, *Gaskiya Ta Fi Kwabo* was intended primarily to counter the Italian and German propaganda aimed at the colonized in Northern Nigeria.

Masquerading in the typical British liberal-humanist outlook, Imam, as the editor of the paper, had explained the objectives of *Gaskiya* as follows:

> To work always for the good of the country as a whole, and not to take side of any one section, neither of Africans against Africans; neither of Europeans against their servants, nor of servants against their masters. God is the protector against the malice of detractors and evil men.[6]

In spite of this avowed orientation, however, the paper was far from being objective or fair. In fact, goaded on by imperialists' apprehension of the effects of the privately owned, southern-based press, the newspaper consistently attacked the 'detractors' and 'evil men' that Imam refers to in the editorial just cited above.

Concealing the real propaganda motives of the colonizers, Imam, as a firm believer in the 'literalization' efforts of the British in Northern Nigeria against all the glaring economic and cultural odds, viewed the establishment of *Gaskiya* purely as a benevolent, humanitarian gesture. Compared to the privately owned Lagos papers whose survival was tied to profits, the "missionary" *Gaskiya* was sold for only a penny, just enough to enable it to offset the cost of printing, papers, photos and salaries.

As a classical propaganda organ of the British Empire, the bulk of the materials in the monthly *Gaskiya* was translated by Imam and others from English newspapers with no editorial intervention of any sort. And in the absence of full-time correspondents in the North, the main sources of domestic news were reporters appointed and approved by the emirs and chiefs, the *Ulama* (clergy), the court judges and district heads, in that order. The pages of *Gaskiya* were not for everybody as such. Perhaps, it is in the handling of World War II and matters related to it that Imam most eloquently expressed his and the paper's avid pro-colonial disposition.

Imam exploited his undoubted felicity in the Hausa language to promote British interests. For example, the portrait of Hitler - the fascist German leader

---

[5] John N. Paden, *op. cit.*, p. 142.
[6] Janheinz Jahn *et al.*, *Who's Who in African Literature, Biographies, Works, Commentaries*, Tubingen, Federal Republic of Germany, Horst Erdmonn Verlag, 1972, pp. 17-18.

of the war years in *Gaskiya* was comparable to that found in the best of the British newspapers during the war. Although the colonialist and imperialist character of World War II was in all likelihood not unknown to Imam, yet to obtain maximum sympathy and support for the British and its allies, he invoked religious images in depicting Adolf Hitler, the alleged sole-perpetrator of the war. Referred to as the 'devil', Hitler was presented as an Islamic religious heretic; a mass deceiver and a great enemy of Muslims in particular.[7]

This religious analogy was constantly employed by Imam to appeal to able-bodied Northerners to offer themselves *en masse* for conscription to fight in the great European War of 1939-1945. Equating the war of the Allies against the Nazis with an actual Jihad (an Islamic religious war or campaign), Imam supplied details of the British recruitment efforts in the North, and of the movements of Nigerian troops in East Africa, Abyssinia, India and Burma. The newspaper also carried a regular obituary column. Those who died were referred to as *'wandanda suka yi shahada'* ('those who died in the cause of Allah').[8]

On the occasion when Abubakar Imam had to respond to a reader's query on why the colonial authorities were censoring letters during the war, Imam rose in spirited defence of the colonial decision.[9] In defence of censorship he argued that in order to protect the people against German terror, letters (to and from soldiers and other local correspondences) had to be checked lest any vital information should stray to the enemies. Contributing to the transferring of the war hysteria and scare in Europe to Nigeria, Imam maintained that censorship was necessary in view of the preponderance of German spies (mice) who had to be checked by trusted censors (cats). Particularly confidential were the location of army formations, troop movements and armament concentration. Pandering to the liberal and humanitarian dispensation of the colonizer, Imam continually cautioned that only the guilty had anything to fear.

Furthermore, Imam and *Gaskiya Ta Fi Kwabo* contributed enormously to the sustenance of the British economy and of the war efforts through consistent exhortations to the peasants to continue to produce groundnuts for export. Growing of groundnuts was central to British industrial growth and the war efforts and Imam's editorials echoed the colonial government's desperate call for extensive groundnut production in the North. While lauding the government's appointment of Commander Carrow as head of the enhanced groundnut production Task Force in 1943, Imam found reason to berate the northern peasants, considering their large number, for the low groundnut output of 1942. Projecting the North as Britain's last hope for groundnuts in the circumstances of the war, Imam argued that increased production of groundnuts was not only

---

[7] See correspondence from the Secretary, Northern Provinces to the Nigeria Secretary, Lagos, dated 18 January, 1949, in G6/SI/Conf. p. 26.

[8] *Gaskiya Ta Fi Kwabo*, 9 November, 1940 and 15 February, 1941.

[9] Ibid.

patriotic but would bring welcome material returns to cultivators. In a passionate tone and the elegant prose characteristic of Imam, he wrote:

> Yanzu kanyan yaki uku ne a Nigeriya, ga bindigar fada, ga ceburin hakar kuza ga kuma garmar u dar gyada. Wanda duk ya diba ya ga baya rike da daya daga cikin wadannan, ya tabbata ya zama kaska ga Jama'a, abincisa jinin 'yan uwa. Allah ya sawwaka. Mu dai nan ofishin Gaskiya Ta Fi Kwabo har mun fara sharar gona, zamu sa gyada mu taimaki sarki.[10]

Now in this Great War, only three weapons are left to us as Nigerians. The first is the gun; followed by the shovel of the tin-miner, and of course the plough used on groundnut farms. Any Nigerian who looks around, discovers he is not involved in any of these three sacrifices, tasks, should acknowledge, without any doubt that he is a parasite, living off the blood of patriots. May Allah protect us from such undesirable elements. All of us working for your favourite newspaper, the *Gaskiya Ta Fi Kwabo*, have already cleared farmland to cultivate groundnuts as our duty to the King of England, our protector against the Germans.

Gaskiya Ta Fi Kwabo also carried a column in which the records of the province by province war levies paid by peasants and workers were made public, thus, engendering inter-provincial rivalries to extort money which went to augment the colonial treasury. This was also followed by the publishing of regular pledges and appeals from all northern emirs and chiefs urging their peasant "subjects" to surpass all previous groundnut production outputs. In so doing, the peasants were expected to overstretch themselves, to please their Emirs and, at the end, the King of England.[11]

The obsession with the war, in fact, led to the slight change in the masthead of *Gaskiya Ta Fi Kwabo* in 1943. Beneath the familiar masthead a new motto dwelling on how critical Nigerian groundnuts were to the survival of the Empire began to appear as from 28 April of that year. Also as editor, Imam began to publish cartoons, supplements and poems on the theme of the need for increased groundnut production to help defeat Hitler and "liberate" Nigerians from the prospects of eternal slavery.[12]

Further evidence of Abubakar Imam's conservative conscience shows during the British Council-sponsored trip to England in June-July 1943. According to Nnamdi Azikiwe's account,[13] the visit was the result of discussions he had had

---

[10] *Gaskiya Ta Fi Kwabo*, 4 April, 1944.

[11] *Gaskiya Ta Fi Kwabo*, 31 March, 1948. p. 72. The English rendition which follows is my own.

[12] *Gaskiya Ta Fi Kwabo*, 3 February, 1943, pp. 2-3.

[13] See *Gaskiya Ta Fi Kwabo* of 9 June, 1943, for verses on groundnuts by the following: Isa Sardauna Gusau, Alhaji Dogondaji Sakkwato and Muazu Hadejia Gumel. Both Dogondaji and Muazu Hadejia were to emerge as major Hausa writers. Samples of groundnut production-inspired cartoons are available in *Gaskiya Ta Fi Kwabo* of 2 August, 1944; while supplements and further poems could be seen in *Gaskiya Ta Fi Kwabo* of 21 June, 1944 and 25 October, 1944.

with one C.F. Dundes of the British Council. The British Council agreed to sponsor the trip as part of their public relations work on both the on-going war and other matters related to colonial rule. Azikiwe and Imam actually shared a ship cabin on the voyage.

Azikiwe, who was the secretary of the delegation, prepared a memorandum on political demands to be presented to the colonial office in London. Members of delegation were required to express their opinion on the draft of the memorandum which included demands for independence for Anglophone West Africa in two stages. The stages were, first, self-government, and then independence, spread over a period of fifteen years, either immediately or sometimes after World War II. The years 1958 and 1960 were suggested for each stage. As Azikiwe admits, the memorandum was actually snubbed by the Colonial Office (but significantly enough, Ghana obtained independence in 1957). Abubakar Imam refused to sign the memorandum on the grounds that it lacked the mandate of the North. When his refusal to sign the memorandum had been widely reported by the southern press, especially *The West African Pilot*, and some of his friends (probably northerners) in Lagos had also expressed their displeasure over the matter, Imam used the pages of *Gaskiya* to justify his action.

Since the memorandum had demanded a graduated independence timetable, Imam was categorical that as the North was not yet ready for independence, owing largely to inadequate awareness of what it involved, not even the colonialists would have made him sign the memorandum. Ever cryptic, Imam wrote of his action:

> *Mutanen Ntgeriya ta arewa sun zabe in, sun aika da ni Ingila, don in je in zama msu makiyayi be, ba don in je in zama musu tunkiya ba.*[14]

> The people of Northern Nigeria elected me and sent me to England, so that I could become their shepherd and not a sheep.

Imam also rejected self-government for Nigeria in 1958 because that would have amounted to exchanging white colonizers for black ones from the South. Imam also kicked against the suggestion in the memo that there should be massive training of school leavers to succeed the British as the North could only boast of a few pupils at Kaduna College, compared to hundreds in the South of the country. Contended with the colonial effort on the educational front, Imam also rejected the free education issue raised in the memo. In an avid defence of the colonial bureaucracy, Imam ridiculed the call for the provision of pension, gratuity and unemployment benefits for Nigerians from the colonial development funds, because, as he reasoned, the taxes and levies collected were

---

[14] Nnamdi Azikiwe, *My Odyssey*, London: C. Hurst and Company, 1970, pp. 357-359. Zik was the editor of the *West African Pilot* at the time of the visit.

too paltry to support the scheme. In the absence of specific complaints from Northerners against psychiatrists, Imam belittled the suggestion that they should be censured. Where the memo recommended the raising of the wages of Nigerian workers and labourers from £3 to £6, and the abolition of discriminatory wages between blacks and whites, Imam also raised strong objections. At the end of his defence, Imam virtually contradicted himself by acknowledging that, on the whole, as editors, they could only exercise advisory, not executive powers. Thus, his signing the memo could not have been the same as practicalizing all the propositions contained in it.

While in England, the delegation had audience with Lord Lugard, the first Governor-General of Nigeria. Imam was later to have a private audience with Lugard, the colonial secretary and other top-ranking colonial bureaucrats, where he freely presented the grievances, fears and problems of the North. He even presented, on request, a memorandum to Lugard on colonial policies and practices as they affected the North.

Although Imam' s views on labour are discernible from his strong objections to wage increases or uniform wages for the same work in the 1943 memorandum, his editorializing on the 1945 workers' general strike[15] clearly exposed his conservative conscience. Starting from the premise that prior to colonization, Nigerians were like blind men in a ditch for whom the colonizer was only a sympathetic and kind rescuer,[16] he urged Nigerian workers to be grateful and to work hard to earn every penny. The colonialists, in his view, could not afford to waste the British tax-payers money on indolent, pleasure-loving Nigerians.[17] Imam went on to argue that the 1945 General Strike had had only adverse effects because everybody had suffered as a result of it. Nigeria, in particular, had retrogressed.[17] In amplifying the official government position, Imam wrote that increases in wages would fuel inflation and that the burden might fall on the poor in form of higher taxes. Imam also defended discriminatory wages to British workers whom he claimed possessed specialized knowledge and skills which Nigerian needed. He portrayed the British staff as agents of development, who deserved to be rewarded appropriately. Imam put his opinion in a cryptic but witty Hausa thus:[18]

---

[15] *Gaskiya Ta Fi Kwabo*, 27 October, 1943, p. 6. The English translation accompanying it is my own Also see *Gaskiya Ta Fi Kwabo* of 11 November, 1943.

[16] The General Strike lasted about 50 days and involved about 500,000 workers. It completely paralyzed economic and social life throughout the country. In political terms, the strike was the biggest uprising against British colonialism. The strike also brought to the fore the revolutionary potential of the working class which the British worked hard to defuse by hastening the process of negotiated independence which came fifteen years later in 1960.

[17] *Gaskiya Ta Fi Kwabo*, 20 August. 1945.

[18] Ibid., pp. 1-3.

> *Mulki na hannun Turawa, suke sama, mu ke kasa*[19]
>
> Power is in the hands of the whites, it's, therefore, foolhardy to agitate or struggle against it. They are on top and we are at the bottom.

Imam, in fact, commended the British love for liberalism, tolerance and democracy for allowing the strike action in the first place. His reasoning was that the words of the colonial authorities should be law and should command the obedience of everybody in Nigeria. In his own opinion, since the strike action was unlawful, he was surprised that it was allowed in the first place. Imam also lamented that the *Gaskiya* newspaper had to be off the streets, the government printers at Kaduna having also joined the strike action.

Quite euphoric about development prospects in post-war colonial Nigeria, Imam believed the colonialists would banish poverty, disease, hunger and ignorance. Northern Nigerians were promised a bountiful existence by Imam on the pages of *Gaskiya*. Probably with the sacrifice of the Nigerians in the war effort at the back of his mind, Imam imagined everybody breathing a sigh of relief and expressing profound gratitude to the English for their colonizing work. Post-war northern Nigeria, he hoped, would be a new world, characterized by meaningful changes in the areas of food, education, good life and prosperity. For these to materialize, however, Imam warned, the British deserved hard work and co-operation of all the colonized.[20]

These views of Abubakar Imam examined so far were obtained from his editorial column titled '*Gaskiya Sunanta Gaskiya*'; 'Truth is the Truth Whatever the Circumstances', in *Gaskiya Ta Fi Kwabo*. Although further references are still to be made to Imam's writings in the *Gaskiya* newspaper, the bulk of the instances which follow emanates from the reading of his most famous three-volume stories, *Magana Jari Ce*.

In terms of chronology, the three-volumes of *Magana Jari Ce,* antedate Imam's career at the *Gaskiya* newspaper. The three volumes were published between 1937 and 1939 when Imam was still teaching at the Katsina Middle School. As it is to be discovered, Imam's conservative opinions in *Gaskiya* had already found articulation in the earlier stories.

Set in an unnamed location somewhere in the East, the narration in the books takes off in the palace of one Emir Abdurrahman. As a result of the intrigues of the Emir's *Waziri* (Vizier, or trusted adviser), Emir Abdurrahman goes off to wage war against a neighbouring Emir, leaving the evil *Waziri* in charge. The Emir's only fortune is that he has also entrusted his only son and heir-apparent, Musa, to an all-seeing, all-knowing, sweet-talking parrot, bought off an Arab. All the stories in the three volumes come through the parrot. For Imam, the parrot embodies wisdom and demonstrates the superiority of the pen over the

---

[19] *Gaskiya Ta Fi Kwabo*, 20 August. 1945.
[20] Ibid.

gun. The craft of wisdom is an invaluable asset, especially for people in power, authority and influence. In effect, those in authority ought to take literature seriously, for its capacity to ward off evil and bad feelings towards them as the parrot's (Imam's?) life as story-teller, journalist and writer illustrates. Imam seems to be saying in the life of the crafty parrot in *Magana Jari Ce* that no amount of money, exaltation or recognition is ever too much for the inimitable resources of a good talker, writer or propagandist.

In the *Magana Jari Ce* stories, activities revolve around palaces, emirs, courtiers and servants, with a substantial dose of the magical and the fantastic. There is a synthesis of fables, legends, fairytales/folktales from a variety of non-Hausa sources which are brought in into the Hausa environment. The dominance of emirs and palaces as the centre of all activities, be they legal, economic, political or cultural in the stories, allows Imam to restate and reinforce the significance of monarchical and traditional leadership.

In glorifying these institutions, Imam presents emirs as the bastions of justice, fair play and the defenders of the people against oppression. They are portrayed as ever-generous. They maintain a retinue of 'slaves,' servants, praise-singers, courtiers and fools, in most cases without visible gainful employment. As evident in a large number of the stories, emirs wield enormous power over life and death of the people; they are seen ordering severe, inhuman treatments, including summary executions of offending 'slaves,' courtiers or other inhabitants of their domains.

While travelling from Zaria to Lagos in the company of the Emir of Zazzau in 1943, Imam told the story of how he was also mistaken for an Emir by their Ibadan hosts, where they had a stop-over. In his mistaken identity as Emir, Imam found all the courtiers and servile conduct of his hosts amazing. He was especially struck by the absence of liberty which royalty involves; he therefore, sympathizes with emirs for the oppression which seems to go with their office. This theme also finds expression in one of the *Magana Jari Ce* stories where the onerous task of being emir is discovered to be too daunting for a doubting visiting chief of the spirits. The fact is that Emirs have no claim to the privacy which those unconnected to royalty only take for granted.

In some of the stories in Volume II, for instance, there is emphasis on the marriage and love relationships of the royalty. The most romantic of love is only obtainable in the circles of emirs, their children and surrogates. In the marriage affairs of emirs, for example, that of one Shahruzzaman, it is the spirits who play matchmakers. One does not marry into the royalty; such marriages are exclusive to their kind, to the fabulously rich, and on very rare occasions, to the offspring of the poor for having undertaken some Herculean tasks!

Imam shows that the court judges and the *dogarai* are closely associated with the traditional leadership institutions. They are the legal expressions of monarchical power. Also portrayed as defenders of the good upholders of law and order, not one *Alkali* (judge) or the emir's policeman *(dogarai)* is presented by Imam as ever overstepping their briefs. The impression one is given of them is of fairness and steadfastness; the cavalier judgements of corrupt judges go without comment.

As far as Imam is concerned the poor masses and peasants of *Magana Jari Ce* ought to remain contented with their status and whatever they may or may not have; striving or struggling to the contrary results in disaster. Not used to wealth, the peasant has the tendency to overreach himself and, in so doing, he gets disgraced. Hard work is, of course, no guarantee to riches, so the labour of the poor generally goes unrewarded; the poor only stumble into prosperity by pure chance or by some default.

The majority of the women in the *Magana Jari Ce* stories manifest a chauvinistic, stereotypical mind at work. In the story of 'Kalala and Kalalatu,' the natural goodness and generosity of the husband, Kalala, is subverted and abused by his wife. In the 'Emir and His Cook' story, also in Volume II, attempts by the Emir to escape the wiles of women by engaging a male cook are seen to be futile. Literally all palace intrigues, wranglings over succession and inheritance are made more intractable by women. In the 'Amjadu and Asadu' story, much suffering is unleashed on an emir and his children on account of the machinations of women courtiers. Therefore, when Amjadu murders one woman admirer bent on luring him to kill unduly, death is presented as the most appropriate penalty for her. Similarly, in the tale of 'Good Sidi and the Good Tanko,' it is Tanko's wife who is the *agent provocateur* leading to the disgrace of her husband. Realizing how his wife had misled him through infinite malice, Tanko murders her and he is in turn executed for that. For Imam, it appears, women are permanently and inherently mischievous, malicious and not worthy of the trust of the menfolk.

Imam's penchant for stereotyping in *Magana Jari Ce*, is also illustrated by how the gullibility of the rural people is exploited by the far more urbane city dwellers. The rural Fulani also fall victim in the story about Jairu in Book II, where, it seems, the nomadic cattle-rearers are shown to be promiscuous, anti-progress, rural and unnecessarily endogamous. The Fulani almost always fall victim of the tricks of the city Hausa man.

Imam's stereotyping is also in evidence in one of the stories in Volume II which is an adaptation from Shakespeare's *The Merchant of Venice*. In the story, the hard-hearted Shylock, the extortionist in the Nigerian context, is seen to be no other than an Igbo man, called Nwanko, who demands a pound of flesh from a Hausa debtor, Malam Bala. Portrayed as a vicious and mean trader, Nwanko plots the downfall of the Hausaman only to end up being defrauded and disgraced when the no less crafty Bala wangles a favourable judgement against Nwanko from a friendly, corrupt judge.[21]

Predictably, Imam is uncompromising over the prevalence of social pro-

---

[21] *Gaskiya Ta Fi Kwabo*, 12 April, 1944.

blems such as prostitution, robbery and theft generally. In many of the *Magana Jari Ce* stories dealing with thieves, (and there are many), thieves are presented as murderous, satanic and mentally retarded people. Carefully obscuring the socio-economic forces leading to these undesirable habits, Imam encourages the reader to believe that virtually all the thieves in *Magana Jari Ce* are of peasant, rural or poor urban social backgrounds. There is the celebrated example of Noma in the story, 'Sarkin Noma and His Children', where armed robbery and stealing are presented as one occupational option available to the poor and their children. Ever concerned about the moral import of his narratives, Abubakar Imam articulates the guiding philosophy of his writings in *Magana Jari Ce* as follows:

> I am careful not to narrate stories which may invite scorn or derision to itself.
> I don't tell stories of promiscuous or wanton women, to avoid sinning.
> Prophetic miracles I avoid as they may be misinterpreted by the untutored.
> Even tales of marauders are restricted to those which the young are unlikely to be attracted to by the antiquated nature of the methods of the thieves[22]

Although the focus of our discussion is the conservative conscience of Abubakar Imam and how this is manifested in his writings in *Gaskiya Ta Fi Kwabo* and the volumes of *Magana Jari Ce,* it is worth noting in conclusion that as a widely travelling, educated man, Imam did possess good ideas on the development of the North in particular and of Nigeria as a whole. For instance, he was a major advocate of education and enlightenment at all levels and was actively involved in the evolution of a post-independent, civilian administration in Nigeria.

---

[22] Abubakar Imam, *Magana Jari Ce*, Zaria, Gaskiya Corporation, 1962, p. 34. This is largely a paraphrase of what Imam says through the parrot.

Chapter 17

The life and works of Sa'adu Zungur

- *Dandatti Abdulkadir*

Introduction

In this introduction I will summarize the role of poetry in Hausa society so that the poetry of Sa'adu Zungur may be seen in context. In the mid-twentieth century, Sa'adu appeared to be the leading poet in northern Nigeria. Before discussing Sa'adu's poems, however, I would like to refer to some poems written in the nineteenth and twentieth centuries. This will enable us to see the development and the types of poetry written at that time and how they differ in theme and content from those of Sa'adu. We can then see Sa'adu's works against the background of these poems.

Poetry acts as a mirror in which the customs and traditions of a people are reflected. When we study Arabic poetry, particularly the *Seven Odey,* we see how the Arab poets reflect their customs and traditions. The culture and history of northern Nigeria is clearly evident in Sa'adu's poems (for example, in *Wakar Bidi'a* and *Arewa Jumhuriya ko Mulukiya*).

The exact time when Hausa poetry began to be written is still problematical. According to Hiskett (seminar paper on "Islamic Influence on the Literary Cultures of Africa"), apart from the *Kirari* of the Kano chronicle, only one example of Hausa verse written before the Fulani Jihad is currently extant. This is a praise song of Bawa Jangwarzo, king of Gobir.

The early nineteenth century witnessed a remarkable literary upsurge in north-western Hausaland. During this period literary writing and poetry were actively encouraged by leaders of the Jihad, such as Shehu Usman Dan Fodio, his brother Abdullahi and his son Muhammad Bello. They wrote on various topics such as education, administration, law and poetry. This can be seen in books like *Infaqul-Maisur*. But among them Abdullahi took the greatest interest in poetry. He wrote poems about his Shaykhs and in celebration of some of the battles during the Jihad. He also wrote poems such as *Wakar Gode Allah* in thanks for God's blessing upon him both before and after the *hijira*.

Most of these works were written in classical Arabic and were later translated into Hausa in Ajami script, a modified form of Arabic script. The exact timing of this process of translation into Hausa is not yet known since no written document exists in support of a particular date. The first person to write extensively in Hausa verse, after the Jihad was Isa, the son of Shehu Usman Dan Fodio. He is said to have translated Shehu's Arabic poems into Hausa verse, while his sister Nana translated Shehu's poems from Fulfulde into Hausa. If it had been customary to write Hausa verse in Ajami before Isa and Nana, the memory of the works, if not the works themselves, would probably have survived.

Most of these early poems were didactic, and the poems of Shehu were primarily modelled along these lines. One also finds, however, writings on the stars (e.g., *Wakar Taurari*). Other poems are mainly concerned with eulogy, *wa'azi*, *tauhid* and *fikh*. The poetry retained its evangelical character in the post-jihad period. It also acquired a further purpose, that of propaganda to uphold the temporal power. In general, these poems urge the masses to obey their natural rulers. A typical example of such poems is *Wakar Bin Shugahanni*.

In the twentieth century, however, the North saw the introduction of a new type of poetry. While the early poetry was composed mainly by the religious teachers, the modern poems were written by men of different professions, most of whom were educated in *boko*. Such people included Na'ibi Wali, a government official, and the late Mu'azu Hadejia, a teacher. There were politicians who wrote poetry, including Sa'adu himself, Aminu Kano, Mudi Sipikin and Akilu Aliyu. The themes of their poems include many aspects of modern life. They wrote poems on social conditions, education, politics and even war. The first in this category was probably the late Aliyu, the Emir of Zazzau, who wrote a poem about his visit to Kano in 1914. In this poem he described vividly all that he saw during the visit. He even made a catalogue of all the emirs he met and the gates he visited.

In the mid-twentieth century, however, Sa'adu became the leading modern Hausa poet in the Northern Region. His poems had a considerable impact on the poets of his society. His poems are generally on current topics, and as a result, they have become very popular. School boys recite and chant his poems, particularly *Maraba da Soja* and *Arewa Jumhuriya Ko Mulukiya*.

Sa'adu Zungur's life history

In any country, one finds that some men, even after their death, are still remembered and their memory always remains fresh in the minds of the people. The people of Britain hold Winston Churchill in high esteem for his valuable contributions to the progress and stability of his country. In America, John F. Kennedy will continue to be remembered for making the United States of

America known throughout the world and for his sound programmes with regard to developing nations.

In Nigeria, too, we have such personalities who will never be forgotten because of the contributions they have made to the progress and development of their country. One of these people is Sa'adu Zungur. During his lifetime Sa'adu played an important role in the political, educational and social activities of his country.

He was born in 1915 in Galadima district, some 40 kilometres away from Bauchi. In 1922 he entered Provincial School in Bauchi. Sa'adu then went to Katsina College in 1926. From Katsina College, he went to Yaba College from 1929-34. He started teaching in Zaria School of Hygiene in 1936. Sa'adu founded the Zaria Literary Society in 1939 and the Zaria Improvement Union in 1941. The Youth Social Circle was formed in 1947 in response to Sa'adu's call. Sa'adu joined the Northern Peoples Congress (NPC) in 1951, the National Council of Nigeria and Cameroons (NCNC) in 1948, the Northern Elements Progressive Union (NEPU) in 1950 and left NCNC in 1952. He led the Bauchi branch of NEPU after 1953. He died in 1958.

Sa'adu's father taught jurisprudence (*fiqh*), theology (*tauhid*), Arabic grammar (*nahawu*), Koran and commentary (*tafsir*). Many students came to study with his father in the Mosque. Sa'adu was born into this religious atmosphere. He showed his intelligence at an early age. He was said to have memorized the Koran at the age of fifteen, which was a remarkable feat for a boy of that age. As a result he became the favourite son of his father, who always took Sa'adu with him whenever he went out to teach in the central Mosque. His father regarded Sa'adu as his successor. During that period people were always reluctant to send their children to modern schools for fear of their being converted to Christianity. (Western education was introduced by the missionaries into Nigeria, so modern education was associated with Christianity in northern Nigeria). Despite this, Sa'adu's father, who was a leading Arabist in Zungur, sent Sa'adu to Bauchi Provincial School. Sa'adu proved to be exceptionally intelligent, and willing to work. He finished in two years instead of the normal four. Then he was sent to Katsina College where he remained for only two years. His teachers then recommended that he go to Yaba College in Lagos. He sat for examination and passed it.

He was the first Northern Nigerian to gain admission to Yaba College. His stay in Lagos influenced him greatly such that whenever he came on holidays to Northern Nigeria, he dressed in a western suit. People expected him to dress in the traditional way. During that period only Europeans and Christians wore European dress, but that did not stop Sa'adu from dressing the way in which he preferred. People were shocked and stunned that, of all people, Sa'adu would wear such clothes. His brother, who was then the Imam of Bauchi, told me that their father called Sa'adu in their presence and asked why he was always wearing a suit instead of his traditional attire. Sa'adu replied that there was nothing wrong with his dressing and explained to his father that people dressed like Arabs or Indians and, similarly, he saw nothing wrong with dressing like Europeans. Sa'adu found it difficult to fit into the society in which he lived. People in this society refused to be realistic and change with the times. Instead they clung rigidly to customs and traditions which retarded their progress. Malam Sa'adu was more progressive than any member of the conservative elite. He was a northern Nigerian who led a simple life and whose time, virtues and life were dedicated to the common people. He tried his best to see that the common man felt the practical link-up of day-to-day life with the revolution that was taking place around him. He did not like to see the common man always waiting to be told what to do; rather, he wanted him to be educated so that he could participate fully in the affairs of his country. This could only be realized through crash educational programmes which were then lacking in northern Nigeria. He knew that the whole idea of the change would be meaningless so long as the masses were left without any basic education, and that the Northerners would lag behind their counterparts in the South. Sa'adu wanted ordinary men to be educated so that they could take a more active part in the affairs of their government. He, therefore, aimed to rid his people of the ignorance in which they found themselves.

After his return from Yaba College, Sa'adu started his career as a teacher in Zaria School of Hygiene. He did not limit himself to the field of education but also tried to awaken his people politically. At the time he was in Lagos, the Nigerian Youth Movement was formed by people like the late Adegoke Adelabu, who later became the leader of the opposition in the Western House of Assembly. Sa'adu fully engaged himself in the activities of the new movement. Consequently, when he returned to Zaria, he introduced the idea of unions in Northern Nigeria. Sa'adu then formed the Zaria Literary Society, the first of its kind in Northern Nigeria. The aim of this society was to enlighten the people about the importance of education in a developing region like Northern Nigeria. He also initiated the formation of the Zaria Improvement Union. Most of the members of these two societies were young people who had been to institutions of higher learning. They set themselves the task of teaching, reading and writing to those who had not been to school. The entrance hall to Sa'adu Zungur's house served as the classroom. He used to organize debates for those who had already acquired modern education. Sa'adu was the first to introduce discussions on current affairs.

He always read from well-known world papers like *The Times* of London or the *Time Magazine*. As a result, educated people always liked to visit him in the evenings to hear more about what was happening in other parts of the world. He was also one of the key men who helped in the formation of *Jam'iyar Mutanen Arewa*. This organization was initially a cultural organization, but was later turned into a political party known as the NPC. At first, all these societies were mainly concerned with the improvement of the educational standard of the people of northern Nigeria, and Sa'adu served as adviser to the authorities concerned.

He also called upon his friends living in different parts of northern Nigeria to form organizations that would help to improve the educational, social and political conditions of the masses. The reaction to his call for the formation of such organizations was seen in Kano when Raji Abdallah, a close associate of M. Sa'adu, formed the Northern Elements Progressive Association in 1943.

In Bauchi, Sa'adu started the Bauchi Discussion Circle. It took the form of a radical movement against the Native Authority, and included men like Aminu Kano, then a teacher in Bauchi Middle School. It was to counter the radicalism of Bauchi Discussion Circle that the Bauchi General Improvement Union was formed which included people like the late Prime Minister, Alhaji Sir Abubakar Tafawa Balewa after the dissolution of BDC in 1944. It also included the Emir of Bauchi and many of his councillors and senior Native Authority officials. It was a moderate organization which believed in gradual reforms in the North. Similar associations soon cropped up in the various Northern Provinces. In Sokoto, the Youth Social Circle was formed in 1947 by people like Sani Dingyadi, Ibrahim Gusau, with people like the late Premier Alhaji Ahmadu Bello on the periphery. In Zaria, the Zaria Youth Association was formed and took the place of the Friendly Society. Attempts to unify these associations into a single region-wide association were made. An invitation from Zaria Association was sent to the Kano and other groups to meet in Zaria. The meeting turned out to be a failure owing to the suspicion of some Native Authority officials who believed that the motive behind the formation of that organization was to destroy the Native Authority. In spite of the fact that the attempt by the Zaria Youth Association to form a region-wide organization proved abortive, Abubakar Imam and Dr. R.A.B Dikko of Zaria continued with their efforts to form an organization that would have branches all over the region.

Their first attempt to that effect was the calling of a meeting of representatives from all over the region in 1948 to discuss the forthcoming changes in the political structure of Nigeria. As a result of this meeting NPC, which was formerly a cultural society, was turned into a political party. At that time Sa'adu was busy in Lagos organizing Jama'iyyar Al'umar Nijeriya ta Arewa (JANA). He led the delegation of JANA to the first convention of the NPC in Kaduna in 1949. A year later another convention was held in Jos. At this meeting Sa'adu demanded that NPC should adopt a radical ideology. Some members objected to the idea as they thought it was premature to call for drastic reforms of the Native Authority system.

Consequently, Sa'adu, Aminu Kano, Maitama Sule and Zukogi broke away from the NPC and formed NEPU in 1950. Its declared objectives were the reform of the Native Authority system, the emancipation of the *talakawa* and the provision of better welfare services in the North. Sa'adu joined the NCNC in

1951, leaving M. Aminu as president of the NEPU and Zugoki became the general secretary.

Sa'adu was full of progressive ideas and thoughts far ahead of his time. He did not believe in gradualism, which he thought was a camouflage for not being ready to accept and implement changes. The North more than any other place in Nigeria needed rapid changes since it was already lagging behind the rest of Nigeria. Others, however, argued that things should be allowed to take their normal course. Sa'adu was known to be very argumentative and for never accepting things at their face value. He always thought over a new idea or ideology, analysed it, and became convinced beyond doubt before he embraced innovations. Some of his critics are of the opinion that Sa'adu lost sight of an important factor: the standard of the people he wanted to enlighten and lead in order to catch up with the southern Nigerians. As he thought well ahead of his time, most of his followers failed to cope with his ideas and consequently they branded him as over-ambitious.

Sa'adu later established contact with well-known Nigerian politicians like Dr. Azikiwe who was the leader of the NCNC. Sa'adu soon joined this party in its crusade against colonialism. He travelled far and wide throughout Nigeria establishing branches of NCNC. His organizational ability, hard work and loyalty gained him the post of the secretary to the party. He paved the way for introduction of its ideology into Northern Nigeria.

The two parties, NEPU and NCNC, and their followers waged a relentless war against illiteracy, backwardness and feudalism. This brought them into conflict with the ruling classes in northern Nigeria, who thought that the aim of Sa'adu and his followers was to destroy them, so they supported NPC and urged the party to safeguard and protect the interests of the ruling class. As a result, the NPC began to express opposition to what Sa'adu and Aminu were doing.

Sa'adu then called upon the masses to throw in their lot with NEPU and NCNC for they were the only parties that would save them from the social evils of northern Nigeria. He emphasized the idea of equality and called for the reorganization of the Native Administrations. He wrote many pamphlets in Hausa so that his message could be understood by the majority of the people. A well-known one is called *Fadakarwa*.

Sa'adu was respected even by members of the NPC, the rival party. This was because Sa'adu used to discuss matters affecting the region and the province with the leaders of the NPC to whom he always gave his honest advice.

In 1948, the NCNC held its annual convention in Lagos, and Sa'adu raised the question of training Northern boys so that they could catch up with their counterparts in the South. He explained further that it was in the best interest of the NCNC to do that, since this would win the party the support of the people of the North. But the leaders of the NCNC appeared not to be keen in this matter.

Sa'adu then resigned his post as secretary and returned to the North. His first reaction against the attitude of the southerners was the composition of his well-known poem, *Arewa Jumhuriya ko Mulukiya*. In this poem, as will be seen later, he alerted both the chiefs and masses to the danger that would follow if they allowed the NCNC to win elections in the North. He toured the region and met emirs, chiefs, and the educated elite, condemning the Southerners who paid only lip service to the welfare of the people of the North. Their only aim, as he explained in the poem, was to see the country become a republic so that they could dominate the people of the North when emirs and chiefs were removed.

Sa'adu also played an important role in the propaganda of Islam. He tried in his lifetime to explain to the people the real meaning of Islam. His brother, who became the Imam of Bauchi, told me that he discussed things like polygamy, the seclusion of Muslim women, and the importance of women's education in northern Nigeria. Sa'adu was opposed to polygamy; he argued that most of our people who are polygamous maltreat their wives in the sense that they discriminate against some of them. And according to Islam, a man is allowed to be polygamous only if he will treat his wives equally.

He also criticized the purdah system in northern Nigeria. He argued that people are not practising what the Koran enjoins. He called upon the *malams*, including his brother, to explain to the people the stand of Islam on this matter. This issue made Sa'adu a very controversial person among the *malams*. In fact, some went to the extent of calling him an atheist, for according to them, Sa'adu deviated from the right teachings of the Koran. It was also related by his brother that Sa'adu wrote a long paper on the question of women's education in northern Nigeria. But unfortunately this was also lost with some of his other works.

He then started to translate the Koran into Hausa, so that people could read it and understand the meaning. He realized that the people learned the Koran by heart but the majority of them did not know the meaning since they did not understand Arabic.

According to Sa'adu, it was not enough to read the Koran; it was essential for one to know the meaning so that one could better understand the message. No previous efforts had been made to translate it into Hausa so that people could understand what they read and only very recently has there been any further effort made to prepare a Hausa translation.

The local *malams* criticized Sa'adu for translating the Koran into Hausa. They argued that once it was translated, the meaning would be lost. Sa'adu also called upon the people to go back to the original Islam, the Islam which was practised during the time of the Prophet and his Khalifs. He realized that people were mixing custom and religion to the extent that customs were stronger than the religion itself.

He observed the infiltration of superstition into Islam; in support of a return to original Islam he was said to have written an article entitled *What is Islam?* Unfortunately, it has disappeared along with many other valuable works, like those on the creation of political assemblies, *The Democratization of Native*

Administration and *The College System in Northern Nigeria.*
Sa'adu was also sceptical about the Native Administrative system in northern Nigeria. He could not see how the North would progress without these institutions being reformed and reorganized. He suggested that the emirs' councils should be composed of elected members who would advise the chiefs and emirs. Perhaps he wanted to see the British system of administration working in northern Nigeria. He expressed the view that unless people in the North woke up and unshackled themselves from laziness, there was no doubt that Southerners would take over the control of the country. A nation that has a high rate of illiteracy will never make any impact on African or world affairs.

Sa'adu saw that the standard of literacy in the North was rather discouraging and still people would not make any effort to remedy the situation. Instead people spent their valuable time playing cards for money or for fun. "It is high time to see on which side our bread is buttered," he once remarked. "If one-fifth of the time our educated people spent on indulging in unnecessary recreations was devoted to educating the masses, this region would within a few years catch up with the other regions in the field of education." He tried to inform the people that they did not have to depend on the government to help them, and started organizing night classes in Bauchi as an example for others.

Most of what he had written in prediction and as warning is now coming to reality and so his works will be remembered by generations yet unborn as works of a far-sighted man. These predictions were made in his poem, *Arewa Jumhuriya ko Mulukiya,* and most of the things he predicted came to pass. For example, he warned the emirs and chiefs that unless they reformed themselves and accepted changes their positions would be weakened. This turned out to be true with the introduction of local government reforms on 1 January 1969, whereby the emirs and chiefs were reduced to the positions of advisors with little real power.

Sa'adu thought that the people of northern Nigeria were lagging behind because of their misguided conception of Islam. They entrusted everything to nature and this, according to him, was contrary to Islamic teaching. He pointed out that Islam is a progressive religion and, since this is the case, it should be brought into the trend of modern civilization. He wanted to see a new approach to Islam in northern Nigeria. He called for the introduction of the Egyptian Koranic system. In the Egyptian system, both religious and secular subjects are taught. It was only some ten years after his death that this system was introduced on a widespread basis, and now such schools can be seen in big cities like Kano, with learned *malams* who translate and interpret the Koran according to the essence of Islam. He argued that the Koran is for all times and as such it should be translated and interpreted in accordance with the essence of Islam.

Sa'adu was a controversial figure, fearless and willing to express his opinion in criticism of various sections of his society. Sa'adu led a very simple life and always liked to be free from interference. He awakened his people so that they might take their rightful position in Nigeria. Sa'adu died after a long illness at the age of forty-three.

Commentary

In his poem *Maraba da Soja,* Sa'adu eulogized the herotic role of the Nigerian army in the war against the regime of Mussolini in East Africa and the Japanese in India and Burma. This action was for the sake of defending freedom which was as stake after the overrunning of France by Hitler's Germany.

The topical structure of this poem can be viewed as follows:

(a) The opening.
(b) Break in the topic for the audience.
(c) State of world disorder before Nigerian troops are called in.
(d) Italians campaigning in Ethiopia.
(e) Japanese advances and retreats ending with the atomic bomb.
(f) Respectful praise for the army and its leaders.
(g) Awe at the power of the atom bomb.
(h) The message of the poem: Freedom.

The poem begins in the traditional way with a dedication formula of two verses.

> Let our prayers and blessing,
>   be upon the most excellent of prophets,
> who is beyond imitation,
>   the leader of all warriors,
> with whom we seek shelter.

Sa'adu starts his poem like most of the Hausa poets by showering praise on the Prophet and his Lord. Sa'adu then goes on to show his intention "Come, friend, I have good news for you, hear my song of victory." This is followed by the description of the hopelessness of the world situation before the Nigerian army was called in to play an active role in the war. Sa'adu, right from the beginning, conveyed to the people clearly what the war was like: "When the war began, a whole unbroken year went by, a year of smoke without red embers." *"Sai hayki ba gaushi:"* this gives the real picture of the struggle and it shows that the war was like a cold war at the beginning and the real war only started when the Japanese had joined.

Then Sa'adu exposes to his readers the kind of campaign the Italians launched.

> Next the Italians took up the sword of enmity

> to aid the Germans, eagerly to leap - they thought, -
> to the bowl of *tuwo* cooked and ready,
> and enemy already dead.

Here Sa'adu shows how the Italians underestimated the power and ability of the allied forces as seen in this idiom – *"Ga tuwo ya nuna sai tushewa."* In Hausa, whenever this proverb is used, it indicates that the task is an easy one and it requires no great effort. He then depicts the picture of the place in which the Nigerian army fought the campaign. This was an attempt to make the people respect the soldiers all the more.

> Army of Liberation in Kenya,
> before you are great rivers,
> trackless mountains. This is no day for diffidence,
> for sluggishness, for hesitation.

Sa'adu then goes on to tell the people how their soldiers fought the war:

> Guns grew busy and men met destruction face to face,
> without fear, without hesitation.

In the last line of verse 12, he uses the word *"kau"* to show his knowledge of Sokoto dialect where one would expect Sa'adu to use *"ko"* which is used in most of the Hausa states, including Bauchi, the poet's home town. Again in verse 13, the poet uses a word *"awa"* in place of which people today will in normal speech use *"kamar."* *"Rundunarmu awa ta dango,"* is more poetic because of the use of archaic word *"awa"* than *"Rundunarmu kamar ta dango."* Here too he uses a good simile to make his poem more effective when he compares the lining up of the soldiers with a swarm of newly hatched locusts. Also his choice of words to describe the command given by the Commander-in-Chief of the Nigerian armed forces shows his ability to use poetic language to create sensation in the mind of his readers:

> *Cif-Kwamanda yai umurni,*
> *Duk a kange dama, hauni*
> *Koguna, sarari, da tsauni*
> *DKar a bar su, susan sukuni*
> *Ko su san zarafin wurin gujewa.*

Here he uses each word with its opposite *"dama, hauni"* *"sarari, da tsauni."* One can give more examples of these words which most of the Hausa like to see especially in poetry, e.g., *"fari da baki, babba da yaro. tudu da kwari waje da ciki, sama da kasa, zaki da daci."* This goes to show that the person not only knows the language but he has mastered it. Here the word *"hauni"* is used to fit the metre. Normally the word *"hagu"* would have been used. It is true that the two words mean the same thing but in ordinary speech one more often hears *"hagu"* than *"hauni."*

Sa'adu discusses the historical development of the war. He praises the effort and the role of the Nigerian army during the war. The gallantry of the Nigerian army was so appreciated by Haile Selassie that he chose some of the soldiers to be his bodyguards after his return from exile.

> The Ethiopian ruler,
>   Haile Selassie showed his noble nature,
> and said, "The Nigerians
>   have excelled all other soldiers,
> they are my choice as palace guards."
>   Imagine our pride and joy!
> The sons of Nigeria had made their name,
>   the army of freedom and peace.
> Lord for the sake of Amina's son, (i.e., Prophet Mohammed)
>   give them your reward that will endure.

Sa'adu then ends this part of his poem by exposing the folly of the Italians in thinking that they would have an easy victory over the allied powers.

> What a rude shock the Italians had!
>   They expected an easy victory,
> without any effort at all,
>   Such were the ideas of a sluggish army,
> Mussolini's corrupt host.
> Their lying was over, their spirits were at low ebb;
>   They were in no mood to endure,
> and submitted their necks to the sword,
>   They were captured without exception.

Sa'adu uses a metaphor here when he says *"Zuciya tasu ta zurare." "Zurare"* is a word used normally when one wants to describe the gushing out of water through a small hole made in a pot. He compares the water gushing out with the lost morale of the Italians.

The next thing the poet conveys to his readers is the treachery of the Japanese and their conspiracy and attempts to deceive the Allied powers.

> Then the Mikado the father of mischief making,
>   whom his people worship,
> called his commander-in-chief,
>   and told him to look for an envoy
> whom he would send to the Americans,
>   Such was their deceitfulness, and guile,
> They sprang most vigorously and fell upon the Americans.

The poet then describes the action of the Allied powers and their armies against the Japanese. The Japanese were paid back in their own coin. They were routed and heavily defeated. The soldiers, particularly those from Nigeria, fought a fearless war under difficult conditions. "They had fierce battles amid jagged mountains and deep rivers."

Sa'adu goes on to tell the soldiers that right from the day they left Nigeria people kept on thinking and praying for them. They fought the battle to preserve freedom and save humanity from destruction. The Nigerians had struggled and won. They also sacrificed their lives for the freedom of their country. He indicated that the memory of the soldiers is always fresh in the mind of the people. "You have filled our thoughts; daily we speak of none but you."

The poet points out that despite the courage and the gallantry of the allied forces, they too suffered casualties.

> The struggle in Burma has indeed been a severe one, without doubt and some are now lying on their right sides (i.e., are dead).

At the end of the poem Sa'adu shows his astonishment at the destruction caused by the atom bomb. He gave the picture of Hiroshima to support his statement.

> What devastation the atom bomb has brought in the city
>   of Hiroshima,
> Fire as far as Wakayama, yes and even to Yokohama;...
>   like the flame of Jahima,
> This bomb is a thing beyond imagination.

The poet ends with the message of the poem which is "freedom". Sa'adu now enumerates certain things which must be eradicated in any society that wants freedom to endure. He says:

> Useless is freedom, where there is poverty,
>   Hopeless to look for trust, where there are those who
> hide envy in their hearts,
>   Worthless is the leadership,
> where there is no honesty
>   Never while men are scorned, never while they are hungry,
> never, till these are ended, can freedom endure.

Here the poet refers indirectly to his own society for most of the evils that he mentioned existed in that society at the time he wrote the poem. The poet reminds the people of Nigeria that their soldiers sacrificed their lives to save those countries attacked by the Germans and the Japanese only to make sure that freedom, justice and prosperity endure. It is now up to Nigerians to rid their society of the ills that retard progress and prevent freedom from enduring. Then Sa'adu emphasizes the fact that freedom will be meaningless when there is poverty and hunger. This will be tantamount to a nation selling its freedom for the purchase of food and other necessities of life. (A good example of this is to be found in the poorer and developing countries of today where the much coveted freedom won at independence was bartered away to receive aid, grants and loans from the richer nations).

Besides, the poem being a general praise of a returning (and victorious) army, it seems to have a higher plane of meaning with a distinct dimension. He observes that it was Nigeria and colonial or minor countries like it that helped to restore order, not between the allies and the axis powers particularly, but within the "advanced nations of the world."

The last verse of the poem tells of another and even higher message and it seems to have been inspired or deliberately preceded by the verse on the atomic bomb. *"Wannan bom babu dama, kaji dan bom mai ragargazawa."* ("This bomb is a thing beyond imagining – this small bomb that pulverizes.") The nature of freedom, that is, after all, what the war was all about, is set out by the poet as his main point. So one finds him saying:

> *Tun da yakin nan ya tashi,*
> *Aka shekara babu fashi,*
> *Sai hayaki babu gaushi.*
> *Sai da anka tushe Faranshi,*
> *Yanci yai sallama da kowa.*

From this one may infer that Sa'adu might have been on the payroll of the British government and propagandist agent of British imperialism. This supposition could be true when we consider his poem, *Wakar 'yan Baka,* which was meant to counteract rumours spread by Hitler's sympathizers. It may be that Sa'adu lacked a clear view or a good knowledge of the balance of power of the world politics at that time.

The issue might have been complicated or misrepresented (but would not it be ridiculous for a colony to fight and sacrifice itself on behalf of a colonial master - all in the name of safeguarding freedom? What has the colony to gain after all? If the colonial master is defeated it would simply mean a change in hands from one master to another). But of course he was writing about events before they had actually materialized. May be he did not have the chance of reflection and consequently was caught unawares. Today there are better means of evaluating things, for we have more time and a better opportunity for seeing things in perspective.

This allegation was expressed by Sa'adu's critics who thought that provided a country is a colony, there is no difference whether it is under one of the Western powers or another. But I think they are being too idealistic, for some countries treat their countries or colonies with respect and prepare them well for their independence, while others rule their colonies for economic exploitation without preparing the people for the responsibilities that lie ahead.

This poem seems to be a plea to the world to recognize the causes of human miseries and to do something about them and in so doing to preserve freedom. It carries a familiar sound but one worth repeating; freedom is useless as an ideal. It is only meaningful when human existence is tolerable. The poem is intensely nationalistic. As an historical interpretation of World War II, it would seem as though the welcomed soldiers had fought the war single-handed. But poetry is not history in the objective sense of the term; it is literature and, as such, this poetic licence is acceptable.

The poem in a sense rewrites an historical account based on the outcome of the war. For example, the Italians are viewed as "stupid" *("Sarkacin Italiyawa")* in verse 18, but the poet conveniently seems to forget how impossible it would have been for such a "stupid" people to get as far as they did. Further, as in all wars, God is on the side of the right (both sides). The Japanese are called pagans *("arna"* in verse 31). The poet says that God preserves our leaders (verse 41) and gives us freedom. This word points the way to the granting of independence. But such thoughts were far ahead of their time. Sa'adu Zungur points to a time when only *Mulkin Kai* (independence) will satisfy the spirit of Nigerian nationalism. The themes of the poem seem to be unusual with respect to the colonial status of Nigeria (a legal and political ward of England at the time), but such forms of mild protest were generally acceptable within the context of artistic expression.

As a praise song about the army the poem is carefully done, and it is to be expected that the soldiers' virtues as warriors should be extolled. But another level of meaning seems evident in the poem, that is, the nature of social intention and the necessity of preserving freedom as a genuine entity.

The form of this poem is traditional but its subject matter is far from being so. The poet also does not use many Arabic words in this poem, however, he uses some English words such as ("Chief-Commander"). Sa'adu builds up the feeling of interest, tension and passion at the end of the poem, becoming more serious with the introduction of some words like *talauci, aminci* and *zumunic.*

Appendix: Samples of Zungur's Poems

Wakar maraba da Soja

Juma'a, mu yi hamdula,
Dukun Sojammu na Indiya da Burma sun komo 6-12-46

Mu yi sulatu da sallumuwa,	*Ga fiyayyen Annabuwa,*
Wanda ya shege kwaikwayawa.	*Shugagab duka jarumawa,*

A gare shi mu ke bidurfakewa.

Allah dai ad da kudura,
Babu tasiri da sutura,

Mulki, iko, du nasara,
Ba tsimi, kuma ba dabara,

Sai da kardin Jalla, mai iyawa.

Zo, aboka, im ma bushara,
'Yan'uwa duka za su rera,

Ka ji wakata ta nasara,
Don yabonmu gami da shukura,

Ga sadaukai, Soja, askarawa.

Marahaban, uhlan wa sahulan,
'Yan Afirika ta Yammu kullan,

Kai maraba da Soja, malam,
Zo, aboka, ka karbi jumlan,

Ayyukun kwazo na jarumawa.

Ka ji gagga, masu hurama!
Sun ciwo tutu ta girma,

Sun buwaya gabas da yamma,
A fagagen nan na fama,

Ku yi maraba da Soja, 'yan Arewa.

Tun da yakin nan ya tashi,
Sai hayaki babu gaushi,

Aka shekara babu fashi,
Sai da anka tushe Faranshi,

'Yanci yai sallama da kowa

Daga nan fa Italiyawa,
Don su taimaki Jamusawa,

Sunka dau takobin adawa,
Wai zatonsu da zaburowa,

Ga tuwo ya nuna sai tushewa.

Welcome to the soldiers

Let our prayers and blessings be upon the most excellent of prophets, who is beyond imitation, leader of all warriors,

        with whom we seek shelter.

With God alone is the ordaining of all things; is power, dominion and victory. There is no causation and no covering, no intelligence and no devising

        save in the strength of the Most High, the all-capable.

Come, friend, I've good news for you; hear my song of victory;
all our brothers will sing, expressing our praise and our thanks

to our knights, our soldiers, our warriors.

Welcome, *uhlam wa sahalan.* Welcome the soldiers, *malam,*
all West African boys! Come, friend and learn the whole tale

of the brave deeds of the warriors

Stalwart fellows and well-equipped, in east and west they prevailed,
winning a glorious banner on the fields of battle.

Men of the North, make the soldiers welcome!

When the war began, a whole unbroken year went by;
a year of smoke without red embers. Then France was crushed

and freedom made its adieu to everyone

Next the Italians took up the sword of enmity
to aid the Germans, eagerly to leap - they thought -
to the bowl of *tuwo* cooked and ready, an enemy already dead.

Daga nun aka ce mu shiryu,	*Duk barade su yi ta niyya,*
Madugui sun share hanya,	*Runduna dada za tu Kenya,*
Can a Isa 'afirka, don tsurewa	
Ga Italiya sun yi haramu,	*Shugabansu yana tu homu:*
"To, sumari, masu zama!	*Yuufu ranar dauka girma,*
"Ga magauta na ta kan isowa."	
Da Janar bubban Kwammunda,	*Yai nufin zai ba da oda:*
"Rundunar bukin Humada,	*Musu yin Kalimur Shahada,*
"Sai kufada kan Italiyan."	
"Rundunar'yanci a Kenya,	*Ga gulube munya-manya,*
"Ga duwatsu babu hanya,	*Yaufurranarfiddukunya,*
"Ba kasala, babu dakatawa!"	
Rundunurmu tu'yan Afrika,	*Suka ketare kan iyaku,Bindigogi na ta*
harka,	*Ga muzuje daf da halaka,*
Ba su tsoro, ba su kau tagewa	
Can Italiya sunka hango,	*Rundumarmy awa ta dango,*
Ba ta niyyar kama zango,	*Sunka farfasa nasu kango,*

Sunka ruga, babu tsuitsayawu

Rundunar'yanci ta bi su,   *Har ta kame madugansu,*
'Yan Nigeriyu sunka bi su,   *Sai Mogadishu, galibinsu,*

Suka wo tunga ta shakatawa

Cif-kwamanda yai umurni,   *Duk a kange dama, hauni*
Koguna, sariri, da tsauni,   *Kar a bar su, su san sukuni,*

Ko su san zarafin wurin gujewa

But then we were told to make ready; the horsemen to prepare themselves
as the caravan-leaders had cleared the roads for the force that was to go to Kenya

        away in East Africa, for our protection

There were the Italians, fully prepared, with their leader boasting
"Youth of Italy, fortune is with you! This is the day when you will win renown!

        See - the enemy is approaching!"
But our general, our commander-in-chief also prepared an order -
"Desert force, men who make the Confession of Belief,

        you will attack the Italians.

Army of Liberation in Kenya, before you are great rivers,
Trackless mountains. This is no day for diffidence,

        for sluggishness, for hesitation!"

Then our force of men of Africa crossed the frontier
and the guns grew busy and men met destruction face to face

        without fear, without hesitation.

The Italians saw our army in the distance like a swarm of newly-hatched
locusts (advancing) with no intention of halting, and scattered, (leaving) their camp
deserted.

        They fled and didn't stop

The army of Liberation pursued them and captured their caravan-leaders.
The Nigerians kept after them all the way to Mogadishu. Most of them

        paused there for a brief rest.

The Commander-in-Chief gave orders to hem them in on the right and on the left across rivers, in the plains, in the mountains; not to permit them any breathing space,

    to prevent them from any opportunity of escape

Babu halin za su dage	*Birbishinsu akwai jiruge!*
Ga su sigina masu hange!	*Rundunarsu ta zam burage,*

    Sai a rumi ba hulinfitowa

Da dare ya yi sunka shirya,	*Madugai suka kintsu kaya,*
Wasu duk aka bar su baya,	*Masu rauni babu jiyya!*

    Ka ji sakarcin Italiyawa

Dada dai kora ta mika,	*Har harar, wasu sunka sheka,*
To, a nan gizo zui yi saka,	*Kaito, ni! Da wagga waka,*

    Za ta san karba ga Editawa

Duniya duk ta yi guda,	*Abyssinia an yi gada,*
Guguwar yaki a murda,	*'Yan Nigeriya sun ka kurda,*

    A kwana ta Somali ba tsayawa.

Habashawa sun yi maye,	*Birni da ruga da kauye,*
Kokawa tasu ta yi kaye,	*Abyssinia, kai ya waye,*

    Am fa karya lagon Italiyawa

Runduna ta Addis-Ababa,	*'Sai ta mika wuya ta tuba,*
Cif-Kwamanada ya yi hudub:	*"Za mu shirya dinar maraba,*

    "Don fa Sarki yau yana shigowa

Shugaban Abyssiniyawa,	*Haile Selassie ya san muruwa,*
Shi ya ce, "Nijeriyawa,	*Sun yi fas bisa askarawa,*

    "Su na zuba nawa dogarawa."

Kai, muna fahari da murna,	*'Yan Nijeriya sun yi suna,*
Rundunar'yanci, amana,	*Rabbi, domin 'Dan Amina,*

    Ba su sakamakonka mai dadewa.

They had no chance to reform their ranks, for the planes were on top of them, and there were the far-seeing signallers. Their army turned into a pack of rats

    trapped in a hole, without hope of getting out.

When night fell they made their preparations; the caravan-leaders packed up;
some were left behind; the wounded were without care -
        such was the stupidity of the Italians!

After that the chase went on. Some of them raced into Harar,
and here a spider was to spin his web for them. (My goodness! I hope
        this song gains acceptance from the editors!)

The world shrilled with joy; with joy the people of Ethiopia danced.
The whirlwind of war spiralled upwards. The Nigerians cleaved
        through to the Somali corner without halting.

The Ethiopians drank freely in city, in encampment and in village,
Their enemy was knocked out, Ethiopia's troubles were over.

        The Italians had lost the game

The force at Addis Ababa submitting itself, yielded.
The Commander-in-Chief gave an address, "We will hold a welcoming
        banquet, for today the Emperor is coming in."

The Ethiopian ruler, Haile Selassie, showed his noble nature
and said, "The Nigerians have excelled all the other soldiers;

        they are my choice as palace-guards."

Imagine our pride and joy! The sons of Nigeria had made their name,
the army of freedom and peace. Lord, for the sake of Amina's son,

        give them Your reward that will endure.

Kai, Italiya sun ga zilla!	*Wui zatonsu su sami galla,*
A ruwan sanyi, su wala,	*Ka ji taron'yan kasala,*
* Rundunar Mussolini, fusikawa*	
Tasu karyan nan ta kare,	*Zuciya tasu ta zurare,*
Babu halin za su daure,	*Sunka mika wuya a sare,*
* Anka kakkama su, ba ragewa.*	
Lokucin da Japan ta ridda,	*Sai ta dorufurofagunda,*
Wai tana son tui shahada,	*Kulfa, im ba a sake oda,*
* Za su sharefagenfada da kowa.*	
Sai Mikado, uban gumaida,	*Wanda shi suka wa ibada,*

Yai kiran Babban Kwamandu,   *Ya cane a dido Jakada,*

    Zaya aikai gun Amerikawa.
Kaji kinibibi da hila!   *Kuji gulma da sunka kulla,Don su*
warware alkawulla,   *Sunka zubura, ba kasala*

    Sunkafada kan Amerikawa.
Sunka zambaci Ingilishi,   *Hong Kong, suka ba ta kas*
hi!Singapore, suka ya da mashi!   *To, Japan, kin dauki bushi,*
    Za ki ninka biya, kina dudawa.
Daga nun suka far ma Burma,   *Suka kama tashar Kohima,Ama suka*
dora homa,   *Suka safuskarsu yamma,*

    Za su mika Hindu, ba tsuyawa.
'Yan masa sukc~aru karka,   *Askurawa, 'yan Afrika,*
Yuufa ne ranar Tabuka,   *Sai ku ketare kun iyaka,*

    Don ku kori Japan zuwa are wa.

What a rude shock the Italians had! They expected an easy victory without any effort at all! Such were the ideas of a sluggish army,

    Mussolini's corrupt host.

Their lying was over, their spirits were at ebb;
they were in no mood to endure and submitted their necks to the sword.

    They were captured without exception.

When Japan's treachery was revealed, they poured out propaganda intending to achieve fame, threatening that if their New Order was not accepted,
    they would take on the whole field.

Then the Mikado, the father of mischief-making, whom his people worship,
called his commander-in-chief and told him to look for an envoy
    whom he would send to the Americans.

For such was their deceitfulness and guile; such their treachery

in breaking their promises! They sprang most vigorously

    and fell upon the Americans.

They outwitted the English; Hong Kong they overwhelmed

and Singapore laid down its arms. Very well, Japan, you've incurred a debt, which you will pay back and with compound interest!

Next they fell upon Burma and captured the railway town of Kohima.
Then the boastfulness of these pagans grew and they set their faces to the west,
    making straight for India without a pause.

But our young men began to stir, our African warrior — "Today is your Tabuk — you must cross the frontier
    to drive the Japanese back to the north!"

Ga duwatsun Arakan Yoma,	*Suka mika har Kohima,*
Haka ne, Mallam Makuma?	*Kai keje ka gano a Bama,*
Duk kasa ce wadda bijigawa.	
An yi daga masu zafi,	*A duwatsu masu katti,*
Da gulabe masu zurfi,	*Kaladun, Chindwin, AIW,*
Dukfagage ne na askarawa.	
Jupanawa, kun yi kunya,	*Don ko mu mun rama gayya,*
Rundunarku tuja da buya,	*Ga ta yau ta ba da keya,*
Sai gudu kuma, babu waiwayuwa!	
Wugga tarzoma ta Burma,	*Babu shakku an yifama,Wasu can suka*
kwanta dama!	*Sun sayo 'yanci—salama,*
Kaji hajja mai wuyur tayawa.	
Koka war ga da sunka kuyur,	*Ruyukan ga da sunka bayar,*
Rundunar ga da sunkajuyar,	*Zuriyar ga da sunka rayar,*
Har kasa ta nude suna tunawa.	
Yan mazuje, masu himma,	*Masu lambobi na zuma,Kun ciro tuta ta*
girma,	*A fagaggen nan na Burma,*
Da Masar, da kasar Italiyawu.	
Tun shigarku cikinjiruge,	*Har isarku zuwafaguge,*
Inda ko wunnetz dage,	*Tun a Arakan kunka zage,*
Kuka kori Japan zuwa Arewa.	
Kuka bar mu da tuntuninka,	*Kullyyaumin, sai batunku,*
Ayyukanku, da lafiyarku,	*Yau muna begen guninku,*

   Rundunar 'yaci, abin yabawa.

There stand the mountains of Arakan Yoma stretching right to Kohima
(It is not so, Malam Makama, for you went to Burma to see and report?)
    It is a country wholly without plains.
They had fierce battles amid jagged mountains

and deep rivers — Kaladan, Chindwin, Alifi

      and were battlefields for our warriors.

Men of Japan, you acted shamefully; for we repaid your treachery,
Your army retreated, and the retreat became a rout,

      and you fled without turning back.

This struggle in Burma has indeed been a severe one, without doubt,
and some are now lying there on their right sides. They bought freedom and peace

      goods which exact a high bid.

They wrestled and won; they gave their lives;
they turned back a host; they gave life to another generation,
      Till the earth is folded and put away they will be remembered.

Young men of zeal! Bemedalled victors!
You have won and brought home banners of glory from the fields of Burma,

      from Egypt and from lands once Italian.

From the day you embarked, till you reached the fields of battle,
wherever you took your stand — right from Arakan — you strove mightily

      and drove the Japanese back to the north.

You have filled our thoughts; daily we speak of none but you,
of your deeds and of your welfare. Today we yearn to see you,

      Army of Liberation, most worthy of praise!

Cif-kwamanda, Allah raini;	*Lord Louis, kai, Allah, sal ni,*
'Yam maza sun kece raini,	*Taka sunnu a dama, hauni,*
* Babu sauran musu kangurewa.*	
Kai, Atom bomb, ya yi shema,	*Can a Birnin Horishima,Gobara har*
Wakuyama,	*Har ta mika Yokohama,Sal ka ce*
harshen Jahima,	*Wannan bom babu dama,*
* Kaji dun bom mal rugurguzuwa.*	
Rabbi domin Mursalima,	*Ambiya, da mukarrabiuna,*
Don waliyyai, salihina,	*A wwalinu, da Ahirina,*
* Ba mu 'yanci babu kuntatawa.*	

Bubu amfuni ga 'yanci	*In akwai hahn tulauci,Babu yin zarafin*
uminci,	*In da musu kwufu a zuci,Babu kyawun*
shugabanci,	*Sai idan da akwai adalci,Babu amfanin*
zumunci,	*Suifa in da akwai kurimic,Kuma babu*
yawan butulct	*Bubu keta, ba sukurci,Bubu ketawur*
mutunci,	*Bubu muiyun war abinci,*

    San nun 'yanci ya ke tsayawu.

Commander-in-Chief, noble sir, Lord Louis, may God preserve and make you joyful!
Our young men are on top of the world! "Tread carefully lest you stumble"—

    those who stubbornly opposed you are no more.

What devastation the atom bomb has wrought in the city of Hiroshima!
Fire as far as Wa'kayama, yes and even to Yokohama;
northwards of Fujiyama, all the way to Tanega and Kogoshima,
like the flame of Jahima. This bomb is a thing beyond imagining —

    this small bomb that pulverises

Lord, for the Messengers, for the Prophets, for Companions,
for the Saints, goodly men all from the first to the last,

    give us freedom without restriction!

Useless is freedom, where there is poverty;
Hopeless to look for trust, where there are those who hide envy in their hears;
Worthless is the leadership, where there is no honesty,
Useless are close human ties, unless there is noble generosity.
Never while ingratitude abounds, never while there is malice or folly;
never while men are scorned, never while they are hungry —

    never, till these are ended, can freedom endure!

Chapter 18

Twilight in the homestead: the drama of Ene Henshaw

- Aderemi Bamikunle

It is a welcome development that Ene Henshaw has, within the last decade been receiving the kind of critical attention that will, hopefully, compensate for the long neglect he has hitherto suffered in the hands of critics. This attention will restore him to his deserved place in Nigeria's literary syllabus. The critical essays on him include Chris Nwamuo's "Henshaw and the Genesis of Literary Theatre,"[1] and "Henshaw and the Development of Nigerian Drama,"[2] "James Ene Henshaw,"[3] by K. Amoaberg and Laskei, and Samson's Amali's "Citation on Ene Henshaw"[4]. There are also Aderemi Bamikunle's "Ene Henshaw and the Beginning of Popular Drama,"[5] "The Politics of the Literary Syllabus, the Marginalization of Ene Henshaw's Plays"[6] and "The Place of Ene Henshaw in Nigerian Drama."[7] An important concern of these essays has been to assess the significant contribution of Henshaw to the development of African drama. Nwamuo's "Henshaw and the Genesis of Literary Theatre" concludes its assessment by emphasizing the areas of dramatic practices where Henshaw blazed the trail for others to follow. In Nwamuo's words:

> Henshaw is the pioneer in the creation of the tradition of Nigerian written drama...first notable playwright who attempts a systematic criticism of tradition-bound life as he does, without the fear of losing identity...the first to explore the conflict of cultures in the lives of Nigerians...and...making African traditional life and experiences the bases of his plays, a tradition that even Wole Soyinka has followed to reach Stockholm...the first to choose the youth as target audiences for any message aimed at bringing about a change

---

[1] *The Literary Criterion*, special issue on African literature, A. *Dhvanya Loka Quarterly*, Vol. XXIII, No. 1 & 2, 1988, pp. 118-130.
[2] *The Guardian*, 10 August 1985, p. 15.
[3] *Critical Survey of Drama*, New Jersey: Salem Press, 1985.
[4] *Nigerian Theatre Journal*, 2, 1985.
[5] *Nigeria Magazine*, Vol. 53,4, 1985.
[6] *Nigeria Magazine*, Vol. 53, 1, 1985.
[7] *Saiwa. A Journal of Communication*, Ahmadu Bello University, 4, 1987.

and innovation in communities, organizations and countries.[8]

This renewed interest notwithstanding, there is an area of the assessment of Henshaw's works that needs emphasis, that is, the revolutionary impact of his art both on his reading public as well as on the medium of drama that he employs to reach that public. In analysing the form of his play, Nwamuo acknowledges Henshaw's efforts to forge a new form of African drama:

> ... the issue of sanctified space in African drama and the unique idioms of mime, drama, ritual song and drumming which have characterized total African theatre today ... were first effectively woven into written drama in English by Henshaw in *'Children of the Goddess*.[9]

What still needs to be emphasized, however, is that behind the artistic practice and choice of form there is a sound social theory and theory of art and culture propounded particularly in the prefaces to Henshaw's plays and his notes on production at the end of the plays. Reading these commentaries, one is immediately convinced that there is nothing that Henshaw writes that is haphazard; everything has its intended function and impact, and is based on certain notions of the relationship between art and life. The choice of form is based on well-reasoned principles of the link between form and social effectiveness of art.

The best way to appreciate the revolutionary role of Henshaw's artistic thinking and practice is to place him within the colonial context in which his writing started and bloomed. As Henshaw himself implies in his prefaces, even though he humbly refers to himself as one who "wandered into playwriting," his plays are basically his reaction to colonialism's cultural assault on the mind and cultural life of African colonial subjects.[10] When Henshaw wrote *This is Our Chance* for staging at Christmas in 1945,[11] Nigeria's independence was fifteen years away. At the time there was very little of Nigerian written literature in English. Ekwensi's collection of short stories, *Ikolo and Other Stories,* the first publicly recognized published creative work, was not published till two years after Henshaw's play. The only well-known published play by a West African at the time was *The Blinkards* by Kobina Sekyi, a Ghanaian, and published in 1923. There was a general absence of scripted plays by Africans. The colonialists took advantage of this vacuum by feeding African theatre lovers on western plays. As Yemi Ogunbiyi found out in a study, theatre lovers at that

---

[8] Nwamuo, "Henshaw and the Genesis of Literary Theatre," *op. cit.*, p. 127.
[9] Ibid.
[10] See prefaces to *This is Our Chance*, Hodder and Stoughton, 1981; *Children of the Goddess,* London: University of London Press, 1966; and *Dinner for Promotion,* London: University of London Press, 1966.
[11] Nwamuo, "Henshaw and the Genesis of Literary Theatre," *op. cit.*, p. 120.

time "were thrilled to a wide range of plays from Greek classics, through Shakespeare, Sheridan to old and long forgotten sensations of London West End."[12] This tied African educated elite to western literary culture, and made it more difficult for them to appreciate African forms of art or establish a tradition of African written drama.

The colonialist knows that usefulness of art as a means of controlling the colonized readers' minds and subtly luring them to accept the world as perceived and presented by the intelligentsia of the West. As Ngugi wa Thiong'o has aptly noted in "Freedom of the Artist: People's Artists Versus People's Rulers,"[13] no art is neutral, every art has some design on the reader's consciousness:

> The arts ... are a form of knowledge about reality acquired through a pile of images. But these images are not neutral. The images given us by the arts try to make us not only see and understand the world of man and nature, apprehend it, but to see and understand it in a certain way or from the angle of vision of the artist.[14]

Most of the time the image which colonialist literature and culture project of African life, culture and civilization is a negative one. This is done ostensibly to make African readers or consumers of this depiction distance themselves from African cultural values. Ngugi's remarks on this are equally apt: "In religious art you'll find that colonialist paintings tend to depict Satan as a black man with two horns and a tail with one leg raised in a dance of savagery: God is a white man with rays of light radiating from his face."[15]

To counter this negative image and replace it with something more positive and objective for the African elite required a literature written by Africans willing to project the truth about Africa from the African perspective. It was the burden of African artists operating within the context of colonialism to assess western culture critically in order to prevent its indiscriminate assimilation by Africans. As Achebe has consistently explained, the pioneer writers deliberately set out to re-interpret Africa to the colonialists and to African victims of colonial alienation. Besides the choice of themes, this project of cultural rehabilitation called for the use of African media of art or at least elements of these art which enhanced resistance to a wholesale dependence and imitation of traditions of Western art. Henshaw's relevance and importance as an artist are best appreciated in his efforts at pioneering the analysis and understanding of the

---

[12] Yemi Ogunbiyi, "Nigerian Theatre and Drama: A Critical Profile," in *Drama and Theatre in Nigeria: A Critical Source Book*, Lagos: Nigeria Magazine, 1981, p. 26.
[13] Ngugi wa Thiong'o, "Freedom of the Artists: People's Artists Versus People's Rulers" in *Barrel of a Pen*, London: Heinemann Educational Books, 1983, p. 57.
[14] Ibid.
[15] Ibid.

contradictions of colonialism and finding solutions to these in his artistic praxis.

The prefaces to his plays are a key to critics' understanding of how Henshaw sees the cultural problems of colonial subjects. In them the problems are viewed predictably as those of production and consumption of art and art works; but the implication of what he says extends beyond the arts to encompass African attitudes to culture as a whole, both in African culture and Western culture. His apprehension of the cultural problem is evident in this remark:

> An important problem which faces all rapidly developing countries is the need to preserve good traditions, and at the same time to graft upon them, where appropriate, the best from other countries.[16]

An African is first and foremost an African, his culture is African even if it should be dynamic enough to open up to, and assimilate from others. According to Henshaw, this should be particularly true of the arts where encouragement should be given to "local arts," but these should "widen the scope to include the arts of neighbouring countries, Europe, and other parts of the world."[17] The need to produce art which is deeply rooted in its cultural surrounding is not only for the sake of the arts alone but for the African audience as well. For Henshaw, drama is not merely for entertainment, "to please the ear and the eye;" but it must "appeal to the intellect and moral aspect" of man. This calls for social situations that both playwright and audience can relate to meaningfully. "There is need," says Henshaw, "for plays to be written and produced in the African's own surroundings and with characters familiar to the ordinary African."[18] Thus, for Henshaw, from the beginning, writing plays was part of the effort to "popularize African drama,"[19] which, in the African context of the time, meant a drama based on forms indigenous to Africa. Through this medium the African can establish the "Africanness" in drama as well as "establish the dignity of the African through literature."[20] African drama, in Henshaw's view, cannot but be functional. Because of the many social problems Africa is facing as a result of colonialism she cannot afford the luxury of "art for art's sake." It is, therefore, obligatory that the playwright use the potential intellectual and moral power in drama to find solutions to Africa's problem. As he puts it:

> The power of literature as an instrument for influencing people and effecting changes is well known. The entire African scene, therefore, provides a challenge to African authors not only as individuals but also as a group.[21]

---

[16] Preface, *This is Our Chance*, p.5.
[17] Ibid.
[18] Ibid.
[19] Preface, *Children of the Goddess*, p. 5.
[20] Preface, *Dinner for Promotion*, p. 5.
[21] Ibid.

African authors must use African works to explain Africa to Africans: "it is far more important today for African writers to explain Africans to each other."²² These are the theoretical principles - social, cultural and artistic -which guide Henshaw's artistic practice, whether we are talking of his choice of themes, his worldview, or his formal, dramatic, and language experimentation.

Commenting on Henshaw's choice of themes, Nwamuo says that this "seems to be in most cases guided by his belief in Nigerian culture and tradition..." This needs clarification, for consistently in his plays it comes out clear that Henshaw accepts the reality of the cultural quality - African and European - in which the African finds himself. Henshaw sees the need to "preserve" what is genuine in African traditions, but realizing at the same time that every living culture must be dynamic, he also recognizes the need to "graft upon, (African traditions) ... the best from other countries."²³ His plays consistently examine African culture for what needs to be retained, what needs to be rejected, and what needs to be grafted to it from western culture to recreate a vibrant and dynamic contemporary culture which will meet the needs of the present as well as the future. The themes of his plays vary according to changing history and according to the needs of the particular period. In the forties, the need to create a cultural harmony out of the conflicting cultures of the West and Africa led to the writing of *This is Our Chance*. The need to reject certain outmoded and barbaric aspects of our cultural past inspired *Companion for the Chief* and the need to reinstate some traditions that had been rejected as a result of western influence is expressed in *Jewels of the Shrine*. With independence the cultural situation of Nigerians changed, and so the focus of Nigerian writing turned to Nigerian politics, political and social institutions and the nature of contemporary life. It is much new concerns that informed the farcical play *Medicine for Love* and the comedy *Dinner for Promotion*. The Nigerian civil war crisis was to lead to the more serious play, *Enough is Enough*.

In *This is Our Chance* the social situation is one in which two tradition-bound societies are on the edge of war over the simple issue of traditions that forbid inter-community marriage. Through this war situation, which was averted in the end, the author explores the conflict between African traditional worldview and the more modern worldview acquired through western education. In the end the tradition represented by two intransigent chiefs, Damba of Koloro and Mboli of Ndura, succumbs to the miracles of western education. A prince was healed by herbal concoction prepared by the teacher, Bambulu. The communities agree to open their societies to schools and their lives to the influences of western education. The advantages of education are many: it brings enlightenment and the chances of reviewing ancient, often obsolete, ideas for the purpose of evaluating their usefulness; the expansion of the scope of

---

²² Ibid., p.6.
²³ Preface, *This is Our Chance*, p. 5.

mind enhances the chances of tolerance and unity, of acceptance of new ideas. Education opens up new possibilities for life to progress and this is the lesson *This is Our Chance* teaches.

Companion for a Chief comes out clearly to condemn the practice of ritual murder at the burial obsequies of an eminent person. Not only is the practice bad in itself, but in this case, it is exploited by Tubaru, the priest, as a means of avenging himself on a rival, Soma, who had married the woman Tubaru wanted. Tubaru had used his position as priest to demand the head of the woman, Adeigra, to accompany the King's corpse into the grave. Luckily, at the end, by a series of dramatic irony, it is the priest whose head is offered in ritual sacrifice, while his would-be victim and her husband escape into exile. The point of the play is that there are aspects of African traditions that are barbaric, even evil, and that need to be discarded.

Jewels of the Shrine, on the other hand, laments the degeneration of certain aspects of African traditional culture. The situation of the old man, Okorie, typifies the cultural dilemma in which most Africans found themselves as a result of the coming of colonialism. This excerpt from one of Okorie's speeches underlines the source of depth of the dilemma:

> You know woman, when I worshipped at our forefather's shrine, I was happy. I knew what it was all about. It was my life. Then the preachers came and I abandoned the beliefs of our fathers. The old ways did not leave me, the new ways did not wholly accept me. I was therefore, unhappy (p. 42).

The younger generation has also abandoned not just the religion but all other social and essential values of traditional societies. As the stranger tells Okorie, "in the town where I came from, a boy of ten riding a bicycle will knock down a man of fifty years without any feeling of pity" (p. 40). Okorie, unable to get the natural sympathy and care that the old expect from the young, has to resort to tricking his grand children, Arob and Ojima, into believing that he has discovered the jewels of a shrine which they might not inherit if they did not treat him as grand children are expected to treat their grandparents. The play, thus, indicates that there is a general lapse in morality and humanness as a result of colonialism and that there is a need to return to these essential values of community life.

Magic in my Blood depicts the trial of a goat thief under the traditional system. The play mocks and satirizes the corruption and inefficiency-infested legal system run by the council of elders. The council of elders consists of drunken old men who doze off between conversation and start off to pronounce whatever sentence comes to their minds, sometimes on the innocent party in the trial. They are selfish self-seekers who condemn a man because the bribe he offers them is small and beneath their dignity. In addition, they will not hesitate to abandon all principles of law and declare a guilty man innocent because of his "supposed" connection by blood with a legendary hero. In this play also,

Henshaw takes a swipe at the idea of woman emancipation. The woman, Afiyu, brought into the council of elders outdoes the men in acts of irrationality and irreverence; all her judicial utterances are based on "feelings in my bones," her condemnation of the thief, Tontiba, is based on intuition while her readiness to condone his crime is done for the respect she had for the supposed blood connection with the legendary hero, Gogadie. On the whole, modernization, Henshaw seems to be saying, has not brought dignity to the traditional legal system.

Probably the most fascinating of the conflict-of-culture plays is *Children of the Goddess* in which traditional religion and Christianity struggle over the soul of a set of twins. Traditional religion regards twins as evil beings that should be destroyed, while the Christians would have them saved for Christ. In the end the Christian religion wins, the twins or their symbols successfully undergo an ordeal. Two leaves placed in a calabash under the scorching sun failed to shrink, indicating the power of the Christian God working miracles to save. The father of the twins, King Amansa, who is also head of traditional religion, gets converted to Christianity and allows that religion to flourish. However, Asari, the twins' mother, insists that the worker of the miracle is the goddess of the sea who gave her the twins in the first instance. The goddess had proved her power earlier when two white feathers she had put in a tray made it too heavy for anyone men or women to lift while she, Asari, the devotee, miraculously lifts the tray with one hand. At the end of the play each religion proves itself and each still has its validity and followers to celebrate its triumph. This end is typical of Henshaw who, though a Christian, does not denounce or totally reject the African religion.

> The events which the play portrays not only strengthen the faith of the young Christian of Labana in their new religion, but confirm the children of the indigenous religion in their traditional worship.[24]

Medicine for Love, is the culmination of the conflict of cultures; but it also explores new themes relating to the politics of contemporary post-independence Nigerian society. What we see is Ekunyah, a highly educated man having to struggle against the habit of relations forcing wives on him without seeking his consent. Thus, Ekunyah, a devoted Christian is compelled by circumstances to rely on diviners' charms and concoctions for his social and political advancement. In exploring these issues Henshaw is emphasizing the Janus-faced cultural life of contemporary Africans. But these themes are closely interwoven with that of contemporary political practice in independent Nigeria, a practice riddled with thuggery, bribery and other forms of fraud. Ekunyah resorts to these means in order to win elections. *Medicine for Love* is a serious indictment of contemporary Nigerian political behaviour.

---

[24] Preface, *Children of the Goddess*, p. 5.

Dinner for Promotion is basically a farcical comedy. However, in its focus on the theme of social self-advancement it reflects in a realistic manner the rat-race prevalent in a society in which the individual stops at nothing to advance his self interests. Seyil and Tikku are friends, flat-mates, and work in the same company. In their effort to advance in the hierarchy of the company, Tikku is ready to exploit his relationship with Sharia, his boss's daughter, to secure promotion. In addition he does not hesitate to do his friend, Seyil, a dirty trick by advising him on actions that he knows would bring about a rupture in his relations with Sharia, his girlfriend. The intention is to enable Tikku to have the girl to himself and use her to secure his promotions. Things do not quite work out in the end and Seyil ends up marrying Sharia and getting the promotion. The play exposes the decline of morality in a society where the thing that matters most is professional and material advancement.

Consistently, Henshaw deals with issues that are topical and of direct relevance to the Nigerian and African society. In the colonial and neo-colonial context which his plays depict changes are inevitable, but Henshaw sees the medium of drama as a means of fostering and controlling the changes. The choice of theme is important in this respect but so also is the dramatic form through which the subjects are explored and dramatized. Henshaw knows that a tradition of written drama has to borrow a great deal from other traditions of drama, in this case the English. Although not a literary man by training, it is clear from the prefaces of his plays that Henshaw has watched many western plays and is familiar with Shakespearean drama.[25] From this knowledge he recognizes that the western tradition of drama as discourse is useful "to catch the conscience" of his audience and readers. His plays, he says, should not only "please the eye and the ear" but must also stimulate interest in African drama, which in the context of his time, meant the drama that incorporates elements of African theatre. Through this dramaturgical experiment he hopes to preserve what is genuine in African culture.

The most obvious elements of African drama preserved in Henshaw's plays are the elements of rituals. Ritual invocations feature prominently in all the plays. From the invocation of the spirit of the ancestors by Kind Damba in *This is Our Chance*, the ritual actions of the funeral obsequies in *Companion for a Chief*, the invocation of the water goddess and her maids in *Children of the Goddess* to the instances of the goddess's intercession in material life, Henshaw "preserves" the African belief in a cosmology in which the spiritual world interacts with the material, gods with humans.

Ritual is an important element of traditional drama for various reasons. Its actions constitute the "dramatic" action upon which the meaning of traditional drama is based. Costumes, colour and movements in ritual represent dramatic spectacle which in traditional drama is not mere decoration but an integral and

---

[25] Preface, *This is Our Chance*, p. 5.

important contribution to meaning. The actions and spectacle, including dances and other body movements, are the basis of the depth of symbolist representation of experience for which ritual is noted, because unlike secular, realistic drama, ritual drama is less dependent on words for its meaning. The narrative which rituals try to enact often embodies the myths and legends and sometimes history of the people transformed into ritual drama. Songs, drumming, dance, miming and poetic invocations are inseparable accompaniments of the ritual process and the dramatic actions that result from it. Whether one is talking of ritual drama proper, or the more secular form of elite and professional theatre that has sprung from it, ritual and its attendant elements are at the core of African drama.[26]

The Africanization of modern written drama, particularly the tradition of written drama in the European languages, can only be through the use of core elements of the tradition of African rituals and ritual drama. In the case of Henshaw his use of African myths, legends, history, songs, drumming, dances and beliefs, is what he refers to as using materials with which the African is familiar, without which audience participation and pleasure are hampered. In this area of drama practice Ene Henshaw is the pioneer that other dramatists such as Clark, Soyinka, Rotimi, have followed.

Closely connected with the issue of authentic African drama is that of appropriate language. From the preface of *Dinner for Promotion,* it is clear that Henshaw was aware of the problem of communication between the author and the audience which can only be solved "by the use of suitable language." The problem, according to him, involves expressing "the thought processes" or "thought habits" of his characters and of himself (playwright) to the audience.[27] Only by this approach can a writer effectively Africanize the language of drama written in European languages. His solution, as he sees it, is "through the transliteration of African phrases, proverbs, or idioms into English" as he does in the speeches of the kings in *This is Our Chance* and of the chiefs in *Magic in my Blood* through the experimentation to evolve a form of language appropriate to the characters wherever necessary, as he does with pidgin English in *Dinner for Promotion.*

There is no doubt that in Nigerian English language drama there are successful playwrights Soyinka, Clark, Rotimi, Osofisan, Sowande, Ogunyemi with more profound social vision and a surer mastery of technique than are often attributed to Henshaw. One, however, will be right to say that whatever any of them has done is really like building on the foundation laid by Ene Henshaw. In whatever form his plays have been found to be "deficient," in contrast to those which came after him, it ought to be recognized that the "deficiency" is not due

---

[26] "See Appendix: The Fourth Stage" in Soyinka, *Myth, Literature and the African World*, London: Cambridge University Press, 1976.

[27] Preface, *Dinner for Promotion*, p. 13.

to lack of talent and artistic capability but to the needs and dictates of his artistic intentions. For example, his characters are said to be simple and lacking in depth of portraiture and that his plots are too simple. But Henshaw's method of characterization and plotting is the best for the kind of plays he writes. Though Henshaw draws a large variety of human characters and depicts many social situations, he is not basically interested in exploring the human psyche. He is interested, rather, fundamentally in the human and social conflicts arising from the colonial encounter. His characters represent social, and sometimes, philosophic points of view, pitted, often, one against another. This kind of work does not require deep, psychological character portraits to achieve its effect. His preference for straightforward plots without sub-plots is best appreciated when seen in relation to the concentration on single conflicts in individual plays which moves towards resolutions at the end. This concentration makes for dramatic intensity and leaves little or no room for distraction from the main arguments and interests.

Henshaw wrote many plays and now that these are receiving the critical attention due to them, his renown as a serious and talented artist is assured in any assessment of Nigerian drama. But perhaps his most important contribution to the development of Nigerian drama derives from his efforts as a theoretician who, from the beginning of his writing career, envisaged a distinct tradition of African drama and understood and addressed the problems of how to create such a tradition. The practice of fusing western tradition of drama with the traditional African ritual drama (with its distinctive elements of dance, drumming, songs, mime and colour symbolism) first found vivid expression in the plays of Henshaw. So also is the experimentation with the language and form of the theatre to move written drama close to the largely "uneducated" audience. Whatever genuine attempt has been made to create a tradition of popular drama (as opposed to elitist, university-orientated drama) in Nigeria also owes a great deal to Ene Henshaw's dramaturgy.

As has been pointed out in the case of the authors of the Onitsha market literary movement, Ene Henshaw sought, through his plays, to understand and resolve the cultural crises that resulted from the colonial situation. Like his contemporaries and successors he did not just decry the evils of colonialism. He made bold and original attempts to arrest the twilight in the cultural homestead in the hope of fortifying the structures of creative adaptation to a new and changing environment. The fate of some of his dramatic personages is a symbolic commentary on the depth of the crisis and the difficulties involved in overcoming it at both individual and social levels. The negligence Henshaw has suffered in the criticism of Nigerian drama in English is one other proof of the persistence and resilience of the colonial twilight over Nigeria's literary production and appreciation.

Chapter 19

The impact of the newspaper and the cinema on Onitsha Market literature

- Emmanuel Obiechina

The newspaper and the cinema are major influences on the Onitsha market literature. This is no surprise, given that both the newspaper and the cinema have enormous popular appeal. Their popularity depends on a very large extent on their accessibility, and this in turn had had to depend on their mode of operating on their audiences.

Certain facts about the newspaper and the cinema as media of communication should be taken notice of here. After four years of systematic education in any language, a man is able to read a newspaper written in that language. Which is another way of saying that a large section of a country's literate population has available to it that country's newspapers. Furthermore, because of their topicality and because they make relatively little demand on the concentration and mental energy of readers, newspapers have a very wide audience. As for the cinema, its appeal to the visual and auditory faculties, as well as its non-insistence on literary skill, combines to make available to it the largest audiences of all.

In West Africa the cinema commands this largest audience of all the mass media, while the local newspapers are read by thousands of the highly educated as well as new literates. This has a direct bearing on the discussion of the Onitsha pamphlet literature, and the impact of the mass media on its development. Both the newspaper and the cinema are familiar to the authors of the pamphlets, as well as to the people about whom and for whom they write. Both, therefore, affect the pamphlet literature. We may well begin with the newspaper.

The tendency of newspapers to popularize certain ideas and expressions and to 'demote' them to clichés everywhere has always been recognized; but in Africa this tendency is even more pronounced because the scope of people's reading is so narrow. For a large number of people, newspapers remain the only reading matter. They pore over newspaper pages as if they contained the rarest words of wisdom. That means that new ideas thrown up in the newspapers are soon picked up, committed to memory and sometimes put to new use by avid newspaper readers.

We shall discuss a few examples here. The 'fundamental human rights' were enunciated in the United Nations Charter and later popularized by the nationalist press and politicians in West Africa during the struggle for independence in the 1940s. The idea gained common currency and was taken up by the pamphlet authors. In the popular pamphlets young women resisting their parents' attempt to impose undesirable husbands on them are made to appeal to it. Other similar expressions popularized by the newspapers are 'That man should not be a wolf to man' (this is the motto of a daily newspaper in Onitsha), or phrases like 'Cock and bull stories.' These and many more like them occur in the pamphlets. Even a relatively new cliché like 'the wind of change' has found a place in the popular booklets. It gained currency after the former British Prime Minister Harold Macmillan's historic speech in the South African Parliament in 1960. Thus, in Thomas Iguh's *The Last Days of Lumumba,* a character is reported as saying 'We have been ruled and exploited by Belgium for donkey long years, but now, I am sorry to say that the wind of change will in no time blow across this great nation of ours.' Ogali A. Ogali, one of the most devoted users of popular newspaper clichés, writes of a girl who has deserted her imprisoned husband: 'With Okonkwo in jail, Caro quickly changed her name back to her maiden names, and what a wind of change!' (*Caroline, the One-Guinea Girl*). In the same novelette we have such newspaper-disseminated phrases as 'Operation UK.' (to indicate a girl's effort to get to the Unite Kingdom at all cost), and 'white college' (to denote the prison yard).

The influence of the newspaper is most evident in the large number of pamphlets dealing with political events and personalities in (and sometimes outside) Africa. This in itself is not surprising, since the growth of the popular press in Africa was inextricably bound up with the fight by African nationalists against European imperialism. Leaders of this fight became continental heroes and were lionized in the popular press. The pages of the popular newspapers were crammed with stories (some of them true, many of them apocryphal) about the exploits of nationalist politicians. Pamphlet authors, as reflectors of popular attitudes and situation, could not ignore a subject of such interest to their readers. The scope of their works concerned with these subjects is indicated by such titles as *Dr. Zik in the Battle for Freedom* (T.O. Iguh); *Zik of Africa, His Political Struggles for Freedom of the Black Race* (Chike Mbadugha); *Boy's Life of Zik, the President of Nigeria Republic* (M. Okenwa); *Heroes of New Africa: Zik, Genius of Today* (Okwu Izuogu); *Dr. Nkrumah in the Struggle for Freedom* (T.O. Iguh); *Dr. Julius Nyerere: A Profile* (T.I. Nduka): *The Struggle and Trials of Jomo Kenyatta* (T.O. Iguh), *Sylvanus Olympio* (R.I.M. Obioha):

The Life of Alhaji Adegoke Adelabu (O.A. Ogali).

Obviously, the people written about are those in whom considerable interest has been built up in the local press, and who have captured the imagination of popular writers and their readers. It is the element of wonder which is often appealed to, and these African nationalists are often invested not only with surprise sagacity in their dealings with the mighty imperialists but also with magical and supernatural powers which enable them to survive.

The leader most mythicized in the pamphlet literature is Nnamdi Azikiwe, the first president of Nigeria. This has to do, as Lindfors has pointed out in 'Heroes and Hero-Worship in Nigerian Chapbooks', with his being a local boy who made good, a successful Igbo from Onitsha, the home of the pamphlet literature. But there is more to it than that. Zik's impact was a national one because his was the first attempt to mobilize the evolving modern class of urban clerks, teachers and artisans into a mass political movement, and to infuse into them a spirit of nationalism. His innovating, sensationalizing style in the press, pointed out by Increase Coker in the article already referred to, created his reputation in the eyes of the generality of the people. His spell-binding, rhetorical style of speaking and writing helped to fire popular imagination which, once roused, vested him with all sorts of virtues and powers, possible and impossible.

Okenwa Olisa's pamphlet, *Many Things You Must Know About Ogbuefi Azikiwe and Republican Nigeria* published in 1964, reflects some of the popular belief in the fantastic qualities attributed to Azikiwe. Thus, giving the simple historic estimate of Zik's earlier position in Nigerian politics in the highly inflated language typical of popular admiration, Olisa writes: 'It is a general fact, and an accepted one, as well, that Nnamdi Azikiwe - "Zik" - was Nigeria's No. 1 hero in the political emancipation of the Federal Republic of Nigeria.

Azikiwe's progress through elementary and grammar school, his attempt to stow away, his scholastic success in the United States, and early brushes with the British administration on his return to Nigeria are seen with the fascinated eye of hero-worship. Zik is projected as an *enfant terrible* to the colonial administration. He is given magical and supernatural powers. Olisa reports that Zik was regarded as a spirit who could change into a fly or any other creature when he met a fatal danger. He was said to be beyond human destruction. These ideas were greatly reinforced by the numerous tales clustering round the story of an assassination plot against him in 1951. To the generality of the common people, in those days of hectic myth-making, the question was always whether Zik was to be regarded as a mere mortal or as a spirit. To which Olisa volunteers the answer that Zik is indeed 'a pure human being with extensive stock of knowledge, talent, democracy, etc.'

One element of the mythicizing of nationalist leaders has been their investment in the pamphlets with messianic qualities. Each of them - Azikiwe, Nkrumah, Lumumba, Kenyatta - is built into a Christ-like figure. Their self-sacrificing heroism is insisted on and woven into the fabric of 'passion' story. For instance, in Ogali's *Patrice Lumumba*, Lumumba is made to address his captors like this:

> You have all sold our hard won freedom back to Belgium and Western powers. I know you have all vowed to treat me shamefully as did the Jews to our Saviour...You have sold the Republic of Congo to Belgium and the Western powers for thirty pieces of silver. But was the Son of Man not sold for that amount by his people?

Elsewhere in the same booklet, Lumumba reproaches Tshombe, who has just slapped him, with 'Was Jesus not slapped even by those who dared not tread where he did?'

The parallel between the lives of nationalist politicians in Africa and the life of Christ is an important aspect in the creation of the charisma of those leaders - a process which they themselves immensely assisted. The political rhetoric of the anti-imperialist campaign period was redolent with messianic references, which worked on the high biblical consciousness of the masses to create the popular estimation of nationalist leaders. Here, for example, is a speech taken from a selection of speeches by Azikiwe. It is heavily laden with references to Calvary, Golgotha, and Gethsemane:

> Gethsemane was there to be conquered. Golgotha was there to be trodden under the feet of man. Calvary was to be overcome. And when a son of the new Africa faced with the travails and tribulations of Gethsemane, and Golgotha and Calvary, there is no need for the spirit to weaken. At this stage of my life, I cannot be mere flesh. I cannot be part of the corruptible phase of man's organism. I am a living spirit of an ideal - the ideal of man's humanity to man. I am a living spirit of an ideology - the ideology of the effacement of man's inhumanity to man.
> (Zik: A selection from the speeches of Nnamdi Azikiwe, cited by Adrian Roscoe in *Mother is Gold: A study of West African Literature*, Cambridge, 1971, p. 158.

The same close parallel between the incidents in the lives of nationalist politicians and the life of Christ was seen in many Gold Coast newspapers on the imprisonment of Nkrumah and his colleagues before the independence of the then Gold Coast. One heated editorial simply announced, *'Obedema goes to Calvary'* and then proceeded to chronicle the tribulations of the saviours of the people and ending with a prophecy of impending resurrection to political power.

The popular pamphlet authors had numerous sources from which to draw in, building up their nationalist heroes. The newspapers, the radio and other mass media were the main source, but these were amply reinforced by the soap-box, the pulpit, and above all, by the biblical tradition. The political heroes themselves were not slow to play on the popular imagination, especially its preference for the fantastic and the picturesque as against the ordinary and the realistic; they vested themselves with qualities which were thereafter elaborated and mythicized. They sometimes inspired the spread of apocryphal tales about themselves and their accomplishments. In this endeavour the organs of mass information were invaluable and they were exploited to the full to influence the information of public opinion.

Even though most of the 'political' pamphlets deal with Africans, a few are about illustrious 'topical' non-Africans. There are, for example, booklets on *The Life Story and Death of John Kennedy* and *The Life History and Last Journey of President John Kennedy* (both by W. Onwuka), based on snatches of information about the murdered American President gleaned from the press and radio. Another pamphlet, *The Trial of Hitler* (S.P. Oloyede), reports a fictitious trial of the German dictator and owes much to the reports of the Nuremberg trials and that of Eichmann.

The major post-independence African crises are widely covered in the pamphlets, especially the Congo and the Nigerian crises. On the Congo crisis of 1960, we have such titles as: *The Last Days of Lumumba* (T.O. Iguh); *Patrice Lumumba* (O.A. Ogali); *How Lumumba Suffered in Life and Died in Katanga* (Okenwa Olisa); *The Life Story and Death of Lumumba* (O. Olisa); *The Trials and Death of Lumumba* (Felix N. Stephen); *How Tshombe and Mobutu Regretted After the Death of Mr. Lumumba* (F.N. Stephen); *Tshombe of Katanga* (T.O. Iguh); *The Ghost of Lumumba* (Ogali A Ogali). Each of the pamphlets dramatizes some aspect of the crisis. On the Nigerian crisis, there are: *NCNC and NPC in Political War Over 1963 Census Figures* (O. Olisa); *The Iniquity and Trial of Awolowo* (C.H.A. Obi Nwala); *The Bitterness of Politics and Awolowo's Last Appeal* (C.H.A. Obi Nwala); *The Famous Treason Trial of Awolowo and 23 Others* (W. Onwuka); *The Complete Story and Works of Military Government and Nigerian Current Affairs, The Record of Northern and Western Nigeria Crisis and the Army Takeover 1966* (Anon).

A detailed study of these pamphlets shows that as well as fostering political consciousness the newspapers have contributed considerably to the conditioning of the attitudes of their readers to political events in Africa and elsewhere. To take for example one of the Congo pamphlets, Olisa's *How Lumumba Suffered in Life and Died in Katanga,* there is no doubt that the chief characters bear out the author's biased opinion of them, and it turns out that what the writer thinks of them reflects opinions widely current in the nationalist press about the *dramatis personae* in the Congo tragedy. Tshombe is portrayed as a wicked and almost inhuman adversary who shoots Lumumba as he kneels down in prayer outside a Katanga jail and then repairs to a pub to celebrate his infamous triumph. He earns the opprobrious name, 'monger', because his motives are regarded as mercenary. Dag Hammarskjold[1] is described as 'one of the main brains behind Lumumba's death.' Lumumba is the stainless hero; patriotic,

---

[1] Secretary-General of the United Nations at the time of the crisis.

brave and full of virtue. Before his death, he delivers a long patriotic speech which ended with these defiant words addressed to the persecutor, Tshombe: 'You can slap, beat, starve and kick me like a football, but I won't ask for mercy.'

What the 'political' pamphlets show is the immense power which the press has acquired to influence public opinion and form the mental and imaginative horizons of people in West Africa, especially those who are not likely to travel beyond their immediate vicinities or to grapple with the higher reaches of political problems. In complete contrast is the handling of the subject of politics by sophisticated West African authors. In place of the popular authors' hero-worship of nationalist politicians, the intellectual novelists and playwrights like Chinua Achebe *(A Man of the People),* Gabriel Okara *(The Voice);* Wole Soyinka *(Kongi's Harvest)* show politicians as corrupt, using their privileged position to corrupt and oppress the people. There is nothing heroic about politicians as portrayed in serious West African literature.

As one of the major influences moulding the attitudes of contemporary West Africans in things like dress, romantic love and material success, the cinema contributes directly in defining the world of values of the pamphlet literature. Commercial films especially (which must be distinguished from documentary or educational films) are aimed at entertainment rather than fostering the adoption of new attitudes, values and styles of life among those who are in search of the 'modern.' The more these films sensationalize the attitudes, styles and values emanating from the West, the more they appeal to the popular imagination and stimulate imitation.

It is the films which portray the glamour and opulence of Hollywood, the devil-may-care toughness of the heroes, and the slick efficiency of the gang-leaders which are most admired. The man who is successful with women, the successful gangster, the man of action, the man of the world who drinks hard, chain-smokes, overdresses and talks tough is the hero after whom film-going adolescents and those adults who are wholly committed to acquiring the new style of life model their lives. Western commercial films are for such people a school where they imbibe, through suggestion, the material side of Western life which they regard as synonymous with progress and civilization. As well as European and American films, there has been, since the war, a large influx of Indian films with their 'romantic' stories and an element of magic and the supernatural, which appeal very much to the popular imagination.

Because the popular pamphlets reflect life on the level at which people are most open to such suggestive influences, their writing conveys unmistakable the direct influence of the cinema. This influence appears in different ways. In the first place, some expressions used by characters in the pamphlets are taken from films. Hence the expression 'Look, old man, play cool' in Ogali's *Eddy the Coal-Boy* or 'Right, you get this, and get it straight...' (Chiazor: *Back to Happiness)* which preludes a girl's quarrel with a despised lover. Some characters emulate the style of tough film-actors, as in this exchange between a forward young lady and her timid lover:

Eliza: Chima. I think you ain't feeling comfortable. 'Well,' Chima hummed.

Eliza: Say on with certainty. Play your rough. Assume this is an opera. Calling on for your own art. Aren't you a generate male?

West African 'intellectual' authors poke fun at the predilection of some youngsters to imitate the speech and behaviour of movie gangsters. In the Wole Soyinka's *The Road,* for example, there is a small-time gang-leader called 'Say Tokyo Kid' who is depicted as an African who has become a miniature American 'tough.' This is how Soyinka introduces this character in the play:

(Enter Say Tokyo Kid)
Say T: (Looks round a little worriedly):
I ain't late am I?
Salubi: Say Tokyo! Say Tokyo Kid!
Say T: Salubi salubrity! Say man, everybody gathered round the ground place. How's business kid?
Salubi: Say Tokyo Charranooga Shoe-shine Boy!
Say T: That's me. I'm all right boy. (Sees the officer and recoils. Makes to pull an imaginary gun from his belt).

Soyinka's excellent eye for the absurd in contemporary Nigeria has not missed the effect of lurid American gangster films on some people. Cyprian Ekwensi also explores some aspects of this impact in his urban novels. Denis of the underworld in *Jagua Nana* is a pocket edition of the big American gang-leader; his style of living, if less opulent, still reflects the excitement and carelessness of those who cynically regard society as a gold mine. The effect of the cinema can also be seen in Ekwensi's *Burning Grass,* which reads in places like an embryonic Western, with Fulani adversaries fighting it out with swords and daggers instead of shooting at one another with guns.

The popular authors are not far behind in portraying gangsters who pattern their lives and actions on film gangsters. For instance, Mille O. Albert in *Rosemary and the Taxi Driver* describes the effect of the cinema on one of his characters: 'Okoro was a film goer. He knew himself that to change a car was an English method of bringing confusion into crime.' Alex Obiorah Okeke explicitly says in the introduction to his play, *I'll Rather Break My Sword and Die:* 'I developed the sense of dramas by daily attendance of film shows and by reading novels, booklets and daily newspapers.'

J.A. Okeke Anyichie's *Adventures of the Four Stars* is closely and consciously patterned on the lives of cowboys and movie-gangsters. The book has a picture of a cowboy on the cover, and the author leaves one in no doubt that he is out to create characters and situations based on those he has seen at cowboy and gangster films. His introduction speaks for itself:

> It is with profound practical experience of what happened in the Old Western countries, the era of Texas gunslingers, the Cow Boys and the Red Indians; the idea with which I set to write the *Adventures of the Four Stars* depicting African guys in a set of Old Lagos Suburb.
> In the Western countries of America they call it Wild Old West, but here in Africa, it is the era of the dope addicts and peddlers; the Bad Boys of Tinubu Square, the Wild Takwa Bar Beach Boys and the jayi-jayi addicts of Idi-Oro suburb. Read of them in thrilling and fascinating adventures packed in one.

Elsewhere in the same pamphlet, the narrator considers that his Nigerian imitation cowboys and gangsters fall short of the originals:

> I let my mind drift to different types of false imaginations. I was just wondering what it means to be tough. The thought of some old celebrated Western Films I used to go (to) began to dawn upon me. I thought of Four Guns to Mesa; Tony Curtis in adventures of Robin Hood; the Caribbean Gold and all sorts of Western Cow Boys of yesteryears.
> But here is black Africa. Where the idea of old Wild West of America, the days of gun slingers and hired gun men, was a mere dream. With these thoughts I decided that it would take another decade to produce tough guns. I mean like Robert Wanger, Billy the Kid, Jessy James and Durango Kid.

The 'tough' talking and 'tough' action which is so widespread in the popular pamphlets can be traced directly to gangster films. Many South African short stories published in *Drum* magazine show, terrifyingly, how deeply the tendency to imitate American gangsters has permeated the lives of young Africans in the urban ghettos and shanty towns of South Africa, stimulating violence, drug-addiction, and crime. In West Africa, the phenomenon is new, but is spreading in the urban areas with the ever increasing influence of the cinema (and of course, industrialization). The Onitsha pamphlet literature bears testimony to that fact.

The association of the cinema with romantic love is equally strong and is equally reflected in the popular pamphlets. This charming passage occurs in R. Okonkwo's *Why Boys Never Trust Money Monger Girls:*

> The film show started at the same time.
> It was a very good and interesting film.
> Joe and Cordelia enjoyed it very much.
> The film was a romancing one and for that it suited their state of love.
> When the actors and actresses in the film kissed themselves,
> Joe and Cordelia kissed each on their own part.

Again, in C.C. Obiaga's *Boys and Girls of Nowadays,* a character hovering at the brink of bankruptcy is reluctantly dragged to a film show by his girl friend. The affair proves a fiasco but it is worth quoting because it bears out the point being made here. This is how the writer describes it:

> Usually while the film was on and there was a part where there was kissing, Jerry would kiss Obiageli as well. But today Jerry was so absent-minded that he forgot to kiss Obiageli during kissing part of the film. Obiageli turned sharply to Jerry and asked him why he didn't kiss her. Jerry was unable to answer. 'Jerry, I think you don't love me any longer,' said Obiageli.

Sometimes attendance at film shows destroys the security which young lovers hope to realize by having their romantic aspirations ratified by the film world and its rituals. Such is the case of Jerry and Obiageli. Nwosu's *Miss Cordelia in the Romance of Destiny* gives an even more typical case of the hazards to which relationships are sometimes put when two people in love draw different and contradictory morals from a romantic film. In this case, the lovers have been seeing the film, 'Samson and Delilah.' The effect on the young man is disturbing and he says ruminatively to his girl friend, 'Did you see another proof to the fact that women have been and will always remain man's greatest source of failure?' The young lady greets the observation with a frown, for she recognizes in it rebuke of herself for dragging him away from his homework. Some of the love situations are diversified by such streaks of irony. Not even the cinema, with its glamorization of romantic love can totally exorcise the pains which sometimes attend personal relations.

One result of the influence of the cinema is a change in the direction of beauty. Film actors and actresses are now the models of beauty for boys and girls. The older generation of African men preferred their women big-framed, tall, with erect carriage, but 'modern' young men prefer their women slim, petite and excitingly made up.

Women used to have to work on the land and carry heavy burdens. This may have helped to determine the criterion in African agricultural societies. Such traditional practices as the grooming young nubile women in fattening chambers may well reflect an aestheticization of an event which had its roots firmly entrenched in economics. The current ideal of beauty differs so conspicuously, especially in relation to size that what pleases the traditionally-oriented eye may actually be repellent to the 'modern,' cinema-conditioned eye.

The popular writers' ideal of feminine beauty is the film actress, and when they describe beautiful women, the wasp-waisted, mascara-groomed, scarlet-lipped woman is their model. But because many of the writers are incapable of finding the appropriate words to describe her, they resort to expedients which are often ludicrous. This is sometimes also the case with their attempts to describe handsome males as the brief extract from Justin Ezimora's *The Lady That Forced Me to be Romantic* shows:

She said that I was wonderfully handsome, my eyes blue, my hair golden and to crown all that, I was so far the best mannered lad she ever met.
In reply I told her that her teeth were as white as snow, her hair like those of a mermaid, her nose pointed, her neck stretched out and attractive and lastly, her general appearance like that of Eve, the first queen on earth. She gave me a warm handshake and vanished.

The features described here are obviously more appropriate to Europeans than to Africans. This is a constant discrepancy in the pamphlet literature.

The popular authors excel in describing the effect of beauty on its beholder. They are then most sure, because most are vague. A good example is the opening passage of Ogali A. Ogali's *Caroline the One Guinea Girl:*

Caroline was an interesting object. She was adored by men - young and old, rich and poor.
In plain language, Caroline was a paragon of beauty. Her smiles sent many young men to the money-lenders.
What for?
Well, the bills - in guineas - must be paid...Caro's acrobatic waist seemed to contain a box of magnetism.
Men who saw her 'throw steps' as she moved along the road generally remarked 'Oh dear! What a nice and attractive waist, I must make a chase!'
'What a Pontiac' men said whenever they were chanced to have a camera look at Caro's nicely set breasts through her nylon blouse.
Her nose?
The Creator was rather very kind and careful when it was made.
Neck?
Good Heavens! Caro's neck was almost six inches long and how crazy were men when they watched her as she turned her neck in order to respond to a caller's greetings.
'Your eyes are rather very romantic, dear Caro,' men remarked times without number. She was at her most romantic form when she 'cut her eyes' in order to entice men.

Caroline is a temptress and a good-time girl who lives by exerting her physical attraction over men. This attraction might evaporate if it were described in concrete terms. The general allusiveness of the description as 'a paragon of beauty,' 'a box of magnetism,' and 'a Pontiac' whose appearance would drive men 'to the money-lender,' leaves the work of perfecting the image to the imagination of the reader. And since the imagination in such matters can be relied upon to prefer the poetic to the objective, allusion proves the best device for describing a provocative, seductive kind of beauty. This is the technique, we all recognize, of the 'romantic' magazine which specializes in the cult of seduction.

Some pamphlet authors go beyond allusive treatment of the physical appearance of their characters. They sometimes dwell on their attention to their toilet, as in Ogu's *How a Passenger Collector Posed and Got a Lady Teacher in Love.* Here is an example:

> Diana coiled her hair in twines and appeared like a stately tower. Her lips were painted red with lip-stick, while her two breasts appeared like two budded roses. Her nose stood straight like that of an Indian film star and lastly but not the least, the face was fancied with the best make-ups that you could not dream of.

The effect is relatively crude. There are Biblical clichés such as 'a stately tower' and 'budded roses'; while the face 'fancied with the best make-ups' might look like a masquerader's; but, this is some attempt at a more concrete description.

The intellectual authors, unlike the popular ones, have only scorn for the uncritical acceptance of the 'modern,' cinema-oriented idea of beauty and 'fashion'. To Achebe, for example, the 'made-up' girls of nowadays are 'painted doll.' Soyinka laughs at the whole business through his misguidedly 'modern' hero, Lakunle, in *The Lion and the Jewel.* Lakunle's idea of 'fashion' is represented by

> High-heeled shoes for the lady, red paint
> On her lips. And her hair is stretched
> Like a magazine photo.

Many of the pamphlets carry photographs of European and Indian film stars on the cover pages. This device is borrowed from the Indian popular pamphlets on which the African equivalents were originally modelled. The practice has been extended by the inclusion of photographs and drawing of young African men and women. Photographs of famous film stars are easily available to the pamphlet authors. Some of them are used as decoration for the backs of hand mirrors and some are even found in such unlikely places as tea-packet and other labels.

Reinforcing the influence of the cinema on the Onitsha Market literature is the part which 'love' songs play in stimulating the idea of romantic love and supplying many of its clichés. The writers of the popular pamphlets show awareness of the existence of the record song books and take many of their sentiments, and sometimes exact expressions, from the songs. In Ugochukwu Ajokuh's *The Chains of Love,* for example, most of the school boys and girls are shown to posses record song books. They place them conspicuously on their parlour tables and spend a considerable part of their holidays singing the songs. The title of the booklet itself is taken from a song of the same name made famous by the American crooner Pat Boone. In Anya's *She Died in the Bloom of Youth,* a ghost is reported as saying:

> Brush away those tears from your eyes, and try to realize that the ache in my heart is

for you,' words taken from 'My Happiness,' a popular song in the song book.

Modern 'progress' transforms tradition-bound attitudes and out-looks into those which 'liberate' individuals and invest them with a certain ubiquitous vitality and assertive autonomy. In the long run the history of that progress is the history of the progress of the mass organs of communication - the newspaper, radio, cinema and television - in the broadening of the vistas of human experience. The restless enthusiasm of the pamphlet authors and of the characters they portray in their pursuit of new experience bears witness to the effect of the organs of communication, in shaking the stability of the traditional psyche and giving it greater mobility. This enthusiasm is expressed through romantic love, the quest for money and a desire for pan-African political solidarity.

There are obviously two sides to the account of this progress towards modernity. On balance, most observers will agree with the pamphlet authors that change is desirable, even though the process may involve pitfalls. We may be tempted to laugh at the pamphlet authors and their crude vision of modern progress fostered by the mass media, but we must remember that debauched as this vision is, it has the strong advantage of being irresistible. The future belongs to the masses. Those who debase mass tastes and depress the spirit through commercially-inspired media will lose their hold when the people realize that a certain moral austerity is essential for real progress and that the organs of mass communication and education which are the principal instruments of true liberation must be put to proper use by those who share their vision of life and aspiration to modern progress. It is only then that they will become the beneficiaries rather than the victims of these media.

Chapter 20

Cultural imperialism and publishing in northern Nigeria: 1903-1960

- Abba Aliyu Sani

Subsequent to the colonization of Nigeria, virtually all facets of the economy and the society became subordinated to those of the conquering imperialists. Cultural imperialism draws specific attention to the mechanism whereby the mass media and the structures of literary discourse exist dominantly in the service of capital. Publishing in the context of this study is restricted to the processes in which written, creative materials are made available to a buying public in newspaper or book form. Also, for the purpose of this work, northern Nigeria refers generally to the geographical area previously known as the Northern Region. This is made of the present nineteen northern states and Abuja. So while 'Northern Nigeria' is the backdrop for examining cultural imperialism and publishing, the bulk of the discourse pertains more to those areas of the North where Arabic-Islamic culture is dominant.

Before the advent of Islam and literacy in Arabic in northern Nigeria in the ninth century A.D., and of capitalist, western style of literacy in the nineteenth century, the oral tradition was the sole embodiment of cultural expression. There may be talk of 'publishing' in pre-capitalist northern Nigeria where generating and circulating oral material was largely communal and participatory. In fact, the phenomenon of 'writing' and, by extension, of 'the book' in the North has its origins in Islam and the Holy Qua'ran generally and the activities of the Algerian Islamic jurist, Mohammed b. Abd al-Karim al-Maghili *(Sadi Fart)*, in the fifteenth century, in particular. Therefore, for much of pre-capitalist northern Nigerian, from the introduction of Islam to the flourishing of the Sokoto Caliphate, the absence of printing facilities meant that Arabic books came to the North through the trans-Saharan trade routes from the Maghreb and the Middle East. The high cost of such Arabic books and manuscripts, among other reasons, necessitated memorization, as obtains in varieties of orature, as a cardinal means of circulating such written materials. For instance, during and after the 19th century *Jihad* led by Uthman Dan Fodio, poetic compositions memorized by Islamic scholars and beggars played an important role in the mobilization for the *Jihad,* while at the same time enhancing proselytizing objectives. Throwing more light on the distribution of creative materials in Arabic in the pre-capitalist Islamic context of the North, a critic has observed:

> It may seem surprising that works in the script (the Arabic Manuscript) had such wide impact as soon as they appeared...the most valuable works were passed from generation to generation in private manuscript collections belonging to families or religious leaders. Students in theological schools copied texts borrowed from their teachers...and then recited or chanted them to the pupils at Koranic Schools. They were overheard by wandering beggars and blind singers, who further disseminated the works.[1]

Internal developments within the Sokoto Caliphate and the heightened activities of European merchants pushed northern Nigeria towards capitalism in the twentieth century. Debunking the assumptions of an egalitarian, pre-colonial North, Robert Shenton notes that on the eve of colonization, the caliphate 'was neither stagnant nor traditional, the possibilities presented by its social relations of production were continuing to unfold on all levels. Urbanization and commercialization continued apace and the class relations of both urban and rural society continued to be elaborated.'[2] Therefore, the formal colonization of the North in 1903 only completed a process of incorporating it, like other parts of Africa, into a dominant, global capitalist system. Colonialism it was which effectively began the undermining of the influence previously wielded by orature and Arabic writing.

On the whole, the subordination of northern Nigerian elite to the likeness of their conquerors was achieved not just through military superiority but also through the subtle structures of education, religion and the technology of writing, printing and the publishing of literature. As in other part of Africa, the missionaries in the cultural arena was supported by the colonialists. Missionary-colonial collections, translations and analyses of northern Nigerian cultures were integral to an overall strategy of subjugating the people.

Essentially, the long-range goal of these missionary-colonial activities was to provide the general foundation of the transformation, from a predominantly oral and Arabic-Islamic scripting, into a Christian, western, bourgeois written culture. Therefore, the advent of printing technology, with its extensive capital requirements as a profit-making enterprise, shifted the North closer to capitalism

---

[1] Stanislaw Pilaszewich, 'The Rise of Written Literature in Africa,' in B.W. Andryzjwski *et. al.* (ed.) *Literatures in African Languages; Theoretical Issues and Samples,* London, Cambridge University Press, 1985, p. 55.

[2] Robert W. Shenton, *The Development of Capitalism in Northern Nigeria,* London, James Currey, 1986, p. 76.

and western culture. Colonial printing not only accelerated the homogenization and standardization of heterogeneous cultures but also propelled their modification. In addition, the finiteness, hardness and seeming inviolability of the print tallied very much with the image of imperious superiority desired by the British.

Printed works of cultural expression and the first colonial printing establishment in northern Nigeria emerged in response to the need for 'inducing' and generating 'literature' among the conquered natives presumed to be in dire need of it. The literature desired was not just intended to mould the minds of the emerging elites, thus assisting efficient exploitation, but also to fulfil public relations work for the imperial government.

In the late 1920s under the governorship of Sir Arthur Richards, the British began to move towards practicalizing the idea of actually generating literature among the 'backward,' "uncultured" peoples of the North. This was to be attained, at the first instance, through the provision of reading materials in English and translation of northern Nigerian languages. The intention also was that such materials were to be used in the colonial schools just being established. Therefore, under the guardianship of a senior education officer, Dr. Rupert East, the Vernacular Section of the Adult Education Department within the Ministry of Education of the northern provinces was assigned the dual task of spreading literacy and generating 'literature.' Much later, the Vernacular Section was converted, enlarged and rechristened the Translation Bureau in 1929. The Bureau, first headquartered at Kano, was later moved to Zaria. The main contribution of the Translation Bureau was the encouragement of indigenous authorship through the translation of story books from Arabic and English sources into northern Nigerian languages, principally Hausa. Thus, from the beginning, the colonialists had begun to influence the precise course of the dominant literate culture in Nigeria by restricting the source for translation materials and actually determining what got translated from English and Arabic literatures and subsequently made available to the literate Nigerian eager to advance himself.

In addition, there was also the choice of Hausa language as the target of the Bureau's translation efforts. Clearly, the fact of relatively more wide-spread use in private and some official interaction, the main reason for the Bureau's emphasis on Hausa, was political. Translation and literary activity in the roman Hausa *(boko),* the language of the dominant ruling classes of the North, had to be encouraged, partly in order to impress on all the other linguistically non-Hausa groups the need to accept the yoke of colonialism. In fact the 'indirect' nature of colonial control in the North, that is through the existing traditional power structures which were preponderantly Hausa, also meant that it was politically more expedient for the colonizer to stimulate modern creating writing activities in Hausa than in Kanuri, Yoruba, Fulani, Nupe or Tiv. But then history had no place for a benevolent colonizer. One does not, therefore, expect the

British to pay equal attention to all the languages and cultures of the peoples of the North. But then owing largely to the perceived successes and potentialities of the Bureau, it was expanded and given the new designation of the Zaria Literature Bureau, in 1933.

Conceived and implemented within the overall scheme of the British for its colonies, the Zaria Literature Bureau (ZLB) functioned, along with other Literature Bureaux in East, Central and Southern Africa, to encourage Africa's cultural dependence on the West and to generate literature. This was effected generally by the weaning of the literate populations away from their pre-colonial cultures. As a result, the major undertaking of the ZLB was, therefore, the sponsoring of a competition in the writing of extended prose fiction in the Hausa language.

As brought out in the case of the literary efforts of the missionaries, the targets of the Bureau's inducement of a secular literature were the first crop of the largely Muslim intelligentsia of the North. This class of people and the Islamic *Ulama* (learned people) were more used to the religious-inspired Arabic script compositions than the secular story-books and poems that Rupert East was trying to promote. Dr. East had, in fact, noted that:

> Since the religious revival of the beginning of the last century, nearly all the original work produced by Northern Nigerian authors had been either purely religious or written with a strong religious motive...The art of story-telling is, of course, well-known to all people of West Africa, but in Northern Nigeria, as elsewhere, it is looked down upon as a pastime for the amusement of women and children, somewhat below the dignity of a man who has attained the status of a Mallam...To these people, therefore, the idea of writing a book which was frankly intended neither for the edification of the mind, nor for the good of the soul, a "story" book which, however followed none of the prescribed forms of story-telling, seemed very strange.[3]

However, despite these initial misgivings by East himself about the attitudes of the northern elites, especially of the Muslim clerics, to his attempt at inducing a secular literary practice in *boko* (the roman alphabets) the 1935 competition did attract several entrants. If nothing else, at least the manuscripts received proved, to both the colonialists and the Nigerians, the viability of the novel roman script *(boko)* to express cultural experiences hitherto confined to the Arabic script. In fact, the attitude of hostility and contempt of the *Mallams* to the European-inspired *boko* education and literature already noticed by East, was largely because *boko* was a threat to the Arabic literature familiar to them. Entries adjudged the best in the competition were subsequently published by ZLB. These included *Shaihu Umar* by Abubakar Tafawa Balewa; *Ruwan Bayaja* ('The Water to Cure all Ills') by Abubakar Imam; *.Jiki Magayi* ('It is the Body

---

[3] Neil Skinner, *An Anthology of Hausa Literature*, Zaria, Northern Nigeria Publishing Company, 1980, p. 171.

which Tells') by John Tafida Wusasa and Rupert East; *Gandoki* by Bello Kagara and *Idon Matambayi* ('The Eye of the Questioner') by Muhammadu Gwarzo.

There is, in all probability, no cause to disagree that the activities of the ZLB further widened the chasm between orature and the emerging written literature in northern Nigeria. This helps to put to rest the assumptions of a smooth, natural transition from the oral to the written or printed form of literature in Africa. The Bureau's works emanating from the competition sought to authenticate themselves culturally by relying on the residues of the oral cultures. As a result, virtually all the works are pervaded by the atmosphere of the fantastic, full of djinns and related creatures of the supernatural. This is, however, far more evident in Bello Kagara's *Gandoki,* Abubakar Imam's *Ruwan Bagaja* and *Jiki Magayi* by East and Tafida Wusasa. With varying emphases, the writers employ techniques from oral story-telling, legends, along with the heavy moralizing characteristic of most oral literature of the area. Basically, the Bureau was to pioneer a new modern literary practice rather than develop the pre-colonial forms.

For a literary competition organized in the high tide of colonialism, it was surprising that the works produced were uniformly mute about colonial violence and repression. For example, Abubakar Tafawa Balewa's *Shaihu Umar* depicts the largely unsavoury life in pre-colonial, Islamized Hausaland and its relationship with eastern, Arab world through the trans-Saharan slave and commodity trade. Without indicting the trade in human beings, there are suggestions in the story that the central character, *Shaihu Umar,* has instead benefited from his sojourn, first as a slave, and later as a freed Muslim *Mallam* in the Middle East. Commenting on Mofolo's *The Traveller,* which was produced in circumstances similar to *Shaihu Umar's,* a critic has observed that in both Balewa and Mofolo,

> ...African society is deemed incomplete and somewhat defective. To become complete and truly human the individuals must acquire certain qualities from other (i.e. European or Arab) societies. Even the partly islamized Hausa community from which Shaihu Umar hails is replete with evil practices. There is internal slavery, inter-tribal war, court intrigue... raidings, hunger, kidnappings, etc.[4]

In Bello Kagara's *Gandoki,* there is the central narrative of the career of the warrior-adventurer, Gandoki, who flees Hausaland in the wake of colonial invasion. He returns to discover the excellent deeds of the Englishmen. They had succeeded in 'pacifying' the natives, established schools and initiated advanced agricultural work. The prodigal anti-hero with the characteristics of Don Quixote sees no option but to praise the colonizers and settle down to relish in

---

[4] Sheikh Adams Abdulahi, 'Literary Tendencies in the Age of Imperialism,' unpublished Ph.D. Thesis, University of Wisconsin at Madison, 1983, p. 208.

the bounty of the British.

On the whole, at the risk of stating the very obvious, Rupert East's efforts to generate a really first class vernacular literature were largely a failure. The writings produced by the Bureau in northern Nigeria of the 1930s (with a very low literacy rate and no precedent in written, extended prose fiction), were excessively elitist. As Donald J. Consentino has observed, Dr. East totally ignored the existing oral cultures and the Arabic modes; instead he toured the North, 'exhorting the Mallams to produce prose narratives of novella length (about 20,000 words), which would not be didactic, and which would not be retold *tatsuniyoyi* (p1.). In short, East proposed that the Mallams imitate the work done two centuries earlier in England; he proposed that they create the Hausa novel.'[5] This was evidently an impossible task, for as Consentino elaborates, 'in effect, he (East) suggested grafting onto a culture with adequate forms of expression an alien genre with no literary, social, or intellectual basis.'[6] However, since the Literature Bureau did not address itself to how the issues of political domination and economic impoverishment of the North were likely to adversely affect the tradition of the 'novel,' the lean harvest of works was only to be expected. Therefore, instead of generating a popular literature for northern Nigeria as had been envisaged, writing, printing, publishing and selling of story-books accelerated the process of incorporating northern Nigeria into the cultural milieu of the West. As Dr. East himself admitted, many of the manuscripts he received were failures. According to him, this was because of the 'failure to bring the tale to a fitting conclusion. The book finishes when the author is tired of it, or thinks he has written enough.'[7]

Furthermore, East was unambiguous about the task he was accomplishing for the British ruling class, which was to undermine the pre-colonial culture of the North by creating a written tradition of literature. The process also advanced the economic interest of colonialism by converting literature to 'a commodity to be bought and used just like anything else which is sold in the market.' One of the salient issues which emerged in relation to the five novellas produced by the Bureau was that, by their production, East believed he had created a culture for northern Nigeria since he viewed literature as the sole determinant of cultural life. We get a clearer view of East's limited perception of the northern Nigerian cultural situation from his correspondence with an English artist he was trying to engage for the Zaria Literature Bureau. In his description of the schedule of work for the artist, East wrote that she was supposed to prepare

> illustrations for stories (local types), adverts, textbook diagrams, simple, etc., and what are wanted are chiefly simple line-drawings easily intelligible to

---

[5] Donald J. Consentino, 'An Experiment in Inducing the Novel Among the Hausa,' *Research in African Literatures*, University of Texas, Volume 9, Number 1, Spring 1978, p. 20.
[6] Ibid, p. 20.
[7] Skinner, p. 172.

primitive, or at least untrained mind.⁸

East added that the artist should be prepared to produce relevant art for primitive African peoples; he hinted that her experience of animal drawings was likely to be especially valuable to her. That artist, Miss J.D. Naeyer, did get the job at the Bureau and left its services in the 1950s as Mrs. Naeyer East.

The 'emergence' of a home-grown written literature in northern Nigeria at the instance of East meant that Europeans were in the natural position to be the literatures' own critics and interpreters. Since colonization, the African and his culture had become prime objects of intellectualization and, consequently, incorporation into the cultural and socio-economic systems of the West. This is the issue of Africa's virtual homogenization into imperialist economic and cultural world system. Further proof of the failure of East's efforts to generate a viable indigenous literature is the fact that none of the five winning authors, except Abubakar Imam who became a staff of the Bureau, wrote any work of worth after the 1933 competition. Once again, Consentino's comments on East's 1933 effort are revealing:

> Although East's goals were commendable, they were also very unrealistic. Literary forms are born out of specific cultural and social matrices. They are freely created, not prescribed. There is nothing inevitable about the novel. It is not the final flowering of a literary tradition, nor the end product of artistic evolution. It may be that Hausa society will never create novelists, but will instead concern itself with other literary forms more relevant to its world view.⁹

Two years after the 1933 contest, one of the winning authors, Abubakar Imam, was recruited to join the ZLB as an editor, in recognition of his writing skills. He left his teaching job in the Katsina Native Authority for the Bureau in 1935. One of Imam's major contributions to the growth of Hausa written literature was the writing of the three-volume stories *Magana Jari Ce* ('The Art of story-telling is a valuable asset') which was published in 1940. The three volumes are linked by the parrot-narrator and the recurrence of key characters. In writing these books, Imam depended heavily on the Arabic *ALFU Laila Wa Laila* otherwise known as *A Thousand and One Nights*, and *Khalila Wa Dinna;* translations of the Grimm's *Household Tales* from Germany. The volumes are thus a celebration of the written literary traditions of the East (Arabian, Indian, Persian, etc.), and of the West, rather than of African literary traditions. Imam was also largely responsible for the commencement of the first Hausa language newspaper, *Gaskiya Ta Fi Kwabo* ('Truth is worth more than a penny') in 1939. Therefore, fully satisfied and supportive of the activities of East and the ZLB,

---

⁸ Correspondence from Dr. R. East to Miss J. de Naeyer, dated 14, July 1944, File G.N. 79, National Archives, Kaduna, p. 14.
⁹ Donald J. Consentino, p. 28.

the colonial government of the northern provinces authorized East to expand the ZLB. In his February 1944 memorandum to the colonial governor, East proposed a broadening of the Bureau's work to include newspapers in a corporation known as Gaskiya Printing and Publishing Corporation.

Established in Zaria under its own ordinance in 1945 with funds from the colonial Development Office, the Corporation took over the functions and property of the Zaria Literature Bureau. Dr. East was charged with the responsibility of acquiring everything for the Gaskiya Corporation, from building plans and printing equipment to staff recruitment. He was specifically mandated to 'choose his own team for the work, and that they should be men with a missionary spirit.'[10] The 'missionary' in the citation simply refers to those with the zeal for political domination. This is because the first editor of the Corporation, Gordon Wilson, was appointed solely on the basis of his varied administrative experience, rather than his literary or journalistic skills.

Operated as an autonomous government subsidiary, Gaskiya was controlled by a Board of Trustees made up of an Emir, a missionary, a trader, one representative of educated young northern Nigerians and a nominee of the chief commissioner of the northern provinces. This pattern of membership allowed for manipulation of the Corporation's work since, in reality, East, the chairman, took all the crucial decisions. For instance, East was in control of everything from authorizing book publishing, translations, and pamphlets to the training of the African staff.

In the Gaskiya charter,[11] its products were expected to follow the tradition of 'clean journalism.' Dr. East is categorical that *Gaskiya* was out to

> lay the foundations of decent and well-informed journalism, with a liberal outlook and critical but unbiased judgement of affairs; to express the views

---

[10] File G 6/Sl/Conf. National Archives, Kaduna, p. 3.

[11] See the Gaskiya Corporation Charter as at 11/8/50. The objects of the paper and Literary Bureau are:
a) To support the general policy of government;
b) To give accurate new, and well-informed and temperate comment on the news;
c) To provide a forum for the view of readers, at the discretion of the Editor;
d) To correct false rumours and misunderstandings that have gained popular currency:
e) To publish such notices and communications government shall require;
f) To publish a reasonable number of informative articles on subjects of general interests;
h) To be broadly educational;
   The paper cannot be limited in its choice of material, except where this is of the following nature:
   a) Attacks on the general policy of Government, though criticism of particular measures may be published;
   b) Personal attacks;
   c) Matter likely to promote religious controversy;
   d) Obviously ill-informed articles (unless corrected by an editorial)
   The discretion in these matters rests with the Editor who is responsible for his decisions to the Board of control.

and gain the support of right-thinking people; to encourage good relations between all sections of the community; and generally to stand for moderation and stability.[12]

The liberal-humanist "objective" outlook of the Hausa paper, *Gaskiya Ta Fi Kwabo,* is brought out by its first editor, Abubakar Imam, in the following words:

> To work always for the good of the country as a whole, and not to take side of any one section, neither of Africans against Africans; neither of Europeans against Africans; neither of rulers against their servants, nor of servants against their masters. God is the protector against the malice of detractors and evil men.[13]

Contrary to the official position, the Gaskiya publications, especially the newspapers, were far from being fair or objective. The "detractors and evil men" were not left to God to deal with. In fact, the 'detractors and evil men' referred to by Imam as well as the 'catchpenny and scurrilous writing' complained of by a top colonial bureaucrat, were innuendoes directed at newspapers based in southern parts of Nigeria. *Gaskiya* was partly established to react against those southern newspapers. In addition, given the then ongoing World War II from 1939-1945, *Gaskiya* performed important propagandist functions by countering Italian and German fascist war propaganda in colonial northern Nigeria. The paper glorified and defended the British and their allies against the "terror" which Germany embodied. The paper informed regularly on the recruitment of natives to fight in the war, highlighted their 'heroism' in the different theatres of war and celebrated the allies' success over the Nazis.

From available records, the Gaskiya Corporation devoted far more energy and resources to its two newspapers, *Gaskiya* and *The Nigerian Citizen** than to the production of novels, poems or plays. For example, only three new novels got published by Gaskiya between 1945 and 1953. This was not simply because the practice of writing was yet to take roots in the North; rather it was because newspapers proved to be better propaganda weapons than the novels Dr East spent years trying to elicit. Once this possibility existed, then the novels had to wait.

However, the project for production of literature was not abandoned in spite of government's complaint about low sales of printed Gaskiya products and the lack of readership among the young educated people. The reasoning was that involvement in literary production was not just economic but was strategic and

---

[12] Correspondence from Dr. R. East to the Secretary, Northern Provinces, dated 27 May, 1950 in G6/Sl/Conf. National Archives, Kaduna, p. 40.

[13] Correspondence from the Secretary Northern Provinces to the Nigeria Secretary Lagos dated 18 January, 1949, in G6/Sl/Conf. National Archives, Kaduna, p. 28.

* Forerunner of the *New Nigerian*

political; the question of opting out, therefore, never arose. As the secretary to the northern provinces rationalized, government subsidy to Gaskiya had to continue because 'the production of good literature for the masses is not at present sufficiently remunerative for a commercial firm to undertake it.'[14]

Like its predecessors, the Gaskiya Corporation still fell short of its own goals in the area of culture and literature. Aside from the low sales, huge debts and 'lack of authors,' the literature for the masses envisaged by Dr East and his sponsors remained an illusion. As of July 1951 Gaskiya's losses amounted to £9,741. In that year, Dr East proceeded on leave from which he never returned. He seemed to have been frustrated out and away.

The propaganda value of Gaskiya newspapers in particular convinced the British of the need for more reading materials and newspapers in a number of northern Nigerian languages. To achieve this, the colonial governor, Sir Arthur Richards, created the Adult Education Committee in 1950. That committee was retained by Richard's successor, Bryan Sharwood-Smith.

In justifying the committee's work, Bryan Sharwood-Smith directed that adult education should be spread among the natives of the North, not just for its own sake, but 'so that amongst other things they shall recognize who their friends are and who are their enemies, and so that they may be protected in the coming years against exploitation, either from within or from without and in whatever guise it may appear.'[15] For this purpose, the North Regional Literature Agency (NORLA) was created in 1953 as the publishing and public relations arm of the adult education committee and the colonial administration. Its functions included a) preparation of material for literary classes in any vernacular, b) preparation of vernacular reading matter for general reading; c) vernacular news-sheets; d) orthographic research; e) publication of vernacular works by independent authors; f) translations.

Conceived as a capitalist, profit-oriented enterprise, the agency was instructed 'to become self-supporting as soon as possible.' The quickest way to do this, however, was to produce only fast-selling materials, and to restrict distribution to thickly populated areas where turnover was highest in relation to expenditure on time and petrol.[16] Although NORLA never succeeded as a business venture, it promoted in the North the rural-urban divide characteristic of other colonial societies. NORLA was also successful in its mass propaganda for the colonial ruling class, especially through the publishing and distribution of the seventeen news-sheets in the major languages of the North. Through these indigenous language papers the colonized were reassured of the immense virtue of colonial bondage and the utter futility of revolt. In fact, the agency was specifically instructed to publish and distribute materials only in the 'public' interest and to avoid 'subversive or obscene' materials.

---

[14] Ibid ,p.28.
[15] *Nigerian Citizen*, 15 January, 1953, p.6.
[16] Appendix 'A' in National Archives, Kaduna, MIA. No. 289.

By and large, the literature texts produced by the agency were true to its objectives. The works enlightened and educated the 'natives' without challenging the structure of capitalist and colonial domination. With the probable exception of Sa'adu Zungur, all the authors promoted by NORLA deemed themselves as having enormous stakes in the survival of the colonial system. They thus preferred either to be silent about oppression or to glorify it in their writings. For instance, virtually all the prose publications were in the apolitical, canonical traditions of Abubakar Imam and Abubakar Tafawa Balewa; while most of the poems were in the Jihad didactic tradition. The poets urged people to piety and to be steadfast in treading the path of Prophet Mohammed and the Imams. There was no doubt that if the *Sunni* variety of Islam prevalent in northern Nigeria was as militant and anti-colonialist at the mahdists were, the tolerant, conciliatory attitude of the colonizers to the indigenous literary effort would have been quite different. So, while NORLA was ostensibly publishing the religion-based literature in Arabic or *ajami* because of its perceived relevance to the people and its literary merit, the real reason for the choice was that the works helped to consolidate colonial exploitation and domination. Owing to the rupture of precapitalist economy, society and culture, NORLA sought some measure of relevance and authentication for its literary works by incorporating aspects of the relics of the oral tradition. As a result, the skeletons of originally total, contextual oral modes found their way into print in the form of individually authored 'texts.' The communality characteristic of oral performance thus became subordinated to that of the individual by printing technology and the capitalist values celebrated in the works.

In the NORLA-sponsored literature works, there is an undue stress on techniques of oral narratives. But in reality, oral narratives were neither the only oral modes surviving in the North, nor were they the most profound. Indeed, the agency deliberately neglected oral poetry and pre-colonial performative forms.

Also, contrary to its avowed objective of making literature available in the major languages of northern Nigeria, NORLA succeeded in promoting only Hausa literature. By so doing NORLA encouraged the emergence of Hausa as a hegemonic culture in the region. This in turn resulted in the Hausa language being the medium of internal colonization. In other words, NORLA was used as an instrument for subordinating all other language groups and nationalities to the cultural suzerainty of the Hausa. The import of this development becomes clearer when contrasted with the Soviet Union situation after the 1917 revolution. Their published literature appeared in 89 languages, 43 of which were unwritten before 1917. In Africa the concentration is on either an imperialist language or one or two African languages. Robert Escarpit has remarked on the cultural crisis which such lopsided development implies:

> The situation is particularly preoccupying in Africa where books in vernacular languages are sadly in the minority. In the United Republic of Cameroon, out of 54 books published in 1978, 40 were in French, 2 in other

foreign languages and only 29 in African languages; in Kenya in 1976, out of 183 books, 121 were in English, 3 were in French, 13 were in other foreign languages and only 46 were in Swahili; in Nigeria, in 1978, out of 1,175 books, 889 were in English and 286 in African languages.[17]

Although NORLA was intended to be an agency for mass education, it ended up accentuating an elitist education and its corollary, literary tradition. And in the absence of mass literacy, no publishing venture could lay claim to startling results. As a consequence of this, the main, and perhaps only, targets of NORLA books throughout its lifespan were the schools. And these were few.

These failures of NORLA were admitted by its editorial superintendent, Neil Skinner, in the following tone of regret:

> In my opinion (and that of the Distribution Manager, Mr. Bobb) it is now proved that at present, public demand for literature is both low and limited. The major source of demand is still what it was in the days of the Literature Bureau - the schools - to which may be added the demand from adult classes for the Hausa primers (but for virtually nothing else).[18]

Dissatisfied with the ailing, indebted NORLA, the colonial administration approved its merger with the Gaskiya Printing and Publishing Corporation, at Zaria, in 1959.

In 1960, following its take-over of the assets and liabilities of NORLA, Gaskiya Corporation faced enormous difficulties. These included the dearth of managerial expertise, labour unrest, poor equipment, low sales and untidy finances. In spite of these, however, Gaskiya still continued to re-issue old and release new literature titles.

Prominent in the new titles were Abubakar Tonau's, translation of Morrier's narrative of his travels in Persia, as *Yawon Duniyar Hajji Baba* ('The Travels of El-Hadj Baba') in 1966. Two plays, *Zamanin Nan Namo* ('These Times of Ours') and *Jatau Na Kyallu* ('Kyallu's Jatau') by the first significant Hausa playwright, Shuaibu Makarfi, were published in 1959 and 1966 respectively.

Quite expectedly, the British were apprehensive that the post-independence ruling class in the North might be susceptible to manipulation from other powers. The British took steps to insure against this by encouraging the Gaskiya Corporation to enter into a 'joint-venture agreement' with Macmillan of London on 19 July 1966.

The immediate outcome of the Gaskiya-Macmillan agreement was the incorporation of a private, limited liability publishing company, known as the Northern Nigerian Publishing Company (NNPC) on 19 October, 1966. With its majority shares of fifty-one per cent to Macmillan's forty-nine, the NNPC was, theoretically, a subsidiary of the Gaskiya Corporation Zaria. But in practice,

---

[17] Escarpit, R.,*Trends in Worldwide Book Development*, 1970-1978, UNESCO, 1972, p. 14.
[18] Skinner, N., NORLA 1954-59,' National Archives, Kaduna.

Macmillan had 'taken over' the NNPC since Gaskiya relinquished the publishing rights it had on over two hundred and sixty Hausa titles to the NNPC in fulfilment of the partnership agreement. A critic of the arrangement has observed that:

> If you look at the agreements signed by the two parties (Gaskiya and Macmillan), it leaves no doubts on the financial skills of Macmillan. Not only did it give them an easier access to the local market but they made huge profits out of their partnership. So whatever amount of help they provided, they deprived the Nigerian Company of 50% of its income when it was most needed since they were trying to develop.[19]

Therefore, contrary to the assumption that the involvement of multinationals was a guarantee of a continuous inflow of foreign capital, the earnings of the NNPC tended to get carted back to the metropolitan colonial headquarters, in the form of dividends and expenditure on the accommodation, salaries and personal allowances of expatriate staff.

Furthermore, besides enhancing the syndrome of general dependency on the former colonizers, rather than develop and use the printing facilities at Gaskiya to the maximum in the process of book production at NNPC as stipulated in the agreements, Macmillan more or less encouraged the decline of Gaskiya's potentials. Much of the printing works of NNPC was done abroad. The age-old complaints of shoddy, delayed, costly jobs were invoked consistently against Gaskiya by Macmillan in order to justify the printing of all NNPC books, including those of Hausa literature, in the United Kingdom or the Far East. Macmillan hardly acknowledged Gaskiya as a leading printer and publisher of Hausa literature. The one-time managing director of Gaskiya Corporation, Labo Yari, explains that 'with the arrival of Macmillan, London, the editorial production and printing of books, including Hausa books, which were formerly done in Zaria, were undertaken in the United Kingdom and Hong Kong.'[20]

Contrary to the claims of multinationals in a Nigerian venture, Macmillan, London, has also proved a failure in respect of facilitating the transfer of technical know-how to Nigerians at the NNPC. Instead of transferring vital publishing skills to Nigerians 'free of charge' in their London office as they had pledged, Macmillan had to be paid in foreign currency for the few who ever got trained. Macmillan recognized the central role of the managing editor in the NNPC structure, and so reserved the prerogative of appointing the first one for the company.[21] However, at the end of the expatriate managing editor's tenure at

---

[19] Monje, C., 'Nigerian Literature in English and the Conditions of its Existence,' a seminar paper presented to the Department of English, Ahmadu Bello University, Zaria, 1986/87 session, p. 5.
[20] Yari, L.,'A Memorandum on Publishing to the Federal Military Government,' undated,, p. 3..
[21] Responsible directly to the General Manager, the Managing Editor's duties include overall superintending of the editorial department, recruitment, training and preparation of publishing programmes for the company.

NNPC, no Nigerian had acquired the necessary skills to succeed him as originally intended in the concept of the partnership. Another Macmillan nominee, therefore, continued to do the work until the early 1980s.

In disregard of the significant contributions of Gaskiya to literary development in the North, especially in its role as the leading publisher of Hausa literature, Macmillan succeeded in helping the relegation of African language literature at NNPC. This was possible because Macmillan paid greater attention to general school textbooks (which bring in greater pro-fits) than to promoting literary works. By discouraging the publishing of works of literature Macmillan actually 'tightened a bit more the garrotte around the neck of indigenous literature.'[22]

---

[22] Claude Monje, p.6.

Chapter 21

The indigenous publisher and the future of culture in Nigeria*

- Kole Omotoso

Language is not only a fundamental of culture, it is the very vehicle of culture. All situations of imperialism are replete with the imposition, first, of the imperialist language. Culture impositions go hand in hand with the imposition of a foreign language on an alien people. It is obvious that if there is to be any cultural liberation, people subjected to imperialism must reassert themselves by re-defining themselves in their own language or group of languages. Thus the fear for the future of culture would not arise in a situation where language imposition did not go hand in hand with colonialism. Or if it arises at all, the problems which have to be dealt with would be of an entirely different nature. The question of the future of culture arises for Nigeria because we are in a situation of neo-colonialism politically, economically and, consequent on all these, culturally. A very obvious priority, therefore, is the decolonization of our culture which should result from political and economic decolonization. This implies seeking redefinition in our own languages. The dissemination of the resultant material in form of books is the duty of a national publishing concern. Short of a national peoples' publishing company, then, a conscious and conscientious publisher, a nationalist educator, is the best placed to do this duty.

From studies as far afield as Ayandele's *The Educated Elite in the Nigerian Society,* Olatunbosun's *Nigeria's Neglected Rural Majority* and Cabral's *Return to the Source: Selected Speeches of Amilcar Cabral,* it is easy to say that we in Nigeria, as in many other countries of Black Africa, come in two cultural moulds. There is the minority of us who have been exposed to the western form of education, who have been educated in foreign languages into foreign forms of

---

* Reprinted from chapter VII of *The Indigenous Publishing for National Development,* edited by G.O. Onibonoje, Kole Omotoso and O.A. Lawal, Onibonoje Press & Book Industries (Nig) Ltd, 1976, pp. 59-70.

perceiving. There is also the majority, put at roughly eighty-five per cent of the total population, who are still illiterate in any language, theirs as well as the foreigners.

At what point in the development of Black society did the slave trading Europeans come into Africa? Why was it so easy to convince the leadership of the Black society that they had no alternative but to co-operate with the foreigners for the sale of their people into perpetual bondage? What were the pre-occupations of the masses of the people which made it possible for them to go along with the fate that their leadership had elected for them? These and many other questions are what should concern African historiography. But what do we find? So-called African historians are attempting to tell the story from the point of view of the African as if it would logically lead to an assertion of the negation: 'And then Africans began to sell the whites into slavery to work in the plantations of the new world!' The fact of the matter is that African society, like many other societies, has always suffered from one major deficiency: the division of the ruled and the rulers and the inevitable division of interests between these two classes. The ruling minority has always been able to join with the foreign adventurer-exploiter to humiliate the ruled majority.

The disintegration of African society just before the slave trade was caused by the internal wrangling of the rulers. The European intervention intensified the wrangling and brought it to almost a situation of permanent war from which both the adventures and their home-based procurers benefited. The benefit of the ruling elite was carried over from the slaving oligarchy to the imperialist rule. Those who could benefit from the imperialist situation at home were those who had acquired position and consolidated it during the previous slave trading situation. The masses of the people were no longer sold into slavery overseas. Rather, they were to serve the terms of their life sentence at home labouring for the foreigner under the whip of the ruling elite at home. If there is anything to learn from *How Europe Underdeveloped Africa* by Walter Rodney, it is that such deliberate underdevelopment was possible by the use and collaboration of the elite at home. Where there was a native elite, the Europeans educated it in its own ways and in its own values:

> From the viewpoint of the colonizers, once the frontiers of a colony were firmly decided, the major problem remained that of securing African compliance in carrying out policies favourable to the metropoles. In colonial Africa, the European bourgeoisie realized that some education would maximize the value of labour. Albert Sarrault, a French Colonial Minister, stressed in 1914 what he termed 'the economic utility of educating the (African) masses.' Several years earlier the French had made a specific statement to the same effect on Madagascar. An ordinance of 1899 indicated that the purpose of schooling was To *make the young Malagasy faithful and obedient subjects of France and to offer an education which would be industrial, agricultural and commercial so as to ensure that the settlers and various public services of the colony can meet their personnel requirements.*

(Our emphasis) In practice, it was not necessary to educate the masses, because only a minority of the African population entered the colonial economy in such a way that their performance could be enhanced by education.[1]

It is noteworthy that it is the education, given for the specific gain of imperialism and colonialism that our historians such as J. Ade Ajayi and Ayandele have emphasized as the gains from the European contact with Africa. One wonders why these eminent historians never query the aim and function of this education.

The organization of any particular exploitative system is based on a small minority encapsulated in a myth with which they (this small minority) manipulate the great majority to do its bidding. This has been repeated in each historical age and can be verified in the history of any time, place or country. This organizational situation existed in Africa before the coming of Europeans. All the Europeans did was to replace the ideological base of the elite and substitute the ideology of their own elite without, except peripherally, touching the masses of the people. Education was the process of carrying out this ideological replacement chore. It is that education which our historians have elected as the most important gain from so many centuries of enslavement and colonialism.

In some African countries where genuine alternatives to the European system have been pursued, it has been necessary to replace the traditional leadership of the chiefs, *oba*, and emirs. Such countries as Guinea-Conakry, Tanzania and the countries of the victorious freedom fighters have dedicated themselves to building a new society by replacing the traditional elite which collaborated with the slave traders, imperialist and colonialist. In doing this they have been accused of destroying the tradition of the African peoples. This accusation does not hold in as far as destruction of an exploitative system, be it as old as the hills of Africa, must be to the good of the majority of the people. In other countries such as Nigeria where public office holders, be they soldiers or politicians, assure the traditional rulers every day of their relevance to the society, we find that the ruling elite use them just as the European imperialists used them before.

Not only this. The most enterprising of these public officers even seek chieftaincy titles from the traditional rulers thus further identifying with the decaying traditional system of exploitation. Is it any wonder then that people, in Nigeria, for instance, have always seen the government, *their* government, as something to cheat and plunder without any sense of guilt? Is it any wonder that political struggle among the elite for power has always left the masses of the people as mere spectators? Can one be surprised that periods of stability are merely

---

[1] Walter Rodney: *How Europe Underdeveloped Africa* (Tanzania Publishing House, 1973) p. 282-283.

periods for the strengthening of the instruments of exploiting the people more and more? Is it too difficult to say that only a situation of conflict (like the civil war, for instance) will offer to the masses of the people the opportunity to snatch their freedom from elite and reconstruct the society for the greater benefit of the greater majority?

Politically, therefore, this minority collaborated with the imperialist powers, who saw them as:

> destined to rule the country. It is their heritage. It is they who must be trained in the art of government so as to enable them to take over complete control of the affairs of their country. Their regime may be delayed, but it cannot be precluded.[2]

This minority passed from being 'collaborators' to being windsowers as soon as they inherited the power of the imperialists. They made promises to the people, promises which they had no notion of how to fulfil and when retribution was demanded of them, it was natural for them to turn to their predecessors, the imperialists, who had installed them in such positions to begin with, and thus bring about a situation of neo-colonialism. The indigenous publisher can choose the faction he wants to join. He can stay with the exploiting minority and provide them with the cultural wherewithal to forget themselves. The indigenous publisher can also choose to stay with the people and make his expertise available to them for the furtherance of their revolutionary struggle. But the indigenous publisher cannot straddle both political walls.

Economically, just as politically, we also encounter the two societies. If we consider some of the traditional economic organizations, we see that they are organized for the relief of the members of the organizations, and not for the greed of a few people. The *esusu* system among the Yoruba and so many other African peoples is an example. This system has also survived outside of Africa among the descendants of Africans in the West Indies and the Americas. It has survived among the greater majority who have to labour for the benefit of the minority. Simply put *esusu* involves contributions from members of the *esusu* group on a regular basis for the benefit of the most pressed for help at particular times. The contributions are not necessarily the same. Rather, shares on a multiple basis are accepted by each member and each member takes back from the group the total of his contribution minus payment made to the organizer who normally does not participate in the *esusu*. This system is still a very popular manner of making money available among the masses for building houses, paying children's school fees or trading. This is the 'banking' system that the masses know about.

Among the elite the situation is different. The European system has been

---

[2] Ayandele quoting Obafemi Awolowo's *Path to Nigerian Freedom*, p. 63 in his *Educated Elite in the Nigerian Society* (Ibadan University Press, 1974) p. 92.

studied and applied with such steadfastness that the elite is prepared to say that this European system is the only form of banking which exists. There is no known example of an African economist who has attempted to fuse the two systems and bring about something unique to Africa. Invariably those economists with whom one has discussed the matter dismiss it as not being sophisticated enough to handle modern problems of economic organization. As if the system they operate evolved overnight! Unfortunately, the European economic order of capitalist exploitation has of necessity permeated the whole society. The majority of the people have had no other alternative than to become slaves to both the city centres of the colony as well as the metropolitan countries of Europe and America. This is not difficult to explain when we realize that the political system has pre-empted any alternatives they could have for the society in which they live.

It is because of this permeation of the same economic attitude throughout the society that it is easy for some members of the elite to say that there is no such division as we have been attempting to document in this chapter and to affirm that both the poor and the rich of Nigeria pray for the same material wellbeing: children, money, cars, houses, positions, etc. And because of this common wish, those who are poor do not see it as their duty to censor those who achieve these legitimate ambitions by illegitimate means. This common identification is one of the problems which the revolutionary movement in this country has to identify in all its ramifications and combat as forcibly as possible because it blunts the revolutionary determination of the people. It has to be stated that there are valid aspirations which any society must grant to its members. Not only this, the society must also be so organized as to make it impossible for only a handful of people to fulfil these aspirations to the detriment of the majority of the society, as it is at present the case in Nigeria.

Economically,

> ...the fundamental problems of Nigeria's rural majority can best be explained from a historical perspective. In doing this the basic aim is to identify colonial development policies which created the dichotomy between the rural poor and the urban affluent and since Nigerian nationals took control of the government apparatus on 1st. October, 1960 they have essentially accepted as given the defective dichotomy which the country inherited, and are mistakenly applying only marginal prescriptions to a fundamental disease. For just as Nigeria itself was regarded as the country-side of the colonial metropolis for the exploitation of its resources, and subsequently, for the transfer of the surplus extracted to the metropolis so also is the rural sector regarded as a primary producer for satisfaction of the food and raw material needs of the urban centres of Nigeria.[3]

---

[3] Dupe Olatunbosun: *Nigeria's Neglected Rural Majority* (Oxford University Press, 1975) p. 49.

All the opportunities created within the new concept of how life should be, as imposed from outside, favour the elite minority. They have continued to work for the maintenance of this advantage and have refused to enlarge the number for whom the opportunity could be open. They have in their turn become an army of occupation who must be dislodged with all the revolutionary weapons education is capable of wielding.

As in the situation of the political duality of our nation to which the indigenous publisher cannot be indifferent, so is the issue of the economic situation. When one considers the area of culture one finds that:

> One part of the middle class minority engaged in pre-independence movements uses the foreign cultural norms, calling on literature and art, to express the discovery of its identity rather than to express the hopes and sufferings of the masses. And precisely because he uses the language and speech of the minority colonial power, he only occasionally manages to influence the masses, generally illiterate and familiar with other forms of artistic expression.[4]

Considering all these political, economic and cultural points, one can understand how Amilcar Cabral could conclude thus:

> Repressed, persecuted, humiliated, betrayed by certain social groups who have compromised with the foreign power, culture took refuge in the villages, in the forests, and in the spirit of the victims of domination.[5]

If the cultural situation is also dual in Nigeria, it is directly derived from the political and economic duality which has been referred to above. The cultural duality is emphasized by the duality of the languages involved and the media consequent on these. On the one hand the educated elite expressed its culture, both what it had inherited from the colonialists as well as the dregs of its own tradition, in the European language which happens to belong to its colonizing master. On the other hand, the majority of the people express their culture in their own language, a language which has begun to reflect its contact with Europe. The medium of the expression of these cultures is for the elite, written and for the majority of the people, oral. For the elite there are the various publishing firms bringing out each day novels, plays and collections of poetry in the European languages. For the majority of the people we have the recording studios and the broadcasting arms of the mass media relaying extracts from novels in Nigerian languages, plays and poetry. The powerful influence of such Yoruba actors as Baba Sala (Mr. Adejumo of Alawada Theatre) and that of Yoruba poets such as Olanrewaju Adepoju are cases in point.

---

[4] Amilcar Cabral: *Return to the Source* (Monthly Review Press, 1973) p. 68.

[5] Amilcar Cabral: *Return to the Source* p. 61.

For twenty years, African writing has been published mainly for the outside world. The speakers for the country have been elected by foreigners who had specific aims in mind, aims which, while coinciding with the aims of the local elite, had no notion of the local majority.

It is obvious that the culture of which we speak in this essay is the culture of that neglected, politically repressed majority rather than the client culture of those who happen to wield political as well as economic power in the country. This is the culture whose future one must be concerned with. This concern must be expressed in political action since culture is not born in a vacuum.

To some extent, the powerful minority inheritors of colonial powers and collaborators with neo-colonialists have realized this. This is the reason behind the so much publicized cultural revival. Under the guise of this cultural revival, villages are rampaged periodically to bring to the urban areas the cream of the rituals, the most profound of the oral literature for the entertainment of the same elite. By the nature of this periodic association with their sources, no effects of these rituals are possible on the elite. Rather, they continue to collaborate in the exploitation of the masses of the people, an aspect of which exploitation this particular cultural revival becomes. The myth and the being, the aspects of these cultural manifestations which have always stood the practitioners in good stead in the process of nation-building, are lost on the elite. Doubtful of their own influence on the city elite, the people move back to their villages with their rituals, with these aspects of their culture which they need not revive since the culture lives with them and they in it.

It is obvious that this culture had no political backing to reassert itself. From this realization one must wonder how it was so easy in the first place for the educated elite to take over everything so completely to the disadvantage of the masses of the people and the denigration of the culture of the people. Furthermore, one must wonder if it would ever be possible for the masses of the people to find enough representatives to fight their fight with them and aid them in the process of reasserting this culture not only for themselves but also for the deluded hybrid inheritors of and collaborators with imperialism.

It is in the possibility of fighting with the masses of the people that I see the role of the indigenous Nigerian publisher. It is not an easy role to play. But it is easy to misinterpret what is expected of the indigenous publisher or any one for that matter who claims to have a conscious awareness of the awkwardness of our Nigerian society, easy for such people to fight *for* the people instead of fighting *with* them. Many of our present-day avowed socialists are merely prepared to fight for the masses of the people. They publish journals in foreign languages addressing their fellow elites while the masses of the people for whom they express such verbally profound feelings know not what their fight is all about. He who must fight with the people must first and foremost, commit them to a programme of literacy. The role of the indigenous publisher is obvious in such a programme. There is no doubt that the culture of the masses itself would undergo a profound alternation during this process of literacy campaign. The accretions from the elite culture would be washed away from it, if it is to be capable of replacing the culture of the elite and providing for the cultural nourishment of all the peoples of the country. Besides this process of washing off the dross of elite culture from the cultures of the peoples, there is also a crying need for profound alteration in the so-called traditional culture itself. For the revolutionary must not be dragged into the same mistake as some of our historians who have been enmeshed into the issue that 'tradition is fixed and at no time absent from the time scale of the indigenous society. The word "tradition" has been used to excuse such anomalies as secret cults in present-day Nigeria without questioning the basis of such a group in a free and egalitarian society - supposedly the dream of this country. Many traditions are in fact opposed to the achievement of a free and just society and such traditions must be changed. The institution of *obas*, emirs, *obis* and all the gradations of the chieftaincy titles must be done away with if indeed a just, egalitarian and free society is to be established. Thus the process of converting the present oral cultural manifestations of the masses of the people into writing must witness radicalizing programmes rather than simply educating them into the existing world-order, which is itself discreditable.

To do this successfully, literacy campaigns must be conducted in the first language of the people. Little has been achieved from the many years of half-hearted literacy campaigns which have been carried out in this country. Even when there had been some measure of success, the programme had been so conservative in content as not to make any difference to the situation of the man who has acquired the literacy. What is meant here is that literacy campaigns must be seen as a cultural action for the freedom of the masses of the people rather than a weapon to aid the oppressed majority in the imitation of their oppressors.

The indigenous publisher can render much service if he is prepared to fight with the oppressed majority. But the contradictions are many and he must be prepared to face these contradictions and decide one way or the other. To begin with, he is committing class suicide when he identifies with the oppressed majority and accepts to fight with them using the effective weapons he, on behalf of the people, controls. But he dies in his class to resurrect in a better, less stratified society. Moreover he does not really lose everything as compared with those who will range themselves on the side of the enemies of the oppressed masses until the tide of the anger of the people drowns them along with the enemy. By making an initial choice on the side of the people, he pre-empts a historical foolishness which makes people fight against the inevitable march of history instead of seeing its trend and lending their weight to keep it on the revolutionary path for the good of all.

Another contradiction which the indigenous publisher must be, and in fact cannot but be, aware of is that profit cannot really be excessive in such an enterprise as this. In our type of incompetent capitalist society, how does one appeal to a man who has invested his money, time and talent in an enterprise, not to take advantage of the situation and enrich himself beyond the recognition of his society? This is a difficult question because it is not a theoretical one. Yet if such a publisher were well grounded on the theoretical aspects of the struggle of the people, he would know that the people's profit is his gain on the long run.

In this connection one must comment on the present trend of book pricing in Nigeria. There are generally two ranges of prices of books in the market. There are those books which are cheap and easily available. They usually sell for under fifty kobo but never above seventy-five kobo. Such books are in subject matter and cultural content unsuitable for the people who find them the most financially accessible of books. The only books of any use in this group are those imported from socialist countries. These are not yet available in such quantities as to make any difference to the market. Religious books also come under this category. On the other side are the books which would be useful but which are completely out of the financial capabilities of most people, including sometimes the elite themselves. This pricing situation is understandable in the declining capitalist countries where every aspect of the books trade is unionized and the resultant increase in production cost, in order to safeguard the profit of the publisher, is passed on to the reader. In such a country, books are no longer cultural materials but articles of trade whose cultural role in society is irrelevant to the publisher.

The type of atmosphere in which the indigenous publisher can conveniently fulfil his role does not, as yet, exist in Nigeria. But the indigenous publisher, as a conscious member of the society, must help towards the creation of such a society, a society in which books, like garri and plantain, will not only be made -available but also made available as cheaply as possible.

Chapter 22

Domestication of an opiate: western paraesthetics and growth of the Ekwensi tradition[*]

- Femi Osofisan

Leisure and Eros...

As opiate, anaesthetic and consoling, functions the entire range of the literary corpus defined as 'paraliterature' or, more commonly, as popular literature. The terms are meant to enclose an almost rebel category of literary praxis, outside the traditional respectable repertoire, but which, increasingly, is turning out to be the dominant current. Thus, paraliterature refers to such works as the novels of adventure, crime and espionage ('whodunit'), war thrillers, SciFi, comic strips, cheap romantic fiction, and so on. They are mostly based in, or around, urban centres, and their central concern is, almost invariably, the cult of Eros. In the city, 'in the anarchy of slums and factories,' as James[1] puts it, ethical restraints unloosen,[2] and a raw and hybrid cosmopolitan culture develops, where lust is king. Thus, though the range of paraliterature appears wide, such dimension is merely deceptive. The motive is always the same, and so is the functional imperative, which is to lure the reader temporarily into a world of sensual fantasy, in which the familiar social and moral order is threatened, but ultimately restores itself, thanks to the reader's *alter ego,* the super-hero. How did all this come about?

---

[*] Reprinted from *Positive Review (A Review of Society and Culture in Black Africa),* Vol. 4, 1981, pp. 1-12
[1] James, Louis, *Fiction for the Working Man* 1830-1850. London, Oxford Univ. Press, 1963, p 168
[2] See Wirth, L 'Urbanism as a Way of Life,' *American Journal of Sociology,* XLIV, (1938), pp 124

All literature is the consequence of leisure.[3] Bourgeois art, which prose fiction is, developed to feed the leisure of bourgeois workers.[4] Correspondingly, class divisions show in the plurality of fictional genres, with paraliterature responding primarily, though not exclusively, to the taste of the lower classes.[5] Modern civilization, in the western world in particular, has gathered vast numbers of the populace into the urban centres, around the teeming industries, and has gradually relieved its workers, through the complicity of technology, of the more harrowing tasks of manual labour. At the same time, in a superbly tragic paradox, it has created a new anguish, the burden of leisure.[6]

Leisure, like nature, abhors a vacuum, and, also like nature, does not always discriminate in its appetite. This is what is anguishing, that leisure and nature consume immeasurable filth.[7] For the lower classes especially, as for most human beings in general, the burden of leisure is relieved usually not through further exertion, whether physical or mental (such as is to be obtained from education, for instance), but rather, by the gratification of our inherent lust. Man at leisure is an exuberant hedonist. *Entertainment* for us (when we are being observed by family, friend or follower), is the synonym of licentiousness. When we leave our offices or workshops, we leave our brains gratefully behind on the desk or in the tool-box. We run to *vice* and *voluptuousness* as desperate men hasten to a deity, or otherwise the majority among us would not know how to fill their spare time. We relax very rarely to enrich our mind, but frequently to stupefy it, to shield it away from the nuisance of consciousness. Always we relax in order to forget, to cushion ourselves from quotidian realities: the doors of carnal abandon open widest at periods of deepest crises. It is no wonder then that the undefinable anguish of the modern industrial state, particularly in the capitalist and capitalist supportive countries, is daily drowned, before the next dawn's rude awakening, in the wash of sex, alcohol, and tawdry art. Paraliterature, like drugs, like television, like a night's whore, creates its own illusion of freedom, a cocoon of assurance for the battered psyche, and it thus partakes of the deceptive ritual of escapism in the modern city. It is because this drama is only a trance, because the catharsis is *manque* and the illusion never lasts, and because the refuge provides no lasting solution to the problems of living, that the literature sold to the masses is appropriately regarded as socio-political opiate.

---

[3] For a Sociology of Leisure, see Murphy J.F. ed.) *Concepts of Leisure*. New Jersey, Prentice-Hall, 1974. See Esp. chapters 4 and 5.

[4] Cf. Stevenson, L. *The English Novel Panorama*. London, Constable & Co., 1960. Also, Condon, I.A. The Movement of English Prose. London, Longmans, 1966. (Esp. pp. 153-165

[5] Cf. Tompkins, J.M.S. *The Popular Novel in England* London, Univ. of Nebraska Press, 1961. Also, Willensky, H.L. 'The uneven distribution of leisure' *Social Problems*, 9,1961. And James, *op. cit.*

[6] Cf. Cosgrove I. and Jackson R. *The Geography of Recreation and Leisure*. London, Hutchinson Univ. Library, 1972.

[7] I am talking of course of unorganized leisure. See, Murphy, *op. cit.* chapters 4 and 5.

The link of any art with its audience cannot, I suppose, be over-emphasized:[8] because there is an urban and suburban milieu, paraliterature exists, and expands with the increase in its consumption time.[9] Consumers of art may not consciously assert this, but it has always been with regards to the response of its particular public that artistic form continuously shapes itself.[10] Obviously no human society is ever completely homogenous; the audience exists in time and space, is subject to historical flux, and the existing social structure itself contains at any given moment manifold stratifications and contending interest groups. Therefore - to echo a point which, since Escarpit,[11] has become a cliché - the forms of literary creation fragment with the history of social classes.[12] In France, for example, the ornate dramas of neo-classicists fit handsomely into the ideology of royal protocol but they yield to the fast prose styles of the Revolution and the fluid syntax of the nascent positivist age, then to the mellow, plaintive cadences of the Romantics: from Racine and Corneille, we move to the essayists and encyclopaedists of the eighteenth century, to Voltaire and Diderot, and then to Hugo and Flaubert, Hegel and Marx. Now paper becomes even cheaper and easier to find, the printing mills improve on their miracle of reproduction,'[13] at the same time as the proliferating proletariat demand, from the depths of their squalid slums, new forms of social and spiritual analgesia. Popular theatres and music halls flourish, newspapers, pamphlets and 'penny dreadfuls flood the market; it is the age of Zola, Dickens and Turgenev, and it is also the age of Eugene Sue and Paul de Kock, of Reynolds and Nicholson, of Fennimore Cooper, Z. C. Judson and H. Ingraham.[14] We need not go on. The literary genres which crowd the modern bookstall, the diverse packages in which they are marketed, their peculiar choice of theme or tone of seduction, all are products of the demographic fluxes of our contemporary capitalist society, of the shifting scales of taste as we travel up or down the ladder of material ease.[15]

Once all these are understood, the historical development of our literature in Africa, and in Nigeria in particular, becomes comprehensible. One can even go further and predict: whatever the past decades may have produced, the 1980s will be the age of pulp and juvenilia. The works of Soyinka, Achebe and Clark

---

[8] Leavis Q.R. *Fiction and the Reading Public*. London, Chatto and Windus, 1965. Esp. pp.118-202.

[9] Delziel, M. *Popular Fiction Hundred Years Ago*. London, Cohen and West, 1957.

[10] Cf. Priestley, in. *Literature and the Western Mind* London, Heinemaun, 1960, pp.113-274. Also, Sartre, J.P. *What Is Literature?* London, Methuen, 1950.

[11] Escarpit, R. *Sociologie de Ia Litterature*. Paris, P.U.F., 1958.

[12] Cf. Leavis, op. cit. Also, Robert. M. *Roman des origines et origines du roman*. Paris, Grasset, 1972.

[13] See Steinberg, S.H. *Five Hundred Years of Printing* London, Penguin, 1961, pp. 214-230.

[14] See James, op. cit. Several other historical studies exist of course.

[15] Escarpit, R. (ed.) *La litteraire et lesociat* Paris, Flammarion, 1970. (See Esp. the contributions from Bouazis, Zalamausky, Escarpit and Estivals). Also, Laurenson D. and Swingewood A. *The Sociology of Literature*. London, MacGibbon & Kee, 1971. Esp. pp. 91-140.

are markedly of a confused ideology;[16] being products of transition, they look more to the past and to the unknowable future. But the works of today have defined their province: they focus graphically on the present alone. The works of the earlier writers consciously crave for the luminous areas of language and metaphor, seek to distil banal experience into crystallized visions, and the anguish of their search cries out in their often tortuous styles and convoluted mechanics.[17] But no more: the newer writers flail their fists aggressively within the limited ethos and coarse reality of contemporary collisions. 'When we started writing we felt a sense of mission about reconstructing our history,' says Munonye, 'but now we must write about the present. We must go into our society, its strong and weak points, its problems, the prescriptions we would like to offer, casting these into art forms.'[18] Thus, instead of *Arrow of God*, the public has *Sacrifice:* instead of *Interpreters,* we have *Violence;* in place of *Ozidi,* so many *Morountoduns* hatch in the theatre's restless womb.[19] My contention, however, is that this distinction is itself misleading: *Sacrifice, Violence* and *Morountodun* are themselves still minority aberrations: louder noises will be heard tomorrow evening from a different category of works, the works which compose our own growing paraliterature. More prominent in the market than Omotoso or Osofisan will grow such writers as Kalu Okpi, Adaora Ulasi, Dilibe Onyeama, and so on,[20] those I have referred to elsewhere as Ekwensi's heirs.[21]

This phenomenon will spring from no miracle but from the reality of our socio-economic development, just as in the history of western art. Soyinka, Achebe, Clark and Okigbo were different, because their world was different. When they began to write, most African states had just come to Independence; the leaders in power were lately comrades of the writers in the fight for freedom. Thus when these leaders turned traitors, the writers denounced them in accents of lingering affection, of nostalgic love. Furthermore, this kinship with the political leaders tended to screen the writers' sight from the truth of the situation, as they saw the problems of the growing nations mostly on the surface in terms of the individual failures of the leaders, rather than in the total system itself.

Meanwhile, however, our nations were sinking fast in the clutches of the

---

[16] Cf. Jeyifo, B. 'Soyinka Demythologized: Notes on a Materialist Reading of a *Dance in the Forest, The Road* and *Kongi's Harvest,* Ife Monographs on Literature and Criticism, Department of Literature in English, University of Ife, 1984.

[17] The 'troika' of critics (to use Soyinka's term for Chinweizu, Madubuike and Jemie) denounce this, but are incapable of seeing it as a product of idcology Being equally implicated by their class values, the solution they propose is just as equally unacceptable, because retrogressive.

[18] Munonye, John. *Dem-Say* (Interviews with Eight Nigerian Writers) edited by Bernth Lindfors. Occasional Publication of the Univ. of Texas at Austin, 1974. p.40.

[19] About these titles. see Bibliography below.

[20] I am talking here of a division based on the levels of consciousness and stylistic sophistication. Ref. my essay, 'The Alternative Tradition: Nigerian Literature after the War,' HALEL, forthcoming.

[21] In fact, Fanon had ably predicted this kind of development in *The Wretched of the Earth*.

capitalist economies of the West. In our peripheral dependency, our societies are splitting up rapidly into more sharply defined, more antagonistic classes; the cities are dividing into ghettoes on one side and well laid out elite plots on the other; 'development' to the ruling class takes shape in the openly promoted westernization of our countries. When the Ibadan-Nsukka artists began to write, class divisions were still in embryo; it was still possible to see all black men as being on the same side of the fence, especially as the 'enemy' was the white colonialist. But a decade later, when our generation began to create, that myth of black consensus or homogeneity of purpose had exploded: there is now clearly a visible back bourgeoisie, as greedy, selfish, parasitic and treacherous as its counterpart in the western world; there is a truly wretched proletariat and sub-proletariat, and there is a fast decaying peasantry.[22] Time has passed, and left the marks of its teeth.

I am concerned in this essay with only the literary, not the political or economic implications of this ongoing dislocation of our society. What it had meant, particularly to the publisher, is an awareness of the corresponding fission of the writer's clientele. Whereas in the 1960s the literate audience was composed in the main of the petty bourgeoisie, by the 1970s the bulk of the reading public was to be found lower down the social ladder, comprising the class of secretaries, nurses and the equivalent spectrum of the lower middle class. The climate of taste has changed; both the aspiring writer and the profit-hungry publisher were bound to take notice. The new public outside the universities devours Hadley Chase, not Shakespeare;[23] it cares little for Okigbo or even Aluko, not to talk of Soyinka and Echeruo: away from the schools' curricula, it is not the Heinemann Educational Series, but the opportunistic collections of Macmillan's 'Pacesetters' and the Fontana Africans novels which top the best-sellers' list.

I have observed, in the essay referred to earlier,[24] of the positive and negative consequences of this novel direction in the movement of our literature, and my aim here is merely to emphasize its *inevitability,* given the factors of our historical development and the example of the western world which we have taken as model, and to show how the apparently neutral factors of aesthetic imagination - the canons of form and mechanics, the internal logistics of genre and medium - are in fact subjective elements within the socio-economic momentum of society.

In this respect, therefore, Cyprian Ekwensi the much vilified, much condemned writer, was paradoxically the most *relevant* (in the sense of

---

[22] Education (interrupted early for various reasons), is also an aspect of the new movement of Literacy. See Ricard, A. 'Rernarques sur la naissance du roman policier en Afrique del'ouest' in Linfors, B. and Schild, U. (eds.) *Neo-African Literature and Culture, Essays in Memory of Jahnheinz Jahn.* Wiesbaden, B. Heyman, 1976. pp.106-110.

[23] Cf. Osofisan, Femi. 'Literacy as Suicide,' *Afriscope,* Lagos (special FESTAC issue), Feb. 1977.

[24] 'The Alternative Tradition ...' *op. cit.*

enduring), and the most contemporary of the authors of the first generation. He was the first to understand the demands of the evolving society, and to make attempts to come to terms with the character of the metropolis. This is why his art - ever so slight - appears to transcend the fragile mortality of his contemporaries, why today's increasing ferment is, in a vivid sense, the legacy of his pragmatic vision.

Cyprian Ekwensi: Eros domesticated...

The movement of our socio-economic development, we thus see, closely parallels the experience of the western countries at the beginnings of their modern industrial period. Correspondingly, therefore, the kind of suburban culture which developed in Europe following the mass migration of people from the countryside into the cities and the upsurge in literacy was bound to have its equivalent in our capitalist-oriented countries. This suburban culture, I have tried to explain, feeds mainly on the art of sensuality, its various formal manifestations, on celluloid or paper. Both the bourgeois and the proletariat demand Eros for their leisure, even if in unequal proportions. Because the culture of Eros deals primarily with the surface of human experience, with the gratuitous exploitation of the senses, it offers only superficial content, the kind of transient oblivion which opiates supply.[25] Hollywood, Indian (and now, Chinese) films, pop music, pulp fiction are, with religion, the drugs which the masses consume in those moments when they are not toiling or starving. And because of the massive spread of western culture into the cities all over the globe, our own masses in the third world have come too to be corrupted by these same inferior, mind-drugging means of entertainment.

Where there is demand, there naturally tends to be an increase in supply, especially with drugs. The supply into our countries of the products of western pop culture has been simply overwhelming. But not only does it come directly, through the unhindered importation of books, magazines, records films an so on, but it also enters in a way that is indirect, but which threatens to become more permanent, through the conscious imitations practised by our own artists. Just as the audience has been seduced by the glittering appeal of western forms of entertainment, so also have the artists. And the first to succumb in this manner was Cyprian Ekwensi.

With Ekwensi, the taste of the opiate occurred early. The literature with which he came into contact during his school days were the classics of western juvenile thrillers, and he fell irresistibly under their spell. As he recalls later: 'I

---

[25] Ricard recounts how the librarian in Lome, out of concern for the education of the young readers, finally took the much-demanded *romans policiers* out of the Borrowing List! See Ricard, A., *op. cit.*

was reading Rider Haggard, Edgar Wallace, Dickens, Sapper and Bates. At the Government College in Ibadan, we could recite whole chunks of *King Solomon's Mines. Nada the Lily* was a favourite; so was *She*, and *Allan Quartermain...* (and *Treasure Island...*)[26]

Ekwensi never woke from the spell. The reason may well be in his choice of careers, for whereas a writer like Soyinka, who also attended the Government College Ibadan,[27] went up to the university to study literature, and thus acquired a more stringent, and more sophisticated critical outlook, Ekwensi's path was much different. He went first to the Yaba Higher College in Lagos, was transferred, during the war, to Achimota in the then Gold Coast, and came back to work as a teacher in Lagos. This was where he wrote his first series of stories, which were broadcast on the radio. Later he took to pharmacy, and went on to England to qualify. And finally in his egregious career, he worked as a forestry officer in various parts of the country, before becoming a broadcaster and director of information both in pre-war Nigeria, and later in the stillborn Biafra. His seems to have been the kind of life which subjected him to the constant pressure of writing. The solitude of the forests in particular was inspiring: '...it was in the forests,' he says, 'that I actually started my writing. Because when you get into the isolation a forest gives you, it's like travelling by sea. You have all of twenty-four hours. I wrote *People of the City* in thirteen nights at sea...I wrote *Jagua Nana* in ten days when I was having a course with the BBC.[28]

Largely, therefore, as far as the growth of his art and craftsmanship is concerned, Ekwensi was self-taught, and had to rely on the influences picked up through chance reading and his own natural predilections. And these were obviously not the Greek classics or the modern surrealists which dominated the old Mbari school. Says Ekwensi, 'In the early stages I was much influenced by Rider Haggard and later by Alexandre Dumas. I liked adventure. I liked people doing things, fighting or digging for gold...Then later on, for the more naturalistic approach to writing, I prized Steinbeck, Hemingway, William Saroyan, Chekhov...(and) Maupassant...'[29] It is thus evident, from this list of choices, what particular techniques would be influential in Ekwensi's ripening aesthetics. All the authors mentioned - except perhaps Chekhov - share certain technical similarities: a simple, lucid prose, composed of short sentences and concrete images; an emphasis for action rather than philosophical discourse; a certain penchant for the sensational and the fantastic; the use of super-large protagonists usually with a dose of cynicism; extraordinary and spectacular events; melodramatic effects, achieved through a clever mixture of adventurous

---

[26] Ekwensi, C. 'Literary influences on a Young Nigerian,' *Times Literary Supplement*, 4 June, 1964, p. 475.
[27] School traditions apparently die hard. When I entered the GCI in 1959, the reading list had not changed much; that's why I feel that Soyinka who was years before me, must have undergone the same influences.
[28] *Dem-Sav, op. cit.*, p. 2.
[29] Ibid, p. 34.

action, physical confrontations and sensuous images - all the ingredients in short, which in an extremely vulgarized form compose the opiate of popular entertainment, and which Ekwensi enthusiastically imbibed at the outset of his career.

But all these ingredients, churning in the young writer's fevered imagination, had to find an appropriate and credible location. Here Ekwensi's scattered upbringing all over the country would serve him splendidly. He knew intimately the prairies of the north, as well as the cult-infested rain forests of the south and particularly, the city of Lagos. Here, his imagination took root, and it would henceforth be his favourite setting, in this Lagos with its girls, cars, dance bands, night clubs and bright lights and the Marina, it was the fairyland of the young and daring and ambitious, for the characters of thrilling romance. And the immediate result of this encounter with the city was Ekwensi's first novelette, *When Love Whispers*. He wrote it in the space of three days, between Friday and Sunday, and it was an immediate roaring success: 'the engine drivers, the foremen and engineers, and those who service trains going up-country, up North...They came, and on their way to work queued up every morning at Chuks Bookshop to buy this booklet.'[30]

That was it then: this work proved seminal to the genre. Apart from indirectly initiating the tradition of the now famous Onitsha chapbooks,[31] the book helped launch Ekwensi on his writing career. It opened his eyes to the three discoveries essential to his art: a mass public, a popular theme (plus the appropriate context to dramatize it in), and thirdly, a suitable writing style. His public from now on would be those masses of urban workers, only partially literate, but avid for entertainment as they lived their intense lives, his theme, the celebration of Eros (both passion and aggression), incarnated in the dashing, liberated lady of the city, living on vice, both exploiter and victim of men and of the city's material lusts; and his style would be the linear episodic plot sequence of the westerns, combining swift, simple prose with highly dramatic action; exploiting suspense, violence and sex, but never really reaching below the surface of experience - a style that is, finally, a domestic variant and cocktail of Rider Haggard, Alexandre Dumas and Hemingway.

Now, with his authorial poise properly established, Ekwensi could move along, and try his hand at the various kinds of popular fiction in the western repertory. Name the peculiar genre of paraliterature, and Ekwensi would invade it, domesticate it: for children's adventure stories, he wrote *Juju Rock, The Leopard's Claw, The Passport of Mallam Illia, Drummer Boy*, etc; for crime

---

[30] Ibid, p.26.
[31] This fact is, surprisingly, acknowledged. But there is a hint of this in Emenyonu, F., *The Role of the Igbo Novel* Ibadan, OUP. 1978. p. xv, and p. 90. (Emenyonu's book signals the rise of a new current in the Nigerian literary milieu, namely, that of the noisy, aggressive cultural and ethnic chauvinist. It is this ridiculous posture that often threatens to rob his work of its significance. See Biodun Jeyifo's review in *Positive Review* (Ibadan), no. 3.

stories and detective fiction, he produced *People of the City, Murder at the Yaba Roundabout;* for love stories and sex romance, at which he excelled, he wrote his major works, such as *When Love Whispers, Jagua Nana, Burning Grass, Beautiful Feathers;*[32] even war thrillers find their echo in his recent *Survive the Peace.* He modulates the content and localizes the action, but as far as form is concerned, he invents nothing; if he wrote tomorrow, it would be a Nigerian version of James Bond or of *Star Wars.*

This in-filling of new material into borrowed forms accounts in the main for the mingling of both the traditional and the modern in Ekwensi, a curious mingling which has confused critics and led to controversy. Ekwensi is indisputably our most modern writer, if only because he has made himself a writer of the modern metropolis. For him the new urban experience is so fascinating that he describes it in terms of a fairy tale. The city, he tells the critic Emenyonu, 'is a den for Ali Baba where forty thieves have stored all their gold, and any one who has the magic words can go and help himself. And sometimes greed traps the sesame and the thieves come back and stab the intruder to death...'[33] Unlike most of his contemporary Igbo novelists, Ekwensi always places the city as his centre of action, with brief, exotic excursions to the village. The Lagos which he portrays is so real, so vivid and alive, that it almost achieves an independent personality, and becomes a hero in its own right. Or as Killam puts it, the city 'is more than a central image...It assumes, as it were, the role of another character, controlling, defining, organizing and often destroying the lives of her people.'[34]

But equally compelling is Eros, as equally powerful in her control of human destinies. In fact, City and Eros mesh inextricably in Ekwensi, to such a point that each assumes the aspect of the other, both feline, seductive, corrupting. One of Ekwensi's characters, Dapo Ladele, celebrates this city-women symbiosis in *Iska,* as he recites a poem to Filia:

> The city is a girl walking
>   walking at dawn
>   handbag over arm, heels down and hungry
> Walking at noon
>   hunger in the vitals
> Walking at dust
>   bracelets all a-glitter
>   heels high and flattering
> The city is a girl walking
>   into offices

---

[32] For a list of Ekwensi's works, see Bibliography below.
[33] Cited by Emenyonu E. *Cyprian Ekwensi.* Evans, 1974, p. 29.
[34] Killam, D., 'Cyprian Ekwensi' in Bruce King (ed.) *Introduction to Nigeria Literature,* Evans & Univ of Lagos, 1971, p. 84.

adventuring into bedrooms
seducing to the top
The city is a girl walking ever walking
ever scheming
ever climbing (. . .)
light skin girl along the street
all made-up from wig to nail paint
head held high and bosom taut
rear end wiggling, calculating,
tantalizing
Eves afire...[35]

This eroticism (which is obviously synthetic), the sensuous context in which it is liberated and concretized, and the props of the action guns, motor cars, wigs, lipstick, etc. - all these place Ekwensi patently in the modern, contemporary situation. They give an immediacy lacking in the writers of the tribal past. And yet Ekwensi is also a most traditional artist, to judge by the mechanics of his composition. The use of the method of collage, for instance, which makes for the loose episodic structure of a work like *People of the City,* is appropriated from the techniques of the griot. Ekwensi's default here may be one of craftsmanship ('the story leaps about spasmodically like a nervous cricket,' complains Laurence[36]) - a fault common to all popular fiction,[37] and in any case not unexpected at a period of the writer's apprenticeship - but the fundamental principle behind his method belongs to traditional aesthetics, more ancient perhaps than *The Odyssey,* and as demonstrated in Fagunwa' s *Ogboju Ode Ninu Igbo Irunmale.* Amusa Sango's double profession of crime reporting and band leader is only an artistic ruse to make plausible our odyssey through the city from one event to the other, a functional equivalent of Mai Sunsaye's 'sokugo,' the dreaded wandering disease which takes him on his wild journey of self-discovery in *Burning Grass,* or even of Jagua's prostitution and nightly visit to the Tropicana, which brings her in contact with various customers and takes her into unforeseen encounters.

Collage and episodic structuring (or, the model of the 'picaresque,' to use Roscoe's apt comparison[38]), dictates, or leads to, the use of stereotypes. 'The

---

[35] Ekwensi, C. *Iska*. London, Hutchinson, 1966, pp. 187-8.
[36] Laurence, M., *Long Drums and Canons* London, Macmillan, 1968 p. 150.
[37] Cf. Dalziel, *op. cit.*, p. 178: 'It is doubtful whether with respect to structure, characterization or style. there is much to choose between popular fiction at different times. The same weaknesses are found, the same stereotyped plots; the same stock situations and characters; at the lowest level the uncertain grammar, at a higher level pretentious writing full of ornate phraseology, inaccurate use of less common words, and ridiculous metaphor; at best a totally undistinguished style. In both cases the reader is confronted with limited, erroneous, insensitive ideas about life and people and their problems.
[38] Roscoe, A. *Mother Is Gold*. Cambridge Univ. Press, 1971 p.87.

popular imagination,' James reminds us, 'is interested in character conceived on a simple, well-defined plane, which exists independent of a complex literary form.'[39] In the performances of the traditional raconteur, the location of the action may shift continually, but never the internal structure or plot sequence, which remains from age to age, and is the link between the generations till it forms the identity mark of the particular genre. Characters wear the same recognizable masks, even if newly repainted; the crises they face, and the options before them, and the solutions they reach are always predictably familiar once the genre is known; it is only the art of the telling that excites.[40] Similarly in Ekwensi, the same drama from book to book endlessly repeats itself namely a character strays into the city, becomes entranced by it, feeds greedily on its sensual attractions even as he is being destroyed by them, but in the end succeeds in escaping into the unreal paradise of his less ambitious beginnings. This 'circular structure,' which Shelton calls 'rebushing'[41] forms the basic pattern of composition all through Ekwensi's writings, whether in the juvenile adventures or in the more serious adult entertainments, and marks his link with the traditional artists and entertainers. It is one way in which his art seeks to domesticate the borrowed form of western popular fiction.[42]

But even more fundamental than these than collage or stereotype is the very impulse behind the domestication itself, the volition which I think has always been reflected in traditional aesthetics. Form, as we agreed earlier, is sacrosanct, and it is only in the manipulation of the interior ingredients that the traditional artist declares his own talent. By borrowing known forms for his own performance, Ekwensi behaves like his traditional counterpart. Within the marked bounds of a familiar tradition, he is content merely to improvise, in localize and domesticate the elements of the performance in an adroit contextual transference. Wherever we may have seen such gestures before, or felt the same tremor of fear or excitement, we know, in Ekwensi's works, that we are trapped inescapably on our own homeland, that the terror may be just across the street:

> Inspector John Faolu walked up to the door and knocked. But he found the door open. There was no one in the room. He pressed the switch. There was no light. His torchlight showed him that there was a bulb in the ceiling, but apparently it had no been connected to the mains. The house was a new one.
> The room was in disorder. There was every sign that the occupants had left in a great hurry. Clothes were carelessly strewn on the bed.
> The books on the table had been disarranged, and beneath this was a box which though closed, had a number of clothes sticking out of it.

---

[39] James, *op. cit.*, p. 47.
[40] Cf. Osofisan, F. 'Drama and New Exotic, the paradox of forte in African theatre.' Paper presented at the Univ. of Ife Staff Seminar. 1978. unpublished material.
[41] Shelton, A.J. cited by Lindfors, *op. cit.* p. 13.
[42] It is perhaps relevant to point out here that this 'circular structure' does not seem to me peculiar to African ethnopoetics, but rather a general feature of the genre.

Faolu took in the scene...[43]

Lindfors[44] is disgusted by the scene, by its cheapness and flagrant plagiarism. Which second-rate American crime fiction does not have such scenes, he asks? But Lindfors is wrong, and the question irrelevant. Crime fiction is cheap, whatever country it comes from, and paraliterature is a tradition of plagiarists and popularizers, right from the various versions of *Pickwick Papers* in later nineteenth century to the present day reformulations of Sherlock Holmes and Maigret, and the metamorphoses of James Bond in Nick Carter, Ian Maclean, Ludlum and John le Carre. What is noticeable in Ekwensi is the extent of the domestication, his attention to detail and verisimilitude, his concern for realistic settings.

Unfortunately, however, this realism, which is his strongest attribute, is not always sustained to the end of the book. More prominent and more sustained is another device he employs for domestication, and which forms another link with the traditional raconteurs. This element is the concern, evident in all his works, to use the story to illustrate an ethical position. Always the stories attempt to retreat from their lurid adventuring into a landscape of primal virtue, and always the attempt is unconvincing. In the West, paraliterature has always been used of course as an ideological weapon, by which the writers shore up the prejudices of their readers against their traditional enemies - the villainous communists, Indians, Niggers, and so on. But the means of such indoctrination is ever so subtle and indirect, always cunningly left to suggestion rather than explicit statement. The result, needless to say, is an ever more effective impact and propagandization. Traditional African raconteurs, on the other hand, are not normally given to insidious tactics in their moral proselytizing. The social or ethical message screams at you, and in case you still have missed it, is summarized graphically for you in memorable aphorisms at the conclusion of the tale.

In domesticating the western popular fiction, Ekwensi has chosen to graft onto the borrowed forms the explicit moral praxis of our raconteurs. Thus the stories are meant not only to entertain, but also to warn the unwary about the dangers inherent in the city, as well as paint a wider critical picture of the conditions of our country, with its socio-political tensions.

Both Killam and Emenyonu are convinced about the deeper psychological implications of Ekwensi's work. 'His novels,' writes the former, 'arise out of his acquaintance with and involvement in the complexities of city living and his attempt to probe with an unflinching realism the superficial delights and real terrors of the city...The tensions in his major novels derive from the attempts of

---

[43] Ekwensi, *Murder at The Yaba Roundabout*. Lagos, 1962 p. 17
[44] Lindfors, 'Cyprian Fkwensi: An African Popular Novelist,' *African Literature Today*, (3): 2-14. See Emenyonu's reply in the 5th issue of the journal, 'African Literature: What does it take to be its critic?' pp. 1-11

their heroes - Amusa Sango, Jagua, Wilson Iyari and Filia Enu, all of whom live on the borderline between success and failure, triumph and collapse - to extract as much pleasure as they can from city living, whilst constantly confronted by the fear of poverty and failure.'[45] Fair enough. Emenyonu, going even further, talks of a quasi-metaphysical exploration: 'In Ekwensi's novels,' he writes, 'man tries to, escape from the knowledge of self-defeat by a reckless immersion in the ecstasies of low life. He goes for sex instead of love, and follows his inclinations with a complete disregard for consequences. He shrinks from labour and awaits the night with all its excitements and oblivion. Man is continuously defeated because he either refuses to fight or avoids his real opponent -self.'[46]

Surely this is the critic's handshake going up to the elbow? I should be glad to meet Emenyonu one day, to ask if he has really read Ekwensi. We have an author of modest means and unpretentious ambitions, whose aim is to reach a popular mass audience. Mostly he succeeds, through his ability to produce 'accurate imitations,'[47] but there is surely no need to take him more serious than he desires. He is not an Achebe or a Soyinka, his imaginative world lacks poetic amplitude, never expands into ontological perspectives. That is why he can be enjoyed on his own levels, for some deeper meaning than its surface emotional titillation and visceral thrill. 'I don't regard myself as one of the sacred writers,' he himself has said again and again to interviewers, 'those writing for some audience locked up in the higher seats of learning. I am just interested in writing about people, events, experiences, deprivations, hunger and so on. So whenever there is an opportunity to write, I write.'[48] Ekwensi will always because of this be easy to read - and easy to forget. That 'self' which Emenyonu mentions, that nebulous, mysterious province of the soul, gateway to the numinous, is what is absent - and *necessarily so* - in Ekwensi's novels. And thanks to that absence, the works are successful pastiche, and their author a successful producer of popular fiction.

Ekwensi's other moralistic intention, namely, to lay bare the inadequacies in our socio-political system is also effusively hailed by Emenyonu: 'Through his realism Ekwensi attempts to confront his society with its social injustices and immoralities, its housing problems, the high-handed and almost inhuman attitudes of its landlords, the get-rich-quick mania which has forced its youth to many corrupt and illegal practices; the robbery and fraud by which the rich enrich themselves more and more at the expense of the poor, crime like material corruption, is everywhere entrenched in the routines of city life.[49]

Still, Ekwensi has written novels, not sociological tracts. And judged by the criteria of art, the best one can say is that there have been profounder

---

[45] Killam, *op. cit.*, p. 79.
[46] Emenyonu, *Cyprian Fkwensi, op. cit.*. p. 13.
[47] Lindfors, *op. cit.*
[48] *Dem-Say, op. cit.* p. 28.
[49] Emenyonu, *Igbo Novel, op. cit.*, p. 98.

testimonies. Furthermore, although he is clearly honest, sincere and concerned by the growing violence and corruption around him, he lacks the proper political vision about the means of transcending the situation. This is why his characters particularly the virtuous politicians, either retreat to the villages,[50] or withdraw into some idyllic limbo. Ekwensi is obviously, for all his concern, a political conservative, with a belief in the old values and a distrust of modernization, which he sees as corrupting. His choice of characters, the carnality and violence that mark their relationships, and his artistic recourse to structural and thematic circularity, all are illuminating indices as to his real political ethos.

III. Coda Ekwensi's heirs, or Eros unleashed...

Ekwensi, to summarize then, is the first Nigerian popularizer of western paraesthetics. In Lagos city, he discovered the equivalent of the fascinating, as well as frightening, urban settings of the western models he sought to domesticate. And in Lagos women, he found the physical and symbolic embodiment of the sensuality central to all works of escapism and social anaesthesia in the tradition of the West. He had also attempted to graft a serious moral purpose onto the format of his stories, but this has not always been successful, either through being too obvious (as in the transparent metaphor of *Beautiful Feathers*) or too contrived (as in *Jagua Nana* or *Iska*).

In recent years, however, a considerable number of writers have appeared on the scene, whose works are cast in the tradition initiated by Ekwensi. The Onitsha chapbooks have already been mentioned earlier, and Obiechina has already made a comprehensive study of them.

But there is also another group of works coming up either from the older or the new publishing houses, which are aimed at an adolescent public. Such are the collections for instance in Macmillan's 'Pacesetters' Series, and some of the reprints being undertaken by Olaiya Fagbamigbe. The Onibonoje and Fourth Dimension publishing houses seem to be more interested in a slightly higher level of literature, but one can fairly predict that, given the nature of the audience, they will soon leap on the bandwagon.

Thematically, the areas explored by these new writers are the same as Ekwensi has pursued i.e. crime (Kalu Okpi's *The Smugglers, On the Road:* the novels of Adaora Ulasi; etc.); romance (Agbo Areo's *The Hopeful Lovers*, Sule's *The Undesirable Element*, Ike's *Toads for Supper*, etc.), not to talk of the innumerable novels of juvenile adventure. Even Heinemann has tries to capture this market, with its publication of Iroh's war thrillers, *Forty-eight Guns for the General*. New villains have sprung out for the heroes to hunt down, as for

---

[50] Much exoticism surrounds the village in the literature of (non-) romantics, aid particularly in the works of negritude. The whole myth crumbles in the realistic picture of decay and squalor painted in Ikem Nwankwo's recent book, *My Mercedes Is Bigger Than Yours*. See Bibliography.

instance South Africa's former BOSS, the target of Kole Omotoso's *Fella's Choice* and Okoro's *The Blood of Zimbabwe*. Omotoso also tries to introduce a new twist in *The Scales,* as his hero, Jogunde of the Third Division, tries to turn against the state, but it reads more at the end like a parable or allegory.

All in all, one can say that there hasn't been much progress from Ekwensi, except that the authors are in some cases far more technically informed, as witness the following scene from Iroh's *Forty-eight Guns*

> Over the northern end of the airstrip, where Rudolf's strong rear base and main body of his troops were concentrated, Boma Wan' s ancient Alouette now creaked and groaned. Charles Chumab's leaflets drifted like a hundred paper kites and Gideon tide's HMG intermittently chattered.
> The ground fire also gathered momentum, barking and chattering. But the Alouette held together with amazing stubbornness.
> Captain tide's ears were jammed by the sputter of his own gun, the croaking of the propellers above him, and the stutter of intense firing from below, added to the whines of flying bullets and the ricochet of lead against the body of the aircraft.
> Colonel Chumab's yells of "Fire!" were lost in the bitter, deafening medley. But tide was firing without urging, his teeth clenched, his body jammed against the door of the aircraft to support his balance as the plane heaved, ducked, banked and manoeuvred from the terror of the ground firing.[51]

This is the kind of realism that would delight Ekwensi. In some cases, however, the progress is backwards from the achievement of Ekwensi. Where he is careful to be authentic, to capture the exact nuances and levels of speech appropriate to a Nigerian setting, it is customary to find the new writers parroting the speech patterns and mannerisms of cheap American gangster novels.

More serious, however, is the total unleashing of Eros, the gratuitous exploitation of sex and violence for their own sake. Ekwensi's ethical concerns, with all their ambiguity, act as a kind of control. Good art, after all, never reveals everything; taste is knowing just how much mystery to maintain in the description of human relations. But such is decadence of the age, that Ekwensi's heirs assault our sensibility continuously with their vulgarity, mistaking such for boldness and originality. This of course is another uncritical imitation of Western pop art, especially as exported from the United States of America. Here for instance is Eros, raw and untamed:

> I hesitated and looked at Sir Brain, who was in the process of stepping out of his trousers. I gave him a long, uncertain look: He nodded assurance, nodding repeatedly and eagerly. Not caring any longer, I mounted the bed, and covered his wife's body with mine, adjusting myself to lie between her legs and pressing my rigid prick against the area of her vagina. I prodded a

---

[51] Iroh, F., *Forty-eight guns for the General*, London-Ibadan, Heinemann, 1976. pp. 205-6.

little and felt myself penetrate ... Sir Brian knelt down against the bed and exhorted "Harder!"

I crushed Lady Dorothy against the mattress and settled down into a cruel, grinding fuck. She groaned loudly and seemed to go berserk..Sir Brain, who had been masturbating, appeared to reach climax first...[52]

Pornography such as this may titillate the reader, but in the final run it only helps to degrade the value of human relationships. To judge by the direction being taken by Western art, however, this popular western art that is serving as model to our authors—it is not unlikely that this unleashing of Eros in all its crudity will soon be common-place among us, and that around it will gather most of our future writers. If that happens, it will be the final ironical tribute to Ekwensi's success as a pioneering artist in the domain of Nigerian paraliterature.

Bibliography: works and authors mentioned (Nigerian)

Achebe, Chinna. *Arrow* of *God,* London, Heinemann, 1964.
Areo, Agbo: *The Hopeful Lovers,* London, Macmillan, 1979.
Clark, J.P. *Ozidi.* London, Oti, 1966.
Ekwensi, Cyprian. *When Love Whispers.* Onitsha, Tabansi Press. 1948.
　　　　Drummer Boy, Cambridge Univ. Press, 1960.
　　　　Passport of Mallam Musa, Univ. Press, 1960.
　　　　Murder at the Yaba Roundabout, Lagos, Tortoise Series, 1962.
　　　　Burning Grass, London, Heinemann Educ. Books, 1962.
　　　　Iska, London, Hutchinson & Co., 1966.
Ike, C., *Toads for Supper.* London, Harvill Press, 1965.
Iroh, F., *Forty-eight guns for the General.* London, Heinemann, 1976.
Iyayi, I., *Violence.* London, Longman, 1980.
Kalu Okpi, K., *The Smugglers.* London, Macmillan, 1978.
　　　　- *On The Road.* London, Macmillan, 1980.
Okoro, F., *The Blood* of *Zimbabwe,* Enugu, 4th Dimension, 1978.
Omotoso, K., *Sacrifice.* Ibadan, Onibonoje Publ., 1978 ed.
　　　　- *The Scales.* Ibadan, Onibonoje Publ., 1976.
　　　　- *Fella's Choice*, Ethiope, Benin. 1975.
Osofisan, F. .*Morountodun.* Play performed in 1979, np.
Onyeama, D., *Sex is A Nigger's Game.* London, Satellite, 1976.
Soyinka, W., *The Interpreters.* I ottdoit, Andre Dcusch, 1965.

---

[52] Onyeama, D. *Sex Is A Nigger's Game*, London, Satellite Books, 1976. pp. 94-5.

Sule, N., *The Undesirable Element.* London, Macmillan 1978.
Ulasi, A.. *Many Thing You no Understand.* London, Fontana, 1973.
- *When Thing Begin For Change,* London, Fontana, 1978.
- *The Man from Sagamu.* London, Fontana,

Chapter 23

The retrospective stage: some reflections on the mythopoeic tradition at Ibadan

- *Omafume F. Onoge and G. G. Darah*

I: Anno FESTAC

OVER the past two years, the University of Ibadan Theatre Arts department has had an impressive list of stage productions. In a social ecology generally bereft of serious cultural activities and attractions other than *idawo* parties, birthday parties, naming parties, wedding parties, wedding anniversary parties, faculty promotion parties, Kung-fu cinema, fake professional wrestling bouts, the under-developed university Zoo, the literate stratum of the petty-bourgeoisie in Ibadan has increasingly come to depend on the university theatre for its cultural diet. A night at the university theatre has also become the only legitimate secular cultural outing permitted our youth in the elite Ibadan secondary schools.

The cultural significance of the university theatre in this largest city in black Africa is enough justification for attempting a critical analysis of its productions. There is yet another necessity for attempting such analysis. This has to do with the new salience which the cultural question has received in Nigeria in our contemporary FESTAC 77 epoch. (Second World and African Festival of Arts and Culture).[1]

The plays which have dominated the university of Ibadan stage in the past two years partake fully in the FESTAC revivalist spirit. The plays either deal explicitly with the pre-colonial past, or explore the contemporary society by a retrospective reference to that past. It is the nature of the retrospective vision of

---

[1] We understand that Wale Ogunyemi's *Langbodo* was being prepared for FESTAC

our culture as portrayed in these plays that is the concern of this essay. We wish to insist that our conclusions about the contents of this retrospective vision has nothing to do with the theatrical and technical merits of these plays.[2]

II: The mythopoeic orientation

The past as represented in these plays is a world dominated by gods and the supernatural. Consider the revealing titles of some of these plays: *Wedlock of the Gods; The Gods Are Not To Blame*. The effective human population of that world are kings and priests. The masses, though typically dignified as 'citizens' in these plays, are virtually effete. When they act their actions are those of animated objects in blind obedience to the kings. Thus for example, the risky adventures undertaken by the hunters' guild which constitutes the entire play, *Langbodo*, have nothing to do with their personalities or the existential demands of their class position in the society. Instead the costly adventures stem from an unquestioning obedience to the directive of their king – a directive which was in fact issued in a most cavalier manner.[3]

The primary interaction of that world is between gods and kings. Seers mediate this interaction. The hierarchy of authority in that world consists of gods, kings, seers, chiefs, court broadcasters (messengers) and the masses in that order. It is in fact truer to say that in these plays, the masses are generally bereft of any authority. In this hierarchised world, gods are the driving forces. 'It is the custom: when the gods command we men must obey, 'say the Ogun priest in *The Gods Are Not to Blame*. Interestingly, for an artistic conceptual representation of the past as supernatural drama, the masses in these retrospective plays, have no direct access to the gods. What the 'gods command' are divined by the kings' seers, and issued as communiqués by the court broadcasters. This dramatises the utter facelessness attributed to the masses in these plays.

Stasis is another crucial feature of that world. This conclusion must seem paradoxical in the light of the elementary fact that theatre is inconceivable outside of motion or dynamics. And to be sure, we do have a visual experience of dynamics when these plays are staged. But what is the quality of this dynamics? It is a pseudo dynamics where the gods who are the propelling

---

[2] In fact, many of these plays have been very successful on stage. We draw particular attention to Wale Ogunyemi's *Langbodo*, and Ola Rotimi's *The Gods Are Not To Blame* which were masterpieces on stage. The excellence of the acting and the technical sophistication are veritable triumphs of the University of Ibadan Stage.

[3] This reminds us of elementary school 'çoncert' plays where commoners are mobilised by King's messengers intoning 'hear Ye! Hear Ye!'

forces, behave in set mythic ways. Where the conflicts in the plays are between gods, their resolutions are already preordained because the attributes of these gods are culturally fixed. Only a cultural outsider may be surprised by the resolutions.

This foreknowledge of resolutions also applies to instances where the combatants are human (usually kings) but with explicit super-natured patrons. As king Odewale says in *The Gods Are Not To Blame*, 'The powers would have failed if I did not allow them to use me.' Where the conflicts take on a more secular character, the conflicting interests are in the nature of palace intrigues whose resolutions do not yield any structural transformations (e.g. *Ijaye* by Wale Ogunyemi). This image of changeless change is what functionalist anthropologists refer to as 'dynamic equilibrium'. A social systemic view where order is primary; where conflicts are non-antagonistic, and where rebellions have as their teleology, the re-affirmation of the status quo.

This Eliotian 'still point' receives its eloquent Africanisation in *The Gods Are Not To Blame:*

> Everything has its own place.
> Why, the tortoise is not tall
> But it is taller than the snail, the
> snail is taller than
> the frog; the frog is taller than
> the lizard; the lizard is taller
> than the fly; the fly is taller than
> the ant; the ant in turn is taller
> than the ground on which it walks;
> Everything has its own place, its
> own level, its standing (King Odewale)

It is this undialectical approach plus the pre-eminence of the supernatural in the artistic representation of the past that we have termed mythopoeic.

III: Consequences for the past

This orientation has, in our view, 'practical' consequences for the understanding of our past and the contemporary situation. First, the past. Consider the assumption of the pre-eminence of the supernatural in our traditional social systems. This assumption which is also a 'scientific' canon of Africanist cultural anthropology and theology[4] states that in Africa, unlike Europe, there is

---

[4] See, for example, Placide Temple's Bantu *Philosophy,* Bolaji Idowu's *Olodumare;* John Mbiti's *African Religions and Philosophies,* Levi-Bruhl's, *Primitive Mentality*

no distinction between the sacred and the profane. The African, unlike Levy-Bruhl's primitives, is steeped in mystical rather than empirio-scientific thought. In fact, in Placide Temple's 'celebrated' *Bantu Philosophy*,[5] the African's exclusive interest is on ontological questions rather than on 'prosaic' issues of economy and politics' Ironically, this thesis has been accepted with exceptional pride by the mainstream of the contemporary African intelligentsia. They see this postulated immanent religiosity as a singular cultural achievement of traditional Africa. Most of our playwrights, poets and novelists have been influenced by this intellectual culture.

However, we must point out that this definition of the traditional African as *homo immobile* before his gods is empirically false. It is a distortion of the cultural heritage. Indeed, a more accurate scientific appraisal of the cultural facts, suggests that Africa, unlike Europe and Asia, is the one continent where man's relation with the supernatural order is primarily instrumental. Let us explain. In Europe, to be religious means a total surrender of the selfhood to god. The religious state of the European Christian, for example, rises in proportion to the degree to which he confesses his sinfulness, unworthiness and *nothingness* in the face of his god. It is only by his continuous unequivocal denial of his very selfhood that he can be assured of attaining the 'state of grace'.

This is the very opposite situation in traditional Africa. To be sure the African observes certain taboos in order to be in a right relationship with his supernatural order. But once he is convinced that he has not transgressed these taboos, the African coaxes, cajoles and manipulates the supernatural partner to fulfil the terms of the 'contract'. There can be no Jobian subservience. An African god, ancestor or cult that fails to deliver the goods is punished either by starvation or extermination.

Because of their awareness of this countervailing power of men over them no indigenous African god dare impose a curse on his human partners without simultaneously providing escape valves. It is in the light of this African cosmological reality, that Ola Rotimi's 'skilful transplantation' of the Oedipus theme into 'African soil' is an artistic error of heretical proportions. We know of no one of the 401 members of the Yoruba Pantheon who would predestine a baby to future patricide and incestuous marriage with his mother. It is in full realization of this cultural fact that Odewale, the authentic African, queries Rotimi's *Ifa*'s voice:

Voice: You have a curse on you, son.
Odewale: What kind of curse, Old One?

---

[5] See also Aime Cesaire's *Discourse on Colonialism* for a critique of Bantu *Philosophy*.

Voice: You cannot run away from it, the gods have willed that you will kill your father, and then marry your mother.
Odewale: Me! Kill my own father and marry my own mother?
Voice: It has been willed
Odewale What must I do then not to carry out this will of the gods?
Voice: Nothing...

The petty-bourgeois Christian audience which shed sentimental tears at this inescapable fate would have walked out of the theatre in wild protest if Yaweh, rather than *Ifa*, were the subject of this misrepresentation. Our impression is that this misrepresentation is capable of reinforcing the paganist stereotypes of African religions in the consciousness of the teenage audience.

A related misrepresentation arising from this conception of the supernatural content of traditional Africa is obvious in the role assigned to magic in the artistic explorations of the Ijaye war. In Ogunyemi's *Ijaye*, military victory and defeat are predicated on which army possesses the magic cloth. Considerations of troop strength, ammunition, military alliances and strategies which had prepared the audience for assessing the outcome of the war suddenly become irrelevant before the non-rational force of the magic cloth. Rotimi's *Kurunmi* shares this fault, though to a lesser degree. Here, the victory of Ibadan over Ijaye is contingent on the power of a spell. We realise that magical beliefs did and do play a part in our wars. It is the primacy accorded it in these artistic instances that we query. The very institutionalisation of the office of military generals in the traditional societies is evidence that our people have always recognised the superiority of rational planning in military campaigns. Chaka's innovations at the levels of military technology and organisation are irrefutable testimonies. To ignore this is to lapse into a reinforcement of the voodoo stereotypes of the traditional heritage.

A second important strand of what we have called the mythopoeic orientation is the undialectical characterisation of the social systems. The systemic goals are mythically set as consensual. This assumption of consensus is particularly striking in view of the fact that the typical society explored in the retrospective plays is the state society. Yet for the playwright the ruling nobilities and subjects in these kingdoms have common interests. There is no intimation of possible cleavages in opposed class interests. For example, the subject population undertakes risky adventures (Langbodo) or goes to war (Ijaye) simply on an *oba*'s appeal prefaced with 'my people!' 'My people we need peace.' 'My people we cannot accept this insult from Oyo' constitute sufficient arguments for mass mobilization in these plays. Moreover, in the rare instances when we get a glimpse of private daily life in these kingdoms, patriarchal culture is intact and celebrated. Individual conflicts are settled on mere invocation of the authority of patriarchy.

The assumption off structural harmony on the social system level is extended to empire systems. For example, in *Ijaye,* the conflict, when it is represented in political terms, is limited to succession disputes. Were Ijaye's secession to triumph, we would merely have an amoeba-like fission where the new autonomous parts are structurally homologous. There are no possibilities of a new ideology or a restructuration of social relationships. Just as *obas* are held to be the custodians of societal consensual aspirations so also are empires seen as achievements of civilization. The concepts of feudality and exploitation with which we may scientifically appraise all state and empire formations are remarkably absent.

'We want peace and unity among the Yoruba' is the only counter slogan offered by those who oppose Kurunmi's in *Ijaye.* No reasons other than the necessity for peace are offered by Kurunmi's opponents for recommending the continuation of the Oyo Empire. The material economic interests such as tributes and the control of trade routes which would be won or lost by the protagonists, at that historical moment of the dawn of mercantilist capitalism in Yoruba land are not raised.

This historiography of the past where antagonistic contradictions do not exist is, in our view, mythic. It cannot explain, for example, instances of slavery as part of the production mode of pre-colonial states. It cannot explain instances of peasant rebellious. It cannot explain politically, population migrations which, in recent African historiography, dominate the stories of origin of many pre-colonial African societies. Under this kind of historiographial outlook, movements such as Agbekoya[6] would have no historical precedent in Yoruba tradition. Rather, they would be seen as artefacts of a post-traditional Yoruba Society. Was peace at all costs the only value of traditional Yoruba politics? Was democracy not a legitimate political value of the masses or political aspirants in the traditional systems?

IV: Consequences for the present

As we have already stated in our introduction, some of the retrospective plays have, as their central interest, critical commentary on the Nigerian political scene. In these plays (e.g. *Langbodo,* and *Day of Deities*), the past affects our

---

[6] The term '"Agbekoya" in Yoruba means "we reject suffering". It is the name of the peasants' movement in the former Western State which organised a mass uprising in 1968 against exploitative taxation. Under the leadership of the late Tafa Adeoye, the peasants stormed the Agodi prisons in Ibadan where many of their comrades were imprisoned on charges of unpaid taxes. All the detainees were set free and the revolt spread to the Government secretariat in Ibadan and major cities in the State. The uprising shook the military government of General Adeyinka Adebayo to its foundations; the oppressive taxes were abolished after negotiations with the revolutionary farmers.

political consciousness of the present.

At the time *Day of Deities* was staged, Nigerian society was experiencing convulsions such as post-Udoji revolts,[7] chaotic sc rambles for fuel at petrol stations, political detentions, kangaroo trials, and the banning of anti-corruption affidavits. During this national disorder, the political solution offered by the Gowon regime was a series of dance and athletic festivals. The political goal was unity and stability. *Day of Deities* faithfully dramatises this anarchy on stage. The solution proffered is to invite powerful deities from the traditional Yoruba Pantheon. (It is remarkable that Brigadier Johnson's solution was also a national invitation to prayer houses.) The gods however keep mute in their statuesque representation throughout the entire play. There is the suggestion that they deny us their 'wisdom' because of our previous neglect of them. There is the further implication, given the mythopoeic conception of the relations of gods and men, that the current anarchy is the punitive act (deserved) of the gods whom we have neglected.

This kind of recourse to the past has serious implications for our contemporary political consciousness. First it is remarkable that it is the gods, rather than the men of the past, that we invite. The mythopoeia consciousness denies political initiative to *real* men in the past and the present. Real working men are invited to political passivity in the present. The recourse to supernature seals off the possibility of exploring rational solutions to the contemporary predicament. Rational variables such as the capitalist-imperialist character of the political economy of oil cartels are not explored as episodes of the play.

No attempt is made to define the specific structure and ideology of the contemporary Nigerian society beyond its mere representation as anarchic. Since these anarchic episodes are not anchored in a specific historically determined social structure, we are back again to the thesis of a universal 'human condition' degeneration. In this specific case, the thesis belongs to that strand of alienation philosophies of the 'fall of man'. It is the case of paradise lost. No sociological and historical accounting is proffered to explain this fall. (At least, Christian alienation philosophers do offer us Adam's transgression of the 'forbidden fruit' taboo as the genesis of the postulated universal fall.)

The non-random and inegalitarian distribution of the miseries in Nigerian society is not indicated. Yet it is common knowledge that the different social classes in Nigerian society do not suffer equally from the national crisis.

---

[7] In 1974, the military junta of General Yakubu Gowon approved generous wage increases for civil servants to stem strikes over high cost of living occasioned by inflation that followed the oil boom of the post-civil war years. The wage panel was headed by Chief Jerome Udoji after whom the policy was named. The gesture temporarily shored up the sagging image of the military regime. Yet the problem of implementation sparked country-wide industrial and social unrest which culminated in the overthrow of the Gowon government in July, 1975.

Indeed, not only is the unequal distribution of theses burdens among social classes hidden, but also the possibilities of class-partisan solutions are sealed off by this metaphorical recourse to deities. The use of deities who, usually, are the common property of all classes in traditional society fosters the illusion of a consensual solution to the contemporary crisis. It is akin to the consensual illusion which our ruling classes have tried to foster by their *selective* usage of those cultural items such as dance, and sports, which tend to transcend class divisions.

With *Langbodo* the crisis of Nigerian society is implied rather than dramatised. The theme, however, is the quest for peace and order. Perhaps the coincidence of this theme with the national slogan of 'peace and stability' renders the dramatisation of the absences superfluous for the playwright. However, the search for the basis of peace and order in this play, takes us through a tour of several societies. Here again it is remarkable that all the societies visited are feudal. They are structurally similar to the society which seeks the peace. Therefore, *ab initio,* no new basis for peace, through a structural reorganisation of society can emerge from this quest. It is feudal peace, rather than the peace which flows from a democratic social order, that constitutes the kernel of this instance of the artistic imagination. Because of this ethnographic constraint, we are not surprised that the peace formulas which the seekers eventually get at Benin are catechised homilies like, 'love your neighbour; trust one another...' of course, as has been historically established the world over, the culture of feudalism can offer no more.

We are aware of the possibility that the ridicule, to which the seekers are subjected on their return, may be the playwright's subtle statement on the hypocrisy of the peace and stability projects in recent Nigerian history. Nonetheless, we insist, that because the ruler and the ruled join in this ridicule from undifferentiated standpoints, in the play, its satirical projection on to contemporary Nigeria would be false. For in the Nigeria satirised, empirical evidence abounds that there is no congruence of standpoints on the issues of national peace and stability.

V: On the uses of history

Retrospective appraisal of Africa's culture-history has been a vital concern in the research production of our intelligentsia. From the perspective of sociology of knowledge, this retrospection has been understandable and necessary, in view of our colonial experience. For the dominant theoretical structure of colonial society denied us a culture–history. Some of their specific theses were:

(a) that we had no complex socio-cultural structure such as kingdoms;
(b) that we had no institutions that could be validly called religious;

(c) that the pre-colonial past was a Hobbesian state of disorder. And because colonial historiography considered state formations, religion and order, as criteria attributes of 'civilization', a tradition of *proving* the existence of these features in our past, has been a mark of African scholarship. It is therefore not surprising that these three themes reoccur in our retrospective plays.

A second source of these topics is related to the *immediate* reality of contemporary Nigeria. Clearly the themes of order and religion readily form part of the characterisation of the contemporary scene. What with the 1967-70 civil war and the inflation in prayer-healing movements. Since art is rooted in society, these themes cannot but be reflected in the playwrights' consciousness. That art mirrors society is now an uncontested claim.

However, in class societies more than one image exists for reflection in the artist's mirror. The various classes project different and contradictory images of the society and its dynamics. The image projected by the privileged exploiter classes *conserves* the status quo, while that projected by the exploited classes *subverts* the status quo. And the burden of our argument has been that, even within the restricted limits of the mirror theory of art the mirrors contained in the contemporary retrospective stage at Ibadan provide only a one-sided reflection of our past and present realities. They reflect only the consciousness of the privileged exploiter.

This one-sidedness is particularly disturbing in view of the fact that the retrospective plays achieve their artistic intensity from their direct linguistic dependence on the idiomatic wealth created by the working people. It is the collectivity of the working people in their necessary daily encounter with nature, rather than rulers living in the Cartesian isolation of palace walls, that produce the acute observations of nature and life codified in the idioms.

If this one-sidedness could ever be defended in the past, it now has no justification whatever in an Africa where the opposing revolutionary consciousness has been empirically realised in Guinea – Bissau, Mozambique and Angola. To be able to incorporate this rising consciousness in its reflection, the artists' mirror must acquire a dialectical surface.

Index

Abalogu, U.N.; 125
Abarry, Abu; vi, ix, xxv, xvii, 129-134
Abdulkadir, Prof. Dandatti; vi, xi, xxxvi, xxxvii, 182, 239-262
Abdullahi, Sheik Adams.; 33, 303
Abimbola, Prof. Wande; xvii, 14, 23
Achebe, Chinua; vi, viii, x, xii, xv-xvii, xxvii, xxix,1, 45, 92, 182, 184, 186, 189, 265, 279, 283, 312, 321, 354
Adali-Morti, Geormbeeyi; 107
Adedeji, J.A.; 189
Adejobi, Oyin; 194
Adekoya, Prof. Segun; v
Adelugba, Dapo; 211
Ademola, Frances; 199
Adeniran, Adekunle; 179
Adeniyi-Jones, Olga; 198
Adepoju, Olanrewaju; 305
Adetugbo, Abiodun; 189
Afigbo, A.E.; 35, 45, 144
Afolayan, Ade; 184
African Oral Literature; xvii
Agbebi, Dr M.; 177
Ahura, Tar; vi, ix, x, xxv, xxvi, 119-128
Aig-Imoukhuede, Frank; vi, 1
Aig-Imoukhuede, Mabel; 199
Ajayi, J. Ade; 301
Ajisafe, Kolawole ;167, 182
Akegwure, P.O.; 72
Akilu, Aliyu; 181
Akinlade, Kola; 145, 211
Akintan, Akintunde ;181
Akpoyoware, Mac; 187
Akwada, Bridget; 197
Alagoa, E.J.; 52, 55, 56, 73
Alcorn, M.W. and Bracher, M.; 10
Almqvist, O'Cathein & O' Healai; vi
Aluko, T.A.; xxxviii, 186, 299
Amadi-Tshiwala, Regina; 125
Amali, Samson; 263
Amayo, Dr Airen; 51
Amoaberg, K. & Laskei, 253

Andrzejwski and Innes; 76, 10, 286
Anene-Boyle, F.A.; 58, 61, 62, 70-73
Anozie, I.P.; 40
Anyadike, Prof. Chima; v
Arens, W.; 31-33
Areo, Agbo; xxxix, xlv, 322, 324
Arinze, F. A.; 144, 149
Asein, Sam; vi, ix, x, xxv, xxvi, xxv, xxvi, xxvii, xxx, xxxi, 118, 161-173, 163
Asekun, Funlayo; 198
Ashiwaju, Garba; 125
Association of Nigerian Authors (ANA); v,
Awolowo, Obafemi; 316
Awoniyi, T. Adedeji; 145, 211
Ayandele, Prof. Emmanuel; xxx, 177, 299, 301, 302
Azikiwe, Dr Nnamdi; xxxi, 217, 218, 244, 274, 275
Azuonye, Chukwuma; vi, viii, x, xxii-xxiv, xxviii, 75-104
Babalola, Adeboye & Gerald, Albert; 180
Babalola, Adeboye ; 127,181, 186, 188
Babayemi, S.O. and Adekola, O.O.; 15, 21
Baker, T.M.; 115
Balewa, Abubakar Tafawa; xxxv, xli, 182, 243, 298, 289, 295
Bamgbose; 219
Bamikunle, Prof. Aderemi; vi, ix, xi, xxxviii, xxxix, 263-272
Banhan, Martin; 197, 190
Banjo, Prof. Ayo; 6
Barber, Prof. Karin; v, viii, ix, x, xxxiv, 181, 207-226
Bascom, William; xvii
Basden, G.T.; 36, 40
Bassir, Olumbe; 187
Batavic epic; xv
Bayajida myth; xvi, xx, 25-32
Beier, U. & Gbadamasi, B.; 125, 186, 190
Beier, Ulli; 6, 107, 198, 199
Bell, Gene H.; 191
Ben-Amos, Dan; xxii, xxv, 51, 60-62, 68, 70

Benin heroic tradition; 49-74
Benin studies; 50
Biodun, Jeyifo; v
Bouquaux, L.; 115, 117
Bowra, C.M.; 72, 103
Bradbury, R.E.; 49, 53, 55, 59
Brotherston, Gordon; 191
Brown, Enitan; 196
Brown, Lloyd; 122
Bunyan, John; 180, 217
Burns, Sir Alan; 175, 176
Cabral, Amilcar; xxxvi, xlii, 299, 304
Campbell, Robert; 177
Carden, Lockwood; 146
Carr, Henry; 153
Cary, Joyce; 186
Caudwell, Christopher; 207
Charle, Patrick; 43
Charlton, L.A; 180
Chase, Hardley; 313
Children's oral literature and socialisation in Yoruba; 151
Chinweizu, Madubuike, & Jemie; viii, 76, 103, 188, 191, 312
Church Missionary Society; 181
Clark, Ebun; 184
Clark, J.P.; viii, x, xxii, xxiv, xxv, xxxiii, xxxviii, xxxix, 51, 66, 67, 71, 105-117, 187, 189, 190, 312, 324
Clay, Bertha; 173
Connah, G.; 50
Consentino, Donald J.; 276, 291
Corelli, Marie; 173
Cosgrove I. and Jackson R.; 310
Crowther, Bishop Ajayi; 180
Cultural imperialism and publishing in northern Nigeria; 285-299
D'Azevedo, Warren L.; 102
Dalziel,; 318
Dan Fodio, Uthman; xxvi, 176, 295
Darah, G.G.; iii, ix, x, xi, xii, xxxi, xxxii, xxxix, xl, xlvi, 185-192, 327
Dark, P.C.; 50
Dathome, O.R.; 127
Davies, Carole and Graves, Adams; 122
Davies, J.G.; 115
Dawodu, E.A.; 182
de Vries, Jan; 101, 104

Delano, Oluwole ; 181
Delziel, M.; 311
Devereux, G; 150
Dickens, Charles; xxxix, xlv, 315
Dike, K.O.; 49
Diop, Birago; 187
Diop, David; 187
Dorson, Richard M.; 103, 121
Dumas, Alexandre; xxxix, xlv, 301, 316
Dunbar, Lawrence; 173
Dundes, Alan; 75, 103
Duse, Mohammed; 173
Eagleton, Terry; xvii, 13, 121, 157
East, Rupert; 119, 120, 228, 287, 298-294
Ebeogu, Afam; vi, x, xxviii, 103, 135-150
Echeruo, M.J.C; xxxviii, 179, 180, 190, 313
Edemode, J.; 58, 65, 66
Edgar, Frank; 180
Egalitarian ethos in Tiv folktales; 119-128
Egharevba, Jacob; xxii, 52, 55-57, 59, 60, 65, 68, 70, 73, 74
Ehrenasft, Philip; 217
Ekwensi, C.; vii, xxxvii, xxxviii, xxxix, xl, xliii-xlv, xlvi, 195, 196, 271, 289, 319-325,
Ekwere, John; 199
Eliade, Mircea; 147
Eliot, T.S.; 105
Emenyonu, Ernest; 182, 316, 320, 321
Enyeribe, Onuoha; 40
Epelle, Keia; 196
Epic in Africa; xvii
Equiano Travels; v
Equiano, Olaudah; v, 40
Esan, Yetunde; 199
Escarpit, Robert; 281, 311
Esli, Obi; 187
Euba, Femi; 188
Ezikeojiaku, Ichie; vi, xx ,xxi, xvii, 35
Fagunwa, D.O.; vi, xxxiv, xxxv, 181, 196, 189, 207-224
Fanon, Frantz; xvi, xxxvi, xlii, 312
Finnegan, Ruth; xxv, 117
Fischer, Ernst; 140
Fletcher, R.S; 180
Fom, S.B.; 116
Forde, D. & Jones, G.I.; 149
Frazer, J.; 127

Frost, Robert; 5
Galbraith, J.K.; 4
Gbadamosi, Bakare; 107
Geertz, Clifford; 151
Goddard, A.D.; 31, 33
Goldmann, Lucien; 207
Graham, Phillis; 145Ati, Tunde; 159
Green, Graham; 186
Green, M.M.; 149
Gugelberger, Georg; xxxi
Gun, H.D.; 115
Gutkind, Peter C.W.; 207
Gwam, L.C.; 153
Gwarzo, Muhammadu; xxxv, xli, 288
Hadejia, Mu'azu ;181
Haggard, Rider; xxxii, xxxix, xlv, 173, 186, 315, 316
Hagher, Iyorwuese; 125
Hallam, W.R.K.; xix, 25-27, 33
Harper, Peggy; 122, 123
Hemingway, E.; xxxix, xlv, 316
Henderson, R.N.; 144
Henshaw, James Ene; xxxviii, xxxix, 185, 253-272
Higo, Aig; 187
Hinderer, David; 180
Hopkins, A.G.; 209
Hopkins, Gerald Manley; 115
Humm, Maggie; 122
Hunt, Prof. Hunt; v
Hurriez, S.H.; 28, 33
Huxley, Elspeth; 186
Ibie, C.O.; 17
Ibitokun, Prof. Ben; v
Ifa; xiv, xv
Igbafe, P.; 54
Igbo birth-songs; 122
Igbo mythopoesis; xx
Igirigiri, Kaalu; xxiv, 87-91, 93, 94, 96-98, 100
Iguh, T.; 254, 277
Iguh, Thomas Orlando; 185
Ihekole, O.N.; 116
Ike, C.; 322, 324
Ikime, Obaro; 51, 53, 57, 60
Ikpo, Kaalu; xxiv, 89, 93, 98, 99
Iloanusi, O.A.; 38, 40

Imam, Abubakar; xxxiv, xxxv, xxxvi, xli, 181, 182, 227-241, 240, 288, 299, 291, 293, 295
Imoukhuede, Mabel; 187
Innes, Gordon; 103
Irele, Abiola; 187
Iri; xix
Iroh, F.; 322, 323
Isichie, E.; 35
Isola, Prof. Akinwumi; vi, x, xxix, xxx, 151-159
Iyayi, F.; 224
Jahn, Janheinz; 229
James, Louis; 309, 319
Jeboda, Femi; 211
Jeyifo, Biodun; 182, 312, 316
Jingo, Mohammed; xv
Jinju, Muhammed; xix, 25, 26, 33
Johnson, Jimi; 190
Johnston, H.A.S.; xxv, 25-27, 117, 180
Jones, Glyn; 105
Joplin, C.; 16
Jordan; 150
Kaalu, Egwu; xxiv, 87, 90, 94, 96, 98-100
Kaalu, Ogbaa; xxiv, 86, 88, 92, 93, 96, 97
Kagara, Bello; xxxv, xli, 290, 289
Kano, Mallam Aminu; xxxvi, xxxvii, 181, 182, 240
Karaye, Maikudi; vi, x, xviii, xx, xix, 25, 29, 31, 33
Keil, Charles; 122
Kellog, Robert; 127
Kennedy, J.F.; xvi, 5, 240
Killam, D.; 303, 320, 321
King, Bruce; 316
Kirk, G.S.; 101, 103
Kirk, G.S.; 127
Kirk-Green, A.H.M.; 179
Kolawole, Prof. Mary; v
Kunio, Yanagida; 2
Ladipo, Duro; 184, 189
Laurence, M; 318
Laurenson D. and Swingewood A.; 311
Lawal, O.A.; vii, 299
Layeni, Ajibola; 168, 183
Leavis Q.R.; 310
Leith-Ross, Sylvia; 123, 150, 149
Levi-Strauss, C.; 27, 29, 33

Levy, Prof. Marion; 2, 4
Levy-Bruhl; 329
Lewis, L.J.; 161, 163
Lewis, Sir Arthur; 3
Lijadu, M.O.; 15, 17, 20
Lijadu, Yemi ;189
Linfors, Bernth; 182, 190, 310, 316-321
Linfors, B. & Schild, U.; 313
Literature and society in Lagos; 161
Literature and the jihadist movement; 176
Lloyd, P.C.; 209, 211
Lord, Albert; 143
Lovejoy, P.E.; 33
Lugard, Frederick; xxxii, 178, 179, 196, 197, 223
MacDiarmid, Hugh; 105
Madubuike, Ihechukwu; viii, 76, 103
Mahmud, K.; 176
Mahood, Molly; 202
Malinowski, B.; 26, 33, 50
Mba, Nina; 122, 123
Mbari Club; 199
Meek, C.K.; 35, 154
Mere, Ada; 159
Misket, Mervyn; 176, 189
Mohammed, Abubakar Sokoto; vi, x, xxxii, xxxiii, 193-218
Moore, Gerald; 190, 190
Morton-Williams, P.; 49
Mphahlele, Ezekiel; 199
Munonye, John; 168, 312
Murphy, J.F.; 319, 310
Myth in Africa; xvii
Na-Mangi, Aliyu; 181
Ndi Igbo cosmology; 37-48
Nduka, Otonti; 164, 166
Nigerian Folklore Society; v
Njaka, E.N.; 35
Njoku, Prof. Eni; 92
Nketia, Prof. Kwabena; 107, 126
Northern Regional Literature Agency (NORLA); xxxv, xli, 180, 228, 324-296
Noss, Philip; 123
Nwala, C.H.A. Obi; 277
Nwamuo, Chris; 263, 274, 267
Nwana, Peter; 182
Nwankwo, Nkem; 168, 174, 322

Nwanodi, Glory; 187
Nwoga & Egudu; 122
Nwoga, D.L.; 37
Nwoko, Demas ;189
Nzekwu, Onuora; 81, 103
Obasa, Adetinikan ;181
Obiechina, Emmanuel; vi, xi, xxxii, xxxv, xxxix, xl, 166, 184, 185, 273-284
Odunju, Folayan ; 181
Ofeimun, Odia; v
Ogali, O.A.; 184, 185, 264, 276, 278, 282
Ogbalu, F.C.; 121, 122
Ogieriaxi, E.; 53
Ogunba, Prof. Oyin; v, 191
Ogunbiyi, Dr Yemi; v, 170, 182, 185, 188, 264, 265
Ogunde tradition; 182
    Ogunde, Herbert; xxxviii, 182-184, 186, 189
Ogundipe-Leslie; Omolara; 187, 220
Ogunmola, Kola; 183, 184
Ogunyemi, Wale; xxxix, 188, 271, 329, 320
Ojaide, Tanure; xxv
Ojo, Ibitoye ;181
Okara, Gabriel; 9, 187, 280
Okediji, Oladejo; vi, xxxiv, xxxv, 207-226
Okigbo, C.; xxxviii, 187, 189, 312, 313
Okoro, F.; 324
Okpewho, Isidore; vi, x, xxi, xxii, xxiii, xix, xxxix, 49, 60, 65, 67, 74, 103
Okpi, Kalu; xxxix, xlv, 312, 322, 324
Olabimtan, Afolabi; 181
Olaiya, Moses; 184
Olatunbosun, Dupe; 300, 303
Olatunji, O.O.; 13
Olawaiye, Nelson; 187
Oleghe, Pius; 187
Olisa, O.; 185
Olisa, O.; 277
Olusola, Elsie; 188
Olusola, Segun; 188
Oluwole, Miss Adunni; 183
Omotoso, Prof. Kole; v, vii, xi, xxxvi, xxxvii, xli, xlii, xlv, 299-311, 323, 324
Omu, Dr F.; 167
Once Upon a Kingdom...; xvii
Onions, C.T.; 37
Onitsha literature renaissance; 184, 190, 272

Onitsha Market Literature; xxxii, xxxix, 184, 273-294
Onoge, Prof. Omafume; v, xi, xxxi, xl-xliii, xlvi, xlvii, 187, 327
Onwuejeogwu, M.A.; 35, 37
Onwuka, W.; 277
Onyeama, Dilibe; 312, 324
Opara, Ralph; 188
Oral Performance in Africa; xvii
Osadebay, Dennis; 186, 187
Osie, Patrick; 188
Osoba, Prof. Segun; v
Osofisan, Prof. Femi; v, vii, xi, xxxix, xl, xliii, xliv, xlvi, 189, 271, 309-326
Otite, Onigu; 51-53
Ottenberg, Phoebe; 149
Oyelana, Tunji; 188
Oyelaran, Prof. Sope; v
Ozidi Saga; xviii, xxii, 56, 66, 107
Paden, John; 227
Palmer, H.R.; 25-28, 33
Paraliterature; xliii, 295, 296, 320
Parry, Adam; 75, 103
Parry, Milman; 103
Pereira, Francesca; 188
Phallocentrism; 15, 17
Phallocracy; 15, 16
Plekhanov, George; 190
Pound, Ezra; 105
Preminger, Alex; 125
Priebe, R.K. and Hale, T.A.; 123
Priestley; 311
Principles of the Igbo oral epic; 75-104
Propp, Vladimir; xvii, 13
Radcliffe-Brown; 50
Rattray, R.S.; 27, 180
Richards, I.A.; 103
Robert, M.; 311
Rodney, W.; 286, 301
Roscoe, Adrian; 187, 318
Rotimi, Ola; xxxviii, xxxix, 257, 320
Rubbingh, Eugene; 120
Ryder, A.F.C.; 50, 55, 57, 59
Said, Edward; xvii
Sala, Baba; 304
Sani, Prof. Abba Aliyu; vi, x, xi, xxxii, xxxv, xxxvi, xl, xli, 285-298
Sartre, J.P.; 311

Satiru revolt; xxxii, xxxiii, 193
Savage, J.A.; 167
Scharfe, Dan & Aliyu, Yahaya; 176, 179
Scheub, H.; xxv, xxvii
Sekoni, Prof. Ropo; v, vi, x, xiv, xvii, xviii, xxii, xxiii, 13
Sekyi, Kobina; 264
Seldan, Raman; 159
Senghor, Leopold; 187
Shagari, President; 2
Shakespeare, W.; 178, 265
Shaw, T.; 36
Shelton, A.J.; 319
Shenton, Robert; 186
Shimuzu, Kiyoshi; 115
Shrub, Harold; xxi
Sidahome, J.E.; xxii, xxv, 51, 57, 61, 63-65, 68, 69-71
Sidi, Emir Dan; 179
Skinner, Neil; 115, 288, 297
Slaughter, Cliff; 156
Smith, Abdullahi; xix, 25, 26
Smith, M.G.; 30, 33
Soares, Tola; 188
Social and ethical values of Berom storytelling; 115
Solzheniskin; 92
Sowande, Sobowale; 181, 271
Soyinka, Wole; viii, xxvi, xxx, xxxviii, xxxix, 186-189, 271, 280, 279, 283, 311, 298, 314, 321, 324
Steinberg, S.H; 311
Stephen, F.N.; 185
Stephen, Felix N.; 277
Stevenson, L; 310
Sule, Maitama; xxxvii, 233
Sule, N.; 325
Talbot, P.A.; 40, 144
Temple, Placide; 329
The Black Victorians; xxx, 177
The intelligentsia and literary development in colonial Nigeria; 175
The Satiru Revolt; xxviii
Things Fall Apart; xii
Thomas, Isaac; 173
Thompson, R. Parris; 77, 93, 104
Tiv and their arts; 121
Toba, Prof. Kinichiro; 4, 5

Todorov, T.; 74
Tokyo Colloquium 1981; 1, 4
Tompkins, J.M.S.; 310
Tonau, Abubakar; 297
Townsend, Rev. Henry; 180
Tremearne, A.J.N; 180
Tutuola, Amos; xxxii, 188, 189, 217
Uchendu, Victor; xx, 35, 38
Ugonna, Nnabuenyi; 121, 122
Ulasi, Adaura; xxxix, xlv, 298, 322, 325
Vansina, S.; 116
Vasquez, Adolfo; 123
Wa Thiongo, Ngugi; 265
Wali, Na'ibi; 181
Walker, B.K. and Walker, S.W.; 116
Wallace, Edgar; xxxii, xlv, 186, 315
Waterman, Peter; 207
Waugh, Evelyn; xxxii, 186

Welch, J.E.; 72
Welek, Rene and Warren, Austen; 121
Whitman, Walt; 6
Willensky, H.L.; 310
Williams, Prof. Adebayo; v
Willis, Roy; 81, 104
Wirth, L.; 319
Wusasa, Tafida; xxxv, xli, 288, 299
Yahaya, Ibrahim; 25, 26, 33
Yai, O.B.; 210
Yamaha, Prof. Abraham; xv
Zaria Literature Bureau; xli
Zarai Literary Society; xxxvii
Zaria Translation Bureau; 228, 277, 288-292
Zukogi, Abubakar; xxxvii, 243, 254
Zungur, Sa'adu; vi, xxxvi-xxxviii, xli, 181, 182, 194, 249-262, 305

www.ingramcontent.com/pod-product-compliance
Lightning Source LLC
Chambersburg PA
CBHW012128010526
44113CB00041B/2642